¡En marcha!

an intensive Spanish course for beginners

Carmen García del Río

Routledge
Taylor & Francis Group

LONDON AND NEW YORK

Contents

Preliminary Unit Pronunciation, Syllabification, Accentuation   3

Unit 1 8	Unit 2 38	Unit 3 70	Unit 4 102
Primeros contactos	**Información personal**	**En donde vivimos**	**La vida diaria**
Learning Objectives	**Learning objectives**	**Learning Objectives**	**Learning Objectives**
A Greetings/farewells Introducing oneself	**A** Family relationships Giving personal information	**A** Expressing destination and purpose Sending a letter Asking for and giving contact details Answering the phone Asking/giving directions	**A** Asking and telling the time (12-hour clock) Discussing parts of the day Discussing the days of the week Discussing frequency of events Discussing daily tasks
B Expressing emotions Spelling Introducing someone Meeting people	**B** Discussing age Discussing dates and birthdays Discussing family	**B** Describing your home Indicating exact location Expressing quantity Identifying colours	**B** Discussing eating habits Eating habits in different countries Opening and closing times Timetables (24-hour clock)
C Discussing nationalities Where are you from? Where do you live?	**C** Describing physical appearance Describing character Talking about others	**C** Describing a city/village Comparing village and city life Discussing preferences Giving reasons Discussing means of transport Counting from 100 to 999	**C** The daily routine Expressing frequency Referring to the recent past
D What language do you speak? Counting from 0 to 99 Saying you do/don't understand	**D** Where you work Discussing jobs and professions	**D** Counting from 1000+ Expressing quantity: *más de, menos de...* Comparing quantities Geographical location Distance Describing a city or a town	**D** Domestic chores Comparison of domestic life with other countries Referring to ongoing actions Making excuses
Grammar	**Grammar**	**Grammar**	**Grammar**
A You in Spanish (*tú/ usted; vosotros(as)/ustedes*) Saying who you are using *Llamarse* Subject pronouns	**A** *Tener:* present tense *Tener:* expressing possession *Ser* and *estar:* expressing marital status Using the definite article to define identities Masculine and feminine nouns The plural	**A** *Ir:* present tense *Ir:* expressing destination Express purpose: *a* + infinitive + noun *Hay* to express existence *Estar* to express location	**A** *Ser* to express the time Days of the week Adverbs Adverbs in *–mente* formed from adjectives Reflexive verbs Irregular verbs: present indicative Totally irregular verbs: *ser, estar, ir and haber* Radical-changing verbs: *despertarse (e>ie), volver (o>ue), pedir (e>i)*

¡En marcha!

First edition published in Great Britain in 2005
By Hodder Education

Published 2013 by Routledge
2 Park Square, Milton Park, Abingdon, Oxon OX14 4RN
711 Third Avenue, New York, NY, 10017, USA

Routledge is an imprint of the Taylor & Francis Group, an informa business

British Library Cataloguing in Publication Data
A catalogue record for this title is available from the British Library

Library of Congress Cataloging-in-Publication Data
A catalog record for this book is available from the Library of Congress

ISBN 13: 978-0-340-80905-1 (pbk)

Typeset in 10/13 pt Helvetica Thin by Fakenham Photosetting Ltd, Fakenham, Norfolk
Illustration by Barking Dog Art, Beehive Illustration
Layouts by Amanda Easter Design Ltd

MIX
Paper from
responsible sources
FSC   FSC™ C013985
www.fsc.org

Printed in the United Kingdom
by Henry Ling Limited

Unit 5	134	Unit 6	166	Unit 7	198	Unit 8	232
Permisos, favores y preferencias		**Gustos y otras cosas**		**Cuéntame que pasó**		**¡Olé!**	

Learning Objectives (Unit 5)

A
Describing objects and their purpose
Expressing possession
Pointing out people and things
Indicating cause, purpose duration, destination

B
Avoiding repetition
Finding out if something has taken place
Discussing the immediate past
Making suggestions and giving advice
Expressing opinions

C
Asking for/granting permission
Seeking information
Asking to borrow something

D
Talking about computers
Giving information about people or things
Understanding and using basic computer terminology

Grammar (Unit 5)

A
¿Cómo + ser (+ noun)?
Ser + adjectives
¿De qué es?
Ser de
Servir/ser para + infinitive
¿De quién(es) es/son
Possessive Pronouns
Adjectives and demonstrative pronouns
Por and *para*

Learning Objectives (Unit 6)

A
Talking about free time
Referring to future plans/ intentions
Apologising and justifying an action
Referring to habitual actions

B
The seasons
Describing the weather
Discussing how the weather affects you
Discussing climate

C
Likes and dislikes
Interests
Agreeing and disagreeing
Opinions on likes and dislikes
Contrasting opinions

D
Discussing travel
Discussing transport
Expressing what you would like to do *me gustaría*

Grammar (Unit 6)

A
Present tense for future intention
ir + a + infinitive
pensar/querer + infinitive
Lo siento (mucho) pero es que…
Soler + infinitive
Quantifiers

Learning Objectives (Unit 7)

A
Discussing past routines
Asking about yesterday

B
Talking about yesterday
Talking about the weekend
Talking about the holidays
Talking about recent events
Referring to what had happened

C
Enquiring about others' past
Locating past events
Discussing the life and works of famous people
Referring to historical events
Events that almost happened

D
Discussing habitual actions in the past
Discussing the past and present
Describing something in the past
Referring to the immediate past

Grammar (Unit 7)

A
Preterite tense of regular verbs
Preterite tense: spelling changes
Preterite of radical-changing verbs: *jugar, buscar, almorzar, leer, oír*
Temporary adverbial phrases

Learning Objectives (Unit 8)

A
Asking for/giving permission
Refusing permission
Discussing traditional and popular music

B
Giving directions, orders and advice
Giving and following instructions
Making recommendations and suggestions
Expressing likes and dislikes
Expressing reactions

C
Discussing the future
Making predictions about the future
Expressing hopes and wishes
Expressing opinions and beliefs
Ignorance/uncertainty about the future

D
Discussing the past, present and future
Expressing purpose
Emotional reactions
Value judgements
Need, possibility and probability
Asking for and giving advice
Giving information about people or things

Grammar (Unit 8)

A
Affirmative imperative
Negative imperative
Imperative + direct and indirect pronouns
Present subjunctive of regular verbs
Prepositions
Prepositional pronouns: *a mí, conmigo, para ti…*

Contents

v

B	B	B	B
Estar, present indicative: expressing how you are The alphabet Using personal titles	Possessive adjectives Months of the year Dates	Ordinal numbers Prepositions and prepositional phrases to express location *¿Cuánto/-a/-os/-as* + noun + verb Verb + quantity *Ninguno* Double negative	Meal verbs Comparison of verbs and adverbs *¿A qué hora…? A la(s)* + time *de* + time + *a* *desde las (la)* + time + *hasta las (la)* + time *entre/sobre/ hacia* + time 24-hour clock

C	C	C	C
Ser, present tense: expressing origin and identity Question and exclamation marks in Spanish Regular verbs in the present indicative	*Ser* + adjective to refer to essential features *Tener* to refer to personal attributes *Llevar:* 'to have' or 'to wear' Qualifying adjectives: gender, number and position *Muy, bastante …* + adjectives to modify quantities *Estar* to indicate a temporary state	Comparison of adjectives and nouns Irregular comparatives: adjectives Present tense: *preferir* *¿Por qué* + clause? *Porque* + clause Cardinal numbers (100–999)	Perfect tense Regular and irregular past participles Time expression used with the perfect tense

D	D	D	D
Y, pero and *no* *¿Verdad?* and *¿no?* Cardinal numbers (0–99)	*Ser* to indicate profession Definite and indefinite article Gender of jobs and professions *Para* + infinitive to indicate purpose *Ser* + adjective to express opinions Shortening of *bueno* and *malo*	Cardinal numbers (1000+) *Estar* to indicate location and distance *¿Cuál?, ¿Cuáles?/¿Qué* + noun The relative superlative The absolute relative	Irregular verbs in the first person singular: *hacer, conocer, dar, saber, ver* Verbs that present double irregularity: *tener, decir, oír, venir* *Estar* + present participle (*gerundio*) Present participle

Culture	**Culture**	**Culture**	**Culture**
A	**A**	**A**	**A**
Buenas tardes Surnames in Spanish	Parliamentary Monarchy	*¿Coger* or *tomar?* Telephone & fax numbers Answering the phone E-mail/Web address	Time expressions Time zones
B	**B**	**B**	**B**
Spanish alphabet Greeting each other	*Las fiestas de San Fermín* Happy Birthday!	*La vivienda* Hispano-American capitals	*Tapas y bocadillos*
	C		
	A dark or fair person		

Acércate al mundo del español:	**Acércate al mundo del español:**	**Acércate al mundo del español:**	**Acércate al mundo del español:**
La lengua española y el mundo	*Así somos*	*Una ciudad para no olvidar: Santiago de Compostela*	*La siesta*

Role plays	**270**
Key to the 'in class or at home' activities	**286**
Glossary of grammatical terms	**296**

Contents

vi

B	**B**	**B**	**B**
Direct object Personal *a* Direct object personal pronouns *Ya , todavía no, aún no* *Acabar de* + infinitive Idiomatic expressions with *tener* *¿Por qué no* + verb? *Saber* and *conocer*	Seasons *Muy, mucho* referring to the weather *Hacer* and *haber* (impersonal)/*llover/nevar* *Estar* and *ser* to discuss weather *Tener frío/calor* *Estar bien* 'If-clauses' *Si* + present indicative	Preterite of *dar, ir, ser, ver* and other irregular verbs Preterite vs perfect tense Pluperfect tense	Present subjunctive: totally irregular verbs, radical-changing verbs, irregular verbs in the first person singular *Si* + present indicative, affirmative imperative/negative imperative Verbs *odiar, detestar, espantar* Exclamation phrases: *¡Qué... !* *Deber* + infinitive *Hay que* + infinitive *Aconsejar/recomendar/sugerir* + *que* + subjunctive
C	**C**	**C**	**C**
¿Poder + infinitive…? *Es que* + explanation *Sí, claro* + imperative Affirmative imperative: regular and irregular verbs Imperative of reflexive verbs Direct object pronouns with the imperative *Prestar/dejar* + noun Indirect object pronouns Order of the object pronous	*Gustar: (a mí) me gusta/n* *Interesar: (a mí) me interesa/n* *También, tampoco, sí, no* *Pues, pero* *(a mí) me parece(n)* + adjective/adverb *(a mí) me gusta(n) más* + noun *preferir*	Years and definite article Placing past events: *hace … años; hace x años que…* The historic present *Por poco* + present tense	Future tense: regular & irregular verbs *Mañana, Dentro de …, En …,* + future *Creer/imaginarse/suponer que* + future *Seguramente (no), probablemente* + future *¡Ojalá* + subjunctive! *Esperar/querer/desear* + *que* + subjunctive or infinitive *Creo/pienso que* + indicative *No creo/no pienso que* + subjunctive *No saber* + *si/cuándo/cómo/cuánto/qué* + future
D	**D**	**D**	**D**
Relative clauses Relative Pronoun *que*	Perfect Tense *Me/te/le… + gustaría* + (infinitive)	Imperfect tense of regular and irregular verbs (*ir, ser, ver*) Adverbial expressions: *siempre, con frecuencia…* Imperfect vs preterite	Time expressions + subjunctive and indicative *¿Para qué* + indicative? *Para que* + subjunctive Expressing emotions + subj. Expressing opinions + subj. Relative pronouns: *el que, la que, los que, las que* Relative adverb: *donde* Relative clause with subjunctive Conditional of regular and irregular verbs
Culture	**Culture**	**Culture**	**Culture**
A			
Nicknames			
	B		**B**
	The climate in Spain and Hispano-America		Greetings
		C	**C**
		Spain: a cultural melting pot	Words of Arabic origin in the Spanish Language
Acércate al mundo del español:	**Acércate al mundo del español:**	**Acércate al mundo del español:**	**Acércate al mundo del español:**
Un país para visitar: Ecuador	*¿Es usted el típico español medio?*	*Un mundo de creadores*	*La música el alma del pueblo*

Acknowledgements

The author would like to thank the following people who contributed in different ways to the project: first, Dr Chris Harris, who worked with the author on the initial proposal of the book and Dr Clare Kearns, who read the entire manuscript and whose comments and suggestions were invaluable; secondly, the Arnold team, with special thanks to Eva Martínez, Lucy Schiavone, Sarah Boas, and Helen Townson; thirdly, Dr Iain Stewart, María João Kay, Rosario Mascato Rey, Dr Pedro Guijarro-Fuentes, Dolores Oria-Merino and Professor Ian Press, whose contributions at different stages of the writing process were very much appreciated. I would also like to thank all my students, who remain the joy and inspiration of my professional life and from whom I have learnt so much throughout my career. Special thanks must go to my family and all my closest friends for being so patient and giving me the support I needed while writing *¡En marcha!*.

Finally, I would like to thank my husband Paul Nicholas Fessler, who makes everything possible and to whom I dedicate this book. Thank you Paul.

The author and publishers would like to thank the following for use of photographs and artwork in this volume:

© Robert Harding **cover and title page**, ©Lucy Schiavone, **pp9** (right), **17** (two top); ©Life File, **pp9** (left), **29** (top left), **54**, **78** (two on left), **87** (bottom), **127** (a and d), **163**, **174** (a and b); ©Photodisk, **pp17** (bottom), **23**, **29**, **67**; ©Ron Watts/CORBIS, **p95** (left); ©Warren Morgan/CORBIS, **p127** (b); ©Jim Craigmyle/CORBIS, **p127** (c); ©Baumgartner Olivia/Corbis Sygma, **p127** (e); ©Paul Steel/CORBIS, **p174** (c); ©Terry W. Eggers/CORBIS, **p174** (d); Diego Rivera, Vendedora de Flores, 1949, Museo Nacional Centro de Arte Reina Sofía Photographic Archive, Madrid ©2003 Banco de México Diego Rivera & Frida Kahlo Museums Trust. Av. Cinco de Mayo No.2, Col. Centro, Del. Cuauhtémoc, México, D.F., **p230**; ©Robbie Jack/CORBIS, **p239**.

¡En marcha!

¡En marcha! 'Let's go!' is a Spanish course book for adult learners who have no prior knowledge of Spanish or who have only a basic knowledge of the language. It provides learners with ample opportunity to develop their listening, speaking, reading and writing skills through exposure to formal and informal Spanish and through carefully structured and graded activities. These integrated components are designed to enable learners to achieve a level of communicative competence by the end of the course sufficient to deal with a wide range of contexts, far beyond the purely transactional. It also aims to provide them with a thorough grounding in the structure of Spanish, taking them step by step from beginner through to intermediate level.

¡En marcha! takes a very pragmatic approach from the beginning. It is highly flexible and has been designed to meet the needs of individual learners and groups, as well as those of tutors.

Structure

The course consists of the following elements:

The preliminary unit, which introduces learners to the special features of Spanish pronunciation and spelling.

Eight further units organised in sections. Every unit has a theme around which the content of the language is developed. All the activities are designed to build confidence by allowing the learner to move forward and consolidate in small stages. Grammar is used as a tool to facilitate communication, not as an end in itself, and the grammatical structures are explained in a clear and simple manner. The author strongly believes in giving students the tools to become independent learners and grammar is just one of these tools.

Each section of *¡En marcha!* starts with a list of essential expressions which can be used by the learner and/or the tutor in various ways: for revision, consolidation or reference purposes. This is followed by a set of activities which introduces new situations, expressions and structures. At the end of the activities, there is a section called *In class or at home* which consolidates what has been studied in class and which learners could tackle independently, working at their own pace. A key to these activities is provided at the back of the book.

Each unit has a section called *Acércate al mundo del español* which includes reading material on a topic related to the cultural theme of the unit. At the end of each unit there is a summary of the most important vocabulary used throughout the unit, called *Essential vocabulary*. The vocabulary is organised thematically to make it easier to learn.

The materials included in each unit have been designed not only to take into account the linguistic needs of the learners, but also to provide broad cultural background information about the Spanish-speaking countries. Learning a language is as much about seeing the world through the eyes of others as acquiring linguistic skills. Throughout *¡En marcha!* there are sections called *C de Cultura* which include notes on cultural points specific to Hispanic countries.

After the units there is a set of worksheets containing 15 role-plays which will enable students to deal in an effective manner with everyday situations such as buying food or clothes, going to a restaurant, seeing the doctor etc. These role-plays are part of the audio material of *¡En marcha!*. The teacher can use them as he/she judges appropriate.

At the end of the book there is an Answer key to the *In class and at home* exercises and a Glossary of grammatical terms. *¡En marcha!* is highly adaptable to the needs of different groups. Groups who are doing a one-year intensive Spanish course, for example, should follow the book systematically from start to finish, while others whose needs are less academic might do some of the writing activities, but possibly focus more on the role-plays.

Note about American Spanish

The author of *¡En marcha!* is from Spain and the Spanish used reflects this. However, within the book there are frequent references not only to the language and culture of Spain, but also to those of Hispano-American countries, in order to reflect the linguistic and cultural wealth of the Spanish-speaking world. The Spanish of Spain is no better or worse than that of Mexico, Chile, Guatemala or Cuba, for example. Spaniards, Mexicans, Chileans understand one another and the learner will be able to understand and be understood by all Spanish speakers, regardless of where they come from.

Support material

Additional material is available freely at the following location: http://cw.tandf.co.uk/languages/en-marcha/. This support material includes audio files and a booklet containing transcripts of the listening passages and a key to the exercises.

Preliminary unit

Before starting the course, you need to have a working knowledge of the basic rules governing Spanish pronunciation, accents and spelling.

Pronunciation

Spanish pronunciation is quite easy compared with that of other languages. The pronunciation of certain sounds varies from region to region and country to country, but these variations are not illustrated here. By learning the standard pronunciation of an educated person from Spain, you will be understood by anybody in the Spanish-speaking world. The best way to start to master the sounds is by listening to the accompanying recording to hear how the words are pronounced and then repeating them, trying to imitate the sound.

1 Vowels

 In Spanish there are 5 vowels: **a**, **e**, **i**, **o**, **u**. Their sound is full, clear and short. Each vowel has only one sound. Listen to how the vowels are pronounced and then repeat them.

a	ala	asa	ama	Panamá	atar
e	ese	mete	de	en	emprender
i	ir	sí	difícil	ti	fin
o	como	corro	son	moto	poco
u	un	su	muro	tú	luna

2 Consonants

You will learn the Spanish alphabet in Unit 1. For now, just concentrate on the pronunciation of some of the letter combinations.

 In Spanish there are 22 consonants. Listen to how the following consonants are pronounced and then repeat them.

b and **v** have the same sound:

vivir	beber	bueno	vuelo	hombre

c + **a**, **o**, **u**, **l**, or **r**:

acá	coma	cuco	clase	crema

qu (silent **u**) + **e, i**:

queso	que	quiero	química	aquí

k Very few Spanish words begin with **k**; most that do are foreign:

| kárate | kilo | kilómetro | kiwi | Kuwait |

c + e, i:

| cero | cerilla | obedecer | cine | piscina |

z + a, o, u:

| zapato | zona | zumo | zarzuela |

Note: **c** and **z** are pronounced as **s** in parts of southern Spain and Hispano-America.

g + a, o, u:

| gato | rogar | gota | hago | gusto |

ch:

| chatarra | cachete | chimenea | chorizo | chusma |

gu + a:

| guapo | agua | guante | guarda |

gu + e, i (silent **u**):

| guerra | Águeda | águila | guitarra | Guillermo |

gü + e, i (a dieresis is placed over the **u** to indicate that the **u** is pronounced):

| cigüeña | vergüenza | averigüé | argüir | pingüino |

h is ALWAYS silent:

| hombre | ahora | humano | huevo | ahumado |

j + a, e, i, o, u:

| jabón | jefe | jinete | jota | justo |

g + e, i:

| gemela | gitano | gimnasia |

ll:

| llamar | llorar | lleno | allá | callar |

Note: **ll** is pronounced as **y** in parts of southern Spain and Hispano-America.

ñ:

| añadir | añejo | señor | niños | España |

r, rr:

r at beginning of a word:	rama	resto	riesgo	Roma	rumor
r in the middle of a word:	arar	eres	arillo	pero	Irene
rr:	parra	perro	tarrito	arroyo	arrugar

s:

| Sara | sello | silla | asomar | sueño |

x:

between vowels: examen exacto boxeo éxito existir

before a consonant: expresión excluir extraer exquisito explicar

Syllabification

A basic knowledge of the structure of the Spanish syllables will help you not only to acquire a good pronunciation, but also to split written words correctly at the end of a line.

A Spanish syllable consists of at least one vowel.

 Vowels

- A vowel or a vowel combination can constitute a syllable:
  Eu-ro-pa   a-la   a-ma-ri-llo
  Spanish vowels are divided into strong (*a, e, o*) and weak (*i, u*) vowels. When two or three vowels are combined, they form either one or two syllables. It is important to understand this in order to know when to use a written accent.

- Two strong vowels (*a, e, o*) do not form a diphthong and are separated into two syllables: r**e-o**   **a-o**r-ta   p**o-e**-ta

- When a strong and a weak vowel are combined, they form a diphthong and unite as one syllable, as follows:

  Strong + weak: **Eu**-ro-pa   r**ei**-na   **ai**-re
  Weak + strong: b**ie**n   se-r**ie**   b**ue**-no
  Weak + weak: v**iu**-do   S**ui**-za   r**ui**-na

- You sometimes also find a union of three vowels, a stressed vowel between two unstressed ones (**i** or **u**) in the same syllable: estud**iái**s Urug**uay**
- A written accent (see Accentuation below) on a weak vowel (*i, u*) breaks the diphthong, separating the vowels into two syllables:
  Ma-r**í**-a   r**í**-o   a-cen-t**ú**-an
- Groups of vowels which form a single syllable cannot be divided in written Spanish.

2 Consonants

- A single consonant forms a syllable with the vowel that follows it:
  ca-sa   me-sa   ro-pe-ro
- **ch, ll, rr** count as single consonants and are never divided between syllables:
  cho-ri-zo   ar-ma-di-llo   pe-rro
- Two consonants between two vowels are separated into two syllables:
  al-**f**a-be-to   cam-**b**iar   E**s**-**p**a-ña

  EXCEPT in the following combinations: **pl, pr, bl, br, fl, fr, tr, dr, cl, cr, gl, gr** which are never split: **bra**-ma   ca-**bri**-to   ha-**bla**
  fru-ta   **cla**-ro   o-**tro**

- If three consonants occur between two vowels, the last one goes with the following vowel: tra**ns**-**f**e-rir   i**ns**-**p**ec-to-ra

3 Practice

Read the text and mark off the **syllables** of each word with a dash (-) between the letters:

Example: Ma-rí-a es es-pa-ño-la (8 syllables)
　　　　　1 2 3 4 5 6 7 8

María es española. Vive en la capital de España, Madrid. Ella estudia en la Universidad Autónoma, estudia inglés y geografía. Tiene dieciocho años. Vive en un piso con unos amigos ingleses. Sus amigos estudian español en la universidad.

Accentuation

1 Basic rules

In Spanish, all words are stressed according to specific rules. Words that don't follow the rules MUST have a written acute accent (´) to indicate the change of stress. The basic rules are as follows:

1 Words ending in a **vowel**, **n** or **s** are stressed on the penultimate syllable: c**a**sa   trab**a**jan   tranqu**i**lo   herm**o**sos

2 Words ending in a consonant other than **n** or **s** are stressed on the last syllable: volad**o**r   pap**e**l   arr**o**z   juvent**u**d

¡En marcha!

ALL words that do not follow these rules MUST have a written accent. So the written accent is an indication that the word does not follow the rules:

- así, ratón, además, cantó, cené, sábado, bolígrafo. All these end in a vowel, **n** or **s**, but the stress falls on another syllable. They do not follow the rule and therefore a written accent is required.
- árbol, hábil, carácter, ángel, López. All these end in a consonant other than **n** or **s**, but the stress falls on the penultimate syllable. They do not follow the rule and therefore a written accent is required.

 Practice

Listen to your tutor and underline the **stressed vowel** of the following words, then write the **written accents**, if required, and explain why.

| **1** lapiz | **2** examenes | **3** escoces | **4** leccion | **5** alumno |
| **6** telefono | **7** examen | **8** atencion | **9** catedratico | **10** deberes |

Special rules

1 The written accent is also used when a combination of vowels that would be expected to form a diphthong does not in fact do so, but instead forms two separate syllables (see diphthongs in Syllabification above) e.g. Ma-rí-a.

2 Words that have the same spelling but a different meaning take a written accent in order to differentiate one from the other:
el (*the*) él (*he, him*)   te (*you*) té (*tea*)   mi (*my*) mí (*me*)
si (*if*) sí (*yes*)   tú (*you*) tu (*your*)
solo (*alone*) sólo (*only*)   aun (*even*) aún (*still/yet*)

3 Question words and exclamations take a written accent.
¿qué? (*what?*); ¡qué! (*what!*); ¿cómo? (*how?*)

 More practice

Listen to your tutor saying the following words. Underline the **stressed vowel** and insert the **written accents**, if required, and explain their purpose.

| **1** libertad | **2** camion | **3** petroleo | **4** palabra | **5** donde |
| **6** jovenes | **7** franceses | **8** carcel | **9** ¿cuando? | **10** Oscar |

Primeros contactos

A Hola, ¿cómo te llamas?

Hello, what's your name?

■ **Expresiones esenciales**	■ **Essential expressions**
Hola	*Hello*
Buenos días	*Good morning (6 a.m. until about midday)*
Buenas tardes	*Good afternoon, Good evening (after lunch till nightfall)*
Buenas noches	*Good evening, Good night (after dark) or after dinner*
¿Cómo te llamas? *(informal)*	*What's your name?*
¿Cómo se llama usted? *(polite)*	*What's your name?*
(Yo) me llamo . . .	*My name is . . .*
. . . es mi nombre	*. . . is my first name*
. . . es mi apellido	*. . . is my surname*
. . . son mis apellidos	*. . . are my surnames*
Adiós	*Goodbye*
Hasta luego	*See you later*
Hasta mañana	*See you tomorrow*

---

1 **Saying 'hello', 'good morning', 'good afternoon', 'good evening', 'good night'**

A Imagine the different times of day (morning, afternoon / evening, night) and greet other people in your class. In turn, respond to their greetings.

B Working with a partner, read the following situations and decide on the appropriate Spanish greeting.

1 It is 6 p.m. and you have just walked into the office and made eye contact with your boss.

2 It is 10 a.m. on Saturday and you have walked into a bar where your friend is already waiting to have breakfast with you.

3 It is 7 p.m. and your evening-class teacher has just smiled at you on your arrival.

4 You are arriving back at your flat at 10 p.m. and you pass a neighbour on the communal staircase.

■ ¡Hola! Buenos días

■ ¡Hola! Buenas tardes

■ ¡Hola! Buenas noches

Listen to these greetings and number them in the order in which you hear them.

a ¡Hola! ☐
b ¡Hola! Buenos días ☐
c Buenas noches ☐
d ¡Hola! Buenas tardes ☐
e Buenas tardes ☐

C de Cultura

■ ***Buenas tardes***

A visitor to Spain will notice straightaway the later times of both the midday meal, which is usually the main meal of the day (rarely earlier than 2 p.m.), and the evening meal (not before 9 p.m.). Shops will close for lunch between 1.30 p.m. and 4 p.m., for example, and will then reopen from 4 p.m. until 8 or 8.30 p.m.. Thus the afternoon runs into the evening and this is reflected in the greeting *Buenas tardes* which means both 'Good afternoon' and 'Good evening'.

2 Saying hello, saying your name and asking someone what his or her name is

A Use this mini-dialogue as a model to find out the names of other people in your class.

■ ¡Hola!
Me llamo Rosa López García.
Y tú, ¿cómo te llamas?

■ ¡Hola!
Yo me llamo Martin Smith.

B El día de la matrícula en una escuela de idiomas
• Registration day at a language school

Read these two dialogues and then with a partner take it in turns to be the secretary (*secretaria*) and the student (*estudiante*).

Secretaria: *¡Hola! Buenos días ¿Cómo te llamas?*
Rosa: *¡Hola!*
Me llamo Rosa López García.
Rosa es mi nombre.
López García son mis apellidos.
Secretaria: *¡Hola! Buenas tardes ¿Cómo te llamas?*
Martin: *¡Hola! Buenas tardes.*
Me llamo Martin Smith.
Martin es mi nombre.
Smith es mi apellido.

C de Cultura

■ **Surnames in Spanish**

Many Spanish-speaking countries have and use two surnames. Traditionally, a person's first surname (*primer apellido*) is the same as their father's, while their second surname (*segundo apellido*) is their mother's maiden name. For example, if Francisco López Martín and Claudia García Pérez have a daughter and they call her Rosa, her full name will be Rosa López García. Tradition, however, no longer corresponds with contemporary Spanish law. The father's surname does not necessarily have to precede the mother's. Parents can choose.

When she marries, a woman keeps her maiden name. However she can add her husband's surname to hers using 'de': Claudia García de López. A woman can also decide to keep both her mother's and her father's surnames: Rosa López-Martín García or Rosa López García-Pérez. But you could end up with an awful lot of surnames!

C Fill in these forms with Rosa's and Martin's details as if you were the secretary.

nombre: _____

apellidos: _____

nombre: _____

apellidos: _____

Now fill in this form with your own details.

nombre: _____

apellidos: _____

D Here are the names of some Spanish people. What would each one say to introduce himself or herself?

Example: Carlos Rivero Blanco

Me llamo Carlos Rivero Blanco.
Carlos es mi nombre.
Rivero Blanco son mis apellidos.

a Miguel Machado Fuentes

b Julio Pinos Cara

c Carmen Navas Martín

d Pilar Vargas Iglesias

e Rosario Peralta Benet

3 'You' in Spanish

A **En Recepción** • In Reception
Listen to this mini-dialogue. In what way is it different from the dialogues you have just been practising? Why do you think this is so?

Recepcionista:	*¡Hola! Buenos días.*
Chris:	*Buenos días.*
Recepcionista:	*¿Cómo se llama usted?*
Chris:	*Me llamo Chris Anderson.*
	Chris es mi nombre.
	Anderson es mi apellido.

G de Gramática

'You' in Spanish

There are different ways of saying 'you' in Spanish according to the number of people you are talking to and the situation in which you find yourself.

you	informal	polite
singular	tú	usted
plural	vosotros / vosotras	ustedes

- In the informal plural, Spanish also distinguishes between:
  you – all female: *vosotras*
  you – all male, or a mix of male and female – *vosotros*
- American Spanish limits the use of *tú* much more closely to family and friends than does European Spanish. *Vos* is used in Argentina, Paraguay, Uruguay, some areas of Chile and Venezuela, Central America and the southern tip of Mexico. *Ustedes* is used for 'you' plural in both formal and informal situations.

B Working with a partner, decide which Spanish word for 'you' should be used when talking to the following people:

a the bank manager
b the hotel receptionist
c your Spanish friend, Ricardo
d a policeman
e Ricardo's sister, Susana
f your friends, Pablo and Margarita
g a group of Spanish delegates
h the section heads of a company

C Listen to these questions and circle whether you are being addressed formally or informally.

a tú / usted   **d** tú / usted
b tú / usted   **e** tú / usted
c tú / usted

4 | **Asking someone else's name**

G de Gramática

■ *Llamarse* **(to be called)**

(yo)	me llamo (*I am called*)
(tú)	te llamas (*you are called, informal*)
(usted)	se llama (*you are called, polite*)
(él)	se llama (*he is called*)
(ella)	se llama (*she is called*)

A Fill in the blanks.

Me llamo Pedro y mi amigo se llama Juan.
Me llamo Alfonso y mi amiga se llama Silvia.

a _____ Ramón y mi amigo _____ Esteban.
b _____ Irene y mi amiga _____ Lola.

B Introduce your partner to the other people in the group.

C How would you ask and answer these questions in Spanish?

1 What's your name? *(informal)*   My name is Martin.
2 What's your name? *(polite)*   My name is Chris Anderson.
3 What's his name?   His name is Michael.
4 What's her name?   Her name is Cristina

D Listen to the recording and complete the following sentences with the appropriate forms of the verb *llamarse* (to be called).

1 Yo _____ Pedro.
2 ¿Cómo _____?
3 ¿_____ usted Pablo?
4 _____ Marta.
5 Mi amigo _____ Vicente.

A Practise saying goodbye to people in your class.

■ Adiós. Hasta luego.

■ Hasta mañana.
   Adiós.

■ Adiós.

Consolidation

A What would you say in order to:
   a Greet someone in the morning.
   b Give your name and surname.
   c Ask someone in your class what his or her name is.
   d Ask an elderly lady what her name is.
   e Greet someone at 7 p.m.
   f Greet someone at 10 p.m.
   g Say your friend's name is Tom.
   h Say goodbye to your tutor.
   i Say 'see you tomorrow' to your friends.

In class or at home

A Complete the following dialogue:

■ ¡Hola!
   ¿Cómo _____?

■ ¡Hola! _____ Marta Suárez Ríos.
   Marta es _____
   Suárez Ríos _____

B Complete the following sentences with the appropriate forms of the verb *llamarse*.
   a Yo _____ Fernando.
   b Él _____ Pedro.
   c ¿_____ usted Carmen?
   d Y tú, ¿cómo _____?
   e (Ella) _____ María.

C What would you say in Spanish in order to . . .
   a greet your flatmate just after 11p.m.?
   b greet someone at breakfast time?
   c ask the grandfather of a friend what his name is?
   d ask someone at a party what his or her name is?
   e ask someone in a work meeting his or her name?
   f say goodbye to your friend?
   g say 'see you later' to your friend?

D Study this table which shows you the subject pronouns in Spanish.

	singular		plural	
first person	yo	(*I*)	nosotros / nosotras	(*we*)
second person (informal)	tú	(*you*)	vosotros / vosotras	(*you*)
second person (polite)	usted	(*you*)	ustedes	(*you*)
third person	él	(*he*)	ellos	(*they*)
	ella	(*she*)	ellas	(*they*)

E Write the questions that correspond to the following answers:

1 Me llamo Julián Cortés Garrido. (*polite*)
2 Me llamo Luisa. (*informal*)
3 Sí, me llamo Rosalía. (*polite*)
4 Sí, ella se llama Dolores.

F ⬤ Listen to the recording of the Preliminary Unit on vowels and consonants and practise their pronunciation.

G Read the phrases and mark off the syllables of each word with a dash (-) between the letters.

1 ¡Hola! Me llamo José Reinoso Cao.
2 Buenos días ¿Cómo se llama?
3 Castaño Cabrera son mis apellidos

■ **Expresiones esenciales**	■ **Essential expressions**
¡Hola! ¿Cómo estás?	*Hello / Hi, how are you?*
¡Hola! ¿Qué tal?	*Hello / Hi, how are things? / How is it going?*
Bien, gracias	*Fine / Well, thanks / thank you*
Muy bien	*Very well*
¿Cómo se escribe tu *(informal)* / su *(polite)* nombre?	*How do you spell your name?*
Mi nombre se escribe . . .	*My name is spelt . . .*
¿Cómo se escribe tu *(informal)* / su *(polite)* apellido?	*How do you spell your surname?*
Mi apellido se escribe . . .	*My surname is spelt . . .*
Éste es (Pedro)	*This is (Peter)*
Ésta es (Marta)	*This is (Martha)*
Éste es el señor...	*This is Mr...*
Ésta es la señora...	*This is Mrs...*
Encantado	*How do you do (man talking)?*
Encantada	*How do you do (woman talking)?*
Mucho gusto	*Pleased to meet you*
El gusto es mío	*The pleasure is mine*

Saying how you are and asking someone how he or she is

A Using the mini-dialogues below, practise asking one another how you are.

- ■ Hola! ¿Cómo estás?
- ■ Bien, gracias. ¿Y tú?

- ■ ¡Hola! ¿Qué tal?
- ■ Muy bien. ¿Y tú?

B Now practise using the polite form of address.

- ■ ¿Cómo está usted?
- ■ Muy bien, gracias. ¿Y usted?

C Look at the different ways María can answer the question *¿Cómo estás?*, depending on how she is feeling.

muy bien	☺ ☺ ☺
bien	☺ ☺
bastante bien	☺
regular	😐
no muy bien	☺ 😐
mal	☹
muy mal	☹ ☹
fatal	☹ ☹ ☹

■ Hola María. ¿Cómo estás?

D Work with your partner and take it in turns to answer the question *¿Cómo estás?*, (How are you?) using the symbols given.

a ☺ ☺ ☺ Estoy muy bien.
b 😐 😐 _____
c ☹ _____
d ☹ ☹ ☹ _____

Now find out how other people in your group are today.

E Look at this verb table and then fill in the blanks to complete the sentences in the exercise below.

Estar (to be)			
(yo)	estoy *(I am)*	(nosotros / nosotras)	estamos *(we are)*
(tú)	estás *(you are)*	(vosotros / vosotras)	estáis *(you are)*
(usted)	está *(you are)*	(ustedes)	están *(you are)*
(él)	está *(he is)*	(ellos)	están *(they are)*
(ella)	está *(she is)*	(ellas)	están *(they are)*

Note: Spanish has two main verbs that mean 'to be': *ser* and *estar*. You will learn when and how to use them in different sections of the book.

1 Hola María, ¿cómo _____?
2 Buenos días, ¿cómo _____ usted?
3 Muy bien, gracias. Y vosotros, ¿cómo _____?
4 Buenas tardes, ¿cómo _____ ustedes?
5 ¿Cómo _____ Roberto?
6 ¿Cómo _____ Roberto y Silvia?

G de Gramática

■ *Estar* (to be)
One of the uses of *estar* is to express how you are (feeling):
Estoy muy bien (I am very well).

2 Spelling your name and asking someone to spell their name

A El alfabeto • The alphabet.

Practise saying the alphabet with your tutor.

Letter	Name	Letter	Name	Letter	Name
a	a	k	ka	t	te
b	be	l	ele	u	u
c	ce	m	eme	v	uve
d	de	n	ene	w	uve doble
e	e	ñ	eñe	x	equis
f	efe	o	o	y	i griega
g	ge	p	pe	z	zeta
h	hache	q	cu		
i	i	r	ere / erre		
j	jota	s	ese		

B Spell out the following names.

  a Ana

  b Juan

  c Santiago

  d Rosario

  e Elvira

C Listen to the recording and tick which of these names is <u>not</u> spelt out:

Carlos   Isabel   Julián   Inés   Hugo

D Listen to the recording and complete the dialogue.

Carmen:	*Hola. ¿Cómo te llamas?*
Estudiante:	*Hola. Me llamo _____*
Carmen:	*¿Cómo se escribe tu nombre?*
Estudiante:	*Mi nombre se escribe _____*
Carmen:	*¿Cómo se escribe tu apellido?*
Estudiante:	*Mi primer apellido se escribe _____.*
	Mi segundo apellido se escribe _____.

E Using the dialogue you have just listened to as a model, take it in turns with a partner to spell out the following names:

  a Ángel Soria Quintos

  b Cecilia Ibáñez Godoy

  c Jorge Celaya Páez

  d Montse Castillo Vázquez

3 Introducing someone

A Study these situations and decide which are informal and which are formal.

- Mira, Marina, éste es Paco.
- Hola, ¿qué tal?
- Hola.

- Mira, Blanca, te presento al señor Romero, director de publicidad.
- Mucho gusto / Encantad**a**.
- El gusto es mío / Encantad**o**.

- Hola papá, mira, éste es mi amigo Pablo.
- Hola, ¿cómo estás?
- Muy bien, ¿y usted?

- Doctor López, ésta es la doctora Grandal.
- Encantada.
- Mucho gusto.

1 What do you think *mucho gusto, el gusto es mío, encantado, encantada* mean?

2 Who says *encantado* and who says *encantada*?

3 Why do you think this changes?

C de Cultura

■ **Greeting people**

In the Spanish-speaking world, women usually kiss one another on each cheek, as do men greeting women. Men will shake hands or slap one another on the back. In formal situations, it is customary to shake hands.

B Complete the dialogues.

- Mira, Elena, éste es Carlos.
- _____
- _____

- Señor Jiménez, ésta es la señora Codesido, presidenta del consejo.
- _____
- _____

C Read the following dialogue, then choose the answers.

Isabel:	*Hola Pedro, ¿cómo estás?*
Pedro:	*Bien, Isabel. ¿Y tú?*
Isabel:	*Muy bien, gracias. Mira, Pedro, ésta es mi amiga Silvia.*
Pedro:	*Hola, ¿qué tal?*
Silvia:	*Hola.*
Isabel:	*Y éste es el señor González, el padre de Silvia.*
Pedro:	*Encantado.*
Sr González:	*Mucho gusto.*

1 When Isabel introduces Pedro and Silvia, will they shake hands or kiss?

2 When Isabel introduces Pedro to Silvia's father, will they shake hands or kiss?

G de Gramática

■ Using personal titles

As in English, personal titles are used in Spanish in formal situations. Some of the more common ones are:

señor (Sr)	*Mr, Sir*
señora (Sra)	*Mrs, Madam*
señorita (Srta)	*Miss, young lady*
doctor (Dr)	*doctor (m.)*
doctora (Dra)	*doctor (f.)*

■ Definite article with personal titles

The definite article is used when talking about someone: *el señor Gil, la señora Ríos, el doctor García Jiménez.*
It is also used to refer to a couple: *Los señores Gil Peña.*
The article is not used if the person is directly addressed: *Entre, señora López.* ('Come in, Mrs López.')

■ Orthography

In Spanish, titles are not capitalised when used with a surname unless they are abbreviated: *la señorita Moreno Díaz* **but** *la Srta. Moreno Díaz.*

D In groups of four and according to your sex, take it in turns to play one of the following people:

> Elvira / Ignacio is introducing these people to Ana / Juan:
> el señor Blas / la señora Blas
> Manolo / Margarita

When you have done this, write out the conversation you have just taken part in.

Consolidation

A What would you say in the following situations:

1 You greet your friend Paco.
2 Paco introduces you to his friend Luis.
3 Luis introduces Mrs Gil to you.
4 You want to know how Mrs Gil is.
5 You want to know how Luis is.
6 You want to know how your partner spells his / her name.
7 You want to know how your tutor spells his / her name.
8 You have forgotten Luis's friend's name; ask him what it is.

B Listen to the recording and tick the phrases you hear.

a	b	c
1 ¿Cómo está?	1 Mira, Luisa, éste es Emilio.	1 Mi nombre se escribe ce, e, ce, i, ele, i, a
2 ¿Cómo están?	2 Mira, Luis, ésta es Emilia.	2 Mi nombre se escribe ese, e, ce, i, ele, i, a
3 ¿Cómo estás?	3 Mira, Luis, éste es Emilio.	3 Mi nombre se escribe ce, e, te, i, ele, i, a

C Here are the answers to some questions. Give the questions.

    1 Me llamo Baltasar. (informal)
    2 Muy bien, gracias. (informal)
    3 Me llamo Claudio Martín. (formal)
    4 No muy bien. (formal)

In class or at home

A What would you say in Spanish in order to:

    1 greet your elderly neighbour in the morning and ask how s/he is.
    2 introduce your friend José to your friend Sofía.
    3 say 'the pleasure is mine'.
    4 say 'pleased to meet you' if you are a woman.
    5 ask 'How do you spell your second surname?' (polite).
    6 introduce Dr Fuentes Ramos to Mr Márquez.

B Complete the following dialogue:

Miguel: *Hola Paul, ¿_____?*
Paul: *Muy bien, ¿Y tú?*
Miguel: *Muy bien, gracias. Mira, Paul, _____ la señora Ventura, la profesora de español.*
Paul: *Mucho gusto.*
Sra Ventura: _____

C Fill in the blanks.
    1 Hola, _____ días.
    2 Buenos días. ¿_____ está?
    3 Muy _____, gracias. ¿Y _____?
    4 Bien, gracias. Mire, señor García, éste es el doctor Sánchez.
    5 Encantado.
    6 _____ gusto.

D What were the questions asked to obtain the following answers?

    1 Me llamo Lola.
    2 Mi primer apellido se escribe *a, ene, a, i griega, a.*
    3 Mi nombre se escribe *a, ene, a.*
    4 Estoy muy bien, gracias ¿Y usted?
    5 Estoy fatal. ¿Y tú?

E Write the abbreviated forms of *señor, señora, señorita, doctor, doctora.*

¿De dónde eres y dónde vives?

Where are you from and where do you live?

■ **Expresiones esenciales**

¿De dónde eres? *(informal)*
¿De dónde es usted? *(polite)*
Soy de + país
Soy + nacionalidad
¿Quién es + nacionalidad?
de
donde
¿Dónde vives? *(informal)*
¿Dónde vive (usted)? *(polite)*
Vivo en . . .

■ **Essential expressions**

Where are you from?
Where are you from?
I'm from . . . (country)
I'm . . . (nationality)
Who is . . . (nationality)?
from, of
where
Where do you live?
Where do you live?
I live in . . .

 Nationalities

A Match the country with the nationality.

País *(country)*

1 Inglaterra	**7** Portugal
2 Estados Unidos	**8** Rusia
3 España	**9** Australia
4 Francia	**10** China
5 Alemania	**11** Argentina
6 Japón	**12** Perú

Nacionalidad *(nationality)*

a argentina	**g** inglesa
b portuguesa	**h** alemana
c australiana	**I** estadounidense
d española	**j** rusa
e peruana	**k** francesa
f china	**l** japonesa

B Read these sentences:

Ricardo es español. Ana es española.

1 Why is Ricardo *español* and Ana *española*?

2 Read the following sentences and look at how the adjective of nationality can change according to the gender of the person. Notice, too, that some do not change.

Rafael es colombian**o**.   Gloria es colombian**a**.
Michel es francé**s**.   Françoise es frances**a**.
Hans es alemá**n**.   Sabine es aleman**a**.
Mike es canadiens**e**.   Margaret es canadiens**e**.

3 Ricardo y Eduardo son español**es**.
Ana y Carmen son español**as**.

Why is it *español**es*** for Ricardo y Eduardo **but** *español**as*** for Ana y Carmen?

4 Complete these sentences.

Rafael es mexicano. Rafael y Juan son _____.

Laura es mexicana. Laura y Teresa son _____.

Jan es holandés. Jan y Pieter son _____.

Mike es canadiense. Mike y Margaret son _____.

C Complete the table below. Make sure that you write the nationality with a lower-case initial letter.

país	nacionalidad			
	singular		plural	
	masculino	femenino	masculino	femenino
Portugal	portugués			
Francia			franceses	
Escocia	escocés			
Gales		galesa		
Irlanda				irlandesas
Italia	italiano			
Grecia			griegos	
Alemania	alemán			
Brasil	brasileño			
Holanda	holandés			
Estados Unidos				

Saying where are you from and asking someone where he/she is from

A Read this mini-dialogue and give your reply.

– ¡Hola! Me llamo Rosa López García. Soy de España. Soy española. Y tú, ¿cómo te llamas? ¿De dónde eres?

– Me llamo Simon. Soy de Inglaterra. Soy inglés. Y tú, ¿cómo te llamas? ¿De dónde eres?

– Yo me llamo . . .

B Find out the nationalities of people in your group.

C Give yourself a new name and nationality, then find out the new names and nationalities of the others in your group. How many have the same nationality as you?

3 Saying where other people are from

G de Gramática

■ **Ser** (to be)

- One use of *ser* is to express **origin**: *¿De dónde eres?* (Where are you from?)
  Soy de China. Soy chino. (I'm from China. I am Chinese.)
- Another use is to **identify**: *¿Quién es?* (Who is (he / it)?)
  Es Ramón. (It is Raymond.)

Ser (present tense)			
(yo)	soy (I am)	(nosotros / nosotras)	somos (we are)
(tú)	eres (you are)	(vosotros / vosotras)	sois (you are)
(usted)	es (you are)	(ustedes)	son (you are)
(él)	es (he is)	(ellos)	son (they are)
(ella)	es (she is)	(ellas)	son (they are)

A Complete these sentences with the correct form of the verb *ser* in the present tense.

1 Me llamo Cristina, _____ italiana.
2 ¿Tú _____ alemán?
3 María _____ portuguesa.
4 Alberto _____ colombiano.
5 Bill y yo _____ canadienses.
6 ¿Rafa y tú _____ españoles?
7 Consuelo y Ricardo _____ argentinos.
8 Jeanne y Marie _____ francesas.

B Rewrite the following sentences using the correct adjective of nationality.

Example: Pedro es de España. Pedro es español.

1 Bob es de Canadá.
2 Michelle es de Francia.
3 Yo soy de Escocia.
4 Somos de Italia.
5 ¿Eres de Portugal?
6 Ellas son de Alemania.
7 ¿Sois de Grecia?
8 Ellos son de Rusia.

G de Gramática

■ **Questions and exclamation marks in Spanish**

In Spanish, question marks and exclamation marks appear twice. At the beginning of the question or exclamation, they are written upside down (¿ ¡) and at the end, the right way up (? !).

¿De dónde eres? (Where are you from?)
¡Qué lástima! (What a pity!)

C Look at these photos, then answer the questions in Spanish.

1 ¿De dónde es Will?
2 ¿De dónde es Emma?
3 ¿De dónde son Mike y John?
4 ¿De dónde es Lisa?
5 ¿De dónde son Sarah y Carmen?
6 ¿Quién es escocesa?
7 ¿Quién es galés?
8 ¿Quién es estadounidense?
9 ¿Quién es española?
10 ¿Quién es irlandesa?

Carmen: España

Lisa: Estados Unidos

Emma: Escocia

Mike: Inglaterra

John: Inglaterra

Sarah: Irlanda

Will: Gales

D Working with a partner, take it in turns to ask and answer the following questions.

Example: ¿De dónde es Bernadette? / Irlanda.
Bernadette es de Irlanda. Es irlandesa.

1 ¿De dónde es Brigida? / Alemania.
2 ¿De dónde es Luis? / España.
3 ¿De dónde eres? / Escocia.
4 ¿De dónde es usted? / Estados Unidos.
5 ¿De dónde son ustedes? / Canadá.
6 ¿De dónde son ellos? / Grecia.
7 ¿De dónde sois? / Inglaterra.
8 ¿De dónde son ellas? / Japón.
9 ¿De dónde son Tom y Jane? / Gales.

4 Saying where you live and asking someone where he/she lives

A You are a member of this class. Study what the teacher and other members of the class are saying, then

1 complete the blank speech bubble with a greeting and information about yourself
2 answer the questions below

- Buenos días.
  Yo me llamo Marta Jiménez Cortés. Soy española, de Málaga pero **vivo en** Madrid.

- ¡Hola!
  Me llamo Alain Tournier.
  Soy francés, de Marsella, pero **vivo en** Londres.

- Buenos días.
  Yo me llamo Robert Rafferty. Soy inglés, de Manchester, pero **vivo en** Londres.

- Buenos días. Me llamo Laura Díaz.
  Soy chilena, de Valparaíso, pero **vivo en** París.

a ¿Dónde vive Laura Díaz?
b ¿Dónde vive Alain Tournier?
c ¿Dónde vive Marta?
d ¿Dónde viven Robert y Alain?
e ¿De dónde es Alain?

f ¿Cuál es la nacionalidad de Laura?
g Y tú, ¿cómo te llamas?
h ¿De dónde eres?
i ¿Dónde vives?

B Introduce yourself to other people in your group and find out where they are from and where they live.

C Listen to the recording and complete the table below.

PERSON 1	PERSON 2	PERSON 3
nombre:	nombre:	nombre:
apellido:	apellido:	apellido:
nacionalidad:	nacionalidad:	nacionalidad:
lugar de residencia:	lugar de residencia:	lugar de residencia:

D Give yourself a new identity: name, surname, place of birth and place of residence. Working in groups of three, ask one another questions in Spanish which enable you to complete the table below.

PERSON 1	PERSON 2	PERSON 3
nombre:	nombre:	nombre:
apellido:	apellido:	apellido:
nacionalidad:	nacionalidad:	nacionalidad:
lugar de residencia:	lugar de residencia:	lugar de residencia:

G de Gramática

Regular verbs in the present indicative			
subject pronouns	-AR estudiar (to study)	-ER beber (to drink)	-IR vivir (to live)
yo	estudio (I study / am studying)	bebo (I drink / am drinking)	vivo (I live / am living)
tú	estudias (you study / are studying)	bebes (you drink / are drinking)	vives (you live / are living)
usted, él, ella	estudia (you study / are studying; he / she studies / is studying)	bebe (you drink / are drinking; he / she drinks / is drinking)	vive (you live / are living; he / she lives / is living)
nosotros(as)	estudiamos (we study / are studying)	bebemos (we drink / are drinking)	vivimos (we live / are living)
vosotros(as)	estudiáis (you study / are studying)	bebéis (you drink / are drinking)	vivís (you live / are living)
ustedes, ellos, ellas	estudian (you study / are studying; they study / are studying)	beben (you drink / are drinking; they drink / are drinking)	viven (you live / are living; they live / are living)

• *Note*: it is not necessary to use the subject pronoun unless you want to emphasise it or avoid ambiguity. The person is in the verb ending.

A Complete the table below.

Regular verbs			
subject pronouns	-AR	–ER	-IR
	hablar *(to speak)*	aprender *(to learn)*	escribir *(to write)*
yo			
tú			
usted, él, ella			
nosotros(as)			
vosotros(as)			
ustedes, ellos, ellas			

B Complete the following sentences with the appropriate form of the verb in the present tense.

1 ¿ _____ matemáticas? (estudiar, tú)
2 Nosotros _____ historia española. (aprender)
3 Pablo y Jane _____ en Madrid. (vivir)
4 Diana _____ italiano y alemán. (escribir)
5 ¿_____ español? (hablar, usted)
6 Elena _____ en Buenos Aires. (vivir)
7 Tu padre, tú y yo _____ mucho. (trabajar)
8 Yo _____ poco. (beber)

¿De dónde eres y dónde vives?

25

1 María es de Madrid. Es española pero vive en Londres. Su primer apellido es Cooper y su segundo apellido es Ramos.
2 Edward y yo somos norteamericanos, de San Antonio, Texas, pero vivimos en España, en Granada. Somos estudiantes. Estudiamos español y aprendemos mucho.
3 Me llamo Stefan Fiedler. Soy alemán pero vivo en Sevilla. Escribo novelas y también estudio español. Aprendo mucho porque hablo mucho.

Rewrite each text with the new subject given.

1 Yo soy de Madrid.
_____
2 Edward y Caroline son norteamericanos,
_____
3 Se llama Stefan Fiedler. Es . . .
_____

Consolidation

A Fill in the missing information.

Example: Luigi es italiano. Natalia es <u>italiana</u>.

1 Brian es inglés. Rachel es _____
2 Alain es francés. Veronique es _____
3 Jim es escocés. Alison es _____
4 Paulo es portugués. Sonia es _____
5 Dieter es alemán. Regina es _____

B How would you say the following in Spanish?

1 Where are you from? (*tú*)
2 What is your name? (*usted*)
3 Rico Colomer is my surname.
4 My name is Fernando Bravo.
5 I am Spanish, from Córdoba.
6 Where do you live? (*tú*)

7 I live in Birmingham.
8 Where do Mr and Mrs López live?
9 Good morning, how are you? (*usted*)
10 We are Italians, from Rome, but we live in Buenos Aires.

C **En la escuela de idiomas** • At the language school. Listen to the dialogue and fill in the blank spaces.

Secretaria: *Buenos días. ¿Cómo _____?*
Estudiante: *Me llamo James _____*
Secretaria: *¿James _____?*
Estudiante: *Sí.*
Secretaria: *¿Cómo se escribe _____?*
Estudiante: *Se escribe be, e, a, te, o, ene.*
Secretaria: *_____.*
Estudiante: *No, se _____ be, e, a, te, o, ene.*
Secretaria: *Gracias.*
Secretaria: *¿ _____?*
Estudiante: *Soy de Inglaterra. Soy _____*

In class or at home

A Make the following sentences singular.

Example: Nosotros somos de Gales. Somos galeses.
Yo soy de Gales. Soy galés.

1 Nosotros somos de España. Somos españoles.
2 Vosotros sois de los Estados Unidos. Sois estadounidenses.
3 Ustedes son de Rusia. Son rusos.
4 Mis amigas son de Argentina. Son argentinas.

B Write the questions that correspond to the following answers.

Example: Ella es española.
¿De dónde es ella?

1 Me llamo Marisa.
2 Soy de Guatemala.
3 Vivo en Ecuador.
4 Jorge y María viven en Oviedo.
5 Yo soy colombiana.

C Conjugate the following verbs.

	1 Regular verbs		
	trabaj**ar** *(to work)*	com**er** *(to eat)*	recib**ir** *(to receive)*
yo			
tú			
usted, él, ella			
nosotros(as)			
vosotros(as)			
ustedes, ellos, ellas			

	2 Irregular verbs	
	estar	ser
yo		
tú		
usted, él, ella		
nosotros(as)		
vosotros(as)		
ustedes, ellos, ellas		

D ¿Qué idiomas hablas?

What languages do you speak?

■ Expresiones esenciales	**■ Essential expressions**
¿Qué idioma(s) hablas? *(informal)*	*What language(s) do you speak?*
¿Qué idioma(s) habla (usted)? *(polite)*	*What language(s) do you speak?*
Hablo . . .	*I speak . . .*
¿Verdad? / ¿No?	*Isn't it? / Do you? etc.*
¿Entiendes (tú)?*(informal)* / ¿Entiende	
(usted)? *(polite)*	*Do you understand?*
No, no entiendo	*No, I do not understand*
Por favor, ¿puede(s) repetir? *(informal / polite)*	*Could you repeat that please?*
¿Puede(s) hablar más despacio, por favor?	*Could you speak more slowly, please?*
Por favor, ¿puede(s) hablar más alto?	*Could you please speak more loudly?*
Perdón, pero no entiendo /	*Sorry, but I don't understand /*
no hablo muy bien el español	*I don't speak Spanish very well*
¿Puede(s) . . . ?	*Could you . . . ?*
¿Qué significa . . . ?	*What does . . . mean?*
¿Cómo se dice *woman* en español?	*How do you say 'woman' in Spanish?*
¿Cómo se escribe tu *(informal)* / su *(polite)* apellido?	*How do you spell your surname?*
¿Cómo se pronuncia tu / su nombre?	*How do you pronounce your name?*

1 Asking someone what languages he/she speaks and saying what languages you speak

A Match each country with its capital and the language spoken there.

País	Capital	Idioma
1 ITALIA	MOSCÚ	FRANCÉS
2 CHINA	MADRID	POLACO
3 ESPAÑA	BEIJING	RUSO
4 REINO UNIDO	LISBOA	CHINO
5 FRANCIA	ROMA	ESPAÑOL
6 POLONIA	ATENAS	ITALIANO
7 PORTUGAL	LONDRES	INGLÉS
8 GRECIA	VARSOVIA	ESPAÑOL
9 RUSIA	CARACAS	PORTUGUÉS
10 VENEZUELA	PARÍS	GRIEGO

B Practise the following mini-dialogues with a partner, first using the informal, then the polite form of address:

■ ¿Qué idiomas hablas?

■ Hablo español y francés

■ ¿Qué idiomas habla usted?

■ Hablo griego y ruso

C Find out how many other people in your group speak the same languages as you.

D Read the self-introductions and answer the questions.

■ Buenos días.
Me llamo Peter.
Soy de Australia.
Hablo inglés, ruso y japonés

■ Buenos días.
Me llamo Carmen.
Soy española.
Yo hablo español e italiano.

■ ¡Hola! ¿Qué tal?
Yo me llamo Alain.
Soy francés.
Yo hablo francés y griego.

■ ¡Hola!
Yo me llamo María.
Soy de Portugal.
Hablo portugués pero no hablo francés.

■ Hola, buenos días.
Me llamo Attilio.
Soy italiano.
Hablo italiano pero no hablo inglés.

Example: ¿Habla Carmen inglés?
No, pero habla español e italiano.

1 ¿Qué idiomas habla Carmen?
2 ¿Habla Attilio inglés?
3 ¿Qué idiomas habla Alain?
4 ¿Habla María alemán?
5 ¿Qué idiomas habla Peter?
6 ¿Cómo se llama el hombre de Francia?
7 ¿Quién es de Australia?
8 ¿Quién no habla francés?
9 ¿Quién habla italiano pero no es italiana?
10 ¿Cuál es la nacionalidad de la persona que habla japonés?

G de Gramática

■ **Connectors**

• **y** = and
Notice that **y** becomes **e** when the next word begins with **i** or **hi**: *Hablo español **e** inglés, Estudio geografía **e** historia.*

• **pero** = but: *hablo griego **pero** no hablo ruso.*

■ **Negation**

• **no** = (i) no (ii) not
¿Hablas ruso? No, no hablo ruso.
(Do you speak Russian? No, I don't speak Russian.)
The first '*no*' = no, the second '*no*' = not. To make a statement negative, all you need to do is put *no* before the verb.

E All of the following statements are false.
Rewrite them in the negative.

1 Carmen es italiana.
2 Pedro aprende ruso.
3 María es española.
4 Attilio habla griego.
5 El hombre francés se llama Michel.
6 Alain estudia francés.

F Listen to the dialogue between a student and the secretary
of a language school, then answer the questions in English.

1 What time of day is it?
2 How did he spell his surname?
3 What languages does he speak?

G Read this dialogue with a partner.

Antonio:	Hola, me llamo Antonio. ¿Y tú?
Sofía:	Yo me llamo Sofía.
Antonio:	¿De dónde eres, Sofía?
Sofía:	Soy española, de Valencia. Tú no eres español, ¿verdad?
Antonio:	No. Yo soy de Iquique en Chile pero ahora vivo en Los Ángeles.
Sofía:	Entonces, hablas inglés muy bien ¿no?
Antonio:	No, no muy bien. Y tú, ¿hablas inglés?
Sofía:	No, pero hablo francés y alemán.
Antonio:	¿Qué tal hablas francés?
Sofía:	Bastante bien.
Antonio:	¿Y alemán?
Sofía:	Muy mal.
Antonio:	Bueno, Sofía, hasta luego.
Sofía:	Adiós, hasta luego.

G de Gramática

¿verdad? or ¿no?

Statements can be turned into questions by adding *¿verdad?*
or *¿no?* (isn't it? / don't you? etc.) and by raising the
intonation in your voice as you say these words.
The same rising intonation is used for questions without using
question words:
¿Hablas inglés? (Do you speak English?)
There is no equivalent of 'Do you ...?' in Spanish. Raising
your voice at the end of the sentence is enough to let the
listener know that you are asking a question.

1 You have already come across the expression *¿Qué tal?*
meaning 'How are things?' What do you think *¿Qué tal hablas
francés?* means?
2 What words are used in the dialogue to answer the above
question? Do you know any other words that can be used to
express different levels of ability?

H Find out what languages people in your group speak and how well
they speak them.

A Study the following cardinal numbers and complete the lists.

0	cero	16	dieciséis	32	
1	uno (un) / una	17	diecisiete	33	
2	dos	18	dieciocho	34	
3	tres	19	diecinueve	35	
4	cuatro	20	veinte	36	
5	cinco	21	veintiuno/a	37	treinta y siete
6	seis	22	veintidós	38	
7	siete	23	veintitrés	39	
8	ocho	24		40	cuarenta
9	nueve	25		50	cincuenta
10	diez	26	veintiséis	60	sesenta
11	once	27		70	setenta
12	doce	28		80	ochenta
13	trece	29		90	noventa
14	catorce	30	treinta		
15	quince	31	treinta y uno		

B Write down the following numbers as words, then read them aloud to your partner.

a 7 _____
b 11 _____
c 19 _____
d 25 _____
e 33 _____
f 48 _____
g 53 _____
h 62 _____
i 71 _____
j 80 _____
k 96 _____
l 99 _____

C 🔊 Circle the numbers you hear on the recording.

0, 7, 19, 21, 33, 47, 59, 60, 74, 82, 95, 9

G de Gramática

■ **Spelling of cardinal numbers:**
- Numbers from 0 to 30 are written as a single word.
- Numbers from 31 to 99 are written as two words linked by *y* except for the tens (20, 30, 40, 50 ...): *treinta **y** uno* (31).

■ **Gender of numbers**
- Numbers are masculine: throwing a six and a four with dice would be **un** *seis* and **un** *cuatro*.
- **¿Uno or una?**
  Uno is replaced by **una** if it is followed by a feminine singular noun: *una libra*: one pound
- **¿Uno or un?**
  Uno is shortened to **un** when it is followed by a masculine singular noun.
  *Tengo **un** euro*: I have one euro
  but
  *¿Cuántos tienes? Tengo **uno**.*
  How many do you have? I have one.

3 Saying you don't understand.

A Read the grammar section below and note the phrases you can use to:

- check whether you have been understood
- say you don't understand and ask for clarification or repetition
- apologise for your Spanish

G de Gramática

■ A question of understanding

- To check whether people have understood, use the verb *entender* meaning 'to understand':
  ¿Entiendes (tú)? (Do you understand?)
  ¿Entiende (usted)?
  ¿Entendéis (vosotros)?
  ¿Entienden (ustedes)?
- If you are having difficulty in understanding:
  No, no entiendo (No, I do not understand) plus:
  Por favor, ¿puede(s) repetir? (Please, could you repeat that?)
  ¿Puede(s) hablar más despacio por favor? (Could you speak more slowly please?)
  Perdón, pero no entiendo / no hablo muy bien el español
  ¿puede(s) ... ?
  (Sorry, but I don't understand / speak Spanish very well, could you ... ?)
- If you have difficulty in hearing:
  Por favor ¿puede(s) hablar más alto? (Could you please speak more loudly?)
- To ask people for the meaning of a word or a phrase:
  ¿Qué significa ... ? (What does ... mean?)
  ¿Qué significa esta palabra / frase? (What does this word / phrase mean?)
- To ask how you say a word or how to spell or pronounce a word:
  ¿Cómo se dice woman *en español?* (How do you say 'woman' in Spanish?)
  ¿Cómo se escribe tu / su apellido? (How do you spell your surname?)
  ¿Cómo se pronuncia tu / su nombre? (How do you pronounce your name?)

B What would you say in the following situations?

1 Ask your doctor to repeat something.
2 Say 'Sorry, I don't understand, I don't speak Spanish very well'.
3 Ask your tutor to speak more slowly.
4 Ask your partner to speak louder.
5 Ask a friend 'how do you say 'friend' in Spanish'.
6 Ask your partner, 'how do you pronounce your name?'

Consolidation

A 🎧 Listen to the recording and write down the numbers.

B How do you ask these questions in Spanish?

   1 What is your name?

   2 Where are you from?

   3 Where do you live?

   4 What languages do you speak?

   5 How well do you speak (French)?

C Use these questions to have a conversation with other people in your group.

D How would you say the following in Spanish?

   1 Sorry, I don't understand, I don't speak Spanish very well.

   2 Do you understand? (to a friend)

   3 Could you speak more slowly please? (to a policeman)

   4 Could you repeat, please? (to your tutor)

   5 How do you pronounce the word 'dog' in Spanish?

   6 How do you write your surname? (to another student)

E Read what Antonio says about himself.

Hola, me llamo Antonio y soy chileno pero no vivo en Chile. Vivo y trabajo en Los Ángeles, Estados Unidos. Hablo español y un poco de inglés. Estudio inglés en una escuela de idiomas en Los Ángeles y aprendo mucho.

F Write a paragraph about yourself. Give your name, your nationality, where you live and the languages you speak and are studying.

In class or at home

A Conjugate the following verbs.

Regular verbs			
	estud**iar** *(to study)*	le**er** *(to read)*	ab**rir** *(to open)*
yo			
tú			
usted, él, ella			
nosotros(as)			
vosotros(as)			
ustedes, ellos, ellas			

B Complete the following sentences with the appropriate form of the verb *ser*.

   a Los profesores ___ de Australia.

   b Ellas ___ chilenas.

   c Vosotros _____ de Buenos Aires.

   d ¿___ usted británico?

   e Nosotros _____ colombianos.

   f Yo _____ portugués, de Lisboa.

Note down, in Spanish, the languages spoken in the following countries. If necessary, use your dictionary.

Países	Idiomas
1 Alemania	
2 Dinamarca	
3 Finlandia	
4 Holanda	
5 Hungría	
6 Islandia	
7 Rusia	
8 Suecia	
9 Turquía	
10 Egipto	

D Write down the numbers, then read them aloud.

a 0 _____   **e** 37 _____   **i** 70 _____

b 6 _____   **f** 40 _____   **j** 88 _____

c 13 _____   **g** 55 _____   **k** 90 _____

d 21 _____   **h** 64 _____   **l** 99 _____

E Complete these sentences, using the verbs in italics.

1 Me llamo Liliana. _____ argentina pero _____ y _____ en Londres, Inglaterra. _____ inglés muy bien.

        hablo   *soy*   *trabajo*   *vivo*

2 Tú _____ estadounidense, ¿verdad? ¿Dónde _____? ¿Qué tal _____ español?

        hablas   *eres*   *vives*

3 Mi amigo cubano _____ Andrés. Andrés no _____ en Cuba, _____ y _____ en Estados Unidos. _____ inglés muy bien.

   vive   *trabaja*   *se llama*   *habla*   *vive*

4 Pepe y yo _____ españoles pero _____ en Edimburgo donde _____ inglés. _____ inglés muy mal.

    hablamos   *somos*   *estudiamos*   *vivimos*

5 ¡Hola amigos! ¿Cómo _____? ¿Qué tal _____ inglés? _____ inglés aquí en Vancouver, ¿verdad? ¿_____ mucho?

    habláis   *estáis*   *estudiáis*   *aprendéis*

6 Gloria y Paco _____ colombianos pero _____ en Nueva York. No _____ ; _____ inglés en una escuela de idiomas y _____ mucho.

    trabajan   *viven*   *estudian*   *aprenden*   *son*

A Before reading the text, read the following information and choose the option which you think is correct.

1 El español es una lengua que procede del:
a latín **b** hebreo **c** árabe

2 El español es:
a la segunda (2da) lengua más hablada en el mundo
b la tercera (3^{era}) lengua más hablada en el mundo
c la cuarta (4ta) lengua más hablada en el mundo

3 El español es una lengua hablada por:
a unos 200 millones de personas
b unos 400 millones de personas
c unos 800 millones de personas

4 El español se habla en:
a 22 países en el mundo
b 18 países en el mundo
c 23 países en el mundo

5 El español es hablado en el siguiente país africano:
a Nigeria **b** Ghana **c** Guinea Ecuatorial

6 El español es lengua oficial en:
a el estado de California y el estado de Florida
b los estados de Kansas y Colorado
c Alaska

B Read the text and check your answers.

Países de habla española

El español, una lengua que procede del latín, es la cuarta lengua más hablada en el mundo, después del chino, inglés e hindú. El español es hablado por más de 400 millones de personas repartidas en 23 países: Argentina, Bolivia, Chile, Colombia, Costa Rica, Cuba, Ecuador, España, algunos estados de Estados Unidos como por ejemplo California y Florida, Filipinas, Guatemala, Guinea Ecuatorial, Honduras, México, Nicaragua, Panamá, Paraguay, Perú, Uruguay, República Dominicana, El Salvador, Puerto Rico y Venezuela. Además, el español es hablado por los judíos sefarditas, los judíos descendientes de los judíos expulsados de España en 1492.

C Look at the map showing the countries in which Spanish is spoken. Some names are missing. Write them down.

Essential vocabulary

(m) = masculine   (f) = feminine

Los países	Countries	Las nacionalidades	Nationalities
Alemania (f)	*Germany*	alemán(a)	*German*
Argentina (f)	*Argentina*	argentino/a	*Argentinian*
Australia (f)	*Australia*	australiano/a	*Australian*
Brasil (m)	*Brazil*	brasileño/a	*Brazilian*
Canadá (m)	*Canada*	canadiense	*Canadian*
Chile (m)	*Chile*	chileno/a	*Chilean*
China (f)	*China*	chino/a	*Chinese*
Colombia (f)	*Colombia*	colombiano/a	*Colombian*
Dinamarca (f)	*Denmark*	danés(a)	*Danish*
Egipto (m)	*Egypt*	egipcio/a	*Egyptian*
Escocia (f)	*Scotland*	escocés(a)	*Scottish*
España (f)	*Spain*	español(a)	*Spanish*
Estados Unidos (m)	*United States*	estadounidense	*American*
Finlandia (f)	*Finland*	finlandés(a)	*Finnish*
Francia (f)	*France*	francés(a)	*French*
Gales (m)	*Wales*	galés(a)	*Welsh*
Grecia (f)	*Greece*	griego/a	*Greek*
Holanda (f)	*Holland*	holandés(a)	*Dutch*
Hungría (f)	*Hungary*	húngaro/a	*Hungarian*
Inglaterra (f)	*England*	inglés(a)	*English*
Irlanda (f)	*Ireland*	irlandés(a)	*Irish*
Islandia (f)	*Iceland*	islandés(a)	*Icelandic*
Italia (f)	*Italy*	italiano/a	*Italian*
Japón (m)	*Japan*	japonés(a)	*Japanese*
México (m)	*Mexico*	mexicano/a	*Mexican*
Perú (m)	*Peru*	peruano/a	*Peruvian*
Portugal (m)	*Portugal*	portugués(a)	*Portuguese*
Reino Unido (m)	*United Kingdom*	británico/a	*British*
Rusia (f)	*Russia*	ruso/a	*Russian*
Suecia (f)	*Sweden*	sueco/a	*Swedish*
Turquía (f)	*Turkey*	turco/a	*Turkish*
Venezuela (f)	*Venezuela*	venezolano/a	*Venezuelan*

Los idiomas (m)	Languages	Palabras para preguntar	Question words
chino	*Chinese*	¿Cómo?	*How?*
español	*Spanish*	¿Cuál?	*Which? What?*
francés	*French*	¿Dónde?	*Where?*
griego	*Greek*	¿Qué?	*What?*
inglés	*English*	¿Quién?	*Who?*
italiano	*Italian*		
japonés	*Japanese*		
polaco	*Polish*		
portugués	*Portuguese*		
ruso	*Russian*		

La identidad	**Identity**
amigo/a	*friend*
apellido (m)	*surname*
hombre (m)	*man*
lugar (m)	*place*
mi	*my*
nacionalidad (f)	*nationality*
nombre (m)	*name*
padre (m)	*father*
persona (f)	*person*
profesor (a)	*teacher*
residencia (f)	*residence*
tu/su	*your*

Parabras útiles	**Useful words**
bastante	*quite*
de	*from; of*
en	*in; at*
éste (m); ésta (f)	*this*
gracias	*thank you*
mucho	*a lot*
muy	*very*
no	*no; not*
pero	*but*
poco	*little, not much*
por favor	*please*
porque	*because*
que	*who; which; that*
sí	*yes*
un poco	*a little*
y	*and*
bien	*fine; well*
fatal	*awful*
mal	*not so good; poorly*
regular	*so-so*

Verbos	**Verbs**
aprender	*to learn*
entender	*to understand*
escribir	*to write*
estar	*to be*
estudiar	*to study*
hablar	*to speak*
leer	*to read*
llamarse	*to be called*
pronunciar	*to pronounce*
ser	*to be*
vivir	*to live*

Información personal

A La familia

The family

■ Expresiones esenciales	**■ Essential expressions**
¿Estás / está casado / casada? *(informal / polite)*	*Are you married?*
Estoy casado / casada	*I am married*
Estoy separado / separada	*I am separated*
Estoy divorciado / divorciada	*I am divorced*
Soy soltero / soltera	*I am single*
Soy viudo / viuda	*I am widowed*
Mi esposo / marido se llama . . .	*My husband is called . . .*
Mi esposa / mujer se llama . . .	*My wife is called . . .*
¿Tienes / tiene hijos? *(informal / polite)*	*Do you have children?*
¿Cuántos hijos tienes / tiene? *(informal / polite)*	*How many children do you have?*
¿Tienes / tiene hermanos y hermanas?	*Do you have brothers and sisters?*
¿Cuántos tienes / tiene? *(informal / polite)*	*How many do you have?*
Tengo . . .	*I have . . .*
Soy hijo único / hija única	*I'm an only child*

C de Cultura

With the death on 20 November 1975 of General Franco, Spain's dictator for 36 years, Spain started a new period in her history: *el periodo de la transición*, a difficult time for the country, which ended in 1982 with the election of a Socialist Government. Juan Carlos I was crowned King of Spain in 1975. On 15 June 1977, the first democratic elections were held; then, on 6 December 1978 the Spanish people approved the Constitution via a referendum and Spain became a *Monarquía Parlamentaria*.

 Talking about families

A Look at the family tree of the Crown Prince of Spain, then read the text and, with a partner, answer the questions that follow.

La familia real en 2004

```
Juan Carlos I = Sofía de Grecia
1938–          1938–
   ┌──────────────┼──────────────────────┐
Elena = Jaime   Cristina = Iñaki     Felipe = Letizia
1963–   1963–   1965–      1968–     1968–    1972–
   ┌──────┐        ┌──────┐            │
Felipe  Victoria  Juan    Pablo      Miguel
1998–   2000–     1999–   2000–      2002–
```

Felipe de Borbón es el príncipe de España. Su padre es el rey Juan Carlos y su madre la reina Sofía. Felipe tiene dos hermanas, Elena y Cristina. Elena vive en Madrid y Cristina en Barcelona. Sus hermanas están casadas y tienen hijos. Elena tiene un niño y una niña y Cristina tiene tres niños. Felipe está casado también, su mujer es española y se llama Letizia. Uno de sus sobrinos se llama como él. Los cuñados de Felipe son españoles. Felipe de Borbón es el heredero de la corona española.

■ **Irregular verbs**

A verb is irregular when it does not follow a fixed pattern in its conjugation. Spanish has a large number of irregular verbs, but only a few are totally irregular. The main ones are **ser, estar** and **ir** (to go). Some verbs like **tener** (to have) present two types of irregularity: in the stem (**e**>**ie**) and in the first person singular (a **g** is added to the first person singular). You will learn more about them in Unit 4.

■ *Tener* (to have)

(yo)	tengo	(I have)	(nosotros / as)	tenemos	(we have)
(tú)	tienes	(you have)	(vosotros / as)	tenéis	(you have)
(usted)	tiene	(you have)	(ustedes)	tienen	(you have)
(él / ella)	tiene	(he / she has)	(ellos / as)	tienen	(they have)

■ **Expressing possession with *tener***

• To express possession or ownership, the construction *tener* + noun can be used: *Tengo dos hermanas.* (I have two sisters.); *Tengo un coche.* (I have a car.)
• To ask about possession: *¿Tener* + noun?: *¿Tienes hermanos?* (Do you have any brothers and sisters?). *¿Tienes un coche?* (Do you have a car?)
• To answer in the affirmative: *Sí, tengo dos hermanas.* (Yes, I have two sisters.)
• To answer in the negative: *No, no tengo hermanos.* (No, I don't have any brothers or sisters.)

■ **Marital status**

To indicate marital status, *ser* and *estar* are interchangeable:
Ser or *estar soltero(a) / casado(a) / separado(a) / divorciado(a) / viudo(a)*
To be single / married / separated / divorced / widowed

• To ask about marital status: *¿Está casado(a)?* (Is he/she married?)
• To answer in the affirmative: *Sí, está casado(a).* (Yes, he/she is married.)
• To answer in the negative: *No, está / es soltero(a).* (No, he/she is single.)

1 ¿Cuántas hermanas tiene el príncipe Felipe?

2 ¿Cómo se llaman las hermanas del príncipe de España?

3 ¿Dónde vive Cristina?

4 ¿Cómo se llama el marido de Elena?

5 ¿Cómo se llama la hija de Elena?

6 ¿Cuántos hijos tiene Cristina?

7 ¿De dónde es el marido de Cristina?

8 ¿Está casado el príncipe Felipe?

9 Y su hermana Cristina, ¿está casada?

B Work with a partner. Find in the text words that denote family relationships and complete the following chart.

Relationship to Felipe	
El rey Juan Carlos	padre
La reina Sofía	
La infanta Elena	
La infanta Cristina	
El hijo de Elena	
El marido / esposo de Cristina	
Letizia	

1 El rey Juan Carlos es el _____ de Felipe y la reina Sofía es su _____.

2 Felipe es el _____ de Cristina y Elena.

3 Elena, Cristina y Felipe son _____ y son los _____ de los reyes.

4 Elena es la _____ de Cristina.

5 Felipe de Borbón es el _____ de los hijos de Elena y Cristina.

6 Los hijos de Elena y Cristina son los _____ del príncipe Felipe.

7 El rey Juan Carlos es el _____ de los hijos de las infantas Elena y Cristina y la reina Sofía es su _____.

8 Los hijos de Elena y Cristina son los _____ de los reyes.

9 La reina Sofía es la _____ de los maridos de Elena y Cristina y el rey Juan Carlos es su _____.

10 Los maridos de Elena y Cristina son los _____ de los reyes.

11 Los hijos de Elena son _____ de los hijos de Cristina.

12 Felipe y el marido de Elena son _____.

D Working with a partner, draw up a family tree using the following information.

• Marta y Paz son hermanas.	• Luis tiene dos primas, Paz y Marta.
• Francisco e Isabel están casados.	• Natalia es prima de Marta.
• Isabel tiene dos hijos y una hija.	• Teresa es la mujer de Javier.
• Su hijo Enrique está soltero.	• Carmen es la madre de Paz.
• Francisco tiene cuatro nietos.	• Javier es hermano de Carmen y cuñado de José.
• Carmen es hija de Francisco.	

G de Gramática

■ **Using the definite article to identify**

You will study the definite article (*el*, *la*, *los*, *las*) in section D of this unit, but note that the definite article is used in the sentences *Teresa es la mujer de Javier* and *Carmen es la madre de Paz* to define the identities of *Teresa* and *Carmen*.

E Form complete, meaningful sentences by selecting one element from each of the three columns.

Francisco e Isabel	es	el marido de Carmen.
Carmen	son	las primas de Natalia y Luis.
Paz y Marta	es	los padres de Enrique.
José	es	el primo de Marta y Paz.
Francisco	son	la hermana de Enrique y Javier.
Luis	es	el abuelo de Luis, Natalia, Marta y Paz.

F Match the questions with the answers.

1 ¿Estás casada? **a** No, no tengo hijos.
2 ¿Cuántos hermanos y
hermanas tienes? **b** Cuatro, dos hijos y dos hijas.
3 ¿Tienes hermanos? **c** No, soy soltera.
4 Tu hermano¿está casado? **d** No, soy hijo único.
5 ¿Tienes hijos? **e** Tengo un hermano y una hermana.
6 ¿Cuántos hijos tienes? **f** No, está divorciado.

G Use the questions from F to talk to other people in your group.

H 🎧 Listen to the three dialogues and fill in the forms below.

1	2	3
Nombre	Nombre	Nombre
Apellidos	Apellidos	Apellidos
Nacionalidad	Nacionalidad	Nacionalidad
Lugar de residencia	Lugar de residencia	Lugar de residencia
Estado civil	Estado civil	Estado civil
Número de hijos	Número de hijos	Número de hijos

I Taking into account the information given in the previous exercise, write a short paragraph about each person.

2 Masculine and feminine

A Write the feminine form of the following nouns:

abuelo padre hijo tío primo cuñado marido

G de Gramática

■ Gender

- All Spanish nouns are masculine or feminine. A general rule is that masculine nouns end in **-o**, and feminine nouns end in **-a**.
- Where a masculine noun ends in a consonant, its feminine counterpart can be formed by adding an **-a**: *profesor*. *profesora*
- Where stress falls on the last syllable of a masculine noun ending in **n** or **s**, it is marked by an accent. This accent is not needed for the feminine form as the stress is now regular. Remember that words ending in a vowel, **n** or **s** are stressed on the penultimate syllable: *marqués*: *marquesa* (see page 6).
- Some nouns have a completely different form for the male and female: *yerno* (son-in-law); *nuera* (daughter-in-law).

- Where a noun has both a masculine and a feminine form, it is the masculine form which is listed first in the dictionary.
- The masculine plural denotes either a group of males, or a mixture of males and females: *el hermano y la hermana = los hermanos*.

These are exceptions to these rules. For example, *día* (day) is a masculine noun, *mano* (hand) is a feminine noun, *tarde* (afternoon / evening) and *noche* (night) are feminine nouns. The gender of such nouns has to be learned as you go along. However, it is helpful to know that most nouns ending in -*ción*, e.g. *estación* (station), -*dad*, e.g. *universidad* (university); -*tad*, e.g. *lealtad* (loyalty); -*ud*, e.g. *salud* (health) are feminine and that many nouns ending in -*ma* are masculine, e.g. *problema* (problem).

B Write the masculine form of the following nouns:

esposa   sobrina   nieta   suegra   hermana   nuera

C Sort the following nouns into masculine (m) and feminine (f) groups:

heredero	niño	amiga	país	chico	ciudad
gato	sistema	apellido	esposa	marido	mano
problema	canción	foto	madre	región	reina

Singular and plural

A Write these nouns in the plural form:

hombre   televisión   idioma   clase   ciudad   tabú   paz   martes

B Write these nouns in the singular form:

mujeres   familias   amistades   sefardíes   países   nueras   lápices

G de Gramática

■ Formation of the plural

Singular nouns ending in a vowel	Add -s	casa	casas
a, e, i, o,u		estudiante	estudiantes
á, é, ó		café	cafés
Singular nouns ending in a consonant or í, ú	Add -es	profesor	profesores
		iraní	iraníes

- Where a noun ends in -z, this changes to -c in the plural: *luz* (light): *luces*
- Where a noun ends in an unstressed vowel plus s, it doesn't change in the plural: *el lunes* (Monday) / *los lunes* (Mondays).

Consolidation

A Put a tick by the word which correctly completes the sentence.

	a	**b**	**c**	**d**
1 El padre de mi madre es mi	abuelo	hermano	tío	hijo
2 La hija de mi madre es mi	tía	abuela	hermana	prima
3 La esposa de mi tío es mi	hermana	tía	sobrina	madre
4 El hijo de mi tío es mi	hermano	sobrino	primo	tío
5 La hija de mi hermana es mi	abuela	tía	madre	sobrina

B Match the masculine noun with its feminine equivalent.

rey	padre	yerno	marido	príncipe
mujer	princesa	madre	reina	nuera

C Rewrite the following text in the masculine version.

La señora Francisca está casada. Su marido es venezolano. Él vive en Caracas y ella vive en Nueva York. Tienen dos hijas. La madre de su marido está divorciada y vive con ella. Su suegro vive en Madrid con su hija.

In class or at home

A Look at Rosario's family tree and complete the information.

1 Pedro es *el abuelo* de los hijos de Rosario y Jorge.
2 Rafael es _____ de Rosario y Jorge.
3 Dolores es _____ de David.
4 Laura es _____ de Dolores.
5 Luisa es _____ de Pedro y Dolores.
6 Iván es _____ de Laura y Victoria.
7 Carlota es _____ de Iván y Marina.
8 Rosario es _____ de Luisa.
9 Pedro y Dolores son _____ de Rafael.
10 Iván es _____ de Pedro y Dolores.

```
              Pedro = Dolores
        ┌────────┬──────────┬──────┐
David = Rosario  Luisa = Jorge   Rafael
  ┌─────┴─────┐      ┌────┴────┬──────┐
Laura   Victoria   Iván  Carlota  Marina
```

B Complete the chart and then write a short paragraph about Rosario and her family.

Nombre del padre	Número de hijos
Nombre de la madre	Estado civil de su hermano Jorge
Número de hermanos	Número de hijos
Estado civil	Estado civil de su hermano Rafael
Nombre del marido	

Your paragraph could start: El padre de Rosario se llama Pedro y su madre . . .

C Complete the sentences by putting the verbs in brackets in the correct form of the present tense.

1 Pedro _____ casado y _____ un hijo. (estar; tener)
2 Margarita y Javier _____ hermanos. (ser)
3 Hola Silvia ¿qué tal _____ ? (estar)
4 ¿Usted _____ casado? ¿ _____ hijos? (estar; tener)
5 Mi marido y yo _____ en Málaga pero nuestra hija _____ en San Antonio. (vivir)
6 ¿De dónde _____ la señora Peralta? (ser)

D Have there been any recent changes in the Spanish royal family tree? If so, update it. To find out you could consult the Internet.

B ¡Cumpleaños feliz!

Happy Birthday!

<table>
<tr><td>

■ Expresiones esenciales

¿Cuántos años tiene(s)? *(polite / informal)*
Tengo . . . años
¿Cuántos años tiene . . .?
Tiene . . . años
¿Qué fecha es hoy? / ¿A qué fecha estamos?
Hoy es . . . / Hoy estamos a . . .
¿Cuándo es tu cumpleaños?
¿Cuándo es el cumpleaños de . . .?
Mi cumpleaños es el . . .
Su cumpleaños es el . . .

</td><td>

■ Essential expressions

How old are you?
I'm . . . (years old)
How old is . . .?
He / she is . . . (years old)
What's today's date? / What's the date today?
Today is the . . . / It's the . . .
When is your birthday?
When is . . .'s birthday?
My birthday is the . . .
His / her birthday is the . . .

</td></tr>
</table>

1 Possessive adjectives: my, your, his, her, etc

G de Gramática

■ Possessive adjectives

These always go in front of the noun in Spanish. Notice that they agree with what is possessed, NOT with the possessor. For example, two boys referring to their aunt will say *nuestra tía*.

	Singular		Plural	
	masculine	feminine	masculine	feminine
my	**mi** hijo	**mi** hija	**mis** hijos	**mis** hijas
your (sing. informal)	**tu** hermano	**tu** hermana	**tus** hermanos	**tus** hermanas
your (sing. formal); his; her	**su** primo	**su** prima	**sus** primos	**sus** primas
our	**nuestro** sobrino	**nuestra** sobrina	**nuestros** sobrinos	**nuestras** sobrinas
your (plural, informal)	**vuestro** tío	**vuestra** tía	**vuestros** tíos	**vuestras** tías
your (plural, formal); their	**su** abuelo	**su** abuela	**sus** abuelos	**sus** abuelas

Note:

• **su** and **sus** each have several possible meanings and normally in speech there is no ambiguity. However, if the meaning is not clear from the context, Spanish will use *de él, de ella, de usted, de ellos, de ellas* or *de ustedes* to avoid the ambiguity:
su padre: el padre de él(ella, usted); sus apellidos: los apellidos de él (ella, usted . . .)

• There is no Spanish equivalent of apostrophe **s** to express ownership or relationships. *Carmen's husband* has to be expressed literally as 'the husband of Carmen': *el marido de Carmen*.

Información personal

unidad 2

44

A Put the following phrases into Spanish.

Example: Your (plural / formal) grandparents:
Sus abuelos

a Our parents
b His uncle
c Your (sing / informal) mother
d My father
e Your (plural / informal) mother-in-law
f Her daughter
g Their sisters
h His brothers

i Your (sing / formal) sister-in-law
j My brothers-in-law
k His niece and nephew
l Your (plural / informal) cousins
m Our aunts
n Their brothers and sisters
o Her grandsons

B How do you say in Spanish:
a Juan's father
b Maribel's sister
c Pedro's parents
d Ignacio's grandchildren

e my brother's wife
f my mother's cousin
g Alberto and Silvia's daughter
h Javier and Liliana's children

C Change the sentences into the plural form.

Example: Mi primo habla español muy bien.
Mis primos hablan español muy bien.

1 Mi amigo es de Cuba.
2 Nuestra tía escribe muy bien.
3 Tu profesor vive en California.
4 Su primo está divorciado.
5 Vuestro cuñado es soltero.
6 Nuestro padre enseña kárate.

2 Saying how old you are and asking someone his or her age

A Practise saying these numbers with a partner.

5	7	11	15	19	24	36	48	51	62	74	86
91	17	29	43	11	82	15	65	22	18	57	2

■ ¿Cuántos años tienes?

B Choose four of the people mentioned below and ask your partner their ages.
a Felipe de Borbón (Príncipe de España, 1968)
b Isabel Allende (Escritora chilena, 1942)
c Antonio Banderas (Actor español, 1960)
d Plácido Domingo (Cantante de ópera español, 1941)
e Sergio García (Jugador español de golf, 1980)
f Carlos Fuentes (Escritor mexicano, 1928)

■ Tengo 27 años.

3 The date

A Complete the calendar with the names of the months.

Los meses del año

abril
agosto
diciembre
enero
febrero
julio
junio
marzo
mayo
noviembre
octubre
septiembre / setiembre

S	M	T	W	T	F	S
						1
2	3	4	5	6	7	8
9	10	11	12	13	14	15
16	17	18	19	20	21	22
23	24	25	26	27	28	29
30	31					

S	M	T	W	T	F	S
			1	2	3	4
5	6	7	8	9	10	11
13	14	15	16	17	18	19
20	21	22	23	24	25	26
27	28					

S	M	T	W	T	F	S
			1	2	3	4
9	10	8	9	10	11	12
16	17	15	16	17	18	19
23	24	22	23	24	25	26
27	28	29	30	31		

S	M	T	W	T	F	S
					1	2
3	4	5	6	7	8	9
10	11	12	13	14	15	16
17	18	19	20	21	22	23
24	25	26	27	28	29	30

S	M	T	W	T	F	S
1	2	3	4	5	6	7
8	9	10	11	12	13	14
15	16	17	18	19	20	21
22	23	24	25	26	27	28
29	30	31				

S	M	T	W	T	F	S
				1	2	3
5	6	7	8	9	10	11
12	13	14	15	16	17	18
19	20	21	22	23	24	25
26	27	27	29	30		

S	M	T	W	T	F	S
					1	2
3	4	5	6	7	8	9
10	11	12	13	14	15	16
17	18	19	20	21	22	23
24	25	26	27	28	29	27
31						

S	M	T	W	T	F	S
	1	2	3	4	5	6
3	8	9	10	11	12	13
10	15	16	17	18	19	20
17	22	23	24	25	26	27
24	29	27	31			

S	M	T	W	T	F	S
	1	2	3			
4	5	6	7	8	9	10
11	12	13	14	15	16	17
18	19	20	21	22	23	24
25	26	27	28	29	30	

S	M	T	W	T	F	S
2	3	4	5	6	7	8
9	10	11	12	13	14	15
16	17	18	19	20	21	22
23	24	25	26	27	28	29
27	28	29	30	31		

S	M	T	W	T	F	S
9	10	8	9	10	11	12
16	17	15	16	17	18	19
23	24	22	23	24	25	26
27	28	29	30			

S	M	T	W	T	F	S
					1	2	3
4	5	6	7	8	9	10
11	12	13	14	15	16	17
18	19	20	21	22	23	24
25	26	27	28	29	30	31

G de Gramática

Note that the months of the year:
- are not capitalised in Spanish
- are masculine: *Enero blanco, mayo florido* (Snow in January, flowers in May)
- do not require an article: *julio tiene 31 días* but **el mes** de *julio tiene 31 días*

B Work with a partner and use these dates to practise asking and giving the date.

- **a** 10 October
- **b** 30 April
- **c** 14 February
- **d** 24 August
- **e** 5 May
- **f** 27 September
- **g** 9 March
- **h** 12 June
- **i** 15 November
- **j** 11 January

G de Gramática

■ La fecha (*the date*)

- Spanish dates are expressed with cardinal numbers, except for the first day of the month which can also be expressed with the ordinal number *primero*: *el 1 (uno) de mayo* o *el primero de mayo.*
- Except in official documents, dates are written in figures: *el 30 de mayo.*

¿Qué fecha es hoy?   Hoy es   el 30 de mayo
¿A qué fecha estamos? (Hoy) estamos a 25 de abril

C 🎧 Listen to the recording and complete the information.

1 El día de Navidad es el _____
2 El día de Fin de Año es el _____
3 El día de la Constitución española es el
   _____
4 El día de Todos los Santos (*All Saints*)
   es el _____
5 El día de la Independencia de México
   es el _____
6 El día de los enamorados es el
   _____
7 El día de San Fermín es el _____

---

4 | ## Saying when your birthday is and asking someone when his or her birthday is

A Using the mini-dialogue as a model, find out from other people in your group when their birthdays are and write them down.

– *¿Cuándo es tu cumpleaños?*
– *Mi cumpleaños es hoy.*
– *¡Oh! ¡Feliz cumpleaños! ¿Cuántos cumples?*
– *Cumplo 28 años. Y tu cumpleaños, ¿cuándo es?*
– *El 12 de mayo.*

B Ask your partner when his / her birthday is.

C 🎧 Listen to the recording and write down the ages and birthdays of these people.

Nombre	Edad	Día del cumpleaños
Alberto		
Laura		
Gabriel		
Manolo		
Remedios		
Gloria		

¡Cumpleaños feliz!

D Read the text and answer the questions.

Mi familia y yo

Yo me llamo Carmen, soy española pero vivo en Escocia, estoy casada con un inglés y no tengo hijos. Mi familia es una familia grande. Tengo cuatro hermanos: tres hermanas y un hermano. Todos mis hermanos están casados y tienen hijos. Mi hermano mayor, Baltasar, está casado con Susana, y tienen un hijo. Mi hermana Julia que sólo tiene diez meses más que yo está casada con Álvaro. Tienen tres hijos – un niño y dos niñas. Álvaro y su hija Julia no aparecen en la fotografía. Mi hermana Elena es mi gemela, está casada con Pedro y tienen cuatro hijos: tres niños y una niña. Mi hermana pequeña Emilia está casada con Ramón. Tienen dos hijos: un niño y una niña. Mis padres, Baltasar y Emilia, viven en La Coruña. Todos mis hermanos, excepto mi hermana pequeña, cumplen años el día doce. El cumpleaños de Baltasar es el 12 de diciembre; el de Julia es el 12 de julio; el de mi hermana Elena es el 12 de mayo y el de Emilia es el 20 de septiembre.

1 ¿De qué nacionalidad es el marido de Carmen?

2 ¿Quién es mayor Carmen o Julia?

3 ¿Cómo se llama una de las hijas de Julia?

4 ¿Cuántas sobrinas tiene Carmen?

5 ¿Dónde viven los abuelos de los sobrinos de Carmen?

6 ¿Cómo se llama la madre de Carmen?

7 ¿Cuándo es el cumpleaños de Carmen?

Consolidation

A Using exercise D as a model, write a short paragraph introducing yourself and your family.

B Complete the sentences as shown in the example.

Example: Jane is talking to Martin and asks: 'Where are your grandparents from?'
      ¿De dónde son . . . abuelos?
      ¿De dónde son **tus** abuelos?

1 Jim and Dorothy get out of the pool. Jim looks and asks, 'Where are our parents?'
      ¿Dónde están _____ padres?

2 Mary, what's your mother called?
      Mary ¿cómo se llama _____ madre?

3 What's his uncle called?
      ¿Cómo se llama _____ tío?

4 Mum, what languages does our neighbour Luisa speak?
      Mamá ¿qué idiomas habla _____ vecina Luisa?

5 How old is her mother?
      ¿Cuántos años tiene _____ madre?

6 What are their sisters called?
      ¿Cómo se llaman _____ hermanas?

7 How old is his brother?
      ¿Cuántos años tiene _____ hermano?

8 Mr Murphy, where is your wife?

Señor Murphy, ¿dónde está _____ esposa?

9 Marta, where do your parents live?

Marta, ¿dónde viven _____ padres?

10 His niece and nephew are called Laura and Liam.

_____ sobrina y _____ sobrino se llaman Laura y Liam.

C Listen to the recording and write down the dates given.

In class or at home

A Write down the names of the months that have 30 days.

B Complete the sentences.

1 ¿Cuántos años _____ tu padre?

2 ¿_____ día _____ hoy?

3 _____ _____ 25 de mayo.

4 ¿_____ _____ el cumpleaños de Marta?

5 ¿Cuántos hermanos _____ (tú)?

6 Mi hermana y yo _____ gemelas. _____ treinta años.

7 Tus tíos _____ siete hijos. Dos hijos y _____ _____.

8 Mi hermano _____ divorciado y _____ en California.

9 Sus sobrinos _____ japonés muy bien.

C Read the text and complete the information.

Julia, Pedro y Alejandro son españoles. El padre de Julia se llama Javier. La madre de Pedro se llama Gema y el padre de Alejandro se llama Jacinto. Javier y Jacinto son cuñados. La madre de Pedro es la esposa de Jacinto.

1 Pedro y Alejandro son _____

2 Julia y Alejandro son _____

3 Gema es _____ de Julia

4 Julia es _____ de Jacinto

5 Pedro es _____ de Julia

6 Gema es _____ de Javier

7 Jacinto es _____ de Gema

8 Jacinto es _____ de Julia

D Rewrite the following paragraph in the third person.

Me llamo Miriam y vivo en Lima. Mi madre es peruana y mi padre es colombiano. Tengo dos hermanos y una hermana. Mi hermano mayor está soltero y mis otros hermanos están casados. Yo no estoy casada pero tengo un hijo. Mi hijo se llama Francisco. Mis hermanos casados tienen dos hijos cada uno. Mi hermana tiene un niño y una niña y mi hermano tiene dos niños. El hijo de mi hermana tiene cinco años como mi hijo. Mis hermanos viven en los Estados Unidos y mis padres en España.

¿Cómo es?

What is he / she like?

■ **Expresiones esenciales**	■ **Essential expressions**
¿Cómo eres/es? *(informal / polite)*	*What do you look like?*
¿Cómo es?	*What does he / she look like?*
Es + adj.	*He / she is . . .*
Soy bajo/a // de estatura mediana // alto/a	*I am short / of medium height / tall*
Llevo gafas	*I wear / am wearing glasses*
Soy demasiado +adj.	*I am too . . .*
Soy bastante + adj.	*I am quite . . .*
Soy muy + adj.	*I am very . . .*
No soy muy + adj.	*I am not very . . .*
Soy poco + adj.	*I am not very . . .*
Soy un poco + adj.	*I am a bit . . .*
No soy nada + adj.	*I am not at all . . .*
¿De qué color tienes el pelo?	*What colour is your hair?*
¿De qué color tienes los ojos?	*What colour are your eyes?*
Tengo el pelo + adj.	*I have . . . hair*
Tengo los ojos + adj.	*I have . . . eyes*

1 | Saying what someone is like physically

A Working with people in your group, practise describing yourself and other people by using the models and vocabulary shown below. Choose one sentence from each section.

G de Gramática

■ **Describing people**

- **Ser** + **adjective** to refer to essential features: *Soy alto.* (I am tall.)
- **Tener** + **article** + **part of the body** + **adjective** to refer to attributes possessed by a person: *Santiago tiene los ojos azules.* (Santiago has blue eyes.)
- **Llevar** + **noun** meaning 'to have' or 'to wear': *La mujer de la fotografía lleva gafas.* (The woman in the photograph has / is wearing glasses.)
- To ask what somebody is like: *¿Cómo es . . . ? / ¿Qué tal es . . . ?* (more informal) *¿Cómo es tu novio? / ¿Qué tal es tu novio?* (What is your boyfriend like?)

Describing your age

¿Cómo eres?

Soy	joven	(tengo 19 años)
	viejo/a	(tengo 80 años)
No soy	joven	(tengo 45 años)
No soy	mayor	(tengo 45 años)

Describing your build and height

Soy	delgado/a	(peso 54 kilos)
	gordo/a	(peso 100 kilos)

Soy	bajo/a
	de estatura mediana
	alto/a

Describing your hair

¿Cómo tienes el pelo?

Tengo el pelo	largo	*long*
	corto	*short*
	liso	*straight*
	ondulado	*wavy*
	rizado	*curly*

¿De qué color (tienes el pelo)?

Tengo el pelo	rubio
	pelirrojo
	castaño
	negro
	gris /
	canoso
Soy	calvo

Describing your eyes

¿Y los ojos?

¿De qué color tienes los ojos?

Tengo los ojos

azules   verdes   marrones / castaños   grises

Describing your face

Tengo la cara

redonda   cuadrada   alargada   ovalada   grande   pequeña

Llevo / Tengo

barba   bigote   gafas

Describing your looks

Soy	guapo/a	*handsome / pretty*
	feo/a	*ugly*
	atractivo/a	*attractive*
	rubio/a	*fair*
	moreno/a	*dark*

C de Cultura

■ **Una persona rubia o morena**

To refer to people with a fair complexion and light-ish hair, Spaniards use the word *rubio(a): mi madre es rubia.* Also this word is used to refer to somebody with blond hair. To refer to people with a darkish complexion the word *moreno* is used: *mi padre es moreno.*

Describing other parts of your body

Read the words referring to the parts of the human body and then write them down beside the correct part of the body.

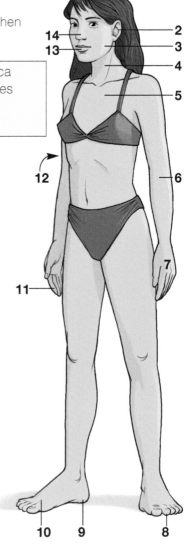

la cabeza	la cara	las orejas	la nariz	la boca
el cuello	la espalda	los brazos	las manos	los pies
los dedos de las manos		el pecho	las piernas	
los dedos de los pies				

Many of the adjectives you have just learned can be also used to describe these parts of the body:

Tengo las manos grandes.   Tengo la nariz larga.
Tengo los brazos cortos.

B Describe somebody in your group and let the others guess who it is.

2 Adjectives and descriptions

A Read the following descriptions and say which describes a man and which describes a woman.

1 Tiene el pelo blanco, corto y liso. Es mayor y bastante gordo. Tiene la cara redonda, los ojos marrones y la nariz pequeña. Lleva gafas y bigote. Es bajo.

2 Es alta, delgada y muy atractiva. Tiene los ojos azules y el pelo negro y largo. Es joven.

Write down in the table the adjectives that describe the man's and the woman's physical appearance.

B Read description **1** again and:

1 Classify the following nouns as masculine (m.) or feminine (f.), singular (sing.) or plural (pl.):
el pelo   la cara   los ojos   la nariz

2 Write down beside each of them the adjectives that describe them, and write down their gender and number.

3 Say how the adjectives agree with the nouns they describe.

4 Do they appear before or after the noun?

Now, read the grammar section carefully.

	adjectives
Man	
Woman	

G de Gramática

■ Adjectives (*Adjetivos*)

Adjectives are words that describe nouns. When we say *Federico es alto y delgado*, the words *alto* and *delgado* are telling us what Federico is like, they give us more information about Federico.

■ Agreement

- Adjectives agree in number (singular and plural) and gender (masculine and feminine) with the nouns they qualify:

  el niño alto   *la niña alta*

  los niños altos   *las niñas altas*

- When a masculine noun and a feminine noun share the same adjective, the adjective is in the masculine plural:

  un hombre y una mujer altos y atractivos.

■ Gender and number

- Adjectives ending in *-o* change to *-a* for the feminine form and add *-s* for plural:

  alto (m.sing.)*;* alta (f.sing.)*; altos* (m.pl.)*; altas* (f.pl.).

- Adjectives ending in other vowels have the same form for masculine and feminine and add *-s* for plural:

  grande (m. f. sing) *grandes* (m. f. pl.);   *amable* (m. f. sing.) *amables* (m. f. pl.)

- Adjectives ending in a consonant have the same form for masculine and feminine and add *-es* for the plural. Adjectives of nationality do not follow this rule (see page 21).

  joven (m. f. sing.) *jóvenes* (m. f. pl.)

  Note that adjectives ending in *-z* change the *z* to a *c* in the plural:

  feliz (m. f. sing.) *felices* (m. f. pl.)

- Adjectives ending in *-ón, -án, -or* (except comparatives) add *-a* for the feminine form:

  trabajador (m. sing.) *trabajadora* (f. sing.) *trabajadores* (m. pl.) *trabajadoras* (f. pl.)

  holgazán (m. sing.) *holgazana* (f. sing.) *holgazanes* (m. pl.) *holgazanas* (f. pl.)

■ Position

- In Spanish the adjective often goes after the noun, whereas in English it usually goes before:

  una señora baja y delgada (a short, thin lady)

- However, some adjectives such as *bueno, malo, grande* can go in front of the noun, undergoing a change in form:

  - *grande* changes to *gran* when it is used immediately before a masculine or feminine singular noun: *un gran chico* (a great boy); *una mujer de gran belleza* (a woman of great beauty).

  - *bueno* changes to *buen* when it is used immediately before a masculine singular noun: *un buen día (a good day)* but *una buena fiesta (a good party).*

  - *malo* changes to *mal* when it is used immediately before a masculine singular noun: *un mal amigo (a bad friend)* but *una mala amiga (a bad friend).*

Note that more often than not a different position suggests a variation of meaning. This is most obvious with adjectives that can be used both before a noun and after a noun but with different meanings. For example,

Grande: *un hombre grande* (a big man) / *un gran hombre* (a great man)

Bueno: *un hombre bueno* (a good man) / *un buen hombre* (a harmless / simple man)

Match the descriptions with the photographs.

1 Es mayor, atractiva, tiene los ojos marrones y el pelo bastante corto y liso. Es delgada y baja.
2 Es bastante joven, tiene el pelo corto y negro. Es guapo.
3 Es joven, atractiva y delgada. Tiene los ojos marrones y el pelo rubio.
4 Es mayor. Tiene el pelo gris, liso y corto. No es gordo y es de estatura mediana. Tiene la cara cuadrada, los ojos marrones y la nariz pequeña.

D Rewrite the following sentences in plural form.

1 Mi sobrino es inteligente.
2 El ordenador es nuevo.
3 El amigo de Pedro es tranquilo.
4 El chico canadiense es amable.
5 La clase es grande.
6 Su marido es feo.
7 Nuestro tío es tímido.
8 Vuestro perro es bueno.

E Write the feminine version of the following sentences.

Example: Nuestro tío es alto.
Nuestra tía es alta.

1 Mi primo es atractivo.
2 Su padre es de estatura mediana.
3 Nuestro amigo es guapo.
4 Tu suegro es bajo.
5 Vuestros maridos son jóvenes.
6 Mis nietos son inteligentes.
7 Su yerno es feo.
8 Tus hermanos son holgazanes.

F Complete each sentence with a suitable adjective.

1 Mi hijo es		**a** grises
2 Juan y su mujer son		**b** interesantes
3 Las pinturas son		**c** vieja y fea
4 Sus ojos son		**d** muy guapo y amable
5 Las profesoras son		**e** feliz
6 La casa es		**f** azules
7 Los elefantes son		**g** trabajadoras
8 Es una persona		**h** aburridos

G Translate the following sentences into Spanish.

1 My daughter has blue eyes.
2 The tall, fat boy is my cousin Pedro.
3 I have an attractive boyfriend.
4 We live in a small, old house.
5 I have a new car.
6 My Spanish teacher, Dolores, is very tall.
7 She has long, curly hair.
8 Rosa and Miguel are happy.

H Complete the text by writing down the appropriate endings to the adjectives.

Mi mujer es muy guap___. No es muy joven. Tiene el pelo rubi___ y ondulad___. Su cara es redond___. Tiene los ojos marron___ y grand___, una nariz pequeñ___ y una boca grand___. Sus manos son muy bonit___. Tiene los dedos larg___ y delgad___.

3 Describing someone's character

A Can you guess what these adjectives mean in English?

introvertido/a	paciente	alegre	activo/a	extrovertido/a	pesimista
simpático/a	trabajador/a	egoísta	interesante	generoso/a	nervioso/a
antipático/a	optimista	holgazán/a	tranquilo/a	aburrido/a	impaciente
organizado/a	pasivo/a	serio/a	desorganizado/a		

B First write down those adjectives which have a positive meaning and then write down their opposites:

+	–
optimista	pesimista

C Listen to the recording and note down personality traits in Spanish as you hear them. Afterwards, describe the personality of any of the three people to your partner.

Mónica   Lionel   Ana

D Read the following information about Marta and guess the meaning of the words that go before the adjective. What do you think these words say about the adjective?

Marta	es	demasiado muy bastante – un poco poco	nerviosa
	no es	nada	

G de Gramática

■ Intensifiers of the adjective

Words like *demasiado* (too much), *muy* (very), *bastante* (quite / rather), *un poco* (a little / a bit), *poco* (not very), *no ... nada* (not ... at all) + adjective modify the adjective by stating to what extent the adjective applies.

Mi hermano es muy alto. (My brother is very tall.)
Marisa es bastante simpática. (Marisa is quite nice.)

■ *Poco* and *un poco*

- *poco* is normally used with adjectives which have a positive meaning:
  Manuela es poco simpática. (Manuela is not very nice.)
- *un poco* is normally used with adjectives which have a negative meaning:
  Sus amigos son un poco antipáticos. (His friends are a bit unfriendly.)

E Now, describe your character and that of your best friend, using some of the adjectives that you have just learned. Complete the table and then share the information with some people in your group.

	Yo soy	Mi mejor amigo/a es
. . . demasiado		
. . . muy		
. . . bastante		
. . . un poco		
. . . poco		
. . . no . . . nada		

F Working in a small group, think of a famous person, and give a description (physical appearance and character) of that person to the rest of your group without saying the name and see if they can guess who you are talking about.

¿Estoy guapo o soy guapo? Ser or estar?

A Read the following phrases and discuss their meaning.

1 Mi marido <u>es muy feo</u> pero hoy <u>está muy guapo</u>.
2 Eleonora <u>es alegre</u> pero hoy <u>está triste</u>.
3 <u>Soy nerviosa</u> pero en estos momentos <u>estoy tranquila</u>.
4 <u>Soy una persona tranquila</u> pero en estos momentos <u>estoy nerviosa</u>.

B Classify the underlined expressions according to whether they indicate an intrinsic characteristic or a changeable state or condition.

C Complete the following sentences with *ser* or *estar* as appropriate.

1 Mi hermano _____ contento, tiene un coche nuevo.
2 _____ preocupada, tengo un examen.
3 Marta _____ atractiva pero hoy _____ fea.
4 Mi profesora _____ muy organizada pero hoy _____ desorganizada.
5 Mi padre _____ activo pero estos días _____ cansado.
6 Mis alumnos _____ trabajadores pero hoy _____ pasivos.

G de Gramática

■ *Ser* or *estar*

• ***Ser*** + **adjective** is used to indicate intrinsic qualities and physical characteristics: *Luisa es guapa e inteligente.* (Luisa is beautiful and intelligent.) (inherent features).
• ***Estar*** + **adjective** is used to indicate a temporary state of affairs, such as a state of mind or mood: *Luisa es tranquila pero hoy está nerviosa.* (Luisa is a calm person by nature (intrinsic quality) but today she is tense.) (state of mind, changeable state).

¿Cómo es?

57

Consolidation

A 🔊 Listen to the recording and write down the missing information.

El abuelo de Claudia

Mi abuelo es un hombre _____ (1) pero tiene un aspecto
joven. Es muy alegre y _____ (2) pero a veces es
demasiado _____ (3). Es de estatura _____ (4) y
fuerte. Tiene el pelo _____ (5) y liso. Su cara es
_____ (6) y proporcionada. Tiene una nariz _____ (7)
y una boca bastante grande. Lleva _____ (8), un bigote
grande. No lleva gafas porque ve bien. Tiene los ojos
_____ (9). Sus ojos reflejan un carácter generoso. Es
_____ (10) y trabajador pero a veces es un poco
desorganizado. Su cuerpo es _____ (11) y musculoso. Sus manos son bastante
_____ (12) pero son fuertes y tienen unos dedos _____ (13) y delgados. La
verdad es que mi abuelo es muy _____(14) y no es nada aburrido.

B Answer the following questions about Claudia's grandfather.

1 ¿Cómo es físicamente?
2 ¿De qué color tiene el pelo?
3 ¿Cómo es su nariz?
4 ¿Lleva gafas?
5 ¿De qué color son sus ojos?
6 ¿Cómo son los dedos de sus manos?

C Underline all the adjectives and classify them according to whether they are describing the physical appearance or the character of Claudia's grandfather.

D Which two expressions in the above paragraph imply negative characteristics?

In class or at home

A Write down the questions to the following answers:

1 Soy baja y bastante delgada.
2 Tengo el pelo pelirrojo y rizado.
3 Tengo los ojos verdes.
4 Sí, soy atractiva.
5 Sí, llevo gafas.

Is this the description of a man or a woman?

B Read the following sentences and give appropriate endings to the adjectives.
a El hermano de María es fe___.
b Mi gata es mal___.

c Juan es baj___ y poco fuert___.

d El coche de Paco es viej___.

e Nuestra abuela tiene unos ojos grand___ y bonit___.

C Read the following description and then write an opposite one.

Mi vecino es un hombre alto y feo. Tiene los ojos pequeños y el pelo rizado. Su nariz es grande y desproporcionada. Es bastante antipático y serio.

D Rewrite the following sentences making them masculine and singular.

1 Las tías de mi madre son mayores.

2 Mis amigas son agradables.

3 Las profesoras alemanas son serias.

4 Nuestras primas tienen los ojos grandes y negros.

5 Las niñas son trabajadoras.

E Match the expressions in the column on the left with the expressions on the right.

1 poco trabajador(a)	**a** pasivo/a
2 nada simpático/a	**b** egoísta
3 poco fuerte	**c** joven
4 poco organizado/a	**d** holgazán(a)
5 nada generoso/a	**e** antipático/a
6 nada activo/a	**f** débil
7 nada mayor/viejo/a	**g** delgado/a
8 nada gordo/a	**h** desorganizado/a

F Translate the following sentences into Spanish.

1 He is an intelligent man.

2 We are quite organised people.

3 Our daughters have dark eyes.

4 His neighbour is rather unpleasant.

5 I am quite tall.

6 She is a very organised woman.

7 My sister is a bit timid.

8 My best friend is very nice.

G Complete the following sentences with *ser* or *estar*, as appropriate.

1 Paco _____ simpático pero hoy _____ muy antipático.

2 Nosotros _____ bien ¿y vosotros?

3 El abuelo de Julia _____ mayor pero _____ muy joven.

4 _____ contenta con mis alumnos: _____ muy trabajadores.

5 Estos días sus hijos _____ bastante nerviosos.

6 Ellos _____ unas personas optimistas pero _____ preocupados.

7 Tú _____ aburrido, pasivo y egoísta. ¡No _____ nada contenta contigo!

H Write down the verbs *ser*, *tener* and *llevar* in the present indicative.

D ¿A qué te dedicas?

What do you do?

1 Professions and jobs

G de Gramática

Ser + **noun of job or profession** is used to indicate profession: *Juan es fontanero.* (Juan is a plumber.); *Laura es dentista.* (Laura is a dentist.)

A ¿Dónde trabajan estas personas?
Link the job title to the place of work.

profesión		**lugar de trabajo**	
futbolista	estudiante	banco	tienda
fotógrafa	médico	editorial	bar
camarero	dependiente	universidad	oficina
profesora de	traductor	hotel	escuela de
idiomas	empleado de	hospital	idiomas
secretaria	banca	equipo de fútbol	
recepcionista		periódico	

B Fill in the missing information.

Guillermo **Irene** **Miguel** **Juliana** **Paco**

1 Paco es _____. Trabaja en un _____.
2 Irene es _____. Trabaja en un _____.
3 Miguel es _____. Trabaja en un _____.
4 Juliana es _____. Trabaja en una _____.
5 Guillermo es _____. Trabaja en un _____.
6 Laura es _____. Estudia en la _____.

Laura

Información personal

unidad 2

Identifying people, places and things. The article.

A Complete the table by inserting the missing forms of the definite article and by writing the corresponding plural forms.

singular	plural	singular	plural
la amiga	las amigas	. . . casa	
. . . hombre		. . . arquitecta	
. . . chico		. . . día	
. . . libro		. . . mujer	
. . . camarero		. . . mano	

B Put the appropriate indefinite article with each noun.

___ padre   ___ príncipe
___ marido   ___ señores
___ abuelos   ___ amiga
___ compañeros   ___ suegras
___ profesora   ___ madre

C Read the sentences below and write in the missing articles.

1 ___ profesor de español se llama Juan.
2 ___ hermanas de ___ príncipe Felipe están casadas.
3 ___ madre de Luis tiene ___ coche italiano.
4 ___ reyes de España hablan inglés muy bien.
5 Tenemos ___ libros en español.
6 ___ español es ___ idioma interesante.
7 Tengo ___amigo en Madrid.
8 ___ abuela de Pedro es de Guatemala.

G de Gramática

■ Definite article

- The definite article is used to refer to something specific: *El profesor de español* (The Spanish teacher).
- The article must always agree in number and gender with its noun.

the	masculine	feminine
singular	el abuelo	la abuela
plural	los abuelos	las abuelas

Note:
The masculine singular article used after *de* must contract thus: *de* + *el* = *del*. *Elena es la hermana del príncipe de España.* (Elena is the prince of Spain's sister.)

- The same rule applies after *a*: *a* + *el* = *al*: *Los niños van al colegio.* (The children go to school.)

■ Indefinite article

- The indefinite article is used to refer to something that is not specific: *Un profesor de español* (A Spanish teacher).
- The article must always agree in number and gender with its noun.

	masculine	feminine
a, an	un profesor	una profesora
some, any	unos profesores	unas profesoras

■ Articles and professions

- Spanish does not use the article when stating a person's occupation:
  Soy profesora. (I am a teacher.) *Es músico.* (He's a musician.)
  An exception to this rule occurs when the article is used to identify or qualify:
  ¿Quién es esa señora? Es la profesora de español. Es una profesora excelente. (Who is that lady? She is the Spanish teacher. She is an excellent teacher.)

Jobs, professions and gender

A Read the grammar section below and then complete the table with the feminine forms. Can you guess their English equivalents?

masculine	feminine	English
a el médico		
b el taxista		
c el jardinero		
d el cantante		
e el abogado		
f el ingeniero		
g el programador		
h el mecánico		
i el deportista		
j el peluquero		
k el traductor		
l el estudiante		

G de Gramática

Many jobs and professions have a masculine and feminine form.

- **Masculine nouns ending in -*o* are made feminine by changing the -*o* to -*a*:**
  el arquitecto (m)   la arquitecta (f)   el carpintero (m)   la carpintera (f)
- **Masculine nouns ending in -*or* are made feminine by adding -*a*:**
  el profesor (m)   la profesora (f)
- **Nouns ending in -*ista*, remain the same in the masculine and feminine:**
  el / la tenista   el / la dentista
- **Many names ending in -*nte* remain the same in the masculine and feminine:**
  el / la estudiante   el / la gerente
  Note that some of these nouns have a feminine form:
  el dependiente   la dependienta   el presidente   la presidenta

Saying what you do for a living and asking someone else what he or she does

A Read the mini-dialogue between Marta and Enrique then answer Enrique's question.

Marta

■ Soy ingeniera. Y tú, Enrique, ¿a qué te dedicas? ¿Estudias o trabajas?

Enrique

■ Soy recepcionista. Trabajo en un hotel. Y tú, ¿qué haces?

B Use the mini-dialogue to find out the occupations of some people in your group.

Listen to the recording and complete the table.

nombre	nacionalidad	estado civil	lugar de residencia	profesión	lugar de trabajo
Laura					
Óscar					
Carlota					
David					
Soledad					
Leticia					

D Adopt a new personality. Complete the form.

NOMBRE _____

APELLIDOS _____

EDAD _____

NACIONALIDAD _____

ESTADO CIVIL _____

LUGAR DE RESIDENCIA _____

PROFESIÓN _____

LUGAR DE TRABAJO _____

CARÁCTER _____

ASPECTO FÍSICO _____

Then, take it in turns with your partner to ask and answer questions to find out who you are now. Write down the relevant questions first.

E Work with a partner and see if you can guess the profession or job of the following people.

Example: José arregla jardines. Es jardinero.

1 Pedro arregla coches. Es _____
2 Celia cura enfermos. Es _____
3 Francisco corta el pelo. Es _____
4 Julián y Emilio diseñan casas. Son _____
5 Elena y Guillermo escriben artículos. Son _____
6 Beatriz canta. Es _____

F Interviewing Pablo. Work with a partner and write the questions that correspond to the answers:

Example: Me llamo Pablo. ¿Cómo se llama?

1 Vivo en Pachuca, México.
2 Sí, estoy casado.
3 Sí, tengo tres hijos, una hija y dos hijos.
4 Tengo 72 años.
5 Soy médico pero ya no trabajo, estoy jubilado.
6 Mi mujer es pintora.
7 Mi hija María es secretaria, mi hijo Manuel estudia medicina y mi hijo Jorge es periodista pero no tiene trabajo, está en paro.

G Now write a short paragraph about Pablo. Start: *Pablo vive en Pachuca, México . . .*

Qualities for jobs

A All the following adjectives could be used to describe the qualities you need in order to do a job. Can you remember what they mean?

extrovertido/a puntual organizado/a paciente activo/a
disciplinado/a dinámico/a creativo/a independiente

How would you define yourself? *Yo soy una persona . . .*

Which qualities do you think are necessary to do the following jobs well:

médico diseñador profesor de matemáticas secretaria
guía turístico taxista estudiante político

Para ser un buen médico es	imprescindible necesario importante aconsejable conveniente	ser	+	adjective

G de Gramática

- **Para** + **infinitive** to indicate purpose: *para ser un buen médico* (to be a good doctor)
- **Ser** + **adjective** is used to express subjective opinions; that is why it can be used to refer to the necessary or desirable qualities for doing a job or an activity:
  Es   *imprescindible* (essential); *necesario* (necessary); *importante* (important);
       aconsejable (advisable); *conveniente* (desirable)
- The adjectives *bueno* (good) and *malo* (bad) lose their last vowel when they are placed before a masculine singular noun: *para ser un buen mecánico* but *para ser una buena mecánica*.

B **Lo bueno y lo malo de un trabajo.** Read the following adjectives and classify them as positive or negative:

monótono	divertido	creativo	aburrido	fácil	interesante
duro	seguro	peligroso	difícil	cansado	

Now complete the information using some of the adjectives you have just learnt:

Yo soy . . .
Mi trabajo es
 . . . demasiado
 . . . muy
 . . . bastante
 . . . un poco
 . . . poco
 . . . no . . . nada

■ Yo soy peluquero y mi trabajo es muy creativo, bastante divertido pero un poco duro
Y tú, ¿a qué te dedicas? ¿Cómo es tu trabajo?

Now ask people in your group about their jobs.

C 🗣 Listen to various people saying what they do for a living and talking about their jobs. Complete the table.

	trabajo	+	—
Elena	profesora	interesante	duro
Amador			
Violeta			
Mario			
Carlota			
Javier			

Consolidation

A Say where these people work:

1 Patricia es camarera. Trabaja en . . .
2 Miguel es fotógrafo. Trabaja en . . .
3 Cecilia es estudiante. Estudia en . . .
4 Santiago es médico. Trabaja en . . .
5 Rosario es recepcionista. Trabaja en . . .

B Complete the following sentences.
1 Mi abuela es mayor. No trabaja, está . . .
2 El hijo de mi prima no tiene trabajo, está . . .
3 Mi padre tiene 68 años. No trabaja, está . . .

C Complete the following information about yourself.

Soy _____, trabajo / estudio en _____. Mi trabajo / profesión es muy _____, bastante _____ pero un poco _____. Mis compañeros de trabajo son _____ y mi jefe es _____ pero a veces es bastante _____.

In class or at home

A Complete the following sentences with the appropriate article and adjectival endings.

1 ___ tía Juana es muy trabajador___
2 Tienes ___ trabajo monóton___
3 ___ jefa de mi marido es un poco impacient___
4 ___ compañeros de trabajo de Emilia son simpátic___
5 Para ser ___ buen___ secretaria es necesario ser organizad___
6 ___ trabajo de Alicia es peligros___
7 Para ser ___ buen estudiante es aconsejable ser disciplinad___
8 ___ profesión de nuestro padre es interesant___

B Say what the following people do for a living or as an occupation .

1 Jaime enseña historia. Es . . .
2 Manuela y Leticia estudian. Son . . .
3 Eugenio traduce libros. Es . . .
4 María trabaja en un bar. Es . . .
5 Jacinto escribe programas informáticos. Es . . .
6 Rosa y Fernando arreglan coches. Son . . .

C Read the text then say whether the statements below are true (*verdaderos*) or false (*falsos*). If false, correct them.

Mis padres, mis hermanos y yo somos una familia típica. Mi padre es inglés y mi madre es de Colombia. Mi madre tiene veintitrés años más que mi hermano y dos más que mi padre. Tengo dos hermanos, un hermano y una hermana. Mi hermano es el mayor, tiene veinticinco años y vive en Nueva York. Mi hermana es la pequeña, tiene nueve años y vive con mis padres. Yo soy el mediano, tengo dieciocho años y estudio en una universidad norteamericana. Mi padre no tiene trabajo en estos momentos. Mi madre trabaja de dependienta en una tienda. Mi hermano mayor arregla coches.

1 Su madre tiene cuarenta y seis años.
2 Su padre tiene cuarenta y nueve años.
3 Tiene dos hermanos.
4 Su madre es colombiana.
5 Su padre tiene un buen trabajo.
6 Su madre es dependienta.
7 Su hermano mayor es mecánico.
8 La persona que habla es una chica.

D Conjugate the following verbs in the present indicative: *arreglar*, *trabajar*, *tener*.

Acércate al mundo del español

A Before reading the text, match the words on the left with their definitions on the right.

1	Los indios de Hispanoamérica	**a**	son de origen negro y blanco
2	Los negros de Hispanoamérica	**b**	son de origen africano
3	Los blancos de Hispanoamérica	**c**	son de origen indio y blanco
4	Los mestizos	**d**	son de origen europeo
5	Los mulatos	**e**	son de origen asiático

B Read the text and then say if the following statements are true or false.

1 En México se habla español, maya y náhuatl.
2 Todos los españoles hablan español y catalán.
3 En Perú y Bolivia hablan aimará, quechua y español.
4 En Ecuador sólo se habla español.

Así somos

El mundo del español es un mundo compuesto por personas de todo tipo. Somos altos, bajos, alegres, melancólicos, simpáticos, antipáticos, guapos, feos .... Somos indios, blancos, mestizos, negros, mulatos. Somos de origen europeo, africano y asiático. Vivimos en países grandes, pequeños, pobres, ricos .... Bailamos flamenco, tango, salsa, merengue .... Hablamos español y otras lenguas.

En Hispanoamérica, el español convive con lenguas amerindias, las lenguas nativas. Las más destacables son:

El náhuatl, la lengua del imperio azteca, que subsiste en México.

El maya es la lengua que se habla en el sur de México, Guatemala y Yucatán.

El quechua, la lengua del imperio inca, que se habla en Bolivia y Perú.

El araucano es la lengua que se habla en Chile.

El guaraní que se habla en Paraguay.

El aimará que se habla en Perú y Bolivia.

Palabras como 'tomate', 'tabaco', 'cacao', 'cacahuete', 'chocolate', 'canoa' vienen de estas lenguas amerindias.

En España, el español convive con el gallego, el catalán, el vasco y el valenciano, lenguas habladas en Galicia, Cataluña, País Vasco y Valencia respectivamente.

El mundo del español es un mundo fascinante y sorprendente.

Essential vocabulary

La familia — *The family*

esposo / marido (m)	*husband*
esposa / mujer (f)	*wife*
matrimonio (m)	*married couple*
padre (m)	*father*
padrastro (m)	*stepfather*
madre (f)	*mother*
madrastra (f)	*stepmother*
padres (m pl)	*parents*
hijo (m)	*son*
hija (f)	*daughter*
hijastro / hijastra	*stepson / stepdaughter*
hijos (m pl)	*children (offspring)*
hijo/a adoptivo/a	*adopted son / daughter*
hermano (m)	*brother*
hermana (f)	*sister*
gemelo/a	*twin*
hermanos (m pl)	*siblings*
hermanastro	*stepbrother*
hermanastra	*stepsister*
abuelo (m)	*grandfather*
abuela (f)	*grandmother*
abuelos (m pl)	*grandparents*
nieto (m)	*grandson*
nieta (f)	*granddaughter*
nietos (m pl)	*grandchildren*
tío (m)	*uncle*
tía (f)	*aunt*
tíos (m pl)	*aunt and uncle*
primo/a	*cousin*
sobrino (m)	*nephew*
sobrina (f)	*niece*

La familia política — *The in-laws, etc.*

suegro (m)	*father-in-law*
suegra (f)	*mother-in-law*
cuñado (m)	*brother-in-law*
cuñada (f)	*sister-in-law*
yerno (m)	*son-in-law*
nuera (f)	*daughter-in-law*
novio (m)	*boyfriend, fiancé, groom*
novia (f)	*girlfriend, fiancée, bride*
pareja (f)	*partner, couple*

Estado civil — *Marital status*

soltero/a	*single*
casado/a	*married*
separado/a	*separated*
divorciado/a	*divorced*
viudo/a	*widowed*

Los meses del año — *The months of the year*

enero	*January*
febrero	*February*
marzo	*March*
abril	*April*
mayo	*May*
junio	*June*
julio	*July*
agosto	*August*
se(p)tiembre	*September*
octubre	*October*
noviembre	*November*
diciembre	*December*
fecha (f)	*date*
mes (m)	*month*
año (m)	*year*
cumpleaños (m)	*birthday*
lugar de nacimiento	*place of birth*

Profesiones — *Professions*

abogado/a	*lawyer, solicitor*
ama/o de casa	*housewife / househusband*
arquitecto/a	*architect*
artista	*artist*
atleta	*athlete*
camarero/a	*waiter / waitress, chambermaid (female only)*
cantante	*singer*
carpintero/a	*carpenter*
cartero/a	*postman / woman*
cocinero/a	*cook*
contable	*accountant*
dentista	*dentist*
dependiente/a	*shop assistant*
director(a)	*manager, director, principal*
electricista	*electrician*
empleado/a	*employee, clerk*
estudiante	*student*
farmacéutico/a	*pharmacist*
fontanero/a	*plumber*
fotógrafo/a	*photographer*
funcionario/a	*civil servant*
gerente	*manager*
ingeniero/a	*engineer*
jefe/a	*boss*
mécanico/a	*mechanic*
médico/a	*doctor*
músico/a	*musician*
policía	*policeman / woman*
profesor(a)	*teacher, lecturer*
programador(a)	*programmer*
recepcionista	*receptionist*

secretario/a	secretary
supervisor(a)	supervisor
taxista	taxi driver
estar en paro	to be unemployed
estar jubilado/a	to be retired

viejo/a	old
mayor	older
menor	younger
mejor	better
peor	worse

Adjetivos para describir el carácter
Adjectives for describing character

aburrido/a	boring
activo/a	active
antipático/a	unpleasant, unfriendly
alegre	jolly, happy
creativo/a	creative
desorganizado/a	disorganised
dinámico/a	dynamic
disciplinado/a	disciplined
divertido/a	funny, amusing
egoísta	selfish
estudioso/a	studious
extrovertido/a	extroverted
fuerte	strong
generoso/a	generous
holgazán(a)	lazy
impaciente	impatient
independiente	independent
inteligente	intelligent
interesante	interesting
introvertido/a	introverted
nervioso/a	nervous
optimista	optimistic
organizado/a	organised
paciente	patient
pasivo/a	passive
pesimista	pessimistic
puntual	punctual
serio/a	serious
simpático/a	nice, friendly, pleasant
tranquilo/a	tranquil, calm
tímido/a	shy
trabajador(a)	hard-working
triste	sad

Adjetivos para describir el aspecto físico
Adjectives for describing physical appearance

alto/a	tall
bajo/a	short
delgado/a	thin
feo/a	ugly
gordo/a	fat
grande	big
guapo/a	good-looking
joven	young
moreno/a	dark
pequeño/a	small
rubio/a	fair

Adjetivos para describir formas
Adjectives for describing shapes

alargado/a	longish / elongated
cuadrado/a	square
ovalado/a	oval
redondo/a	round

Adjetivos para describir los colores
Colour adjectives

azul	blue
blanco/a	white
castaño/a	brown (of hair)
gris	grey
marrón	brown
negro/a	black
pelirrojo/a	red-haired
verde	green

El cuerpo humano
The human body

boca (f)	mouth
brazo (m)	arm
cabeza (f)	head
cara (f)	face
cuello (m)	neck
dedo (m)	finger / toe
espalda (f)	back
nariz (f)	nose
mano (f)	hand
ojo (m)	eye
oreja (f)	ear
pecho (m)	breast / chest
pierna (f)	leg
pie (m)	foot

llevar gafas (f pl)	to wear glasses
llevar barba (f)	to have a beard
llevar bigote (m)	to have a moustache

En donde vivimos

A ## Cosas de ciudad

In the city / town

■ **Expresiones esenciales**	**Essential expressions**
¿Adónde va(s)? *(polite / informal)*	*Where are you going?*
Voy a la farmacia a comprar aspirinas	*I'm going to the chemist's to buy aspirins*
¿Dónde vive(s)? *(polite / informal)*	*Where do you live?*
Vivo en la calle / la plaza / la avenida . . .	*I live in [. . .] street / square / avenue*
¿En qué número?	*At which number?*
En el número . . .	*At number . . .*
¿Cuál es tu / su dirección? *(informal / polite)*	*What is your address?*
Mi dirección es . . .	*My address is . . .*
¿Qué (número de) teléfono tiene(s)?	*What is your phone number?*
(polite / informal)	
¿Tiene(s) teléfono / fax / correo electrónico?	*Do you have a phone / fax / e-mail?*
(polite / informal)	
Mi teléfono / fax / correo electrónico es . . .	*My phone / fax / e-mail is . . .*
Oye, perdona / Oiga, perdone *(informal / polite)*	*Excuse me!*
¿Hay un / una (+ lugar) por aquí?	*Is there a (+ place) around here?*
¿Dónde está el/la (+ lugar)?	*Where is the (+ place)?*
La primera / segunda / tercera calle	*The first / second / third street*
a la derecha / a la izquierda	*on the right / on the left*
Todo recto	*Straight on*

1 ### Amenities

A Here is a list of places and amenities in a town. Can you guess
their meanings?

El ayuntamiento	El hotel	El teatro
La calle	La Oficina de Turismo	El cine
La avenida	La Oficina de Correos	El banco
La plaza	El hospital	Las tiendas
El parque	La farmacia	El supermercado
La estación de	La cafetería	El mercado
autobuses	El restaurante	Los grandes
La parada de autobús	El bar	almacenes
La estación de tren	La catedral	
El aeropuerto	La iglesia	
El aparcamiento	El museo	

B Now classify the places in Ex. A under the following headings:

Places to stay	Information	Streets, etc	Shops	Bank/Post office

Public buildings	Health	Culture & entertainment	Transport	Eating and drinking

C Complete the sentences with the appropriate form of *ir* (to go) and a place from the list above.

¿Adónde vas?

Example: (Yo) *voy al aeropuerto* a coger / tomar un avión.

1 (Yo) _____ a ver una película.
2 (Mi novio) _____ a tomar café con mis amigas.
3 (Mi hermana) _____ a comprar aspirinas.
4 (Ella) _____ a echar una carta.
5 (Nosotros) _____ a sacar dinero.
6 (Vosotras) _____ a comprar fruta.
7 (Los niños) _____ a comprar chocolate.
8 (Tú) _____ a coger / tomar un autobús.
9 (Usted) _____ a reservar una habitación.
10 (Ustedes) _____ a ver una exposición de pintura.

G de Gramática

■ Expressing destination and purpose

- To ask about destination: **¿Adónde + ir?** (literally where to + to go?). ¿Adónde vas? (Where are you going?) The verb *ir* (to go) is an irregular verb. Its conjugation is as follows:

Ir (to go)			
(yo)	voy (*I go / am going*)	(nosotros(as))	vamos (*we go / are going*)
(tú)	vas (*you go / are going*)	(vosotros(as))	vais (*you go / are going*)
(usted)	va (*you go / is going*)	(ustedes)	van (*you go / are going*)
(él / ella)	va (*he / she goes / is going*)	(ellos(as))	van (*they go / are going*)

- To answer: **Ir a + definite article + noun** (to go to + noun)
  Voy al banco. (I go / am going to the bank.)
- To express purpose: **a + infinitive + noun**:
  *Voy al banco **a sacar dinero***. (I go / am going to the bank to withdraw money.)

C de Cultura

■ *Coger* or *tomar*?

The word *coger* meaning 'to take', 'to catch' (*coger un autobús*, to catch a bus) is a taboo word in some Hispano-American countries, for example, in Mexico and Argentina, and should be avoided there. Use *tomar* (*tomar un autobús*) instead of *coger*.

D Asking for an address and giving your address.
Read and listen to the following mini-dialogues.
- ¿Dónde vives?
- Vivo en la calle San Andrés.
- ¿En qué número?
- En el 15. Y tú, ¿dónde vives?
- Vivo en la plaza de Pontevedra, número 28.

- ¿Cuál es su dirección?
- (Mi dirección es) Avenida de Pescadores, número 12.

Now find out where people in your group live.

E Read the envelopes and underline the abbreviations for the following words: *calle, avenida, plaza, número, código postal, señor, señora, doctor.*

F Now complete the information for the first envelope:

Nombre *Juana* Apellidos _____ _____

Calle _____ Nº _____

C.P. _____ Población _____

Provincia _____

País _____

1

Sra Juana del Río Moreno
C / Almeda , Nº 25
14098 Santiago de Compostela
La Coruña
España

2

Dr Fernando Costa Suárez
Avda. de América, 101
Veracruz
México

3

Sr Fuentes Márquez
Pl. Mayor, Nº 32
C.P. 32008
Córdoba
Argentina

2 **Asking for and giving contact details**

A Read the mini-dialogue.

■ ¿El teléfono del aeropuerto, por favor?

■ ¿Noventa y uno dos cuatro cero veinticinco catorce

■ Gracias, adiós.

C de Cultura

■ **Telephone and fax numbers**
Telephone and fax numbers are said in tens or in pairs whenever possible:
943 64 55 78 *nueve cuatro tres sesenta y cuatro cincuenta y cinco setenta y ocho* or
nueve cuatro tres seis cuatro cinco cinco siete ocho.

■ **Answering the phone**
In Spain: *¿Diga?* or *¿Dígame?* In Mexico: *¿Bueno?*
In most parts of South America: *¿Aló?* or *¿Sí?*

In Argentina and Uruguay: *¿Hola?*
In Mexico: *¿Bueno?*

■ **Giving an e-mail or web address**
E-mail is *correo electrónico* and is widely used. Web address is *dirección de web.*
c.garota@hispano.es : ce punto garota (una palabra) arroba (@) hispano punto e ese
http:/ / www.luz.chile:hache, te, te, pe, dos puntos barra barra uve doble uve doble uve doble punto luz punto chile

B Listen to the conversations and write down the phone numbers.

nombre	número de teléfono
Instituto de idiomas	
Ayuntamiento	
Restaurante 'El Sol'	
Embajada de España en Londres	

C Listen to the e-mail and web addresses and write them down.

a Mi correo electrónico es . . .
b El correo electrónico de mi trabajo es . . .
c La dirección de web de mi empresa es . . .
d La dirección de web de mi universidad es . . .

D Tick the e-mail and web addresses that you hear.

a K.goma3@inter.com **d** http: / / www.vidasol.urt
b g.goma33@inter.co.uk **e** http: / / www.vida.rust
c j.gema33@interna.com **f** http: / / www.vidasole.urs

E Read the following business cards and answer the questions.

1 ¿A qué se dedica Concepción?
2 ¿Cuál es el móvil de Concepción?
3 ¿Cuál es su dirección?
4 ¿Cómo se llama la agencia de Felipe?
5 ¿Tiene móvil?
6 ¿Cuál es su correo electrónico?
7 ¿Cuál es su dirección de web?

> **1**
>
> *Concepción Porta Colomer*
> **Abogada**
>
> Avda. de las Ciencias, nº 2, 27090 Valencia,
> Tef. 96 347 86 23, Móvil: 892 42 65 87   Fax: 96 347 86 24
> Cporta@contact.es

> **2**
>
> **LUZ 2** AGENCIA DE PUBLICIDAD
>
> **Felipe Maroto Jiménez**
> Director
>
> Pl. Central 7
> Comuna Sol
> Santiago
> Chile
> Fono: 27 43 12
> Fax: 27 54 72
> Luz2@mailchile.com
> Web: http: / / www.luz.chile

F Read the mini-dialogue and then find out the contact details of some people in your group.

– ¿Qué (número de) teléfono tienes?
– El 94 78 65 76. ¿Y tú?
– El 94 87 33 04 ¿Tienes correo electrónico?
– Sí, es j.nunez@carline.com ¿Y tú?
– No, no tengo.

3 Asking for and giving directions

A 🔊 Listen to and read the following mini-dialogues.

1 **Mónica:** Oye, perdona ¿la calle Real, por favor?
Chico: Sí, mira, la primera calle a la izquierda.
Mónica: Gracias.

2 **Mónica:** Oiga, perdone, el restaurante Castaño está por aquí ¿verdad?
Señor: Sí, mire, la segunda a la derecha.
Mónica: Gracias.
Señor: De nada.

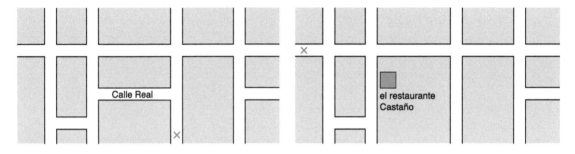

3 **Mónica:** Perdona, por favor, ¿hay un banco por aquí?
Chico: Sí, hay uno al final de esta calle, a la derecha.
Mónica: Gracias.

4 **Mónica:** Perdone, ¿hay una farmacia por aquí?
Señor: Sí, mire, en la calle Sol.
Mónica: Y ¿dónde está la calle Sol?
Señor: Todo recto, la tercera calle a la izquierda.
Mónica: Muchas gracias.

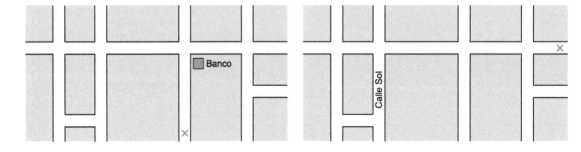

Now write down the phrases used in the mini-dialogues to
  a attract attention: *Oye, perdona . . .* (informal)
  b give an explanation: *Sí, mire . . .* (polite)
  c ask if there is a place as in 'is there a chemist?':
  d ask about the exact location of places:
  e give directions:
  f say thank you:

En donde vivimos

unidad 3

74

B Complete the sentences with *hay* or *está*.

1 Perdone, ¿el cine Avenida _____ por aquí?
2 Perdone ¿_____ un cine por aquí?
3 Oye ¿_____ una parada de autobús en esta calle?
4 Por favor ¿dónde _____ el estadio?
5 Perdona, la Oficina de Correos _____ en esta plaza, ¿verdad?
6 Oiga, por favor, ¿_____ un hospital por aquí?

C Read the following mini-dialogues and look at the map below.

1 –¿La calle Libertad, por favor?
  –Sí, mire la segunda a la derecha.

2 – Perdona, ¿hay una estación de tren por aquí?
  – Sí, hay una, la primera calle a la izquierda.

3 –La Plaza Mayor está por aquí ¿verdad?
  –Sí, todo recto.

4 – Oiga, ¿dónde está el hotel San Juan?
  – La segunda calle, a la derecha.

D Now work with a partner. Look at the street map and ask and say where the following places are. Start from the bus station each time.

a La Oficina de Turismo
b Un supermercado
c Una parada de metro
d El Ayuntamiento
e Un restaurante
f La catedral
g La calle Fuegos
h El teatro
i El bar Luna

G de Gramática

■ Hay or estar

- **Hay** ('there is / there are') is the impersonal form of the verb *haber* in the present indicative. It is invariable so can be either singular or plural. It is used to denote existence.
  ¿Hay un banco / una farmacia por aquí? (Is there a bank / chemist near here?)
  Sí, hay uno / una en esta calle. (Yes, there is one in this street.)
  No, no hay. (No, there isn't one.)
- **Estar** expresses the location of something whose existence is presupposed.
  ¿Dónde está la farmacia / el banco? (Where is the chemist / bank?)
  La farmacia / El banco) está al final de la calle. (The chemist / bank is at the end of the street.)

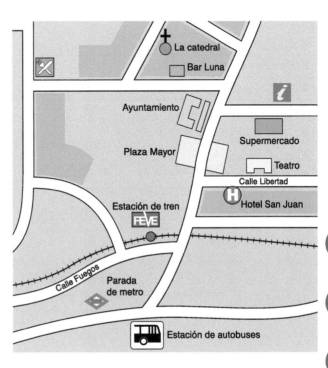

Consolidation

A Work with a partner. Ask him or her the relevant questions in order to complete the following form. Use the polite form *usted*.
¿Cómo se llama? What is your name?

NOMBRE _____   CÓDIGO POSTAL _____

NACIONALIDAD _____   TELÉFONO _____

PROFESIÓN _____   MÓVIL _____

DIRECCIÓN _____   FAX _____

CIUDAD _____   CORREO ELECTRÓNICO _____

B Draw a sketch map of your local area and mark some of the places and streets. Work with your partner. Ask for and give directions to some of these places. Start from the railway *(estación de tren)* or bus station *(estación de autobuses)* or another central landmark.

In class or at home

A Fill in the missing information.

tú	usted
1 ¿Cómo te llamas?	_____
2 _____	¿A qué se dedica?
3 ¿Dónde vives?	_____
4 _____	¿Cuál es su dirección?
5 ¿Tienes móvil?	_____
6 Perdona, ¿Hay un banco, por aquí?	_____
7 _____	Oiga, por favor, ¿dónde está la catedral?
8 ¿Adónde vas?	_____

B Write sentences following the example given.

Example: ¿Adónde ir Carmen?
  ¿Adónde va Carmen?
  Carmen ir supermercado comprar pan *(bread)*.
  Carmen va al supermercado a comprar pan.

1 ¿Adónde ir (tú)?
  (Yo) ir mercado comprar vegetales.

2 ¿Adónde ir Leticia y Laura?

Ir restaurante comer

3 ¿Adónde ir (vosotros)?

(Nosotros) ir estación tren tomar tren.

4 ¿Adónde ir José?

Ir Oficina de Correos enviar carta.

C Read the business card and then complete the form.

NOMBRE: ....

APELLIDOS: ....

....

PROFESIÓN: ....

DIRECCIÓN: ....

CIUDAD: ....

CÓDIGO POSTAL: ....

TELÉFONO: ....

FAX: ....

CORREO ELECTRÓNICO: ....

D Write down Sofía's telephone and fax numbers in words.

Sofía Pérez Domingo
Abogada

Pl. Delicias 16, 45078
Madrid, España
Tel: 91 319 32 65 90
Fax: 91 320 32 78 00
Sofi3@entel.com

E Look again at the map in Ex. 3D and complete the mini-dialogues.

1 – Perdona, ¿dónde _____ la calle Fuegos?

– La primera _____

2 – Perdone, ¿_____ un teatro por aquí?

– Sí, la _____ calle _____

3 – Oye, por favor, el Bar Luna está por aquí, ¿verdad?

– Sí, _____ recto, la _____ calle, _____

B Mi casa
My house

■ **Expresiones esenciales**

¿Dónde vive(s)? *polite / informal*

Vivo en un piso / una casa / un adosado

Mi vivienda está en el centro / a las afueras

Mi piso tiene . . .

Mi piso es . . .

Mi piso mide . . .

¿A qué piso va(s)? *(polite / informal)*

Voy al (+ número ordinal)

¿Dónde está?

¿Qué hay?

Hay un / una . . .

Tiene un / una

¿Cuántos / as . . . hay?

Hay uno / dos / tres . . .

No hay ningún / ninguna (+ noun)

No hay ninguno / ninguna

Essential expressions

Where do you live?

I live in a flat / house / semi-detached house

My home is in the (town) centre / on the outskirts / in the suburbs

My flat has . . .

My flat is . . .

My flat measures . . .

Which flat are you going to?

I'm going to . . . + ordinal number

Where is (it)?

What is there? / What has it got?

There is a . . .

It has a . . .

How many . . . are there?

There is one / are two / three

There is / are no . . .

There isn't one / aren't any

1 Housing

A ¿Dónde vives? Read the mini-dialogue.

Un piso

Una casa

un adosado

■ Vivo en un piso, en el centro, ¿y tú?

■ Vivo en un adosado, a las afueras.

Find out in which type of dwellings people in your group live.

C de Cultura

■ **La vivienda**

In Spanish and Hispano-American urban areas, most people live in flats (*un piso*) which in Hispano-America is called *un apartamento*. In Spain *un apartamento* is a relatively small flat.

En donde vivimos

u n i d a d 3

78

B Look at the plan of a flat.

C Listen to Maite describing the house where she and her family live. Underline what you hear.

Maite y su familia **viven en**:
un piso   un adosado   una casa

Su vivienda **está**:
en el centro   cerca del centro   lejos del centro   a las afueras

Tiene:
un dormitorio   dos dormitorios   tres dormitorios
un cuarto de baño   dos cuartos de baño
un salón   un comedor   un salón-comedor   un estudio
una cocina pequeña y moderna   una cocina grande y moderna
calefacción   garaje   ascensor

Es:
grande   pequeño/a   bonito/a   nuevo/a   viejo/a

Mide:
80m^2 100m^2 120m^2 160m^2

D Now describe your house to your partner. Then listen and take notes of his/her description. Describe his/her house to other people in your group.

E Look at the advertisement for a flat and write a description of it. Now imagine you want to sell your flat. Write an advertisement to put in your local newspaper.

VENDO PISO
C / Buena Vista, nuevo, 3 dormitorios, cocina moderna, salón-comedor, calefacción, garaje. Céntrico. Barato (cheap). Interesados llamar al teléfono 964 547809.

Mi casa

F In the lift. *En el ascensor*. Read the mini-dialogue.

- ¿A qué piso va?
- Voy al cuarto piso, ¿y usted?

- Voy al primer piso.

 Now listen to three people in a lift and say, *¿A qué piso van?*

a Señor 1 **b** Señora **c** Señor 2

G de Gramática

■ Ordinal numbers

primero (1º) segundo (2º) tercero (3º) cuarto (4º) quinto (5º)
sexto (6º) séptimo (7º) octavo (8º) noveno (9º) décimo (10º)

- Ordinal numbers agree in gender and number with the nouns they modify:
  el segundo piso   la tercera casa
  los segundos hombres   las quintas personas
- The ordinal numbers *primero* and *tercero* drop the final *-o* before masculine singular nouns: *el primer piso* the first floor   *el tercer piso* the third floor
- Ordinal numbers are seldom used after *décimo*.

---

2 Describing your home

A Here is a list of some basic items in a house. With the help of a dictionary and your tutor, find out their meanings.

en la cocina	en el salón	en el comedor	en el dormitorio	en el cuarto de baño
una cocina	un sofá	una mesa	una cama	un baño
un horno	un sillón	una silla	una mesilla de noche	una ducha
un fregadero	una librería	una lámpara	un armario	un lavabo
una nevera	una televisión	una estantería	una moqueta	un váter
una lavadora	un cuadro	una alfombra	unas cortinas	un espejo

B Look back at the plan of the flat. Choose one room and describe it to your partner:

- ¿Qué habitación es?
- ¿Tiene un / una . . . ?
- Es el / la . . .
- Sí / no.
- Hay un / una . . .

C Read the text and answer the questions in English.

Los españoles y la vivienda

La mayoría de los españoles viven en pisos. A la hora de comprar un piso nuevo, los factores más importantes son: el precio, la calidad de la construcción y la distribución de la vivienda. Para los españoles, la situación geográfica y la tranquilidad de la zona también son importantes: prefieren una vivienda cercana a su trabajo. El número de dormitorios más buscado es de tres, seguido de cuatro. El piso mide entre 70 y 120 m² y tiene dos cuartos de baño.

En donde vivimos

1 In which type of housing do most Spaniards live?

2 What are the three most important factors mentioned when buying a new flat?

3 What factor is important when considering geographical location?

4 How many bedrooms are they usually looking for?

5 And how many bathrooms?

6 What size flat are most people looking for?

 ## Indicating precise location

A Identify which drawing each description refers to and write the numbers in the boxes

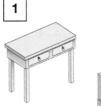   

- El libro está debajo de la mesa. ☐

- El libro está encima de / en / sobre la mesa. ☐

- La mesa está enfrente de / delante de la televisión. ☐

- El libro está dentro del / en el cajón . ☐

G de Gramática

■ Prepositions and prepositional phrases

Prepositions (e.g.'of') and prepositional phrases – one or more prepositions combined with an adverb or a noun (e.g.'in front of') – are used to link a noun, a noun phrase or a pronoun with the rest of the sentence to indicate location, direction, time, etc.

Prepositions are tricky. You are advised to memorise prepositions as vocabulary. Note that every language uses prepositions differently.

■ Showing exact location

- **enfrente de** 'opposite': *El banco está enfrente de la catedral.* (The bank is opposite the cathedral.)
- **detrás de** 'behind': *El libro está detrás de las cortinas.* (The book is behind the curtains.)
- **delante de** 'in front of': *Mi jefe está delante de tu mujer.* (My boss is in front of your wife.)
- **dentro de, en** 'inside': *El dinero está dentro de / en la bolsa.* (The money is inside the bag.)
- **debajo de** 'under': *El perro está debajo de la mesa.* (The dog is under the table.)
- **en, sobre, encima de** 'on': *El periódico está en / sobre el sofá, encima del sofá.* (The newspaper is on the sofa.)
- **al lado de** 'next to': *Mi novio está al lado de Raúl.* (My boyfriend is next to Raúl.)

B Colours. Look at the picture and link the words on the left with the phrases on the right:

¿De qué color es / son . . . ?

1 Las camisas	**a)** es verde
2 Los zapatos	**b)** son rojas
3 La silla	**c)** es amarilla
4 Las cortinas	**d)** es gris
5 Los pantalones	**e)** son blancas
6 La puerta	**f)** es negra
7 El sofá	**g)** son marrones
8 La chaqueta	**h)** son azules

C Ask somebody in your group where some of the items are and what there is on / in / under / next to things.

¿Dónde está la guitarra roja? La guitarra roja está encima de la cama.

Encima de la cama ¿qué hay? Encima de la cama hay un / una . . .

4 — How many things are there in . . . ?

A Look at the picture of the bedroom above and say:

	guitarras	
	libros	
	cuadros	
¿Cuántos	periódicos	hay?
¿Cuántas	camisas	
	personas	
	bicicletas	
	niños	

Hay uno / una / dos / tres / cuatro . . .
No hay ninguno / ninguna.
No hay ningún pantalón / ninguna chaqueta.

G de Gramática

■ **Asking questions about quantity**

To ask questions about quantity the interrogative adjective **_cuánto_** 'how much' or 'how many' is used.

• **_Cuánto_** changes to agree in number and in gender with the noun(s) which it modifies:

¿_Cuánto, -a, -os, -as_ + noun + verb ?

¿Cuánto dinero tienes? (How much money do you have?)

¿Cuánta gente hay? (How many people are there?)

¿Cuántos libros compras? (How many books do you buy? / are you buying)

¿Cuántas sillas hay? (How many chairs are there?)

■ **Responding to questions about quantity**

• Affirmative response: **verb** + **quantity:**   _Tengo tres euros._ (I've got three euros.)

Hay mucha (gente). (There are a lot (of people).)

Compro tres libros. (I buy / am buying three books.)

Hay siete (sillas). (There are seven (chairs).)

• Negative response: **_ninguno_** ('no one', 'no', 'none', 'not … any'). This can appear before a noun as an adjective and therefore agrees with the noun in number and gender. _Ninguno_ drops the final **-o** before a masculine singular noun.

No tengo ningún dinero. (I don't have any money.)

No hay ninguna gente. (There isn't anyone. / There's nobody.)

No tengo ningún libro. (I don't have any / a single book.)

No hay ninguna silla. (There is no chair. / There isn't a (single) chair.)

• **_Ninguno_** can appear as a pronoun referring back to a noun which has already been mentioned or which is understood. It agrees in gender with the noun that it replaces.

No tengo ninguno. (I haven't got one.)

No hay ninguna. (There isn't one.)

No compro ninguno. (I don't buy any.)

■ **Double negatives**

Note that in Spanish, unlike in English, if a negative word follows the verb, the verb must also be preceded by a negative word:

No tengo ninguno. (I don't have any / (a single) one.)

<u>B</u> Complete the sentences with _cuántos, cuántas, un, una, uno,_
ningún, ninguno o ninguna.

1 ¿_____ mesas hay?

Hay _____ mesa.

2 ¿_____ salones tiene tu casa?

Tiene _____.

3 ¿_____ cuartos de baño tiene tu casa?

Tiene _____ cuarto de baño.

4 ¿_____ camisas rojas tienes?

No tengo _____.

5 ¿_____ revistas hay?

No hay _____.

6 ¿_____ pisos tienes?

¡Yo! No tengo _____ piso.

Consolidation

A Describe your ideal home to your partner.

B Describe what there is in your sitting room to your partner.

C Look at the drawings and write down the expressions that correspond to each of them.

a _____ b _____ c _____ d _____

e _____ f _____ g _____

al lado de, encima de, enfrente de, debajo de, delante de, dentro de, detrás de

D Answer the following questions.
- **a** ¿Cuántos sofás tienes?
- **b** ¿Cuántos garajes hay en tu casa?
- **c** ¿Cuántas bicicletas tienes?
- **d** ¿Cuántos Rolls-Royces tienes?
- **e** ¿Cuántos pisos tienes en las Seychelles?

In class or at home

A Write the ordinal numbers in words.
- **a** El 3° piso
- **b** La 2° mesa
- **c** El 5° sofá
- **d** El 1° estudiante
- **e** Los 1° alumnos
- **f** La 10° lección
- **g** El 8° rey
- **h** La 6° canción

B Complete the text. Add the missing endings and articles.

Yo vivo en ___ piso a las afueras de Toledo. Mi piso tiene dos dormitorios bastante pequeñ___ pero tiene ___ salón grand___ y ___ cocina muy bonit___. ___ cocina mide 14 m². Es cuadrad___. Tiene dos ventanas y en ella hay un horno, ___ cocina eléctrica, dos fregaderos, ___ nevera grand___, ___ lavadora y ___ mesa. Además, mi piso tiene dos cuartos de baño. Tiene ascensor pero no tiene garaje.

C Look up in the dictionary the words that you don't know and say what colour the following items are:

a Los limones son _____   **e** Los elefantes son _____

b La hierba es _____   **f** Las naranjas son _____

c La nieve es _____   **g** El carbón es _____

d El cielo es _____   **h** La sangre es _____

D Look at the drawings and write down the expressions that correspond to each of them.

a _détras de_ _____   **b** _____   **c** _____   **d** _____

e _____   **f** _____   **g** _____

detrás de, dentro de, debajo de, enfrente de, delante de, al lado de, encima de

E Complete the following sentences with _un, uno, una o ningún, ninguno, ninguna._

1 No tengo _____ dinero.

2 Aquí no hay _____ silla.

3 ¿Hay _____ Coca-Cola en la nevera?
Lo siento, no hay _____.

4 En mi habitación no hay _____ libro.

5 ¿Tienes _____ televisión en la cocina?
Sí, tengo _____.

6 Yo no tengo estudio èn casa ¿y tú?
Sí, yo tengo _____.

F Complete the sentences with _cuántos_ or _cuántas_.

1 ¿_____ camisas tienes?

2 ¿_____ ascensores tiene tu casa?

3 ¿_____ cuartos de baño hay en tu piso?

4 ¿_____ lenguas hablas?

5 ¿_____ primos tienes?

La ciudad y el pueblo
The city, the town and the village

Expresiones esenciales	**Essential Expressions**
El pueblo / la ciudad (no) es + adjetivo	*The village / the city or town is (isn't) + adjective*
En el pueblo / la ciudad (no) hay + noun	*In the village / in the city or town there is (isn't) / are (aren't) + noun*
El pueblo / la ciudad (no) tiene + noun	*The village / the city or town has (hasn't) + noun*
El pueblo es más tranquilo que la ciudad	*The village is quieter than the city*
En el pueblo hay menos discotecas que en la ciudad	*In the village there are fewer discos than in the town*
El pueblo es tan divertido como la ciudad	*The village is as much fun as the town*
El pueblo tiene tantos problemas como la ciudad	*The village has as many problems as the town*
¿Dónde prefieres vivir y por qué?	*Where do you prefer to live and why?*
Prefiero vivir en el campo porque es más barato	*I prefer to live in the country because it's cheaper*
Ir en autobús / bicicleta / coche / metro	*To go by bus / bike / car / underground*
Ir andando / Ir a pie	*To walk / To go on foot*

 Talking about cities, towns and villages

A Think about where you live and then, using some of the adjectives that appear below, describe *la ciudad y el pueblo*.

El pueblo (no) es . . .
La ciudad (no) es . . .

aburrido/a	divertido/a
caro/a	barato/a
pequeño/a	grande
peligroso/a	seguro/a
estresante	relajante
monótono/a	estimulante
sucio/a	limpio/a

Now say some of the things that there are or aren't *en la ciudad o el pueblo:*

En el pueblo (no) hay . . .
En la ciudad (no) hay . . .

edificios altos	contaminación
tráfico / muchos coches	contacto con la naturaleza
ruido	mucha / poca gente
oportunidades de trabajo	actividades culturales
vida nocturna	

En donde vivimos

unidad 3

86

El pueblo (no) tiene . . .	bares	tiendas
La ciudad (no) tiene . . .	cafeterías	cines
	restaurantes	espacios verdes
	discotecas	problemas
	museos	casas pequeñas

Comparing

<u>A</u> Look at the photographs and then complete the sentences below. You can use some of the vocabulary in 1A.

Higher degree: El pueblo es más tranquilo que la ciudad.

1 El pueblo es   **más** _____ **que**   la ciudad.

2 En el pueblo hay   **más** _____ **que**   en la ciudad.

3 El pueblo tiene   **más** _____ **que**   la ciudad.

Lower degree: En el pueblo hay menos discotecas que en la ciudad.

4 El pueblo es   **menos** _____ **que**   la ciudad

5 En el pueblo hay   **menos** _____ **que**   en la ciudad.

6 El pueblo tiene   **menos** _____ **que**   la ciudad.

Same degree: El pueblo tiene tantos problemas como la ciudad.

7 El pueblo es   **tan** _____ **como**   la ciudad.

8 En el pueblo hay   **tanto** _____ **como**   en la ciudad.

    tanta _____ **como**

9 En el pueblo no hay   **tantos** _____ **como**   en la ciudad.

10 El pueblo tiene   **tantas** _____ **como**   la ciudad.

G de Gramática

■ **Making comparisons**

To form a comparative adjective (e.g. taller) in Spanish, you use *más* (more) or *menos* (less): *más alto* (taller, lit. more tall); *menos alto* (less tall).

a) Comparison of adjectives

Higher:	*más* + adjective + *que*	*El pueblo es más tranquilo que la ciudad.*
Lesser:	*menos* + adjective + *que*	*La ciudad es menos tranquila que el pueblo.*
Same:	*tan* + adjective + *como*	*La ciudad es tan tranquila como el pueblo.*

b) Comparison of nouns

Higher:	*más* + noun + *que*	*En la ciudad hay más gente que en el pueblo.*
Lesser:	*menos* + noun + *que*	*En el pueblo hay menos trabajo que en la ciudad.*
Same:	*tanto/a/os/as* + noun+ *como*	*En el pueblo hay tantos problemas como en la ciudad.*

Note:

- *no* + verb + *tan* + adjective + *como* is equivalent to *menos* + adjective+ *que*:
  La ciudad no es tan tranquila como el pueblo. = La ciudad es menos tranquila que el pueblo.

- *no* + verb + *tanto/a/os/as* + noun + *como* is equivalent to *menos* + noun + *que*
  En el pueblo no hay tanto trabajo como en la ciudad. = En el pueblo hay menos trabajo que en la ciudad.

B Complete the following sentences using the irregular comparatives.

1 El pueblo es _____ que la ciudad. Es más tranquilo.

2 La ciudad es _____ que el pueblo. Hay más problemas.

3 Mi hermano tiene 42 años. Yo tengo 33. Mi hermano es
_____ que yo.

4 David tiene 23 años. Diego tiene 26 años. David es 3 años
_____ que Diego.

5 Rigoberta habla inglés muy bien, Juan no. Rigoberta habla
inglés _____ que Juan.

6 La vida en una capital es _____ que en una ciudad
pequeña. Es más divertida.

G de Gramática

■ Irregular comparatives

The following adjectives have irregular comparative forms:

		Irregular comparative adjectives		
		singular	plural	
bueno/a/os/as	(good)	mejor	mejores	(better)
malo/a/os/as	(bad)	peor	peores	(worse)
grande (s)	(big)	mayor (or más grande)	mayores	(bigger / greater)
pequeño/a/os/as	(small)	menor (or más pequeño)	menores	(smaller)

Note:

- ***mayor*** can mean 'elderly', 'grown up' and 'elder' as well as 'older':

Soledad es mayor que Paco.	Soledad is older than Paco.
Una señora mayor.	An elderly lady.
Mi hermano mayor.	My elder brother.
Mis hijos son ya mayores.	My children are grown up now.

- ***menor*** can mean 'younger':

| *Paco es menor que Soledad.* | Paco is younger than Soledad. |
| *Mi hermano menor.* | My younger brother. |

Expressing preferences

A Read the mini-dialogue and then tell your partner where you prefer living and why.

– ¿Dónde prefieres vivir en un pueblo o en una ciudad?

– Prefiero vivir en un pueblo.

– ¿Por qué?

– Porque el pueblo es más tranquilo. En la ciudad hay más cosas que en un pueblo. Hay más tiendas, discotecas, museos, etc. pero la vida es más estresante y más cara. La ciudad no es tan agradable como el pueblo.

G de Gramática

■ Expressing preferences

The verb **preferir** *(to prefer)* is used to express preference. This verb is a 'radical changing verb' because there is a change in its stem: **e>ie** in all the persons except the first and second person plural (nosotros / as, vosotros / as). You will learn more about radical-changing verbs in Unit 4.

Preferir (e>ie)					
(yo)	prefiero	(I prefer)	(nosotros(as))	preferimos	(we prefer)
(tú)	prefieres	(you prefer)	(vosotros(as))	preferís	(you prefer)
(usted)	prefiere	(your prefer)	(ustedes)	prefieren	(you prefer)
(él / ella)	prefiere	(he / she prefers)	(ellos(as))	prefieren	(they prefer)

■ Enquiring about preferences

- To ask about preferences you can use **¿qué + preferir ... ?**
  ¿Qué prefieres el campo o la ciudad? (What do you prefer: the countryside or the city?)

■ Enquiring about cause or reason

- To ask for the cause or the reason of something you can use **¿por qué ... ?** (why?)
  ¿Por qué prefieres vivir en el campo? (Why do you prefer to live in the country?)

■ Giving reasons

- To express reason you can use **porque** (because) + *clause:*
  *Prefiero el campo (**a** la ciudad / la ciudad **al** campo) porque ...*
  (I prefer the countryside (to the city / the city to the countryside) because ...)

B Listen to Carlos talking about why he prefers the city to the country and say if the following statements are true (V for *Verdadero*) or false (F for *Falso*).

1 La ciudad es más divertida que el campo. ☐
2 En la ciudad hay menos cosas que en un pueblo. ☐
3 En la ciudad hay más cines que en un pueblo. ☐
4 En la ciudad hay mucha tranquilidad. ☐
5 Vivir en una ciudad es más barato que vivir en un pueblo. ☐

4 Getting around: means of transport

A First, read the list of types of transport and the related adjectives. Then, working in a group, use this vocabulary to compare the advantages and disadvantages of the various ways of getting around.

Ir en bicicleta es más sano y barato que ir en coche pero es menos rápido.

	bicicleta	ecológico	ir	andando	cansado
	coche	barato	ir	a pie	relajado
	autobús	incómodo			
ir en	moto	rápido			
	metro	cómodo			
	taxi	lento			
	tren	caro / sano			

B Complete the following sentences.

1 Marta prefiere la ciudad _____ pueblo _____ la ciudad es más divertida.

2 Mis abuelos _____ el taxi _____ autobús porque el taxi es _____ cómodo.

3 Prefiero la moto _____ bicicleta _____ la moto es más rápida.

4 Vosotros _____ el coche _____ metro, ¿verdad?

C Now ask people in your group which means of transport they prefer and why.

■ ¿Qué prefieres ir andando o en autobús?

■ Prefiero ir andando porque es más relajado.

5 Cardinal numbers (100–999)

A Study the following cardinal numbers, then complete the table.

100 cien	**300** trescientos/as	**700** *setecientos/as*
101 ciento uno / una	**400** cuatrocientos/as	**800** ochocientos/as
200 doscientos/as	**500** quinientos/as	**900** novecientos/as
201 doscientos uno / una	**600** seiscientos	

549 quinientos/as (500) cuarenta y nueve (49)	**124**
363	**809**
918	**777**
465	**612**
286	**515**

B Take it in turns with a partner to write down numbers between 100 and 999 and say them to one another.

C Look at these numbers and say them in Spanish. Then listen to the recording and put a tick by the ones you hear.

380   525   267   931   742   102   875
603   427

D Write the following numbers in words.

a 105 dólares   **e** 888 ciudades
b 543 pueblos   **f** 405 hombres
c 999 euros   **g** 923 habitantes
d 100 personas   **h** 667 coches

G de Gramática

• ***Ciento*** is shortened to ***cien*** before a noun or an adjective but not before another number, except ***mil***.
  cien estudiantes (a hundred students)
  ciento una familias (a hundred and one families)
  los cien mejores libros (the hundred best books)
  ciento treinta casas (a hundred and thirty houses)
  ciento un estudiantes (a hundred and one students)
  cien mil habitantes (a hundred thousand inhabitants)
• In Spanish, hundreds agree in gender with a following noun:
  Doscientas mujeres (two hundred women)
  Doscientos hombres (two hundred men)

Remember that compound numbers from 31 to 99 are written as two words linked by ***y***:
treinta y uno (31), *doscientos treinta y uno* (231)

En donde vivimos

unidad 3

90

Consolidation

A Listen to Elisa and Enrique talking about their preferences and complete the table.

Elisa / Enrique:	¿Qué prefieres el pueblo o la ciudad?
	¿Por qué?
Elisa:	La ciudad es . . . el pueblo es . . .
Enrique:	La ciudad es . . . el pueblo es . . .
Elisa / Enrique:	¿Qué prefieres ir a pie o en metro, en coche o en bicicleta?
Elisa:	Prefiero . . . el metro es . . . .
Enrique:	Prefiero . . . la bicicleta es . . . el coche es . . .

In class or at home

A Rewrite the sentences following the example given.

La bicicleta no es tan rápida como el coche.
La bicicleta es menos rápida que el coche. La bicicleta es más lenta.

1 El autobús no es tan cómodo como el metro.
2 El coche no es tan caro como el taxi.
3 La ciudad no es tan limpia como el pueblo.
4 Ir a pie no es tan cansado como ir en bicicleta.

B Complete the following sentences.

1 Yo pref___ la bicicleta al coche porque la bicicleta es más barat___
2 Vosotros pref___ el tren ___ coche ¿verdad?
3 Ellos pref___ el campo a la ciudad. El campo ___ menos problemas.
4 En el pueblo no ___ muchos cines.
5 ¿(Tú) pref___ el metro o el autobús?
6 Pref___ el metro ___ es más rápido.

C Complete the following sentences using the irregular comparatives.

1 La bicicleta es _____ que el coche. Es más segura.
2 Pablo es _____ que tú. Tiene diez años más.
3 El tráfico es _____ en Madrid que en Oviedo. Madrid tiene demasiados coches.
4 El metro es _____ que el autobús. Es más rápido.
5 Cecilia es _____ que su hermana Juana. Tiene siete años menos.

D Write the following numbers in words.
a 100 españoles.
b 978 personas.
c 432 euros.
d 299 alumnas.
e 927 programas.
f 505 lenguas.
g 760.
h 310 médicos.
i 141 jardineros.
j 815 arquitectas.

D En la ciudad

In the city/town

■ Expresiones esenciales	■ Essential expressions
¿Dónde está + lugar?	*Where is + place?*
Está en el centro / en el norte	*It's in the centre / in the north*
en la costa	*on the coast*
en el interior	*inland*
cerca de / lejos de . . .	*near to / a long way from . . .*
a X kilómetros de . . .	*X kilometres (away) from . . .*
¿Cuántos habitantes tiene?	*What is the size of its population?*
Tiene unos . . .	*It has around . . .*
menos de+ cantidad	*fewer than / under + quantity*
más de + cantidad	*more than / over + quantity*
casi . . .	*almost . . .*
aproximadamente . . .	*approximately . . .*
muy grande	*very large*
grandísimo/a/os/as	*extremely large*
el/la más poblado(a); los/las más poblados(as)	*the most heavily populated*
el/la menos alto/a; los/las menos altos/as	*the least high / tall*
el/la mejor; los/las mejores	*the better / best*
el/la peor; los/las peores	*the worse / worst*
el/la mayor; los/las mayores	*the older / elder / eldest / greater / greatest*
el/la menor; los/las menores	*the younger / youngest / lesser / least*

1 Cardinal numbers (1.000 . . .)

A Study the following cardinal numbers.

1.000	mil
2.000	dos mil
10.000	diez mil
100.000	cien mil
159.748	ciento cincuenta y nueve mil (159.000)
	setecientos cuarenta y ocho (748)
500.000	quinientos /as mil / medio millón
1.500.000	un millón (1.000.000) quinientos/as mil
	(500.000) / un millón y medio
25.667.477	veinticinco millones (25.000.000)
	seiscientos/as sesenta y siete mil (667.000)
	cuatrocientos setenta y siete (477)

Now write out the following numbers.

a 1.205 hoteles
b 6.000 pesos mexicanos
c 10.100 dentistas
d 101.513 bicicletas
e 430.098 habitantes
f 500.321 personas
g 1.911.718 niños
h 1.500.000 habitantes

B 🔊 Listen to the recording and write down the numbers you hear.

C Read the following expressions and work out what they mean.
a 7.480.740 habitantes
b <u>unos</u> siete millones y medio de habitantes
c <u>menos de</u> siete millones y medio de habitantes
d <u>más de</u> siete millones de habitantes
e <u>casi</u> siete millones y medio de habitantes
f siete millones y medio de habitantes <u>aproximadamente</u>

Now match each number on the left with a phrase on the right.

1 6.511.780   **a** más de ocho millones y medio
2 3.899.677   **b** casi seis millones
3 5.999.000   **c** seis millones y medio aproximadamente
4 432.000   **d** menos de cuatro millones
5 8.756.214   **e** unos cuatrocientos mil

D Say the name of the country of each capital and read the number of inhabitants out loud:

capital	número de habitantes
a Buenos Aires	2.960.000
b Canberra	234.700
c Caracas	1.290.000
d Londres	6,755.000
e Madrid	3.188.300
f México	20.000.000
g Beijing	11.000.000
h Ottawa	304.500

G de Gramática

- The word ***mil*** is invariable when plural thousands are being expressed.
  veinte mil habitantes (twenty thousand inhabitants)
  But can appear in the plural in the expression ***miles de*** (thousands of)
  miles de habitantes (thousands of inhabitants)
- Unlike English, ***mil*** is not preceded by an article.
  Tengo mil dólares (I have a thousand dollars)
- To refer to two million or more, Spanish uses the plural of *millón*. **millones.**
  un millón (one million)
  dos millones (two million)
- The expression 'million + noun' is ***un millón de / x millones de*** **+ noun.**
  medio millón de casas (half a million houses)
  un millón de hombres (one million men)
  tres millones y medio de trabajadores (three and a half million workers)
- When writing numbers in Spanish, a comma is used where a full stop appears in English and vice versa:
  3, 465 euros (three thousand four hundred and sixty five euros – English convention)
  3.465 euros (*tres mil cuatrocientos sesenta y cinco euros* – Spanish convention)
  3.465 (three point four six five – English convention)
  3,465 (*tres **coma** cuatrocientos sesenta y cinco* – Spanish convention)
- The full stop is not used when writing years.
  13 de agosto de 2005 (13 August 2005)

2 Expressing location and distance with *estar*

Mar Cantábrico

Océano Atlántico

Islas Baleares

Mar Mediterráneo

Islas Canarias

Islas Canarias (ver cuadro)   Ceuta   Melilla

1 La Coruña	13 Navarra	25 Ávila	37 Valencia
2 Lugo	14 Zamora	26 Madrid	38 Huelva
3 Asturias	15 Valladolid	27 Guadalajara	39 Córdoba
4 Cantabria	16 Segovia	28 Teruel	40 Jaén
5 Vizcaya	17 Soria	29 Tarragona	41 Murcia
6 Guipúzcoa	18 La Rioja	30 Cáceres	42 Alicante
7 Pontevedra	19 Zaragoza	31 Toledo	43 Sevilla
8 Orense	20 Huesca	32 Cuenca	44 Cádiz
9 León	21 Lérida	33 Castellón	45 Málaga
10 Palencia	22 Barcelona	34 Badajoz	46 Granada
11 Burgos	23 Gerona	35 Ciudad Real	47 Almería
12 Álava	24 Salamanca	36 Albacete	

G de Gramática

■ Expressing location with *estar*

- Asking where people, places or things are:
  ¿Dónde + está/están... ?
  ¿Dónde está Lima? (Where is Lima?)
  ¿Dónde están las llaves? (Where are the keys?)
- Saying where people, places or things are: **está/están en...**
  Lima está en Perú. (Lima is in Peru.)
  Las llaves están en la mesa. (The keys are on the table.)

Note that the preposition **en** has different meanings.

■ Expressing distance with *estar*

- **Está a** + distance: *Santiago está a 66 kilómetros de La Coruña.* (Santiago is 66 km from La Coruña.)
- **Está lejos / cerca (de)**: *Buenos Aires está cerca de Montevideo.* (Buenos Aires is near Montevideo.)
  Bilbao está lejos de Madrid. (Bilbao is a long way from Madrid.)

A Work with a partner. Read the following sentences, look at the map and give the names of the cities described.

1 Está en el centro de la Península Ibérica. Es la capital de España.
2 Está en el sur de España, en la costa atlántica, cerca de Málaga pero lejos de Madrid.
3 Está en el este de España, en la costa mediterránea, cerca de Alicante.
4 Está en el oeste de España, a 210 kilómetros de Madrid.
5 Está en el noreste de España, en la costa mediterránea, lejos de Madrid.
6 Está cerca del norte de Portugal, en el noroeste de España, en la costa atlántica.

B Fill in the compass points.

C Read the sentences again and write down the expressions that indicate:
a Location: **b** Distance:

D Choose four cities from the map and ask your partner where they are?

- ¿Dónde está Málaga?
- Málaga está en el sur de España, en la costa mediterránea cerca de Cádiz.

Norte

3 Describing a city or town

A Look at the photographs and say the adjectives that come into your mind as you study them.

B Read the descriptions and then answer the questions.

México D.F. (Distrito Federal), la capital de la República de México, es la ciudad más grande de Latinoamérica. Tiene más de 18 millones de habitantes. Está en el centro de México y a 2.309 metros sobre el nivel del mar. En ella hay muchos lugares y monumentos históricos, entre los que destacan la Plaza del Zócalo, la plaza más antigua y grande de la ciudad. Es una ciudad interesantísima.

La Habana, la capital de Cuba, es la ciudad más grande del Caribe, tiene unos dos millones de habitantes. Es una ciudad de estilo colonial y su parte antigua 'La Habana Vieja' es Patrimonio de la Humanidad (UNESCO 1982). Está en el norte de la isla en la costa del Golfo de México. Es una ciudad bellísima.●

1 ¿Cuál de las dos capitales es la más grande?
2 ¿Qué capital está en la costa?
3 ¿En qué costa?
4 Según el texto, La Habana ¿es una ciudad fea?

C Complete the following sentences with either *qué* or *cuál*.

1 ¿_____ es la plaza más grande de México DF?
2 ¿_____ ciudad es la más poblada de Cuba?
3 ¿_____ de las dos ciudades está en el interior?
4 ¿_____ ciudad tiene casi 20 millones de habitantes?

G de Gramática

■ *¿Cuál? ¿Cuáles?* / *¿Qué + noun?*

• *¿Cuál?* is an interrogative word meaning 'which one?' It implies a choice between two or more alternatives and conveys the idea of selection.
¿Cuál de las dos capitales está en el Caribe? (Which of the two capitals is in the Caribbean?)
¿Cuáles son las ciudades más contaminadas del mundo? (Which are the most polluted cities in the world?)

• *¿Qué + noun...?* like *¿cuál?*, can convey the idea of selection. *¿Qué capital está en el Caribe?* (Which capital is in the Caribbean? is equivalent to *¿Cuál de las dos capitales está en el Caribe?*).

D 🎙 Listen to Lionel and Carmela talking about the cities where they live and complete the tables on the next page.

Lionel	Carmela
Nombre de la ciudad	Nombre de la ciudad
Nombre del país	Nombre del país
Situación	Situación
Número de habitantes	Número de habitantes
¿Cómo es?	¿Cómo es?
Monumento o lugar histórico	Monumento o lugar histórico

E Choose a question word to complete each question.

¿cuántos?   ¿dónde?(2)   ¿cómo?(2)   ¿qué?(2)

1 Y tú ¿_____ vives?

2 ¿_____ se llama tu ciudad?

3 ¿En _____ país está?

4 ¿En _____ ?

5 ¿_____ habitantes tiene?

6 ¿_____ es?

7 ¿_____ monumento o lugar histórico importante tiene?

Now ask people in your group about the place where they live and talk about where you live.

4 Superlatives

A Read the following sentence. What do you think it means?

México D. F. es la ciudad más grande de Hispanoamérica.

Can you find any similar sentences in the descriptions that you have read in Ex 3B (page 95)?

Now read the Grammar section on the next page and do the following exercises.

B Write sentences following the example given.

Madrid es una ciudad grande (España)

Madrid es la ciudad más grande de España.

1 Lima es una ciudad grande (Perú)

2 Carolina es rubia (familia)

3 José Luis es bueno (grupo)

4 Gran Bretaña es una isla grande (Europa)

5 Estados Unidos es un país muy poblado (Norteamérica)

6 Mi tío Manuel es bajo (mis tíos)

7 Francisco es joven (familia)

8 Es un hospital malo (ciudad)

C de Cultura

■ Capitals of Hispano-America

The capitals of most Hispano-American countries are where the vast majority of the population is concentrated. Industrialisation and the rural exodus have produced the phenomenon of hyperurbanisation. These vast urban concentrations bring many serious problems to their inhabitants. All the urban problems – pollution, sanitation, housing, transport, education, poverty ... are aggravated because of the size of the cities.

■ The superlative

As in English, the superlative expresses a quality in its greatest possible degree.

There are two ways of expressing the superlative: the relative superlative and absolute superlative.

■ The relative superlative

To express ideas such as 'the biggest', 'the most' and 'the least', the definite article (**el, la, los**, or **las**) followed by **más** (most) or **menos** (least) and the corresponding adjective, plus the preposition **de** is used. In this way an element is identified as having a quality in its highest or lowest degree amongst a group:

- **definite article + (noun) + más / menos + adjective + de**

  La Habana es la ciudad más grande de Cuba. (Havana is the biggest city in Cuba.)

  Mi novio es el chico más guapo de todos. (My boyfriend is the most handsome of all.)

Note that the Spanish **de** translates the English **in** or **of** after a superlative.

■ Irregular superlatives

The following adjectives can have an irregular superlative:

		Irregular superlatives	
		singular	plural
bueno/a/os/as	(good)	el (la) mejor	los (las) mejores
malo/a/os/as	(bad)	el (la) peor	los (las) peores
grande(s)	(big)	el (la) mayor (or más grande)	los (las) mayores
pequeño/a/os/as	(small)	el (la) menor (or más pequeño)	los (las) menores

Pedro es el mejor de la clase. (Peter is the best in the class.)

■ The absolute superlative

The absolute superlative intensifies the meaning of an adjective. In Spanish it is formed as follows:

- **muy + adjective**: *México DF es muy grande.* (Mexico DF is very big.)
- **adjective + ísimo a/os/as**:

  If the adjective ends in a consonant, *-ísimo/a/os/as* is added:

  difícil (difficult) *dificilísimo a/os/as* (very difficult)

  If the adjective ends in a vowel, the vowel is removed and *-ísimo/a/os/as* is added: *grande* (big) *grandísimo a/os/as* (very big / enormous)

Note spelling changes with adjectives ending in **-go**, **-co**, or **-z**:

  largo (long)   *larguísimo* (very long)

  seco (dry)   *sequísimo* (very / extremely dry)

  feliz (happy)   *felicísimo* (very happy)

C Write sentences following the example:

  El mar Caspio es un lago grande.
  El mar Caspio es un lago muy grande / grandísimo.

1 El Everest es una montaña alta.
2 El Nilo es un río largo.
3 Tokio es una ciudad poblada.
4 La Ciudad del Vaticano es un país pequeño.
5 El desierto de Atacama es un desierto seco.

D Now complete the following sentences

  El mar Caspio es <u>el lago más grande</u> del mundo.

1 El Everest es _____ del mundo.
2 El Nilo es _____ del mundo.
3 Tokio es _____ del mundo.
4 La ciudad del Vaticano es _____ del mundo.
5 El desierto de Atacama, en Chile es _____ del mundo.

Consolidation

In groups of three or four, choose a city of the world. Describe it to the other people in the group and see if they can guess which city you are describing.

In class or at home

A Here are some Spanish cities and their approximate populations:

Cádiz: 136.000	Lugo: 89.500	Murcia: 378.000
Barcelona: 1.527.000	Sevilla: 704.000	Zaragoza: 615.000

Match the phrases on the left with the phrases on the right.

1 Lugo no tiene tantos habitantes	**a** pero más que Lugo.
2 Barcelona tiene más habitantes	**b** como Murcia.
3 Sevilla tiene más habitantes que Zaragoza	**c** pero menos que Barcelona.
4 Zaragoza tiene menos habitantes que Barcelona	**d** que Sevilla.

B Complete the questions and then answer them.

1 ¿_____ de las cinco ciudades es la más pequeña?
2 ¿_____ es la más grande?
3 ¿_____ ciudades están en la costa?
4 ¿_____ ciudades están en el sur de España?

C Complete the following description.

Barcelona _____ una ciudad español__. _____ en el noreste de España, en _____ mediterránea. Tiene _____ de millón y medio de habitantes. Es una ciudad modern__ y dinámic__. Tiene una vida cultural variad__. En ella hay museos important___. Tiene varias universidades y en ella se hablan dos lenguas, el español y el catalán. _____ 620 km de Madrid.

D Write sentences following the example given.

El inglés es difícil.
El inglés es muy difícil / dificilísimo.

1 El español es fácil.
2 La ciudad de México está contaminada.
3 Mi pueblo es feo.
4 Mi jefe es aburrido.
5 Nuestro padre es rico.
6 La ciudad de Nueva York es grande.
7 Su profesor es simpático.

Acércate al mundo del español

Una ciudad para no olvidar: *Santiago de Compostela*

Santiago de Compostela, la capital de la Comunidad Autónoma de Galicia, es una ciudad situada en el noroeste de España.

Santiago es una ciudad moderna, viva y alegre. Tiene una población de más de 105.000 habitantes de los cuales unos 35.000 son estudiantes universitarios. Su universidad, fundada en 1504, es una de las más antiguas del mundo.

El descubrimiento del sepulcro del Apóstol Santiago en el año 813 convierte a Santiago en uno de los centros de peregrinación más importantes del mundo católico. Durante siglos, peregrinos de todo el mundo han recorrido el Camino de Santiago partiendo desde diferentes puntos de Europa.

Santiago tiene unos magníficos edificios, entre los que destaca su catedral, verdadera joya arquitectónica, y sus plazas. Es un lugar para visitar y no olvidar.

La fiesta de la ciudad es el 25 de julio: 'Día del Apóstol' y cuando el 25 de julio coincide en domingo se celebra el llamado Año Santo Compostelano.

A Answer the following questions.

1 ¿Dónde está Santiago de Compostela?
2 ¿Por qué es Santiago un centro de peregrinación?
3 ¿De qué siglo es la Universidad de Santiago?
4 ¿Cuál es el edificio más importante?
5 ¿En qué día y mes se celebra el Día del Apóstol?

B Do you know anything about *El Camino de Santiago*? Would you like to find out more about it? Go to the Internet and read about it.

Essential vocabulary

Lugares
aeropuerto (m)
aparcamiento (m)
avenida (f)
Ayuntamiento (m)
banco (m)
bar (m)
cafetería (f)
calle (f)
catedral (f)
cine (m)
estación (f)
  de autobuses
  de tren
estadio (m)
farmacia (f)
grandes almacenes (m pl)
hospital (m)
hotel (m)
iglesia (f)
mercado (m)
metro (m)
museo (m)
Oficina (f)
  de Correos (m)
  de Turismo (m)
parada (f)
  de autobús (m)
  de metro (m)
parque (m)
plaza (f)
restaurante (m)
supermercado (m)
teatro (m)
tienda (f)

Places
airport
parking
avenue
Town hall
bank
bar
coffee shop
street
cathedral
cinema
station
bus station
train station
stadium
chemist
department stores
hospital
hotel
church
market
underground railway
museum

Post Office
Tourist Information Office

bus stop
underground stop
park
square
restaurant
supermarket
theatre
shop

Direcciones y números de contacto
código (m) postal
correo (m) electrónico
dirección (f)
número (m)
  de fax (m)
  de móvil (m)
  de teléfono (m)

Addresses and contact numbers
postal code
e-mail
address

fax number
mobile number
telephone number

Para dar direcciones
a la derecha
a la izquierda
al final de . . .
todo recto

To give directions
on the right
on the left
at the end of . . .
straight on

Números ordinales
primero/a
segundo/a
tercero/a
cuarto/a
quinto/a
sexto/a
séptimo/a
octavo/a
noveno/a
décimo/a

Ordinal numbers
first
second
third
fourth
fifth
sixth
seventh
eighth
ninth
tenth

Vivienda
adosado (m)
casa (f)
piso (m)

Housing
semi-detached house
detached house / house
flat / floor

Habitaciones
entrada (f)
dormitorio (m)
cuarto de baño (m)
salón (m)
comedor (m)
salón-comedor (m)
estudio (m)
cocina (f)
calefacción (f)
garaje (m)
ascensor (m)

Rooms
hall
bedroom
bathroom
sitting room
dining room
lounge-dining room
study
kitchen
heating
garage
lift

Para expresar situación espacial
al lado de
debajo de
delante de
dentro de, en
detrás de
en, sobre, encima de
enfrente de

To express location

next to
under
in front of
inside
behind
on
opposite

Medios de transporte
autobús (m)
bicicleta (f)
coche (m)
metro (m)
moto / motocicleta(f)
taxi (m)
tren (m)

Means of transport
bus
bike
car
underground
motorbike
taxi
train

Adjetivos	*Adjectives*
barato/a	*cheap*
cansado/a	*tired, tiring*
caro/a	*dear, expensive*
cómodo/a	*comfortable*
ecológico/a	*ecological*
estimulante	*stimulating*
estresante	*stressful*
incómodo/a	*uncomfortable*
lento/a	*slow*
limpio/a	*clean*
monótono/a	*monotonous*
peligroso/a	*dangerous*
rápido/a	*quick*
relajado/a	*relaxed*
relajante	*relaxing*
sano/a	*healthy*
seguro/a	*safe, sure*
sucio/a	*dirty*

Situación geográfica	*Geographical situation*
norte (m)	*north*
noroeste (m)	*northwest*
noreste (m)	*northeast*
sur (m)	*south*
suroeste (m)	*southwest*
sureste (m)	*southeast*
centro (m)	*centre*

Para expresar distancia	*To express distance*
a x kilómetros	*x kilometres away*
cerca (de)	*near* (to)
lejos (de)	*far* (from)

Verbos	*Verbs*
coger	*to catch / to take*
ir	*to go*
preferir	*to prefer*
tomar	*to catch / to take*

La vida diaria

A ¿Qué hora es?

What time is it?

<table>
<tr><td>■ Expresiones esenciales</td><td>■ Essential expressions</td></tr>
<tr><td>¿Qué hora es?</td><td>What time is it?</td></tr>
<tr><td>¿Tiene(s) hora? (polite / informal)</td><td>Have you got the time?</td></tr>
<tr><td>Es la una</td><td>It's one o'clock</td></tr>
<tr><td>Son las dos / tres . . .</td><td>It's two / three o'clock</td></tr>
<tr><td>en punto</td><td>exactly / on the dot</td></tr>
<tr><td>y cuarto</td><td>quarter past</td></tr>
<tr><td>y media</td><td>half past</td></tr>
<tr><td>menos cuarto</td><td>quarter to</td></tr>
<tr><td>de la mañana / de la tarde / de la noche</td><td>in the morning / afternoon / evening / night (after stated time)</td></tr>
<tr><td>por la mañana / por la tarde / por la noche</td><td>in (= during) the morning / afternoon etc</td></tr>
<tr><td>al mediodía</td><td>at midday</td></tr>
<tr><td>a medianoche</td><td>at midnight</td></tr>
<tr><td>¿Qué día es hoy?</td><td>What day is it today?</td></tr>
<tr><td>Hoy es + día</td><td>Today is + day</td></tr>
<tr><td>despertarse / levantarse / acostarse</td><td>to wake up / get up / go to bed</td></tr>
<tr><td>temprano / tarde</td><td>early / late</td></tr>
<tr><td>bañarse / ducharse / vestirse</td><td>to have a bath / shower / get dressed</td></tr>
<tr><td>rápidamente / tranquilamente</td><td>quickly / calmly</td></tr>
</table>

1 **Telling the time (*la hora*) using the 12-hour clock**

A Read the mini-dialogues and look at the clocks.

■ ¿Qué hora es?   ■ ¿Tiene(s) hora?

■ Es la una en punto.   ■ No, lo siento.

■ Son las dos y cuarto.   ■ Sí, son las cinco menos cinco.

G de Gramática

¿Qué hora es? / ¿Qué horas son? (in many Spanish-speaking countries) 'What time is it?'
Note that in Spanish:

- **Es** is used with **una**: *es la una y cuarto* (1:15).
- **Son** is used with the other hours: **son** *las tres en punto* (3:00).
- The feminine article **la / las** is always used before the hour, because it refers to *la hora*.
- The hour is given first, then the minutes: *son las cinco* (hour) *y diez* (minutes) (5:10).
- Time **after** the hour is expressed with:
  the hour + y + minutes

- Time **before** the hour is expressed with:
  the hour + menos + minutes.
- In Hispano America the expression **un cuarto para** *las ocho* (7:45), **cinco para** *la una* (12:55) is often used.
- The equivalent of *half past* is **y media**: *es la una y media*.
- The equivalent of *quarter past* is **y cuarto**: *es la una y cuarto*.
- The equivalent of *quarter to* is **menos cuarto**: *son las seis menos cuarto*.
- The equivalent of *o'clock precisely* is **en punto**: *son las siete en punto*.

C de Cultura

■ Time expressions

- **mediodía** (midday) is a term that refers to 'noon' but is often used to refer to a period of time between noon and lunch time.
- **de la tarde, de la noche** (in the afternoon, in the evening) will change with the season of the year, **de la tarde** from noon to nightfall and **de la noche** from nightfall to midnight.

- **de la mañana** (in the morning **or** in the early hours) covers the time from midnight to noon. The expression **de la madrugada** is also used to refer to the early hours.

■ Time zones

The Canary Islands are one time zone to the west of mainland Spain. This means that when it is midday in Spain it is 11 a.m. in the Canary Islands, and when it is midday in the Canary Islands it is 1 p.m. in mainland Spain.

Now look at the diagram on the right and say the following times in Spanish:

a 1:25   **b** 3:00   **c** 5:20   **d** 6:30

e 7:45   **f** 8:20   **g** 9:50   **h** 11:05

en punto
cinco   cinco
diez   diez
cuarto — menos   y — cuarto
veinte   veinte
veinticinco   veinticinco
media

B Listen to the recording and tick the times you hear.

a 12:30 ☐   **b** 2:30 ☐   **c** 5:10 ☐   **d** 7:40 ☐   **e** 9:20 ☐

f 11:15 ☐   **g** 12:05 ☐   **h** 3:00 ☐   **i** 5:50 ☐   **j** 4:25 ☐

Which times have not been said on the recording?

C Read the information below.

■ ¿Qué hora es?

Son las once y cinco	**de la mañana**. (a.m.)
Son las once y cinco	**de la noche**. (p.m.)
Son las cuatro y cuarto	**de la tarde** (p.m.)
Son las cuatro y cuarto	**de la mañana**. (a.m.)
Es **mediodía**.	Son las doce **del mediodía**. (p.m.)
Es **medianoche**.	Son las doce **de la noche**. (a.m.)

Now look at the times below and answer the question *¿Qué hora es?*

Example: 2.30 p.m. Son las dos y media de la tarde.

a 3:05 p.m.   **b** 7:15 a.m.   **c** 11:20 p.m.   **d** 8:30 a.m.

e midnight   **f** 5:50 p.m.   **g** midday   **h** 10:10 p.m.

D Say what time it is in the following cities if it is 3.30 p.m. in Madrid.
Say *¿Qué hora es en . . .?*

a Chicago (siete horas menos)
b Londres (una hora menos)
c La Habana (seis horas menos)
d París

e Tokio (siete horas más)
f Ciudad del Cabo
g Manila (seis horas más)
h Buenos Aires (cinco horas menos)

2 Days of the week and parts of the day

A *Los días de la semana*. Read the mini-dialogue and say what day it
is today.

■ ¿Qué día es hoy?

■ lunes
　martes
　miércoles
■ Hoy es　jueves
　viernes
　sábado
　domingo

G de Gramática

■ **Days of the week**
Note that the days of the week:
• are not capitalised in Spanish: *lunes* (Monday)
• are masculine: *el lunes*
• ending in **s** don't change in the plural: *el lunes / los lunes*
• Mondays to Fridays are *días laborables*
• the weekend is *el fin de semana*

B Say if the following statements are true (*verdadero*) or false (*falso*).

	verdadero	falso
1 Hoy es viernes.	☐	☐
2 El sábado es un día del fin de semana.	☐	☐
3 Los domingos hay clase.	☐	☐
4 El jueves es un día del fin de semana.	☐	☐
5 La semana tiene seis días.	☐	☐
6 Hay cinco días laborables.	☐	☐

C Parts of the day. Read the information about a day in the life of
Carolina and Jaime and say what Spanish time expressions
correspond to the English expressions *in the morning, at noon, in the
afternoon, in the evening*. Put the sentences in chronological order.

Un lunes en la vida de Carolina y Jaime

Carolina y Jaime

comen en un bar **al mediodía**　　**por la noche** van al gimnasio

van a clase **por la tarde**　　trabajan **por la mañana**

D Now you and the people in your group take it in turns to answer
the question *¿qué hacéis los lunes?*

E Complete the phrases with the prepositions *de* or *por*.

1 Son las ocho ___ la mañana.
2 Juan y Pedro estudian ___ la noche.
3 En Canarias son las cinco ___ la tarde .

4 ___ la tarde voy al cine.
5 Tenemos un examen ___ la tarde.

3 Saying how, when and where

A Read the grammar section below. Add *-mente* to the following adjectives and complete the sentences.

enérgico   constante   único   horrible   divino

1 Estos días Manuel habla _____ con su amigo Enrique.
2 Tus amigos cantan _____.
3 La madre de Pedro cocina _____, su comida es riquísima.
4 Trabajamos_____.
5 Vosotros viajáis _____.

B Correct the following sentences.

1 Mi profesor habla respetuosamente y amablemente.
2 Paul lee español correctamente pero lentamente.

G de Gramática

■ Adverbs

To refer to how, when and how often something is done or happens.

Adverbs are invariable words (i.e. they never change), that modify verbs, adjectives or other adverbs by saying how, when, where, how much or how often something is done or happens. In Spanish, adverbs normally have the same functions as in English. Words like *bien* (well), *mañana* (tomorrow), *aquí* (here), *bastante* (enough), *siempre* (always) are adverbs.

Adverbs can also consist of groups of words that behave in the same way as an adverb: *de repente* (suddenly), *por la tarde* (in the afternoon), *a la derecha* (on the right).

- **To refer to how something is done or happens**
  bien (well); *mal* (badly); *regular* (so-so / all right); *deprisa* (fast); *despacio* (slowly); *claramente* (clearly); *así* (in this way, thus) ...
  Many adverbs which express how something is done or happens are formed by adding **-mente** to the feminine singular form of an adjective or to the singular form if the adjective is invariable. This form corresponds to the English adverbial ending *-ly*.

masculine	feminine	adverb
tranquilo	tranquila	tranquila**mente** (calmly)
amable	amable	amable**mente** (kindly)

Note that when an adjective has a written accent, it is kept in the adverb.

| rápido | rápida | rápida**mente** (quickly) |

When two adverbs ending in *-mente* appear together, the first one loses the *–mente* ending.
Elena habla rápida pero claramente. (Elena speaks quickly but clearly).

- **To refer to when something is done or happens**
  pronto (soon); *temprano* (early); *tarde* (late); *antes* (before); *después* (later, afterwards); *ahora* (now); *ayer* (yesterday); *hoy* (today) ...

- **To refer to how often something is done or happens**
  siempre (always); *casi siempre* (almost always); *normalmente* (normally); *a menudo* (often); *a veces* (sometimes) *casi nunca* (almost never); *nunca* (never)

C Look at the pictures and read the verbs that illustrate the actions.

Julián y yo ¡qué vidas tan diferentes!

levantarse

Julián se levanta temprano, se ducha rápidamente, se lava los dientes, se afeita, se viste y va a trabajar. Por la noche, se acuesta temprano. Yo me despierto tarde, me baño tranquilamente, me peino, me visto y voy al café a leer el periódico. Por la noche, me acuesto tarde.

¿Y tú

te levantas temprano / tarde?

te vistes rápidamente / tranquilamente?

te duchas / te bañas rápidamente / tranquilamente?

te acuestas temprano / tarde?

ducharse

lavarse los dientes

D Tell your partner what you do:

Yo me levanto . . .

Then check what your partner does and tell the people in your group:
Mi compañero se levanta temprano . . .

afeitarse

Now check what your partner and you have in common and write it down:
Mi compañero y yo, nos acostamos temprano / tarde . . .

Check what two other people in your group do and write it down:
Mary y tú, os acostáis temprano / tarde . . .

vestirse

Then tell the people in your group what they do:
Mary y John se acuestan temprano / tarde . . .

E What do you think the verbs *despertarse, levantarse, ducharse, bañarse, peinarse, afeitarse, vestirse* and *acostarse* have in common?

acostarse

G de Gramática

■ Reflexive verbs

Verbs like *despertarse* (to wake up), *levantarse* (to get up), *peinarse* (to comb), *acostarse* (to go to bed / to lie down) are always accompanied by a reflexive pronoun (**me, te, se, nos, os, se**) (myself, yourself, himself, etc.). These verbs express actions done by the subject for or to himself / herself: *me despierto* (I wake up), *te levantas* (you get up). The reflexive pronoun changes according to the subject of the verb, as below:

Present tense of *levantarse:*					
(yo)	**me** levanto	(I get up)	(nosotros(as))	**nos** levantamos	(we get up)
(tú)	**te** levantas	(you get up)	(vosotros(as))	**os** levantáis	(you get up)
(usted)	**se** levanta	(you get up)	(ustedes)	**se** levantan	(you get up)
(él / ella)	**se** levanta	(he / she gets up)	(ellos(as))	**se** levantan	(they get up)

■ Irregular verbs

Irregular verbs are verbs which do not follow the normal pattern. Some verbs are always irregular but others are irregular only in some tenses.

Ser, estar, ir and **haber** (to have) are examples of irregular verbs.

■ Radical-changing verbs

Radical-changing verbs can be grouped initially like any others as **-ar**, **-er** or **-ir** verbs. However, these verbs undergo a spelling change in the stem. The stem change affects all persons except the first and second person plural.
Here are examples of the three types.

	e > ie	**o>ue**	**e>i**
	despertarse (*to wake up*)	**volver** (*to return*)	**pedir** (*to ask for*)
(yo)	me despierto	vuelvo	pido
(tú)	te despiertas	vuelves	pides
(usted)	se despierta	vuelve	pide
(él / ella)	se despierta	vuelve	pide
(nosotros(as))	nos despertamos	volvemos	pedimos
(vosotros(as))	os despertáis	volvéis	pedís
(ustedes)	se despiertan	vuelven	piden
(ellos(as))	se despiertan	vuelven	piden

Note that **jugar** (to play) with a stem vowel **u**, follows the same pattern as verbs with stem vowel **o**: **jue**go, **jue**gas, **jue**ga, jugamos, jugáis, **jue**gan.

Other radical-changing verbs

e >ie

calentar (to heat); *cerrar* (to close); *comenzar* (to begin); *empezar* (to begin); *fregar* (to wash up); *merendar* (to have a snack / picnic); *pensar* (to think);
divertirse (to enjoy oneself); *entender* (to understand); *encender* (to switch on, to light); *perder* (to lose); *querer* (to want, to love); *tener* (to have); *preferir* (to prefer);

o>ue

acostarse (to go to bed, to lie down); *costar* (to cost); *probar* (to prove / to taste / to try on); *mover* (to move); *soler* (to be in the habit of / to 'usually'); *dormir* (to sleep); *morir* (to die)

e>i

corregir (to correct); *elegir* (to choose); *medir* (to measure); *repetir* (to repeat); *seguir* (to follow); *vestir* (*se*) (to dress)

Note: *corregir / elegir* **g>j** before **o**: *corrijo, corriges, corrige, corregimos, corregís, corrigen*
seguir **gu>g** before **o**: *sigo, sigues, sigue, seguimos, seguís, siguen*

F Choose a verb from the grammar section, say the infinitive and a subject (e.g. *probar, yo*) and your partner will say the corresponding form. Then she/he chooses another infinitive and subject and so on.

G Complete the sentences with the appropriate form of the verb.

1 Yo _____ tarde del trabajo. (volver)
2 Tú _____ muy temprano los fines de semana. (despertarse)
3 Vosotros _____ mucho dinero. (invertir)
4 Elena y Carmen no _____ al tenis muy bien. (jugar)
5 Nosotros no _____ los platos todos los días. (fregar)
6 Usted _____ ir a Madrid ¿verdad? (querer)
7 ¿Cuánto _____? (costar)
8 ¿Por qué Sara _____ siempre lo mismo? (repetir)

Consolidation

A 🎧 Listen to the recording whilst reading this paragraph.

El domingo de los señores Costa

El domingo es un día tranquilo. Normalmente nos despertamos tarde, sobre las diez y media. Por la mañana vamos al parque a caminar un poco y después vamos a un bar a tomar algo. Por la tarde nos quedamos en casa, vemos la televisión o dormimos la siesta. A veces, nuestros amigos vienen a casa. Por la noche nos acostamos temprano.

B Underline all the adverbs and adverbial phrases used in the paragrah above to express frequency and time.

C Rewrite the paragraph in the first person singular.

D Now tell your partner about your Sundays.

In class or at home

A Complete the mini-dialogues.

1 ¿Qué hora _____?

_____
(1:30)

2 Luisa ¿_____ hora?

Sí, (10:20)

3 Por favor, señor, ¿_____ hora?

Sí, (18:45)

4 Señora por favor, ¿_____ hora?

No, _____

B Write out the following times.

Example: 11:25 a.m. Son las once y veinticinco de la mañana.

a 6:10 p.m.	**b** 12 p.m.	**c** 1:15 a.m.	**d** 10:40 p.m.
e 12:55 p.m.	**f** 8:30 a.m.	**g** 7:35 p.m.	**h** 1:00 p.m.
i 5:20 a.m.	**j** 4:45 p.m.		

C Make correct sentences by adding the necessary words.

Example: ¿Levantarse (tú) / temprano / sábados?   ¿Te levantas temprano los sábados?

   a Juan / vestirse / rápidamente
   c Divertirse (nosotros) / mucho / aquí
   e Siempre / acostarse (yo) / tarde / sábados / noche
   g ¿Querer (usted) / siempre / comer?
   i Ustedes / siempre / acostarse / temprano / fines de semana?

   b ¿Cuánto / costar / libros?
   d Mis padres / despertarse / muy temprano
   f ¿Entender (vosotros) / español?
   h Niños / jugar / bien / fútbol
   j Tu hijo / medir / 2m

D Write down the days of the week.

   a l_____   **b** j_____   **c** s_____   **d** m_____
   e v_____   **f** d_____   **g** mi_____

E Add *-mente* to the following adjectives and complete the sentences.

perfecto   correcto   silencioso   elegante   maravilloso

   1 Siempre hacéis los ejercicios _____.
   2 Irene camina _____, parece una modelo.
   3 Rosa y Roberto bailan _____.
   4 ¿Por qué siempre te vistes tan _____?
   5 Los gatos se mueven _____.

F Read again the text **'El domingo de los señores Costa'** and rewrite it in the third person plural.

G Conjugate the following reflexive verbs: *depertarse, ducharse, vestirse, acostarse*.

H Complete the table with the appropriate forms of the verbs.

	infinitive	regular verbs			irregular verbs		
		-ar	-er	-ir	-ar	-er	-ir
yo	entender / desayunar / escribir / comer / ir / contar	desayuno					
tú	ser / estudiar / pedir / estar / beber / vivir						
Ud. / él, ella	subir / tener / preferir cerrar / aprender / hablar						
nosotros (as)	describir / levantarse / estar / volver / comer / corregir						
vosotros (as)	seguir / completar / recibir / cerrar / ser / correr						
Uds. / ellos, ellas	repartir / pensar / cocinar / deber / ir / querer						

B Los horarios
Timetables

Meals in Spain

A Before reading the text, match the English words with their Spanish counterparts.

Food	Comida	Drinks	Bebidas
1 butter	**a** sopa	**1** beer	**a** agua
2 cereals	**b** tapas	**2** coffee	**b** refresco
3 cheese	**c** tortilla	**3** fizzy drink	**c** vino
4 eggs	**d** mantequilla	**4** water	**d** café
5 fish	**e** tostadas	**5** wine	**e** cerveza
6 fruit	**f** queso		
7 meat	**g** huevos		
8 marmalade	**h** arroz		
9 rice	**i** cereales		
10 salad	**j** fruta		
11 snacks	**k** pescado		
12 soup	**l** ensalada		
13 Spanish omelette	**m** mermelada		
14 toasts	**n** carne		

La vida diaria

unidad 4

110

G de Gramática

■ 'Meal verbs'

'Meal' verbs such as *desayunar* mean not only *to have breakfast* but also *to have for breakfast*:

– ¿A qué hora desayunas?	At what time do you have breakfast?
– Desayuno a las ocho	I have breakfast at eight
– ¿Qué desayunas?	What do you have for breakfast?
– Desayuno café y tostadas	For breakfast I have coffee and toast.

B 🎧 Listen to and read the text about the eating habits of the Spaniards. Underline any words or expressions that you don't understand. Then read the text again and try to work out the meaning from the context. Finally, before asking your tutor or consulting a dictionary, talk to other people in your group to see if, together, you can understand the text.

Los españoles desayunan entre las siete y media y ocho y media de la mañana. El desayuno no es abundante; muchos toman sólo un café o un vaso de leche, algunos toman además cereales o tostadas con mantequilla y mermelada. A media mañana, sobre las once, toman otro café o alguna bebida y luego hacia la una, antes de comer, toman el aperitivo que consiste en alguna tapa y una copa de vino, una cerveza o un refresco. Al mediodía, entre las dos y tres de la tarde es cuando toman la comida principal. Muchos españoles comen en casa. La comida es abundante y suelen tomar dos platos. El primer plato consiste en una sopa, ensalada o arroz y el segundo plato suele ser un plato a base de carne o pescado. También toman postre: fruta o algo dulce y por último café. La comida se acompaña con vino o agua. Por la tarde, los niños, después del colegio, entre las cinco y media y seis de la tarde, meriendan un bocadillo y los adultos toman un café con algo dulce. Muchos españoles, después de trabajar, a partir de las ocho de la tarde van a un bar con los amigos y toman una bebida y alguna tapa. Por la noche, entre las nueve y las diez y media, cenan. La cena: sopa, huevos, tortilla, ensalada, queso, fruta … es más ligera que la comida.

Las comidas

C de Cultura

■ Tapas y bocadillos

Bocadillos or *bocatas* (m.) are sandwiches made with a baguette. They can be served cold with simple fillings such as cheese or ham. They can also be served hot with fillings such as squid or a type of black pudding known as *morcilla*. If you see a sign for a 'sandwich', this is likely to refer to something made with sliced bread and toasted. *Tapas* are snacks which, in the past, were given free with every drink you bought. From a huge variety you might have been given a small piece of Spanish omelette (*tortilla*), a few olives (*aceitunas*), a few peanuts (*cacahuetes*), a slice of cured ham (*jamón serrano*) on a small piece of bread, a hot croquette or a small serving of seafood such as prawns (*gambas*) or anchovies (*anchoas*). Today very few bars offer any *tapas* (other than olives) free. Instead, you are more likely to buy a slightly larger portion known as a *ración* (f.) or *media ración*. Prices, sizes of servings and variety can vary depending on where you are. The Basque Country is one of many regions where cuisine of this sort (and every other sort) tends to be excellent. All Spanish regions have their speciality dishes.

C Complete the information in the table and then compare Spanish eating habits with those of your country and your own habits.

		españoles	tu país	tú
El desayuno	**¿cuándo?** **¿a qué hora?**	por la mañana entre las 7.30 y las 8.30		
	¿cuánto? **nada / poco / bastante / mucho**	poco		
	¿qué?	café vaso de leche cereales tostadas con mantequilla y mermelada		

A media mañana	**¿a qué hora?**			
	¿qué?			
Antes de comer, el aperitivo	**¿a qué hora?** **¿qué?**			

La comida	**¿cuándo?** **¿a qué hora?**			
	¿cuánto? **nada / poco / bastante / mucho** **¿qué?**			

La merienda	**¿cuándo?**			
	¿a qué hora?			
	¿qué?			
Antes de cenar	**¿a qué hora?**			
	¿qué?			

La cena	**¿cuándo?**			
	¿a qué hora?			
	¿cuánto? **nada / poco / bastante / mucho**			
	¿qué?			

D Compare the eating habits of different countries.

    Example: Los españoles desayunan menos que los ingleses.

                  Los españoles comen más tarde que los portugueses.

                  Los españoles cenan menos que los estadounidenses.

E Compare your eating habits with those of other people in your class.

    Example: Yo desayuno menos que mi compañero. Él desayuna cereales, un vaso de leche y café y yo desayuno un café.

G de Gramática

■ Comparing verbs and adverbs

In Unit 3, section C, you learnt how to compare adjectives and nouns. Now you are going to learn how to compare verbs and adverbs.

a) Comparison of verbs:

Higher degree	verb + *más que*	*Yo como más que tú,* (I eat more than you.)
Lesser degree	verb + *menos que*	*Los españoles desayunan menos que los ingleses.* (The Spanish eat less for breakfast than the English.)
Same degree	verb + *tanto como*	*Pablo cena tanto como su padre.* (At supper, Pablo eats as much as his father.)

b) Comparison of adverbs

Higher degree	*más* + adverb + *que*	*Los españoles se levantan más tarde que los griegos.* (The Spanish get up later than the Greeks.)
Lower degree	*menos* + adverb + *que*	*Yo salgo menos temprano que tú de trabajar.* (I leave work later [lit. = less early] than you.)
Same degree	*tan* + adverb + *como*	*Los españoles comen tan abundantemente como los franceses.* (The Spanish eat as much as the French.)

Irregular comparatives of adverbs

bien = *mejor*	*Yo como mejor que tú,* (I eat better than you.)
mal = *peor*	*Pedro cena peor que su hermano* (At supper, Pedro doesn't eat as much as [lit. = dines worse than] his brother.)

Opening and closing times in Spain

G de Gramática

■ Time expressions

- To express the time at which something happens, the construction **a + la / las** is used:

  ¿A qué hora abre el banco? (At what time does the bank open?)

  A las diez.   (At ten.)

- To refer to work schedules or hours of business, the constructions **de . . . a** or **desde las . . . hasta la / las** are used:

  ¿Qué horario tiene la biblioteca? (What are the library's opening times?)

  ¿Cuándo está abierta la Oficina de Correos? (When is the Post Office open?)

  De nueve a cinco. / Desde las nueve hasta las cinco. (From nine to five.)

  ¿De qué hora a qué hora trabajas? / ¿Desde qué hora hasta qué hora trabajas? (What are your working hours?)

  (Trabajo) de ocho a una. / (Trabajo) desde las ocho hasta la una. (I work from 8 until 1.)

- To express approximate time

  entre (between): *entre las siete y media y ocho y media de la mañana*

  sobre (around): *sobre las once*   *hacia* (about): *hacia la una*

A Read the following text and answer the questions.

El horario español

En España la mayor parte de las tiendas abren de diez a dos y de cinco a ocho. Cierran al mediodía para comer. Este horario puede variar según las zonas y las estaciones del año. Así en verano muchas tiendas en las zonas turísticas no cierran hasta las diez de la noche.

Los grandes almacenes abren todo el día y no cierran para comer.

Muchos museos cierran al mediodía pero en las grandes ciudades algunos de ellos permanecen abiertos todo el día. Los lunes suelen estar cerrados.

Los bancos abren desde las nueve de la mañana hasta las tres de la tarde.

Muchas oficinas públicas tienen un horario intensivo de nueve a tres y no abren por la tarde.

En la universidad hay clases por la mañana y por la tarde pero no al mediodía ya que es la hora de comer.

Los bares y discotecas cierran muy tarde. Muchas discotecas están abiertas hasta las tres o cuatro de la madrugada y algunas de ellas no cierran en toda la noche.

B Say if the following statements are true or false.

1 Todas las tiendas en España cierran al mediodía para comer.
2 Muchos museos no abren los lunes.
3 Los bancos no abren hasta las diez.
4 Las universidades tienen clases de dos a cuatro.
5 Los bares y discotecas tienen un horario estricto.

C Answer the following questions.

En tu país:
1 ¿de qué hora a qué hora están abiertas las tiendas?
2 ¿a qué hora cierran los bancos?
3 ¿desde qué hora hasta qué hora están abiertas las discotecas?
4 ¿qué horario tienen las oficinas públicas?

D Write six sentences in which you compare typical working hours, timetables and shop opening times in Spain with those of your home country.

Examples:
En mi país los bancos abren de . . . a . . .
En mi país los bancos abren más horas que en España.
En mi país los bancos no cierran al mediodía.

E Ask your partner five questions about opening and closing hours in his/her country.

G de Gramática

■ The 24-hour clock

Official time expressed in news bulletins, newspapers, bus, train and plane schedules, TV programmes and so on, uses the 24-hour clock. Expressions such as *de la mañana, de la tarde*, are omitted. The words *hora / horas* and *minuto / minutos* are normally used.

El tren sale a las 14:00 (catorce horas)

El avión llega a las 22:35 (veintidós [horas] treinta y cinco [minutos])

El autobús sale a las 14:02 (catorce cero dos/catorce horas y dos minutos)

A Read the grammar section and then the bus timetable.

ESTACIÓN DE AUTOBUSES DE LA CORUÑA

HORARIO DE AUTOBUSES

Largo recorrido
Salidas:

Oviedo, Avilés, Gijón, Santander y Bilbao: *9,14 y 16.*

Bilbao, San Sebastián e Irún: *14.*

Madrid: *8:30, 11:15, 14:30 y 22.*

Orense: *7:45 y 15:30.*

Lugo: *6:45, 12:30 y 15:30* (laborables); *8, 10:30 y 17:30* (diario).

Viveiro: *18* (laborables); *16:45* (domingos y festivos).

Santiago: *de 7 a 21*, todas las horas.

Pontevedra y Vigo: *8, 9:30, 11, 13, 18 y 20.*

Al aeropuerto de Lavacolla (Santiago)

Salidas: *5:50, 7:15, 12 y 16:45*, todos los días.

Salidas aproximadas del aeropuerto: *8:45, 13.30 18 y 19:45* los martes, jueves y sábados; *8:45, 13:30, 18 y 20*, los demás días de la semana.

B Look at the bus timetable and answer the questions.

1 ¿A qué hora sale el primer autobús para Madrid?

2 ¿A qué hora sale el último autobús para Santiago?

3 ¿Qué días hay autobuses para Viveiro?

4 ¿Qué días hay un autobús que sale del aeropuerto de Lavacolla a las 20h?

5 Los domingos, ¿a qué hora sale el último autobús para Lugo?

C 🔊 Listen to the recording and complete the table.

Salidas (*departures*) Andén (*bay*) Destino (*destination*) Retrasar (*to delay*)

	destino	hora de salida	número de andén
1			
2			
3			
4			
5			

Consolidation

A Complete the following sentences about your eating habits:

1 Por la mañana tomamos el . . .
2 Antes de comer tomamos el . . .
3 Al mediodía tomamos la . . .
4 A media tarde los niños toman la . . .
5 Por la noche tomamos la . . .

B Choose the right option to complete each sentence.

1 Mi hijo cena _____ su padre.
   a tanto que   **b** tanto como   **c** tanto de
2 Los argentinos comen _____ los australianos.
   a más que   **b** más de   **c** más
3 Los bancos abren _____ temprano _____ las tiendas.
   a más .. de   **b** más . . . que   **c** más . . . como
4 Los padres comen _____ los hijos.
   a más mal que   **b** peor que   **c** más mal de
5 Carlitos merienda _____ su hermano pequeño.
   a menos de   **b** menos como   **c** menos que

C Take turns with your partner to ask the questions which correspond to the following answers. Write the times in full.

1 El primer tren para Veracruz sale a las 13:00h.
2 Trabajo de las 9h a las 14h.
3 Esta farmacia abre desde las 16h hasta las 22h.
4 El último autobús llega a las 23:45h.
5 La oficina está abierta de 08:00h a 13:30h.

In class or at home

A Write down what the Spanish have for breakfast, aperitif, lunch and dinner. If you need help, refer to the text in Ex.1B.

B Complete the information about what time the Spanish have their meals.

1 Los españoles desayunan . . .
2 Los españoles comen . . .
3 Los españoles cenan . . .

C Write down comparative sentences following the examples given.

Examples: Mi hermano desayuna cereales y tostadas. Yo desayuno un vaso de leche.
Mi hermano desayuna más que yo.
Yo desayuno menos que mi hermano.
Juan se levanta a las seis de la mañana. Luis se levanta a las ocho.
Juan se levanta más temprano que Luis.
Luis se levanta más tarde que Juan.

1 Mike come un sandwich. Pablo come dos platos y postre.
2 Mi hermano pequeño cena una tortilla. Yo ceno una tortilla.
3 Teresa se viste rápidamente. Jacinto se viste despacio.
4 Mi abuela merienda un café. Mi abuelo merienda un café y un croissant.
5 Elena trabaja diez horas al día. Carmen trabaja siete horas al día.
6 El banco abre a las diez. El supermercado abre a las nueve.

D Read the bus timetable again (p.115) and answer the questions. Write down the times in full using the 24-hour clock.

1 ¿A qué hora sale el último autobús para Gijón?
2 ¿A qué hora sale el primer autobús de la tarde para Madrid?
3 Los lunes ¿a qué hora sale el primer autobús para Lugo?
4 Los martes ¿a qué hora sale el autobús para Viveiro?

La rutina diaria

Daily routine

■ Expresiones esenciales	■ Essential expressions
¿A qué hora + actividad?	*At what time + activity?*
¿A qué hora te levantas?	*At what time do you get up?*
Me levanto a las . . .	*I get up at . . .*
¿A qué hora empiezas a trabajar?	*What time do you start work?*
Empiezo a trabajar a las . . .	*I start work at . . .*
(Luis) empieza a trabajar a las . . .	*(Luis) starts work at . . .*
¿Quién cena antes / se acuesta más tarde?	*Who has supper before / goes to bed later?*
¿Te has levantado temprano?	*Did you get up early?*

1 **Describing your daily routine**

A Here is Luis's daily routine. Can you complete the missing information?

> Luis siempre se despierta a las siete y media de la mañana (7:30 a.m.) pero se levanta a las _____ (7:45 a.m.), a continuación se ducha y _____ (8:10 a.m.) desayuna un café. Sale de casa _____ (8:20 a.m.). Llega a la oficina _____ (9:00 a.m.). A veces, _____ (11:15 a.m.), toma un café en el bar con los colegas. _____ (1:30 p.m.) sale de la oficina y casi siempre vuelve a casa a comer.
>
>   Normalmente come _____ (2:30 p.m.). Por la tarde empieza a trabajar _____ (4:25 p.m.). Termina de trabajar _____ (8:00 p.m.), a menudo toma algo con sus amigos en un bar. Después regresa a casa _____ (10:00 p.m.), cena, nunca ve la televisión y siempre se acuesta _____ (12:00 p.m.)

B Listen to Luis talking about his daily routine and check your answers.

C Write down the four reflexive verbs and their infinitive forms that appear in the text and indicate which two of the four have a stem change.

La vida diaria

unidad 4

118

D Write down the three verbs and their infinitive forms that refer to the main meals of the day.

E Read the text again and write down the expressions that indicate:
  a leaving a place
  b arriving at a place
  c coming back to a place
  d starting to do something
  e finishing doing something

F **¿A qué hora . . . ?** At what time . . . ? Answer the following questions.

  1 ¿A qué hora empieza Luis a trabajar por la mañana?
  2 ¿A qué hora sale de casa por la tarde?
  3 ¿A qué hora termina de trabajar?
  4 ¿A qué hora regresa a casa por la noche?
  5 ¿A qué hora se acuesta?

G In groups of four talk to the people in your group and find out at what time they do the various things:

Example:

¿A qué hora te levantas?   Me levanto a las ocho y media de la mañana. ¿Y tú?

	Tú	compañero 1	compañero 2	compañero 3
levantarse				
desayunar				
salir de casa				
empezar a trabajar las clases				
comer				
terminar de trabajar las clases				
regresar a casa				
cenar				
acostarse				

H Answer the following questions:

  1 ¿Quién de vosotros se levanta más temprano?
  2 ¿Quién se acuesta más tarde?
  3 ¿Quién sale antes de casa?
  4 ¿Quién cena antes?

To express frequency

A Read again what Luis does every day and write down the expressions used to refer to how often something is done or happens in descending order of frequency.
Example: *siempre* (always)

B Rewrite these sentences using one of the following expressions: *pocas veces, de vez en cuando, casi nunca, poco frecuentemente, nunca*

1 Los fines de semana siempre me levanto temprano.
2 Mi hijo va de viaje muchas veces.
3 Nuestro profesor llega tarde a clase a menudo.
4 La abuela casi siempre duerme la siesta.
5 Mi coche se estropea muy frecuentemente.

C Say three things that you always do on Monday morning and three things that you never do.

Referring to the recent past

A Answer the following questions, by ticking the relevant boxes.

	Sí	No
1 Esta mañana:		
¿Te has levantado temprano?	☐	☐
¿Has leído el periódico?	☐	☐
¿Has ido a clase?	☐	☐
¿Has ido a trabajar?	☐	☐
2 Esta semana:		
¿Has ido al cine?	☐	☐
¿Has dormido bien?	☐	☐
¿Has salido por la noche?	☐	☐
¿Has estudiado mucho?	☐	☐

	Sí	No
3 Este año:		
¿Has aprendido a conducir?	☐	☐
¿Has comprado un coche?	☐	☐
¿Has hecho mucho deporte?	☐	☐
¿Has ido de viaje?	☐	☐

B Answer the following questions and then read the grammar section on the next page about the perfect tense.

1 Do all the above questions refer to events in the present, past or future?
2 Have all these events happened in a period of time that includes the present?
3 Is this period of time considered finished?

La vida diaria

unidad 4

120

■ **The perfect tense**

As in English, Spanish uses different tenses to refer to the past. The perfect tense is one of them. It is formed, as in English, by adding the **past participle** to the present tense of **haber** (to have). Example: *He hablado* (I have spoken).

Formation of the past participle

The past participle is formed by adding the endings *-ado* or *-ido* to the stem of the verb:

Verbs ending in *-ar*:	*-ado*	(hablar)	→	habl*ado*
Verbs ending in *-er / -ir*:	*-ido*	(tener)	→	ten*ido*
		(salir)	→	sal*ido*

	Present of haber	Past participle	Present of to have	Past participle	
(yo)	he		I	have	
(tú)	has		you (familiar)	have	
(usted)	ha	estudiado	you (formal)	have	studied
(él / ella)	ha	bebido	he / she	has	drunk
(nosotros(as))	hemos	recibido	we	have	received
(vosotros(as))	habéis		you (familiar)	have	
(ustedes)	han		you (formal)	have	
(ellos(as))	han		they	have	

Irregular past participles

In Spanish there are a few common irregular past participles that you will have to learn.

Infinitive	Past participle	Infinitive	Past participle
hacer (*to do / to make*)	hecho	cubrir (*to cover*)	cubierto
volver (*to come back*)	vuelto	escribir (*to write*)	escrito
ver (*to see*)	visto		
poner (*to put*)	puesto	decir (*to say*)	dicho
romper (*to break*)	roto	morir (*to die*)	muerto
abrir (*to open*)	abierto		

The past participle is invariable and is not conjugated in this tense: *Elena ha recibido una carta. Luis ha recibido una carta.*

However when used as an adjective after the verbs *ser* and *estar* and nouns, the past participle agrees in number and gender with the noun it refers to:

El banco está cerrado. (The bank is closed.)   *La ventana está cerrada.* (The window is closed.)

El lunes pasado. (Last Monday.)   *La semana pasada.* (Last week.)

■ **Use of the perfect tense**

To refer to completed past actions or events, in a time frame that includes the present:

¿A qué hora te has levantado esta mañana?   (What time did you get up this morning?)

Este año habéis aprendido mucho.   (This year you have learnt a lot.)

Note: The Perfect Tense is often accompanied by **time expressions** that include the present:

hoy (today)

recientemente (recently)

últimamente (lately)

esta mañana/tarde/semana (this morning/afternoon/week)

este mes/año/siglo (this month/year/century)

estas vacaciones (these holidays)

<u>**C**</u> Now read your partner's answers from Ex. A and write a summary of what he/she has done. Then tell the other people in your group what he/she has done.

Example: Esta mañana Mike se ha levantado temprano, no ha ido a clase porque ha ido a trabajar. Esta semana no ha salido pero ha estudiado mucho. Este año ha aprendido a conducir y ha comprado un coche.

<u>**D**</u> Rewrite the verbs in these sentences in the plural.

1 Esta mañana he ido a desayunar con mi tío Pablo.
2 ¿Has terminado de comer?
3 Hoy usted ha trabajado poco y mal.
4 Ella ha estado en mi casa toda la tarde.
5 Recientemente, he asistido a muchos conciertos.

<u>**E**</u> Translate the following sentences into Spanish.

1 This morning the bank opened late.
2 Did you (singular, familiar) go to the cinema this week?
3 Today we came from Venezuela.
4 This afternoon Marta and Marisa had a coffee in my house.
5 Did you (plural, formal) have a *siesta* today?

Consolidation

<u>**A**</u> Complete the information.

1 Yo siempre desayuno a las diez pero hoy . . .
2 Los niños juegan al fútbol los miércoles pero este miércoles no . . .
3 Siempre cenamos a las diez pero hoy . . .
4 Normalmente nuestra profesora es muy puntual pero esta mañana . . .

<u>**B**</u> Choose one element from each column to make correct sentences:

Últimamente	hemos visitado	al teatro
Este fin de semana	he ido	muy cansada
Hoy	hemos llegado	nada
Esta tarde, después de trabajar	no han hecho	muchos problemas
Recientemente	ha tenido	dos veces El Salvador
Este año	he estado	tarde a una reunión

In class or at home

A Read the sentences. First write down the times and then write down the questions to the following answers.

Example: Siempre me levanto 8:30 a.m.
    Siempre me levanto a las ocho y media de la mañana.
    ¿A qué hora te levantas?

1 Mi hermano y yo siempre desayunamos 11:10 a.m.
2 Francisco normalmente termina las clases 7:00 p.m.
3 Mi familia come a menudo 2:15 p.m.
4 Julio y José casi siempre van al bar 9:45 p.m.
5 El abuelo a veces cena muy tarde, cena 11:45 p.m.
6 Las clases empiezan demasiado temprano, empiezan 8:00 a.m.

B Read the text and write the verbs in brackets in the present or perfect tense.

María siempre _____ (1 *levantarse*) temprano pero hoy _____ (2 *levantarse*) muy tarde. Normalmente _____ (3 *desayunar*) en casa pero esta mañana _____ (4 *desayunar*) en una cafetería con unas amigas. Al mediodía, siempre _____ (5 *volver*) a casa pero hoy _____ (6 *tener*) que comer en la oficina. Casi siempre _____ (7 *terminar*) de trabajar a las ocho y después _____ (8 *ir*) a un bar a tomar algo pero hoy _____ (9 *trabajar*) hasta las diez y después _____ (10 *ir*) directamente a casa.

C Complete the table with the appropriate form of the verbs in the perfect tense.

		Perfect tense		
	Infinitive	**-ar**	**-er**	**-ir**
yo	desayunar / comer / vivir	*he desayunado*		
tú	estudiar / beber / escribir			
usted, él / ella	trabajar / aprender / salir			
nosotros(as)	estar / ver / ir			
vosotros(as)	hacer / tener / decir			
ustedes, ellos(as)	acostarse / ser / abrir			

D | Tareas domésticas
Domestic chores

■ **Expresiones esenciales**   ■ **Essential expressions**

¿Qué haces en casa?	*What do you do at home?*
Limpio / friego / plancho	*I clean / wash up / iron*
¿Qué está(s) haciendo? *(polite / informal)*	*What are you doing?*
Estoy duchándome	*I'm having a shower*
Me estoy duchando	
¿Qué está haciendo Luis?	*What is Luis doing?*
Luis está haciendo la cama	*Luis is making the bed*

1   **Domestic chores**

A *Luis hace la limpieza.* Match the following expressions with the appropriate illustration.

limpiar el polvo   limpiar el cuarto de baño

pasar el aspirador   fregar los platos   poner la lavadora

colgar la ropa   planchar   hacer la cama

a)

b)
c)
d)
e)

f)

g)

h)

G de Gramática

■ **Irregular verbs in the first person singular**

A number of verbs are irregular in the first person singular (*yo*) of the present tense, the other persons follow a regular pattern:

- **Some verbs add *g* to the first person singular:**
  hacer (to do, to make): *ha**g**o, haces, hace, hacemos, hacéis, hacen*
  Other verbs following this pattern are: *poner* (to put), *salir* (to go out), *valer* (to be worth, to cost), and all their derivatives.

- **Some verbs add *z* to the first person singular.**
  These include verbs ending in *-acer* (except *hacer*); *-ecer, -ocer* (except *cocer*) and *–ucir:*
  conocer (to know): *cono**z**co, conoces, conoce, conocemos, conocéis, conocen*
  Other verbs: *agradecer* (to be grateful), *parecerse* (to look

like), *crecer* (to grow), *obedecer* (to obey), *conducir* (to drive), *producir* (to produce), *traducir* (to translate), etc.

- **Other irregular verbs in the first person singular:**
  dar (to give): *do**y**, das, da, damos, dais, dan*
  saber (to know): *s**é**, sabes, sabe, sabemos, sabéis, saben*
  ver (to see / to watch): *v**e**o, ves, ve, vemos, veis, ven*

■ **Verbs that have a double irregularity**

These verbs present two types of irregularity: both in the first person and in the stem.

tener (to have): *ten**g**o, t**ie**nes, t**ie**ne, tenemos, tenéis, t**ie**nen*
decir (to say, to tell): *di**g**o, dices, dice, decimos, decís, dicen*
oír (to hear): *oi**g**o, oyes, oye, oímos, oís, oyen*
venir (to come): *ven**g**o, v**ie**nes, v**ie**ne, venimos, venís, v**ie**nen*

B Listen to Clara talking about what she does at home. Tick the appropriate box.

	hacer la cama	limpiar el polvo	pasar el aspirador	fregar los platos	colgar la ropa	poner la lavadora	planchar	limpiar el cuarto de baño	cocinar
siempre									
todos los días									
casi siempre									
frecuentemente									
a menudo									
alguna vez									
una vez a la semana									
casi nunca									
nunca									

C Look at the table above and write down five things that Clara does at home.

Example: Clara siempre hace la cama.

D Write sentences about five things that you never do at home or you don't do very often.

Example: Yo nunca hago la cama.
Yo no hago nunca la cama.
Yo no hago la cama nunca.

Note the position of the word *nunca*. All the above sentences are synonymous.

2 Division of labour

A Read out aloud the following article about domestic chores and answer the questions.

Los españoles y las tareas domésticas

La sociedad española ha cambiado mucho en los últimos años pero todavía tiene que cambiar más. La casa y su cuidado todavía es cosa de mujeres. Un porcentaje muy elevado de mujeres hace las tareas domésticas. Muchas mujeres que trabajan fuera de casa encuentran todo sin hacer cuando regresan a casa, el marido y los hijos en el sofá viendo la televisión, porque claro ella es la que tiene que hacer la cena y organizar la casa. Planchar, fregar, cocinar, poner la lavadora, colgar la ropa ... han sido tradicionalmente labores femeninas y no es fácil cambiar la mentalidad de los hombres pero tampoco de las mujeres. Para conseguir la igualdad tenemos que cambiar todos.

B Say if the following statements are true (*verdadero*) or false (*falso*). Correct the false ones.

1 La sociedad española ha cambiado poco en los últimos años.
2 La limpieza de la casa es responsabilidad de toda la familia.
3 En España, los hombres organizan la casa.
4 Muchas mujeres hacen las tareas domésticas.
5 Los hombres tienen que cambiar de mentalidad.

C Say what the situation is in your country. Tick the statements that apply and compare with others in your group.

En mi país:

a muchas mujeres son amas de casa / muchas mujeres trabajan fuera de casa.
b más hombres que mujeres trabajan fuera de casa.
c más mujeres que hombres trabajan fuera de casa.
e los niños ayudan en casa más que las niñas.
f las niñas ayudan en casa más que los niños.
h las tareas domésticas son la responsabilidad de la mujer / del hombre / de toda la familia.
i las mujeres / los hombres / todos tienen que cambiar de mentalidad.

Talking about ongoing actions in the present

A Read the grammar section below and do Ex. B.

G de Gramática

■ Referring to ongoing actions

To refer to events taking place as we speak, Spanish uses the construction **estar + gerundio** (present participle).

Teresa está hablando por teléfono. (Teresa is speaking on the phone.)

Nosotros estamos colgando la ropa. (We are hanging out the washing.)

Note the position of the reflexive pronoun and the written accent when the gerund and the reflexive pronoun form one word. The reflexive pronoun can be either in front of the verb or attached to the present participle.

*Luis **se** está duchando.* (Luis is having a shower.)
*Luis está duch**á**ndose.*

The present participle is invariable and is not conjugated.

Formation of the present participle

The present participle is formed by adding the endings **-ando** or **-iendo** to the stem of the verb:

Verbs ending in **-ar**: **-ando** (hablar) → habl**ando**
Verbs ending in **-er / -ir**: **-iendo** (tener) → ten**iendo**
(salir) → sal**iendo**

Note: Most verbs ending in a vowel + **-er**, **-ir** become **-yendo**.

leer → le**yendo**
oír → o**yendo**

Radical-changing verbs behave as follows:

decir → diciendo   poder → pudiendo
venir → viniendo   dormir → durmiendo

B Look at the photographs and say what is happening.

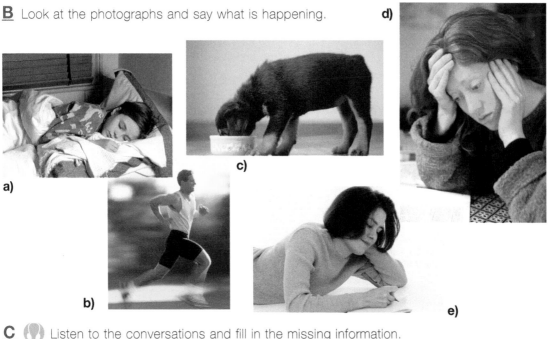

a)

b)

c)

d)

e)

C Listen to the conversations and fill in the missing information.

	¿Qué está haciendo . . . ?
Sofía	
Carlos	
Juan	
La profesora Jiménez	
Corina	

D Making excuses. Read the examples and then complete the mini-dialogues.

1 Pablo, ¿vienes al parque?

No, no _____, en estos momentos _____ (escribir) una carta.

2 Dígame.

¿El señor Fuertes Romero?

Lo _____ pero en estos momentos _____ (hablar) por teléfono.

3 Hugo ¿vienes a cenar?

No, no _____, _____ (estudiar).

4 Sra Muñoz ¿viene a tomar un café con nosotros?

Lo _____ pero en estos momentos _____ (esperar) una llamada de teléfono.

5 ¿Venís de excursión mañana?

Lo _____ pero no podemos _____ (terminar) un trabajo.

Jorge, ¿vienes al bar?

No, no puedo; estoy viendo una película en la tele.

Dígame. ¿El doctor García Jiménez, por favor?

Lo siento pero en estos momentos está atendiendo a un paciente.

Consolidation

A  Paco is very pleased with himself because he has spent most of the day cleaning the house. Marta arrives home in the evening and Paco is dying to tell her about what he has done. Listen and tick what he has done in the grid.

¿Qué ha hecho Paco hoy?	ha hecho	no ha hecho
Ha arreglado el salón		
Ha limpiado el polvo		
Ha pasado el aspirador		
Ha fregado los platos		
Ha limpiado el cuarto de baño		
Ha hecho la cama		
Ha arreglado el dormitorio		

B Put the verbs in brackets into the present participle form and then answer the questions, as in the example.

Example: ¿Luis está (ducharse)? (hacer la cama)
¿Luis se está duchando / está duchándose?
No, no se está duchando / no, no está duchándose, está haciendo la cama.

1 ¿Luis está (colgar) la ropa? (cocinar)
2 ¿Estás (leer) el periódico? (ver la televisión)
3 ¿Los abuelos están (dormir)? (jugar a las cartas)
4 ¿Estáis (estudiar)? (descansar)
5 ¿Elena está (pasar) el aspirador? (limpiar el cuarto de baño)
6 ¿Ustedes están (aprender) francés? (aprender español)
7 ¿El profesor está (corregir) los ejercicios? (explicar el gerundio)
8 ¿Estás (escuchar) la radio? (hacer los ejercicios de español)

In class or at home

A Write the verbs in brackets in the present tense.

1 Los británicos _____ a la izquierda (conducir).
2 Nosotros _____ del inglés al español (traducir).
3 Yo no _____ España (conocer).
4 Yo _____ clases privadas de japonés (dar).
5 Vosotros no _____ la televisión por la tarde (ver).
6 Lola e Irene nunca _____ los deberes (hacer).
7 Yo siempre _____ la verdad (decir).
8 ¿_____ (tú) a tomar café? (venir).
9 Nosotros no _____ dinero (tener).
10 Yo no _____ conducir (saber).

B Link up the three parts of each sentence.

Example: El médico está atendiendo al paciente.

1 El médico	está diseñando	la casa
2 La profesora	está hablando	por teléfono
3 Los estudiantes	estáis haciendo	los coches
4 Nosotros	está enseñando	al paciente
5 Vosotros	están arreglando	un puente
6 La secretaria	estamos limpiando	matemáticas
7 La ingeniera	está atendiendo	la cena
8 Los mecánicos	están haciendo	un examen

C Complete the sentences putting the verbs in brackets in the present or the perfect tense, according to the meaning.

1 José Luis siempre _____ (llegar) puntualmente al trabajo pero esta mañana _____ (levantarse) tarde y no _____ (llegar) a tiempo.

2 Esta semana yo _____ (estar) ocupadísimo, por eso, hoy sábado _____ (estar) tan cansado.

3 Mi madre casi siempre _____ (cocinar) pero hoy no _____ (cocinar).

4 Hoy mi profesor _____ (devolver) los exámenes en clase. ¡ _____ (sacar) un diez!

5 Esta mañana Marta no _____ (ir) a trabajar porque esta tarde _____ (tener) una boda.

6 Mis hijos _____ (estudiar) todas las tardes pero hoy no _____ (poder) estudiar porque _____ (tener) una fiesta en el colegio.

7 Yo normalmente _____ (traducir) del inglés al español pero hoy _____ (tener) que traducir del español al inglés.

8 Nosotros _____ (limpiar) la casa los domingos pero este domingo _____ (descansar).

D Say what time it is and include the time of day.

Example: 4:30 p.m.
  Son las cuatro y media de la tarde.

a 8:00 a.m.   **d** 11:35 p.m.
b 7:15 p.m.   **e** 6:10 p.m.
c 5:30 a.m.

E Complete the following mini-dialogues with the correct form of *estar* + present participle.

1 – *¡Paco! ¿qué* _____*? (hacer)*
   – _____ el periódico (leer).

2 – *María, ¿vienes?*
   – No puedo, _____ (vestirse).

3 – *¿Qué hace el niño?*
   – El niño _____ al fúbol con sus amigos? (jugar).

4 – *Marla, ¿ves a Juan?*
   – Sí, _____ con un señor (hablar).

5 – *Dígame.*
   – ¿El señor Romero, por favor?
   – Lo siento pero en estos momentos _____ (descansar).

F Rewrite the sentences in the perfect tense, as in the example given.

Example: Desayunamos con el director (esta mañana).
             Esta mañana hemos desayunado con el director.

1 Comemos a las dos y cuarto (hoy).
2 Marta escribe una novela (este año).
3 Vosotras tenéis exámenes (este mes).
4 Usted llega tarde (esta mañana).
5 Ellos ven el partido de fútbol (esta tarde).
6 Estoy muy estresado (últimamente).
7 Tú estudias mucho (este curso).
8 Nosotros resolvemos muchos problemas (recientemente).

Acércate al mundo del español
La siesta

A Before reading the text, tick the boxes which apply to you or express your opinion:

	Sí	No
1 Duermo la siesta.	☐	☐
2 La gente de mi país duerme la siesta.	☐	☐
3 La siesta es buena.	☐	☐
4 La siesta la duerme la gente perezosa.	☐	☐

B Before reading the text, make sure you know the meaning of the following words. Use a dictionary, if necessary.

un invento   el rendimiento   el sueño
la mente   el placer

C Read the text and then say four positive things about la siesta.

D Find out if the people in your group *duermen la siesta*.

Una siesta, ese invento tan español

Dormir después de comer, además de un invento genuinamente español, es una necesidad del organismo grabada biológicamente en los genes. El ser humano está programado para dormir por la tarde sin que eso suponga ningún prejuicio en nuestro rendimiento. Muy al contrario, numerosos estudios han demostrado que este paréntesis permite aumentar la concentración, el rendimiento, la productividad e incluso la creatividad. Existe una predisposición natural en el ritmo circadiano, el ciclo del sueño, del ser humano para dormir por la tarde, lo que permite aumentar la capacidad física e intelectual, relajar los músculos y la mente y, para qué negarlo, disfrutar de este pequeño placer en la mitad del día.

Source: http:// www.elmundo.es/elmundosalud/2002/11/21medicina/1037880803.html (adapted)

Essential vocabulary

Para expresar la hora	*To express the time*	**Adverbios**	*Adverbs*
¿Qué hora es / son?	*What time is it?*	así	*in this way, thus*
Es la . . . / son las . . .	*It is . . .*	bien	*well*
en punto	*o'clock*	claramente	*clearly*
y cuarto	*quarter past*	deprisa	*fast*
y media	*half past*	despacio	*slowly*
menos cuarto	*quarter to*	mal	*badly*
de la mañana	*in the morning*	regular	*so-so / all right*
de la tarde	*in the afternoon / evening*	tranquilamente	*calmly*
de la noche	*at night*	ahora	*now*
de la madrugada	*in the early hours*	antes	*before*
Partes del día	*Times of the day*	ayer	*yesterday*
por la mañana	*in (during) the morning*	después	*later, afterwards*
por la tarde	*in the afternoon*	hoy	*today*
por la noche	*in the evening / at night*	pronto	*soon*
al mediodía	*at midday*	tarde	*late*
a medianoche	*at midnight*	temprano	*early*
Los días de la semana	*Days of the week*	a menudo	*often*
lunes (m)	*Monday*	a veces	*sometimes*
martes (m)	*Tuesday*	casi nunca	*almost never*
miércoles (m)	*Wednesday*	casi siempre	*almost always*
jueves (m)	*Thursday*	normalmente	*normally*
viernes (m)	*Friday*	nunca	*never*
sábado (m)	*Saturday*	siempre	*always*
domingo (m)	*Sunday*	**La rutina diaria**	*Daily routine*
días (m) laborables	*working days*	acostarse	*to go to bed /*
días festivos	*bank holidays*		*to lie down*
fin (m) de semana	*weekend*	afeitarse	*to shave*
Los horarios	*Timetables*	bañarse	*to have a bath*
¿a qué hora . . . ?	*at what time . . . ?*	despertarse	*to wake up*
a la(s) . . .	*at + time*	ducharse	*to have a shower*
de . . . a	*from . . . to*	empezar	*to start / to begin*
entre / sobre / hacia . . .	*around/between/about*	levantarse	*to get up*
desde las (la) . . .	*from . . . to*	peinarse	*to comb*
hasta las (la) . . .		terminar	*to end / finish*
22:35: veintidós (horas)	*22:35 Twenty-two*	vestirse	*to get dressed*
treinta y cinco	*hours thirty-five*	**Verbos relacionados**	*Meal verbs*
(minutos)	*minutes*	**con las comidas**	
destino (m)	*destination*	cenar	*to have (for) dinner*
andén (m)	*bay / platform*	comer	*to have (for) lunch / to*
llegada (f)	*arrival*		*eat*
salida (f)	*departure*	desayunar	*to have (for) breakfast*
largo recorrido (m)	*long distance*	merendar	*to have (for) an afternoon*
diario/a (adjetivo)	*daily (adjective)*		*snack / tea*
cada hora	*hourly*	**Las comidas**	*Meals*
Verbos relacionados	*Verbs related to*	aperitivo (m)	*aperitif*
con los horarios	*timetables*	cena (f)	*dinner*
abrir	*to open*	comida (f) o almuerzo (m)	*lunch*
cerrar	*to close*	desayuno (m)	*breakfast*
llegar	*to arrive*	merienda (f)	*tea / snack*
salir	*to leave / to depart*		

Comida / Alimentos	*Food*
arroz (m)	*rice*
carne (f)	*meat*
cereales (m)	*cereals*
ensalada (f)	*salad*
fruta (f)	*fruit*
huevos (m)	*eggs*
mantequilla (f)	*butter*
mermelada (f)	*marmalade*
pescado (m)	*fish*
queso (m)	*cheese*
sopa (f)	*soup*
tapas (f)	*snacks*
tortilla (f)	*omelette*
tostadas (f)	*toast*
Bebidas	*Drinks*
agua (f)	*water*
café (m)	*coffee*
cerveza (f)	*beer*
refresco (m)	*fizzy drink*
vino (m)	*wine*
Tareas domésticas	*Domestic chores*
cocinar	*to cook*
colgar la ropa	*to hang out the washing*
fregar los platos	*to do the washing up*
hacer la cama	*to make the bed*
limpiar el polvo / el cuarto de baño	*to dust / clean the bathroom*
pasar el aspirador	*to vacuum-clean*
planchar	*to iron*
poner la lavadora	*to set the washing machine*
Para expresar cantidad	*To express quantity*
nada	*nothing*
poco	*little*
bastante	*enough*
mucho	*a lot*

Permisos, favores y preferencias

A Objetos

Objects

<table>
<tr><td>

■ **Expresiones esenciales**

¿Cómo es (+ objeto)?

Es redondoa

¿De qué es (+ objeto)?

Es de plástico / de madera

Es / Sirve para cortar / comer

¿De quién es (+ objeto)?

¿Es tuyo / suyo? *(informal/polite)*

Sí, es mío

No, no es mío, es de él / Lola

¿Es el tuyo / el suyo? *(informal/polite)*

¿Son las tuyas / las suyas? *(informal/polite)*

Sí, son las mías

¿Cuál prefiere(s) ésta, ésa o aquélla?
(polite/informal)

Prefiero ésta de aquí / ésa de ahí / aquélla
de allí

</td><td>

■ *Essential expressions*

What's . . . like?

It's round

What's . . . made of?

It's made of plastic / wood

It's / It's used for cutting / eating

Whose . . . is it? / Whose is the . . . ?

Is it yours?

Yes, it's mine

No, it's not mine, its his / Lola's

Is it yours (lit. your one)?

Are they yours (lit. your ones)?

Yes, they're mine (lit. my ones)

*Which one do you prefer: this one, that one or
that one over there?*

*I prefer this one here / that one there / that
one over there*

</td></tr>
</table>

1 Objects around us and their description, purpose or use

A Read the descriptions and say which of the following objects each describes.

un abrigo   una calculadora   una pelota   un lápiz
un cepillo de dientes   un bolígrafo

1 Es estrecho, largo, duro y de color rojo. Es de madera y sirve para escribir, dibujar y pintar.
2 Es redonda, de color blanco y negro. Es de piel y sirve para jugar al fútbol.
3 Es rectangular y dura. Es de plástico y sirve para calcular.
4 Es amarillo, estrecho, largo y ligero. Es de plástico y sirve para lavarse los dientes.
5 Es amarillo, estrecho y largo. Es de oro y sirve para escribir.
6 Es negro y blando. Es de lana y sirve para protegerse del frío.

G de Gramática

■ Describing objects and their purpose

- **¿Cómo + ser + (noun phrase)?** To ask what things are like:
  ¿Cómo es el espejo? (What is the mirror like?)
- **Ser + adjective** To refer to essential features, size, form and colour. Notice that the adjective AGREES with the object (noun) described:
  El espejo es cuadrado. (The mirror is square.)
  La mesa es cuadrada. (The table is square.)
- **¿De qué es + (noun phrase)?** To ask what something is made of.
  ¿De qué es el espejo? (What is the mirror made of?)
- **Ser de + noun** To refer to the material something is made of:
  El espejo es de cristal. (The mirror is made of glass.)
- **Para + infinitive** To express purpose or use:
  Sirve / es para mirarse. (It's used for / is for looking at yourself.)

C de Cultura

In Spain and Hispano-America certain names have diminutives, for example: José: Pepe; Dolores: Lola; Manuel: Manolo; María Luisa: Marisa; Francisco: Paco; Enrique: Quique.

B Listen to *Pepe*, *Lola*, *Manolo* and *Marisa* describing some of the objects shown below. Complete the chart and then match each description to the object being described.

una mochila

un espejo

un sombrero

unas gafas

un paraguas

un plato

	¿Cómo es?	¿De qué es?	¿Para qué sirve?	Objeto
Pepe				
Lola				
Manolo				
Marisa				

C Describe the two remaining objects.

D In groups of three or four, choose two or three objects and describe them to the rest of the group.

Objetos

2 Expressing possession

A Read the mini-dialogues and underline the words or expressions which indicate possession.

1 – *¿De quién es el bolígrafo?¿Es tuyo?*
  – *No, no es mío, es de mi abuelo.*

2 – *¿De quién son las llaves? ¿Son de tu hermano?*
  – *No, no son suyas. Son mías.*

3 – *¿De quiénes son los libros? ¿Son vuestros?*
  – *No, no son nuestros. Son de ellos.*

4 – *Juan, este ejercicio ¿es el tuyo?*
  – *Sí, es el mío.*

B Read the grammar section about how to express possession.

C Replace the words in italics with possessive pronouns.

Example: Trabajo con *tu ordenador.*   Trabajo con *el tuyo.*

1 Aquí tiene *sus llaves.*
2 *Vuestros libros* no están en el salón.
3 ¿Podéis dejarme *vuestra maleta*?
4 ¿Dónde están *tus ejercicios*?
5 Yo tengo *mi pasaporte* en la habitación del hotel.
6 Pedro no consulta *su agenda* a menudo.
7 Dejo *mis cosas* aquí.
8 ¿Es éste *el billete de Emilia*?
9 ¿Vendéis *vuestra casa*?
10 Prefiero *nuestra habitación a la de ellos*.

G de Gramática

■ **Expressing possession with *ser***

• ***¿De quién(es) es / son* (+ noun phrase)?**
¿De quién es? (Whose is it?)
¿De quién es este libro? (Whose is this book?)
¿De quiénes son estas mochilas? (Whose are these rucksacks?)

• ***Ser de* + noun**:
Es de Pedro. / Es de tu padre. / Es del niño (It's Pedro's. / It's your father's. / It's the child's.)

• ***Ser* + possessive pronoun**:
Es mío. / Es el mío (It is mine.)

■ **Possessive pronouns**

In Unit 2 we studied the possessive adjectives *mi, tu, su, mis, tus, sus, nuestro/a, nuestros/as, vuestro/a, vuestros/as, su, sus.*
Remember they precede the noun and they agree with that noun and not with the possessor:

mi casa (my house)   *nuestra casa* (our house)
mis casas (my houses)   *nuestras casas* (our houses)

Permisos, favores y preferencias   unidad 5

G de Gramática

■ Formation of possessive pronouns

	singular		plural	
	masculine	feminine	masculine	feminine
mine	el mío	la mía	los míos	las mías
yours (informal)	el tuyo	la tuya	los tuyos	las tuyas
yours (polite)	el suyo	la suya	los suyos	las suyas
his / hers	el suyo	la suya	los suyos	las suyas
ours	el nuestro	la nuestra	los nuestros	las nuestras
yours (informal pl.)	el vuestro	la vuestra	los vuestros	las vuestras
yours (polite pl.)	el suyo	la suya	los suyos	las suyas
theirs	el suyo	la suya	los suyos	las suyas

■ Usage

- **Possessive pronouns agree in gender and number with the possessed thing,** not with the person who possesses it, i.e. they agree with the noun they replace:

  Tengo tus llaves. (I have your keys.)

  ¿Las mías? (Mine?)

  Sí, las tuyas. (Yes, yours.)

  He recogido su equipaje. (I have picked up your (polite) luggage.)

  *¿El mío? (*Mine?)

- ***El suyo***, ***la suya*** and ***los suyos***, ***las suyas*** each have several possible meanings and normally in speech there is no ambiguity. However, if the meaning is not clear from the context, Spanish uses the **definite article** + ***de*** + appropriate form of the **personal pronoun** or the **name of the person** to avoid the ambiguity:

Mi casa es más grande que (la suya) la de él / la de Paco		= his / Paco's
My house is bigger than ...	*la de ella*	= hers
	la de ellos / as	= theirs
	las de usted(es)	= yours

■ The possessive pronoun after *ser*

- **The definite article is normally omitted:**

  ¿De quiénes son los libros? ¿Son vuestros? (Whose are these books? Are they yours?)

  No, no son nuestros. Son de ellos. (No, they are not ours. They are theirs.)

- **But the article is kept for contrast or emphasis:**

  Juan, este ejercicio ¿es el tuyo? (Juan, is this exercise yours?)

  Sí, es el mío (Yes, it is mine.)

D In groups of three or four, one person describes an object belonging to somebody in the group and the rest of the group has to guess what the object is and who owns it. Use the mini-dialogues from Ex. 2A as models.

Objetos

137

3 Pointing out people and things

A Read the following mini-dialogue:

- ¿Qué camisa quieres, ésta o ésa?
- Ni ésta ni ésa; quiero aquélla, la amarilla.

1 What do you think the words *ésta, ésa* or *aquélla* mean in English?

2 What is the difference in meaning between them?

3 Now read the grammar section to check.

G de Gramática

■ Demonstrative adjectives and pronouns

Demonstratives are words to indicate relative proximity of people, animals or things to the speaker, either in space or in time. The demonstratives allow us to:

- Select somebody or something from a group: **esta** *casa* (this house)
- Refer to a specific place or time: **aquel** *año* (that year)

Spanish demonstratives are marked by both gender and number. English demonstratives are marked by number only.

Spanish, like English, distinguishes between

- **adjectives** which qualify a noun: *este coche* (this car). Demonstrative adjectives agree in gender and number with the noun they qualify: *estas fotografías* (these photographs).

  and

- **pronouns** which refer back to a noun: *¿Cuál, éste?* (which one, this (one)?); *¿Cuáles, éstas?* (which ones, these (ones)?) Demonstrative pronouns agree in gender and number with the nouns they refer to: *éste* (masculine, singular pronoun) refers to *coche* (masculine singular noun); *éstas* (feminine, plural pronoun) refers to *fotografías* (feminine, plural noun).

Formation of demonstratives

Pronouns have the same form as adjectives in the masculine and feminine, but pronouns also have a neuter form (see below). Accents may be used to distinguish the adjective from the pronoun (*esta foto / ¿ésta?*), however, it is acceptable in modern Spanish to omit the accent on these forms when the context makes the meaning clear.

DEMONSTRATIVES				
	Singular		Plural		Examples

	Masc.	Fem.	Masc.	Fem.	Examples
Nearer to the speaker in time and space	este	esta	estos	estas	-Quiero este coche. (*I want this car.*) *¿Cuál?* (*Which one?*) *Éste.* (*This one.*) *Este año vamos a Perú.* (*This year we are going to Perú.*)
Nearer to the listener in time and space	ese	esa	esos	esas	-Quiero esas camisas. (*I want those shirts.*) *¡Ésas!* (*Those ones!*) *Ese año fuimos a Perú.* (*That year we went to Perú.*)
Far away from the speaker and the listener in time and space	aquel	aquella	aquellos	aquellas	*Aquellos pisos son carísimos.* (*Those flats [over there] are very expensive.*) *¿Aquéllos?* (*Those ones over there?*) *Aquel verano fue maravilloso* (*That summer [many summers ago] was wonderful.*)

■ The neuter forms of demonstrative pronouns

These pronouns are *esto, eso, aquello*. Their forms are invariable. They don't have a gender.

They refer to unspecified situations, ideas or things: 'this / that thing':

¿Puedes darle esto a tu madre? (Could you give this to your mother?)

¿Y eso qué es? (And what's that?)

Eso es todo. (That's it. That's all.)

Aquello es mío. (That [over there] is mine.)

B Transform these sentences, following the example:

Example: Esa mesa es la mía.

Mi mesa es ésa.

1 Aquella mochila es la suya.

2 Esta clase es la vuestra.

3 Esos deberes son los tuyos.

4 Esa bicicleta es la nuestra.

5 Aquel coche es el suyo.

6 Estas camisas son las mías.

7 Este postre es el tuyo.

8 Este dormitorio es el vuestro.

9 Ese piso es el mío.

10 Estos relojes son los nuestros.

C Complete the following sentences with the appropriate demonstrative adjective or pronoun:

Example: ¿Quiere *este* libro?

No, quiero *ése* de ahí.

1 ¿Quieres leer esta novela? No, quiero leer ____ de ahí.

2 ¿Prefieres ese vídeo? No prefiero ____ de aquí.

3 ¿Ves ____ casas de allí?

4 ____ estudiantes son alumnos de español, ____ de ahí son de francés y ____ de allí son estudiantes de italiano.

5 ¿Qué fotografía preferís ____ o ésa? Ninguna de las dos, sino ____ que está sobre la mesa.

6 ____ año hacemos deporte todos los días.

7 ¿De quién es ____ coche que está allí lejos? ____ coche es de mi amigo Pedro.

8 ____ chico que está ahí, es mi hermano.

D Can you say the following in Spanish?

1 That's terrible!

2 What is that over there?

3 This is mine.

4 Do you understand that?

Objetos

4 Indicating cause, purpose, duration, destination. Some uses of *por* and *para*

A Read the following sentences and then read the table in the grammar section in which some of the uses of *por* and *para* are explained. Then categorise the sentences according to type.

Example: Este coche es *para* el jefe = to indicate whom or what something is for.

1 Este regalo es para mi abuela.
2 Este regalo es por tu cumpleaños.
3 Estudio para aprender.
4 Canto por no llorar.
5 Este autobús pasa por tu pueblo.
6 Este autobús va para tu pueblo.
7 Tengo una cita para el jueves.

8 Llegamos para Navidad.
9 Llegamos por Navidad.
10 ¿Por qué vas al médico?
11 ¿Para qué vas al médico?
12 Vamos para Málaga el sábado.
13 Pasamos por Málaga el sábado.

G de Gramática

■ Prepositions

A preposition is an invariable word which links together two other words or groups of words to indicate a relationship of time, space, possession, etc.:

*Llego **por** la mañana.* (I arrive in the morning.)   *Este perro es **de** mi hermano.* (This dog is my brother's.)
*El coche está **enfrente de** tu casa.* (The car is outside [lit. = opposite] your house / home.)

Prepositions can consist of two or more words: *enfrente de* (opposite), *alrededor de* (around); *junto a* (next to).

■ *Por* and *para*

The prepositions ***por*** and ***para*** both correspond to the English 'for', and because of this, it is difficult for English speakers to decide which one to use. Bear in mind that they may also correspond to other English prepositions or expressions.
Here are some of the main uses of ***por*** and ***para***:

Por	Para
To indicate cause or motive *(because of, on account of, on behalf of)* Este dinero es por tu trabajo *This money is for (=because of) your work.* Hoy Carlos trabaja por su padre. *Today Carlos is working on behalf of his father.*	**To indicate for whom or what something is intended** El libro es para Paco. *The book is for Paco.* Carlos trabaja para su padre. *Carlos works for his father.*
To indicate movement through / along / up / down / in / into Camino todos los días por el parque. *Every day I walk through the park.*	**To indicate movement or destination** El tren va para Gerona. *The train is bound for Gerona.*
To indicate approximate duration 'for the period of' Siempre llegan por mi cumpleaños *They always arrive around my birthday.*	**To indicate a deadline 'by or for a certain time'** Siempre llegan para mi cumpleaños. *They always arrive in time for my birthday.*
To indicate cause (What for? Because . . .) ¿Por qué te vistes así? *Why are you dressed like that?* Porque tengo frío. *Because I'm cold.*	**To indicate intention** ¿Para qué te vistes así? *Why are you dressed like that?* Para no tener frío. *So as not to be cold.*

B Insert *por* or *para* in the following sentences.

1 El metro pasa ____ el aeropuerto.
2 El autobús va ____ el aeropuerto.
3 Camino ____ la playa con mis amigos.
4 Este telegrama es ____ Rosario.

5 Fran está enfermo y Paco canta ____ él.
6 El tenor canta ____ el público.
7 Salimos ahora ____ Guadalajara.
8 ¿____ dónde pasa el tren?

Consolidation

A Work with a partner. Here are the answers to some questions. Read them and write the corresponding questions.

Example: No, (ese reloj) no es mío, es de mi hermano.
¿De quién es este reloj? ¿Es tuyo?
Sí, (esta chaqueta) es la mía.
¿Esta chaqueta es la suya?

1 No, ese coche no es mío, es de mi compañera.
2 Sí, (el pasaporte) es el mío.
3 No, esos libros no son nuestros, son de ellos.
4 Sí, (las fotos) son nuestras.
5 Sí, (las llaves) son las mías.
6 No, (la tarjeta de crédito) no es nuestra, es del señor Freijanes.
7 No, la mía es (la pintura) aquélla.

B With your partner, take it in turns to look around and choose an object. Without naming it, describe it to your partner and see if he/she can guess what it is. Your partner can ask you questions about shape, colour, material, origin, etc.

In class or at home

A Insert the appropriate demonstratives.

1 ¿Cuál quieres: esta camisa o ____?
No quiero ésta, ni ésa; quiero ____, la verde.
2 En esta fotografía de aquí estás más guapa que en ____ de ahí.
3 ____ programa es mejor que ése.
4 ¿Quién es tu jefe: ese señor, o ____ que está allí?
Es el que está allí
5 ¿Qué coche prefieres? ¿Éste de aquí o ése de ahí?
Hmm . . . ninguno de los dos, prefiero ____ que está allí.

B Insert *por* or *para* in the following sentences.

1 Salgo ____ Guatemala mañana.
2 Este mini-bus va ____ la estación de tren.
3 Paseamos ____ la ciudad todas las tardes.
4 Necesito el dinero ____ el sábado.
5 Este paquete es ____ tu tía Juana.

B

Terminar o no terminar

To finish or not to finish

■ Expresiones Esenciales

¿Ya has terminado el libro?

Sí, lo he terminado esta mañana

No, no lo he terminado todavía / aún

No, todavía no / Aún no lo he terminado

Acabo de llegar / salir / comer

¿Tienes frío? ¿Por qué no . . . ?

¿Conoces a Marisa? *(informal)*

¿Sabes español? *(informal)*

¿Sabe cantar? *(polite)*

■ Essential Expressions

Have you finished the book yet?

Yes, I finished it this morning

No, I still haven't finished it / I haven't finished it yet

No, I still haven't / I haven't . . . yet

I've just arrived / left / eaten

Do you feel cold? Why don't you . . . ?

Do you know Marisa?

Do you speak Spanish?

Can you sing?

---

1 Avoiding repetition

A Read the grammar section and then insert personal *a* where needed:

1 ¿Conocéis ____ la casa nueva de Pablo?

2 El presidente llama ____ los ministros.

3 Queremos ____ un billete de ida y vuelta.

4 No conozco ____ nadie en esta fiesta.

5 Tenéis ____ dos hijos, ¿verdad?

6 Buenos días, quiero ____ un café con leche.

7 Veo ____ tu perro.

8 No queremos ____ nada.

9 El médico atiende ____ el enfermo.

10 Conocemos ____ la directora del banco.

G de Gramática

■ Direct objects

These are nouns or pronouns that are on the direct receiving end of the action. In the sentence *tengo las tijeras aquí* (I have the scissors here), *tijeras* is the direct object.

■ Personal *a*

In Spanish, a direct object noun referring to a **specific person** or an animal is preceded by the preposition '**a**'. This is called the **personal *a*** and it does not have an English translation:

*Veo **a Juan**.* (I see Juan.)

but *Veo la casa.* (I see the house.)

*Busco **a mi amigo**.* (I'm looking for my friend.)

*Conozco **a tu profesor**.* (I know your teacher.)

Mi tía quiere mucho ***a su perro***. (My aunt loves her dog a lot.)

The personal *a* is used before the interrogative words ***¿quién?*** and ***¿quiénes?*** when they are direct objects:

¿A quién / A quiénes ves? (Whom are you seeing?)

The personal *a* is also used with pronouns denoting people even if their identity is not specified:

*No veo **a nadie**.* (I see nobody.)

Note that the personal *a* is not used when the noun refers to an indeterminate person:

Busco un dentista. (I'm looking for a dentist. [=any dentist])

or after *tener*.

Tengo hijos . (I have children.)

B Read the following mini-dialogues.
  1 Underline, in each bubble, the words that replace *las tijeras* and *a Juan*.
  2 Say where they appear in the sentence.

■ Pedro, ¿tienes las tijeras?

■ Oye, ¿has visto a Juan?

■ Sí, las tengo aquí.

■ No, no lo he visto.

C Now read the grammar section on direct object pronouns.

G de Gramática

■ Direct object pronouns

Direct object pronouns are pronouns that replace the direct object:

*Miguel ve **la televisión**.* (Miguel is watching television.)
*Miguel **la** ve.* (Miguel is watching it.)

Note that with the third person pronouns singular and plural (see table below), the pronoun agrees in number and gender with the noun that it replaces:

*Paco ve <u>la televisión</u>. Paco **la** ve.*
*Paco ve <u>el partido</u>. Paco **lo** ve.*
*Paco compra <u>los alimentos.</u> Paco **los** compra.*
Josefa recibe <u>las notas</u>. Josefa **las** recibe.

In Spanish, the direct object pronouns are:

subject	direct object	examples
yo (*I*)	**me** (*me*)	Carlos me admira. (*Carlos admires / is admiring me.*)
tú (*you*) familiar sing.	**te** (*you*)	Luis te quiere. (*Luis loves you.*)
usted (*you*) formal sing.	**lo** (masc.) **la** (fem.) (*you*)	Lo llamo mañana. (*I'll phone you tomorrow.*) ¿La llevamos a la estación? (*Shall we take you to the station?*)
él (*he / it*) ella (*she / it*)	**lo** (*him / it*) **la** (*her / it*)	Lo compro mañana. (*I'll buy it tomorrow.*) La conocemos muy bien. (*We know her very well.*)
nosotros(as) (*we*)	**nos** (*us*)	¿Nos enseñas a bailar? (*Will / you teach us to dance?*)
vosotros(as) (*you*) familiar pl.	**os** (*you*)	No os veo. (*I don't / can't see you.*)
ustedes (*you*) formal pl.	**los** (masc.) **las** (fem.) (*you*)	El director los espera. (*The director is waiting for you.*) Las veo esta tarde. (*I'll see you this afternoon.*)
ellos(as) (*they*)	**los** (masc.) **las** (fem.) (*them*)	Los mando mañana. (*I'll send them tomorrow.*) ¿Las queréis? (*Do you want them?*)

Position of object pronouns

As a general rule the direct object pronoun is placed before the conjugated form of the verb.

*Marta **me** recoge a las ocho.* (Marta is picking **me** up at eight o'clock.)
***La** veo.* (I see **her / it**.)

Note that with the perfect tense, object pronouns, reflexive pronouns and negative words are always placed directly before the form of ***haber***.

***No lo** he visto.* (I haven't seen him / it.)
***Se** ha vestido rápidamente.* (She got dressed quickly.)

In constructions in which an infinitive or present participle is preceded by a conjugated form of a verb, the pronoun can be placed either before the conjugated form of the verb or attached to the infinitive or present participle:

La** quiero ver. / Quiero ver**la (I want to see her / it.)
***Lo** tenéis que hacer. / Tenéis que hacer**lo**.* (You have to do it.)
***Las** estamos terminando. / Estamos terminándo**las**.* (We are finishing them.)

Note that a written accent has to be added to *termin**á**ndolas* in order to preserve the stress.

Redundant direct object pronouns

When the direct object comes before the verb, it is usually repeated as a pronoun:

*Las tijeras **las** tengo yo.* (I've got the scissors.)
*El coche **lo** compro mañana.* (I'll buy the car tomorrow.)

D Replace the words in *italics* by direct object pronouns.

Example: Hago *la cama*.
La hago.

1 Veo *a ti* por la ventana.
2 Llaman *a mí* por teléfono.
3 Han llamado *a José* por teléfono.
4 Entiendo *el ejercicio*.
5 Hemos alquilado *una casa*.
6 Oigo *a vosotros*.
7 Comprendéis *a los estudiantes*.
8 Han criticado *a usted* (Sra Gil).
9 Queremos comprar *una televisión*.
10 Tenemos que alquilar *un vídeo*.
11 Estáis cambiando *las cosas*.
12 Tiene que escuchar *a nosotros*.

E Insert the direct object pronoun where necessary:

Example: Este libro leo yo primero
Este libro *lo* leo yo primero.

1 Los ejercicios corrijo yo.
2 Apago la televisión.
3 La cena hace Rosario.
4 Los muebles compramos nosotros.
5 Ellos mandan el regalo.
6 El paquete envian ellos.
7 La conferencia dais vosotros.
8 Vosotras cerráis la tienda.

G de Gramática

■ *lo/le, los/les*
Note that in some areas of Spain speakers use **le/les** in preference to **lo/los** when referring to men.

| Veo a Pedro | Lo/Le veo. BUT |
| Veo el coche. | Lo veo |

2 To find out if something has already taken place

■ Sí, (lo he terminado) esta mañana.

■ ¿Ya has terminado el libro?

■ No, todavía no / aún no (lo he terminado). /
No, no lo he terminado todavía / aún.

G de Gramática

■ *Ya, todavía no, aún no.*
To find out if something has just taken place use **¿Ya +
perfect tense . . . ?**
¿Ya has terminado el libro? (Have you just finished the book?)
Sí, lo he terminado esta mañana. (Yes, I finished it this morning.)

Sí, esta mañana (Yes, this morning.)
No, no lo he terminado todavía / aún (No, I still haven't finished it. / I haven't finished it yet.)
No, todavía no / aún no lo he terminado.
No, todavía no / aún no (Not yet.)

A Answer the questions as in the example, using the direct object pronouns *la, lo, las, los* and the expressions *todavía no / aún no* where appropriate:

Example: ¿Ya has vendido el coche?
No, todavía no. / Aún no lo he vendido. / Sí, lo he vendido hoy.

1 ¿Ya has aprendido los verbos irregulares? No, _____.
2 ¿Ya habéis terminado el proyecto? Sí, _____ esta mañana.
3 ¿Ya han visto al dentista? No, _____.
4 ¿Ya has hecho la cena? Sí, _____ a las nueve.
5 ¿Ya has visto esta película? Sí, _____ el jueves.
6 ¿Ya han vendido la casa? No, _____.
7 ¿Ya has mandado el correo eléctronico? Sí, _____ a las diez de la mañana.
8 ¿Ya has colgado la ropa? No, _____.

B Think of three or four daily tasks (*limpiar la casa, hacer la comida, hacer los deberes*) and find out if your partner has already done them or not.

 To express what you have just done or what has just happened

A Read the following mini-dialogues and see if you can guess what the expression *acabar de* means, then read the grammar section.

■ ¿Está María?

■ No, lo siento, acaba de salir.

■ ¿El tren a Guadalajara?

■ Acaba de salir.

■ ¡Cuidado! El agua acaba de hervir.

G de Gramática

■ *Acabar de* **(to have just)**

To express what you have just done or what has just happened in Spanish, you should use the expression: *acabar de* + **infinitive**:

El avión de Tokio acaba de llegar. (The plane from Tokyo has just landed.)
Acaba de salir el sol. (The sun has just come out.)
El gobierno acaba de abrir un nuevo aeropuerto. (The government has just opened a new airport.)

Note that the infinitive is the only verb form that can follow a preposition in Spanish.

B Choose a phrase from the list to complete
the sentences, using the correct form of
acabar.

Acabar de perder el campeonato	Acabar de hervir
Acabar de perder el último tren	Acabar de encontrar su primer trabajo
Acabar de cobrar	Acabar de comer
Acabar de comprar un coche	Acabar de despegar
Acabar de llegar de viaje	Acabar de entrar en una reunión

Example: No quiero ir porque **acabo de** llegar a casa.

1 Estoy cansado porque _____.
2 Lo siento, no puede hablar con el director porque _____.
3 Mi padre está contento porque _____.
4 Isabel está preocupada porque _____.
5 El agua está caliente porque _____.
6 Podemos ir de compras porque _____.
7 No tienen hambre porque _____.
8 Nuestra hija está feliz porque _____.
9 No puedes ver el avión porque _____.
10 Los jugadores están tristes porque _____.

C Work with a partner. Read the grammar section at the top of p.147
and respond to the following questions, as in the example.

Example: ¿Tienes frío? ¿Por qué no enciendes la calefacción?
La acabo de encender. / Acabo de encenderla.

1 ¿Tienes hambre? ¿Por qué no comes la pizza que he preparado?
2 ¿Tienes sed? ¿Por qué no bebes el zumo que he comprado?
3 ¿Tiene sueño? ¿Por qué no duerme la siesta?
4 ¿Tienes prisa? ¿Por qué no llamas un taxi?
5 ¿Tiene calor? ¿Por qué no abre la ventana?
6 ¿Tienes frío ¿Por qué no cierras las ventanas?
7 ¿Tienes ganas de salir? ¿Por qué no llamas a tu novia?

G de Gramática

■ Expressions with *tener* (literally 'to have')

Sometimes the English construction **to be** + **adjective** is expressed in Spanish using the construction **tener** + **noun**. You have already used one idiomatic expression with *tener*. *tener x años* (to be x years old). Here are some more.

tener frío (to be / feel cold)
tener calor (to be / feel hot)
tener hambre (to be / feel hungry)
tener sed (to be / feel thirsty)
tener sueño (to be / feel sleepy)
tener prisa (to be in a hurry)
tener ganas de + infinitive (comer / salir ...) (to feel like eating / going out ...)

Adjectives such as ***mucho*** (much) and ***poco*** (little) can be used with the nouns and must agree with them:

Tienes mucho / poco frío. (You are very / a bit cold.)
Los niños tienen mucha hambre. (The children are very hungry.)
Tengo muchas / pocas ganas de ir al cine. (I very much want / don't want to go to the cinema.)

Making suggestions and giving advice

The phrase *¿Por qué no + verb?* (Why don't you ...?) is commonly used to make suggestions or give advice.

Si tienes hambre, ¿por qué no haces un sandwich? (If you are hungry, why don't you make a sandwich?)
No tenéis dinero, ¿por qué no buscáis un trabajo? (You don't have any money (so) why don't you look for a job?)

Saber and conocer

A Read the mini-dialogue and say what you think the reply means.

B Read the grammar section and then complete each sentence with the correct form of *conocer* or *saber*:

1 El señor Garrido ¿_____ latín?
2 Mis amigos _____ Bolivia muy bien.
3 ¿_____ (tú) qué hora es?
4 ¿_____ (usted) a qué hora llega el tren?
5 Usted, no _____ a mi esposa, ¿verdad?
6 Mi compañero de clase _____ jugar al tenis muy bien.
7 Vosotros _____ todos los bares.
8 El presidente no _____ a este artista.
9 ¿Quieres _____ a mi mejor amigo?
10 Yo no _____ mucho de arte pero _____ la obra de este pintor.
11 ¿_____ (vosotros) a alguien en esta fiesta?
12 ¿A quién _____ mejor, a Pedro o a Marta?

■ ¿Conoces a la nueva directora?

■ No, no la conozco pero sé que es alemana.

G de Gramática

■ *Saber* and *conocer*

The verbs *saber* and *conocer* both mean 'to know' in English.

Saber is used to express

- **knowing facts or pieces of information:**
  Sé donde vives. (I know where you live.)
  Sabemos que este museo es muy bueno. (We know this museum is very good.)
- **knowing something by heart**
  ¿Ya sabéis los verbos irregulares? (Do you already know the irregular verbs?)
  Sé las tablas de multiplicar (I know my multiplication tables.)
- **knowing how or being able to do something.**
  Mi padre sabe patinar muy bien (My father knows how to skate / can skate well.)
  ¿Saben jugar al ajedrez? (Can they play chess?)

Conocer is used to express

- **being acquainted with people, places or things**
  Conocen La Habana, ¿verdad? (You know Havana, don't you?)
  ¿Conoces a mi tía Carmen? (Do you know my Aunt Carmen?)
- **meeting people for the first time**
  ¿Quieres conocer a mi novia? (Do you want to meet my girlfriend?)

Note that both verbs are irregular in the first person singular of the present tense: *Conocer: conozco*
   Saber: sé

Terminar o no terminar

147

Consolidation

A Answer the questions using a direct object pronoun as in the example.

Example: ¿Has visto mi mochila?
No, no la he visto.

1 ¿Has terminado el trabajo?
2 ¿Habéis recogido los paquetes?
3 Pedro, ¿ha recibido el telegrama?
4 Los niños ¿han llamado a sus amigos?
5 ¿Has enviado el mensaje?
6 ¿Habéis visto a Luis?
7 Juan ¿has encontrado mis gafas?
8 ¿Has devuelto los libros?

B Say what or whom these people know. Use *saber* or *conocer*. Follow the model given.

Example: Yo no _conozco_ a nadie aquí. ¿Tú _conoces_ a alguien?
No, yo tampoco.

1 Yo no _____ al novio de Marta. ¿Tú lo _____?
Yo sí, es muy simpático.
2 Fran ¿tú _____ traducir del inglés al español?
Un poco pero no muy bien.
3 Yo no _____ conducir ¿y tú?
Yo sí.
4 ¿_____ (vosotros) bailar flamenco?
5 Nosotros _____ al presidente de esta compañía.
6 Sra. Ríos, ¿_____ adónde tiene que ir?
7 Por favor, ¿_____ (usted) a qué hora llega el tren de Soria?
8 Yo no ____ cocinar ¿y tú?
Yo tampoco.

In class or at home

A Write personal *a* where needed:

1 Nosotras conocemos ____ mucha gente aquí.
2 Hoy he recibido ____ tu carta.
3 Esta semana he invitado ____ mis suegros a cenar.
4 Estos días no hemos visto ____ nadie.
5 El jefe ha llamado ____ Manolo a su despacho.
6 Buenas tardes, quiero ver ____ la directora.
7 No tengo ____ hijos.
8 El recepcionista ayuda ____ los clientes.

B Replace the words in *italics* with direct object pronouns.

Example: Cerramos *la puerta*.
La cerramos.

1 Mandamos *el dinero* mañana.
2 Recibe *a mí* por la tarde.
3 He acabado *la novela* por la mañana.
4 Tenéis *el examen* el lunes.

5 Ellos llevan *a Pablo* al aeropuerto.

6 Usted ha entendido *los problemas*.

7 Queremos alquilar *un piso*.

8 Está haciendo *la comida*.

9 Tenemos que devolver *los libros* hoy.

10 Veo *a ti* a las diez.

11 Estamos escuchando *las noticias*.

12 Están viendo *el partido*.

C Insert the direct object pronoun where necessary:

Example: Este paquete abro yo.
Este paquete *lo* abro yo.

1 Este pastel como yo.

2 Nosotros llamamos a Pedro.

3 La clase da la profesora de biología.

4 A los compañeros informáis vosotros.

D Answer the questions, as in the example, using the direct object pronouns *la, lo, las, los* and the expressions *todavía no / aún no,* when appropriate.

Example: ¿Ya has hecho el ejercicio?
No, todavía no / aún no lo he hecho / Sí, lo he hecho por la tarde.

1 ¿Ya has cortado la hierba?   No, _____.

2 ¿Habéis empezado las clases?   Sí, _____ esta semana.

3 ¿Ya han terminado la reunión?   No, _____.

4 ¿Ya has leído el documento?   Sí, _____ al llegar.

5 ¿Ya han visto a su tía?   Sí, _____ esta mañana.

E Write sentences, following the model.

Example: ¿Tener frío? ¿Cerrar la ventana? (tú)
¿Tienes frío? ¿Por qué no cierras la ventana?
La acabo de cerrar. / Acabo de cerrarla.

1 ¿Tener hambre? ¿Hacer un bocadillo? (tú)

2 ¿Tener sed? ¿Comprar una botella de agua? (vosotros)

3 ¿Tener sueño? ¿Dormir una siesta? (usted)

4 ¿Tener prisa? ¿Terminar la reunión? (ustedes)

5 ¿Tener calor? ¿Encender el aire acondicionado? (tú)

F Say what or whom these people know. Use *saber* or *conocer* and the direct object pronouns *la, lo, las, lo* when appropriate. Follow the model given.

Example: Nosotros <u>*conocemos*</u> Nueva York muy bien. ¿Y tú?
Sí, yo también. / No, yo no <u>*lo conozco*</u>.

1 Yo no _____ a la nueva jefa. ¿Y tú?
Sí, yo _____, es muy agradable.

2 Ustedes ¿_____ hablar español?
Sí, _____ hablar muy bien.

3 Yo _____ bailar salsa ¿y vosotros?
No, nosotros no _____.

Permisos y préstamos

Permissions and loans

■ **Expresiones esenciales**	■ **Essential expressions**
¿Puedo encender la televisión?	*Can I switch on the TV?*
Es que quiero ver el partido	*It's just that I'd like to watch the match*
Sí claro, enciéndela	*Yes, of course, switch it on*
¿Me / Le / Nos / Les das una hoja?	*Could / Would you give me / him / her / us / them a sheet of paper (please)?*
¿Me / Le / Nos / Les prestas el coche?	*Could / Would you lend me / him / her / us / them the car (please)?*
¿Me / Le / Nos / Les deja llamar por teléfono?	*Could / May I / she / he / we / they use the phone?*
No, lo siento, es que . . .	*No, I'm sorry, you see . . .*

1 Seeking and granting permission

A Read the following mini-dialogues.

■ Carmen ¿puedo encender la televisión? Es que quiero ver el partido.

■ ¿Puedo llamar por teléfono? Es que tengo que llamar a casa.

■ ¿Podemos pasar?

■ Pasad, pasad.

■ Sí claro, enciéndela.

■ Sí claro, llama.

1 Notice the expressions used to ask for permission to do something.

2 What type of verb forms are used here to give permission (*enciéndela, llama, pasad*)? To find out read the grammar section.

G de Gramática

■ **Asking for permission**

Use **poder** + **infinitive**. Remember *poder* (*o > ue*) is a radical-changing verb, in which the stem changes apply to all persons, except the first and second person plural.

> *¿Puedo encender la televisión?* (Can / May I switch on the television?)
> *¿Podemos comer algo?* (May we have something to eat?)

Very often when we request permission to do something, we justify it. One of the expressions used is **es que** + explanation:

> *Es que quiero ver el partido.* (It's just that I want to watch the match.)
> *Es que no hemos comido aún.* (It's just that we haven't eaten yet.)

G de Gramática

■ The imperative

One way of granting permission in Spanish is to use the expression

Sí, claro + verb in the imperative:

Sí, claro, enciéndela. (Yes, of course, switch it on.)

The word *enciende* is in the **imperative mood.** (For a definition of 'mood' see the Grammar Glossary on p. 296). As well as being used to give permission, the imperative is also used to give positive instructions, orders and advice.

There are two forms of imperative in Spanish, informal and polite, the choice of which depends on whether you are addressing someone as *tú* or *usted*. In this unit we look at the informal positive form. The polite form and the negative forms are covered in Unit 8.

Formation of the informal imperative

The singular form *tú* is identical to the third person singular of the present indicative.

Infinitive	Present Indicative	Imperative
	third-person sing.	tú
Hablar	él / ella habla	habla
Comer	él / ella come	come
Escribir	él / ella escribe	escribe
Cerrar	él / ella cierra	cierra
Dormir	él / ella duerme	duerme
Pedir	él / ella pide	pide

Note that radical-changing verbs such as *cerrar, encender, dormir, pedir* have the same irregularity in the imperative as in the indicative.

There are eight verbs that have an irregular *tú* form in the imperative:

Infinitive	Imperative (tú)
decir	di
hacer	haz
ir	ve
venir	ven
poner	pon
salir	sal
ser	sé
tener	ten

The plural form **vosotros** is formed by changing the final **-r** of the infinitive to **-d**:

Infinitive	Imperative
	vosotros
Hablar	hablad
Comer	comed
Escribir	escribid
Cerrar	cerrad
Dormir	dormid
Pedir	pedid

Note: In Hispano-America and the Canary Islands, the *vosotros* form of the imperative is not used; the *ustedes* form which you will learn in Unit 8 is used instead.

Imperative of reflexive verbs

The pronoun of the reflexive verb is added to the end of imperative forms as follows:

Infinitive	Imperative (tú)	Imperative (vosotros)
ducharse	ducha + te: dúchate	duchaos
levantarse	levanta + te: levántate	levantaos

Note that a written accent has to be added to the *tú* form (*dúchate*) in order to preserve the stress. And also note that the final **-d** of the **vosotros** form is dropped. The only exception to this rule is **irse** (to go away), which becomes **idos** (go away!) in the imperative.

Direct object pronouns with the imperative

The direct object pronouns are added to the imperative form:
• *Enciéndela* (switch it on); *ábrelo* (open it)

■ Main uses of the imperative

• **To give directions:**
  Coge / Toma la primera calle a la derecha. (Take the first street on the right.)
• **To give instructions:**
  Corta las patatas en cuadrados, lávalas y sécalas. (Cut the potatoes into cubes, wash and dry them.)
• **To give orders:**
  ¡Salid inmediatamente! (Leave immediately! / Get out – now!)
• **To give advice:**
  Antes de tomar el sol, pon crema solar. (Before sunbathing, put on sun cream.)

Permisos y préstamos

151

B Change the infinitives of these sentences into the positive informal imperative (*tú* and *vosotros*).

	Tú	*Vosotros*
Example: Estudiar más.	estudia	estudiad

1 Apagar la televisión.
2 ¡Levantarse de una vez!
3 Cerrar la puerta al salir.
4 Lavarse las manos.

5 Hacer ejercicio todos los días.
6 Pedir dinero a tu hermano mayor.
7 Decir la verdad.
8 Acostarse pronto.

C As in the previous exercise, change the infinitives of these sentences into the positive informal imperative (*tú* and *vosotros*), but this time, in addition, substitute the direct object with the appropriate direct object pronoun.

	Tú	*Vosotros*
Example: Comer el bocadillo.	cómelo	comedlo

1 Hacer la cena.
2 Limpiar el coche.
3 Vender los pisos.
4 Terminar las listas.

5 Llamar un taxi.
6 ¡Mandar el correo electrónico!
7 Poner la mesa.
8 Aprender los verbos.

D Complete the following dialogues. Insert the correct form of the imperative and add direct object pronouns where necessary.

1 – ¿Puedo coger la silla?   – Sí claro, _____.
2 –¿Podemos usar tu ordenador? Es que tenemos que mandar un mensaje urgente.
   – Sí, _____.
3 – ¿Puedo consultar este diccionario?   – Sí claro, _____.
4 – ¿Podemos escuchar música?   – Sí, sí, _____.
5 – ¿Puedo salir un momento?   – Sí claro, _____.
6 – ¿Podemos encender la luz? Es que no se ve bien.   – Claro, _____.
7 – ¿Puedo entrar?   – _____.

2 Asking for things, seeking information and asking to borrow things

A Read the following dialogues. Which words are used to say who benefits from the actions?

– ¿Me prestas treinta euros por favor? Te los devuelvo mañana.
– ¡30 euros! Lo siento, te puedo dejar 20.

– ¿Me das un chicle?
– Sí claro, toma.

– ¿Me dejas un bolígrafo rojo?
– Sí, toma.

– ¿Le prestas el coche a tu hijo esta noche? Es que su coche está en el garaje.
– Vale, pero me lo tiene que devolver mañana a primera hora.

– ¿Me da su número de teléfono?
– Sí, es el 981 786509.

B Now read the grammar section about two sorts of object pronouns.

G de Gramática

■ Asking for things or seeking information

The present tense of **dar** (to give): *doy, das, da, damos, dais, dan)* is used with an indirect object pronoun preceding the verb, normally in an interrogative sentence:

¿Me das una hoja? (Could / May I have a sheet of paper?)

¿Me da su dirección? (Could / Would you give me / could / may I have your address?)

If you want to borrow something, the present tense of the verbs **prestar** or **dejar** + **noun** is used with an indirect object pronoun:

¿Me prestas el coche? (Could / Can / May I borrow the car?)

¿Le dejo el diccionario de español? (Shall I lend you (polite) the Spanish dictionary?)

Note also that **dejar** can be used to ask for permission to do something:

¿Me deja llamar por teléfono? (Do you (polite) mind if / May I use the phone?)

■ Indirect object pronouns

These stand for the indirect object, i.e. the person or object that benefits or loses as a result of an action.

Le compro un coche. (I'll buy him a car).'Him / her' (*le*) is the indirect object who benefits from the verbal action.

*Juan, ¿**le** prestas el coche **a tu hijo** esta noche?* (Juan, are you lending the car to your son tonight?)

*Vale, pero **me** lo tiene que devolver mañana.* (OK, but he must return it to me tomorrow)

Note that the direct (*lo …*) and the indirect object pronouns (*me …*) can appear in the same sentence. See below.

subject	indirect object	examples
yo (*I*)	**me** (to / for) me	*¿Me compras un pastel?* (Will you buy / Are you buying me a cake?)
tú (*you*) informal	**te** (to / for) you	*Te da el dinero mañana.* (He'll give you the money tomorrow.)
usted (*you*) polite	**le** (to / for) you	*Le pago más tarde.* (I'll pay you later.)
él (*he / it*) ella (*she / it*)	**le** (to / for) him / it **le** (to / for) her / it	*Le presto mi casa.* (I'm lending my house to him / to her.)
nosotros(as) (*we*)	**nos** (to / for) us	*¿Nos haces la cena?* (Will you make / Are you making dinner for us?)
vosotros(as) (*you*) informal	**os** (to / for) you	*No os prestamos el portátil.* (We won't lend / aren't lending you the laptop.)
ustedes (*you*) polite	**les** (to / for) you	*¿Les envuelvo el regalo?* (Should I wrap the present for you?)
ellos (*they*) ellas (*they*)	**les** (to / for) them	*Les enseño español.* (I teach Spanish to them.)

Note that the first person and second person informal singular and plural have the same form as the direct object pronouns.

Position of indirect object pronouns

The rules for the position of these are exactly the same as for the direct object pronouns. Generally they are placed before the conjugated form of the verb. But, in constructions in which an infinitive or present participle is preceded by a conjugated form of a verb, the pronoun can be placed either before the conjugated form of the verb or attached to the infinitive or present participle:

*¿**Me** dejas un libro de cocina?* (Could / May I borrow a cookery book?)

***Os** queremos dar las gracias.* (We want to thank you.)

*Queremos dar**os** las gracias.*

*Estamos haciéndo**les** un gran favor.* (We're doing them a big favour.)

***Les** estamos haciendo un gran favor.*

Note that a written accent has to be added to *haci**é**ndoles* in order to preserve the stress.

- Remember that with the Perfect tense, object pronouns, reflexive pronouns and negative words are always placed directly before the form of **haber**.

***No le** he prestado la bicicleta.* (I haven't lent him / her the bicycle.)

- With the positive imperative, the indirect object pronouns as well as the direct object pronouns MUST be attached to the end of the imperative:

  ¡Dame el libro! (Give me the book!)

  ¡Dámelo! (Give it to me!)

Note that a written accent has to be added to *dámelo* in order to preserve the stress.

■ Order of object pronouns

When direct and indirect object pronouns appear together in a sentence, whether before the verb, or added to the end of it, the indirect one is always first in the sequence.

  Me la *presta.* (S/he lends it to me.)

  Te lo *tengo que arreglar. Tengo que arreglár**telo***. (I must sort it out for you.)

  *Enví**amelo** pronto.* (Send it to me quickly.)

Note that when there are two object pronouns together in an English sentence, the sequence is often the other way round:

te lo doy (lit. it-to you I give)

Se replacing *le* or *les*

The indirect object pronoun *le* or *les* becomes **se** before the direct object pronouns *lo, la, los, las*:

Carmen compra un coche *a su sobrina.*

(Carmen buys a car for her niece.)

*Carmen **le** compra un coche.*

(Carmen buys her a car.)

*Carmen **se lo** compra.*

(Carmen buys it for her.)

Avoiding ambiguity

- In Spanish, a prepositional phrase is sometimes used, together with the object pronoun, in order to avoid ambiguity or for emphasis: *a él, a ella, a ellos, a ellas, a usted, a ustedes, a Pedro, a tus padres …*

- *Marta se lo da* could be ambiguous; it could mean 'she / he gives it to him / her / you / them / you'.

  If we add *a ella* the ambiguity disappears: *Marta se lo da a ella.* (Marta gives it to her.)

C 🔊 Now you are going to listen to five people asking to be given or to borrow some of the items listed below. Fill in the items and say whether the requests are granted.

	¿Me dejas / Me prestas … ?	¿Me das … .?	Sí	No
Dialogue 1				
Dialogue 2				
Dialogue 3				
Dialogue 4				
Dialogue 5				

tu ordenador   un bocadillo   tu cámara   una guía de teléfonos
la goma de borrar   tus notas de clase   un vaso de agua
el periódico   tu correo electrónico   un poco de champú
una calculadora

D Now, work with your partner and ask him/her for some of the items in Ex. C. Decide whether you want to be given or simply to borrow some of these items.

- ¿Me dejas el periódico?

- Sí, toma. / No, lo siento, es que lo estoy leyendo en estos momentos.

Using indirect and direct object pronouns

A Replace the words in *italics* with the appropriate indirect object pronouns.

Example: Compro un piso *a mi hija.*
Le compro un piso.

1 No presto un libro *a ti.*

2 Entregan los exámenes *a los estudiantes.*

3 Mandamos el paquete *a vosotros.*

4 He escrito un poema *a mi novia.*

5 Sr Sánchez ¿ha vendido la casa *a sus vecinos?*

6 Explica el problema *a mí.*

7 Lee el periódico *a su abuela.*

8 No ha comprado una bicicleta *a vosotros.*

9 Tengo que comprar un regalo *a los niños.*

10 Quiere prestar un libro *a su padre.*

11 Paga (tú) la cena *a tu hermano.*

12 Haced el favor *a vuestros amigos.*

B Replace the words in italics with the appropriate direct object pronouns.

Example: Compro *un portátil.*
Lo compro.

1 Como *un helado.*

2 ¿Habéis hecho *la cama?*

3 Reciben *a los invitados.*

4 Usted mete *el dinero* en el banco.

5 ¿Han mandado ustedes *el telegrama?*

6 Enseño *latín* a los niños.

7 ¿Tomas *cereales* por la mañana?

8 Él no ha llamado a *Carolina.*

9 Quiero dejar *el paquete* en casa.

10 No tengo que llevar *corbata.*

11 Enciende (tú) *la radio.*

12 Apagad *el televisor.*

C Read the list of sentences in A and replace the direct and indirect objects with the appropriate direct and indirect object pronouns.

Example: Compro <u>un piso</u> *a mi hija.*
Se lo compro.

Consolidation

A Ask your partner for permission to do some of the following. Give a reason to justify your request. Take turns.

1 Abrir la ventana. Hacer calor.

2 Encender la radio. Querer oír las noticias.

3 Quedarme en tu casa a dormir. Perder las llaves de casa esta mañana.

4 Llamar por teléfono. Tener que hablar con Marta.

5 Consultar el diccionario de español. No saber lo que significa . . .

6 Subir el volumen de la televisión. No oír muy bien.

7 Llevarme a la estación. Tener mucha prisa.

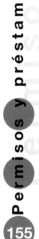

Permisos y préstamos

B Ask your partner his/her address, telephone number, mobile number and e-mail. Take turns.

C Take turns with your partner, asking to borrow his/her bicycle, a green pen, 20 euros, his/her laptop.

In class or at home

A Link the questions with the appropriate answers.

1 ¿Puedo poner música?
2 ¿Puedo hacer un café?
3 ¿Puedo usar tu ordenador?
4 ¿Puedo entrar?
5 ¿Puedo tirar estos papeles?
6 ¿Puedes prestarme dinero?
7 ¿Me puede dar su nombre?
8 ¿Les puedes prestar tu gramática?

a Sí claro ¿cuánto quieres?
b Juan López Merino.
c No, lo siento, la necesito.
d Sí, tíralos, tíralos.
e No, lo siento, estoy ocupada.
f Sí claro, ponla.
g Lo siento, pero no tengo.
h Sí claro, úsalo.

B Change the infinitives in these sentences into the positive form of the informal imperative (*tú* and *vosotros*). Then replace the direct objects with the correct object pronouns.

	tú	**vosotros**
Example: Secar los platos.	seca	secad
	séca<u>los</u>	secad<u>los</u>

1 Poner la mesa.
2 Colgar la ropa.
3 Ordenar la habitación.
4 Hacer la comida.

5 Pasar el aspirador.
6 Limpiar el cuarto de baño.
7 Comprar pan.
8 Fregar los platos.

C Replace the words in *italics* with the appropriate indirect object pronouns. Then replace the direct object with the direct object pronoun.

Example: Leo un cuento *a mi sobrino*.
      Le leo un cuento.
      Se lo leo

1 Doy dinero *a ti*.
2 Envías el paquete *a tus hijos*.
3 No prestamos la casa *a Jorge*.
4 ¿Habéis mandado el recibo *al Sr Mariño*?
5 ¿Han entregado las notas *a los estudiantes*?
6 Regala (tú) un piso *a mí*.
7 Leed las noticias *a vuestro tío*.
8 Juan compra un helado *a los niños*.

Permisos, favores y preferencias

Los ordenadores
Computers

■ **Expresión esencial**
Un ordenador es un objeto que sirve para . . .

■ **Essential expression**
A computer is an object that is useful for . . .

1 Talking about computers and their components

A Read the text below out loud and then define the following terms:

a Informática **d** Software

b Ordenador **e** Dispositivos externos

c Hardware **f** Dispositivos internos

El ordenador y sus componentes

El término '**informática**' proviene de la unión de dos palabras: INFORmación y autoMÁTICA. La informática es la ciencia que estudia el tratamiento automático de la información por medio de ordenadores e incluye, además, su teoría, diseño y fabricación.

El ordenador es una máquina que puede realizar automáticamente conjuntos de operaciones aritméticas y lógicas.

La tecnología informática afecta a todas las áreas de la vida moderna. Los ordenadores tienen muchos usos y cada día aparecen nuevas aplicaciones. Esta tecnología se aplica a la industria, la medicina, el ocio, la educación, y al mundo de los negocios.

El término **hardware** se refiere a todos los componentes físicos que integran el ordenador: monitor, ratón, teclado . . . La palabra **sofware** se refiere a las instrucciones que dirigen las operaciones llevadas a cabo con el hardware: guardar un documento; copiar un texto . . .

Básicamente, la finalidad de un ordenador es recibir información, procesarla, almacenarla y devolverla. Para ello, cuenta con multitud de dispositivos, cada uno especializado en realizar una tarea concreta: algunos de ellos están dentro del ordenador (dispositivos internos) mientras que otros están fuera de él (dispositivos externos).

Educación secundaria. Tecnología Informática. R.Gonzalo et al. Anaya multimedia. *(Adapted)*

B Here is a list of some of the parts of a computer. Look at the
picture and label each component.

El disco duro

La disquetera

Los disquetes

La impresora

El monitor

El ratón

El teclado

La unidad de CD-ROM

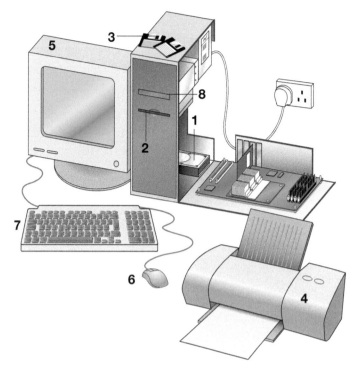

<u>C</u> Read the following definitions of the functions of some of the
computer's components. With a partner, write down the name of
the component described.

Example: El dispositivo que permite introducir caracteres en el
ordenador es *el teclado*.

1 El dispositivo que permite ver la información es el _____.
2 El dispositivo que permite plasmar en papel la información es la

_____.

3 El dispositivo que permite transmitir órdenes al ordenador es el

_____.

4 El dispositivo que almacena multitud de información, sobre todo
programas es el _____.
5 El dispositivo que controla el funcionamiento de los dispositivos
y procesa datos es la _____ o el _____.

D Prepare with your partner a brief summary of what you have just
learnt about computers and present it to the group.

Permisos, favores y preferencias   unidad 5

Giving information to clarify, specify or identify

A Read the following sentences.

1 La informática es la ciencia _que estudia el tratamiento automático de la información por medio de ordenadores_.

2 El dispositivo _que permite introducir caracteres en el ordenador_ es el teclado.

3 La joven _que acabas de ver_ es experta en informática.

What purpose do the underlined words serve? Do they clarify, specify or identify?

B Now read the grammar section to check your answers.

G de Gramática

■ Clarifying, specifying, identifying

We often need to give additional information and one way to do this is by using **relative clauses** which work in a similar way to an adjective, i.e. qualifying a noun, adding additional information about the noun.

La informática es la ciencia que estudia el tratamiento automático de la información por medio de ordenadores.

(Information Technology is the science that studies the automatic processing of information by means of computers.) The underlined phrase tells us something about _ciencia_, in the same way as an adjective does.

Relative clauses are introduced by a relative pronoun, adjective or adverb. For now you will learn about the relative pronoun _que_ ('that' or 'which').

■ Relative pronoun _que_ (that, which, who, whom)

Que has two functions:

• **As a pronoun.** Used in this way it is invariable and it refers back to a person or thing mentioned in the main clause (antecedent _ciencia_).

• **As a link** between two clauses. The clause introduced by the relative pronoun is called a relative clause.

Que can be used with short prepositions such as **a, con, de, en**, with reference to a non-human antecedent:
El piso **en que** vivo es pequeño. (The flat in which I live is small.)

Differences between the use of relative pronouns in Spanish and English

• The relative pronoun is never omitted in Spanish whereas it frequently is in English.
La joven que acabas de ver es experta en informática.
(The young lady [whom] you have just seen is an expert in IT.)

• In Spanish, prepositions must always immediately precede the relative pronoun. They cannot be placed after the verb, as they can in English.
El coche con que normalmente viajo es confortable.
(The car which I normally travel in is comfortable.)

C Form sentences using the relative pronoun _que_. Follow the example.

Example: El francés es una lengua. El francés se habla en Francia.
El francés es una lengua _que se habla en Francia_.

1 El italiano es un lengua. El italiano se habla en Italia.
2 Pedro es un amigo de la familia. Pedro vive en Buenos Aires.
3 Éste es el restaurante. En este restaurante se come bien.
4 Carmen es la tía de Pedro. Carmen vive en Venezuela.
5 Ésta es la máquina. Esta máquina limpia muy bien.
6 Ésta es una vecina. Veo a la vecina todos los días.

D Rewrite the paragraph below, inserting the following relative clauses in the appropriate places:

- que tiene un carácter complicado
- que estoy leyendo
- que está con ella por su dinero
- que hace muebles de cocina
- que tiene una vida difícil

> El libro es muy interesante. El personaje principal es una mujer. Esta mujer es dueña de una factoría. Gana mucho dinero pero no es feliz. Su marido no la quiere. Él es un hombre. Su marido ha contratado a un asesino pero ella se ha enterado de ello y ha decidido …

E Go back to the text *El ordenador y sus componentes* (p.157) and identify all the relative clauses that appear. There are four of them. Identify the antecedent of each.

 3 ## Basic vocabulary of Windows

A You might find yourself in a situation where you need to use a computer in Spain or in a Hispano-American country. So you should familiarise yourself with some of the terminology. Look at the Start Menu and match the Spanish terms with the English ones listed below:

Programs
Favourites
Documents
Control panel
Search
Help
Run
Log off
Turn off computer

Start

Stand by
Re-start
Restart MS-DOS
Yes
Cancel

Inicio
Programas
Favoritos
Documentos
Configuración
Buscar
Ayuda
Ejecutar
Cerrar sesión
Apagar el sistema

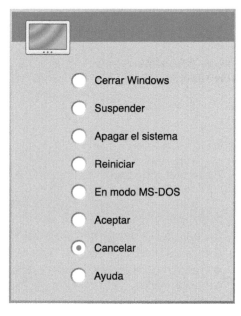

○ Cerrar Windows
○ Suspender
○ Apagar el sistema
○ Reiniciar
○ En modo MS-DOS
○ Aceptar
◉ Cancelar
○ Ayuda

B Look carefully at the toolbar on this screen and work out the English equivalents of the Spanish terms:

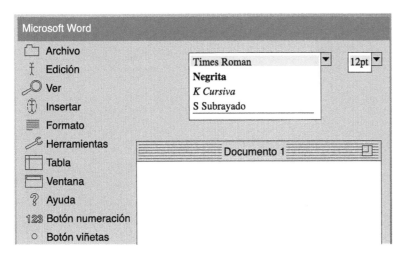

C Read the list of terms below and write their English equivalents.

Abrir
Copiar
Copiar formato
Cortar
Deshacer
Guardar
Imprimir
Ortografía y gramática
Pegar
Rehacer
Vista preliminar

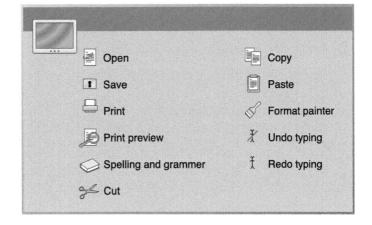

Consolidation

A Define the following words, using relative clauses. Follow the examples.

Examples: Un lápiz es un objeto que sirve para escribir.
Un(a) médico/a es una persona que cura a los enfermos.
La climatología es la ciencia que estudia el clima.

a Un cuchillo
b Un diccionario
c Un(a) futbolista
d La musicología
e Un jarrón

f Un(a) escultor(a)
g Una televisión
h La zoología
i Una cama

In class or at home

A Complete the following sentences with the appropriate relative clause from those listed below.

que tenéis en casa
que te he dejado
que ves
que ha comprado
que ha entrado
que tiene bigote
que sirve para reproducir imágenes y sonido
en que he viajado

1 La casa _____ es de mi padre.
2 La mujer _____ es la directora de la empresa.
3 Una vídeo-cámara es una máquina _____.
4 Ese señor _____ es el profesor de matemáticas de mi hijo.
5 El libro _____ es de mi tío.
6 El coche _____ Pedro es muy lento.
7 El avión _____ hoy por poco tiene un accidente.
8 La litografía _____, ¿es de Dalí?

B Rewrite the paragraph, inserting the following relative clauses in the appropriate places.

que está a unos trescientos kilómetros de la capital
que vive en México
que siempre está de buen humor
que está construido cerca de una playa fantástica
en que vive

Mi tío Julián es el hermano menor de mi madre. Es un hombre alegre. La ciudad es una ciudad grande. Él está casado pero no tiene hijos. Es dueño de un hotel. Viene a España una vez cada dos años. Cuando está en España viaja mucho.

C Read the following list of computer terms and write down the Spanish equivalents:

a	Control panel	**i**	Monitor
b	Documents	**j**	Mouse
c	Floppy disk	**k**	Printer
d	Hard disk	**l**	Programs
e	Help	**m**	Run
f	Keyboard	**n**	Search
g	Log off	**o**	Turn off computer
h	Microprocessor		

Acércate al mundo del español
Un país para visitar

A Read the text.

Ecuador

Ecuador está entre el hemisferio norte y el hemisferio sur, en América del Sur. Limita al norte con Colombia y al sur y al este con Perú. Al oeste limita con el Océano Pacífico. La extensión del país es de 256.370 kilómetros cuadrados. La zona de la costa del Pacífico es llana. La cordillera de los Andes atraviesa el país de sur a norte. Las grandes elevaciones se producen del centro al norte del país. Entre las montañas más altas destacan Chimborazo de 6310m sobre el nivel del mar y Cotopaxi de 5897m.

Las islas Galápagos pertenecen a Ecuador. Estas islas están situadas en el Océano Pacífico a casi mil kilómetros al oeste de Ecuador. Las Galápagos constituyen una de los paraísos naturales del planeta. Son de origen volcánico. Su fauna y flora son únicas y tienen mucho interés científico. Entre sus muchos animales característicos podemos destacar la tortuga gigante, también llamada galápago, que vive unos 150 años y llega a pesar 3.000 kilos.

Ecuador es una nación multiétnica y multicultural. En este país conviven 14 nacionalidades indígenas. En ciudades y pueblos viven principalmente mestizos, blancos y afroecuatorianos. Su población sobrepasa los 12,6 millones de habitantes.

El idioma oficial del país es el español, pero hay lenguas indígenas como el quichua, shimi, awapit, záparo, etc. Su capital es Quito.

B Answer the following questions.

1 Why are the *islas Galápagos* so named?
2 Why are these islands important?

C Have you visited any Hispano-American country? If so, which one? Describe it to some people in your group.

Essential vocabulary

Objetos	*Objects*
abrigo (m)	*coat*
agenda (f)	*diary*
bandeja (f)	*tray*
billete (m)	*ticket, banknote*
bolígrafo (m)	*pen*
calculadora (f)	*calculator*
camisa (f)	*shirt*
cartera (f)	*wallet*
cepillo de dientes (m)	*tooth brush*
chaqueta (f)	*jacket*
diccionario (m)	*dictionary*
disco (m)	*record*
equipaje (m)	*luggage*
espejo (m)	*mirror*
flores (f pl)	*flowers*
fotografía (f)	*photography, photograph*
gafas (f)	*glasses, spectacles*
lápiz (m)	*pencil*
libro (m)	*book*
llave (f)	*key*
maleta (f)	*suitcase*
mesa (f)	*table*
mochila (f)	*backpack*
ordenador (m)	*computer*
papelera (f)	*waste-paper basket*
paquete (m)	*parcel*
paraguas (m)	*umbrella*
partido (m)	*game, match*
pasaporte (m)	*passport*
pelota (f)	*ball*
plato (m)	*plate*
reloj (m)	*clock, watch*
sombrero (m)	*hat*
tarjeta de credito (f)	*credit card*
televisión (f)	*television*

Adjetivos para describir	*Describing adjectives*
forma	*shape*
rectangular	*rectangular*
tamaño	*size*
largo/a	*long*
color	*colour*
amarillo/a	*yellow*
plateado/a	*silver*
rojo/a	*red*

Materiales	*materials*
cristal (m)	*crystal, glass*
madera (f)	*wood*
piel (f)	*leather*
plástico (m)	*plastic*

textura	*texture*
blando/a	*soft*
duro/a	*hard*
ligero/a	*light*

Expresiones con tener	*Expressions with tener*
tener frío	*to be / feel cold*
tener calor	*to be / feel hot*
tener hambre	*to be / feel hungry*
tener sed	*to be / feel thirsty*
tener sueño	*to be / feel sleepy*
tener prisa	*to be in a hurry*
tener ganas de comer / salir	*to feel like eating / going out*

Verbos	*Verbs*
acabar de . . .	*to have just . . .*
conocer	*to know*
dar	*to give*
dejar	*to leave*
encender	*to switch on / to light*
prestar	*to lend*
saber	*to know*
terminar	*to finish*

El ordenador y sus componentes	*The computer and its components*
informática (f)	*computing*
hardware (m)	*hardware*
software (m)	*software*
CPU (f) o el microprocesador (m)	*CPU or microprocessor*
disco (m) duro	*hard disk*
disquetera (f)	*disk drive*
disquete (m)	*floppy disk*
impresora (f)	*printer*
monitor (m)	*monitor*
placa base (f)	*motherboard*
ratón (m)	*mouse*
teclado (m)	*keyboard*
unidad (f) de CD-ROM	*cd-rom drive*

Herramientas para operar el programa Windows	*Tools to operate Windows*
abrir	open
aceptar	yes
apagar el sistema	close down, turn off computer
archivo (m)	file
ayuda (f)	help
botón (m) numeración	numbering
botón (m) viñetas (f)	bullets
buscar	search
cancelar	cancel
cerrar sesión (f)	log off
cerrar windows	shut Windows
configuración (f)	control panel
copiar	copy
copiar formato (m)	format painter
cortar	cut
deshacer	undo typing
documento (m)	document
edición (f)	edit
ejecutar	run
favoritos (m)	favourites
formato (m)	format
guardar	save
herramientas (f)	tools
imprimir	print
inicio (m)	start
insertar	insert
K (cursiva)	I (italics)
n (negrita)	b (bold)
nuevo documento (m) en blanco	new blank document
ortografía (f) y gramática (f)	spelling and grammar
pegar	paste
programa (m)	program
rehacer	redo typing
reiniciar	re-start
reiniciar en modo ms-dos	restart ms-dos
s subrayado	u underline
suspender	stand by
tabla (f)	table
ventana (f)	window
ver	view
vista (f) preliminar	print preview

essential vocabulary

Gustos y otras cosas

A El tiempo libre

Free time

■ **Expresiones esenciales**

¿Qué hace(s) en tu / su tiempo libre?

Hago deporte

Veo la televisión / voy a bailar

Voy al cine / voy de compras . . .

¿Qué piensas hacer la semana que viene?

La semana que viene voy a . . .

El año próximo quiero ir a . . .

Lo siento mucho pero es que . . .

Los fines de semana suelo ir / quedarme . . .

■ **Essential expressions**

What do you do in your free time?

I do sport

I watch television / go dancing

I go to the cinema / shopping

What are you thinking of doing next week?

Next week I'm going to . . .

Next year I want to go to . . .

I'm very sorry, but (the thing is) . . .

At weekends, I usually go / stay . . .

---

1 **Free time**

A *¿Qué hace(s) en tu / su tiempo libre?* Match each of the following sentences to the appropriate picture.

- Voy a bailar • Voy al cine • Hago deporte • Navego por Internet • Salgo de copas con mis amigos • Veo la televisión

a _____   c _____   e _____

b _____   d _____   f _____

B Now write the sentences in the third person singular.

C Read these statements and say if they are true (*verdadero*) or false (*falso*) for you. If any of them is false, give the correct information.

¿Qué haces en tu tiempo libre?	V	F
1 Los fines de semana siempre me levanto a las siete de la mañana.	☐	☐
2 Hago deporte de vez en cuando.	☐	☐
3 A menudo voy de compras.	☐	☐
4 Veo la televisión de vez en cuando.	☐	☐
5 Voy de excursión todos los fines de semana.	☐	☐
6 Voy de copas pocas veces.	☐	☐
7 Voy de compras muchas veces.	☐	☐
8 Navego por Internet todas las noches.	☐	☐
9 Casi nunca leo.	☐	☐

D Using the information from the previous exercise, write a short paragraph about what you do in your free time. You can follow the model given below.

■ Yo hago deporte casi todos los días, cuatro o cinco veces a la semana; veo la televisión de vez en cuando; leo todas las noches; salgo con mis amigos a menudo; siempre voy de copas los fines de semana y voy de compras de vez en cuando. ¿Y tú?

■ Yo ...

E Now listen to Pablo and Irene talking about what they do in their free time and fill in the missing information.

Pablo   **Irene**

Actividad	Frecuencia	Actividad	Frecuencia
va de paseo			todos los sábados y a veces los jueves también
hace deporte			casi nunca
ve la televisión			todas las noches
lee			casi siempre
va al cine			pocas veces
sale de copas			nunca
va de compras			los domingos

Plans and intentions

A Read the mini-dialogues and say:

1 whether the information asked for refers to present, future or past events

2 which verbal structures have been used

■ *¿Qué haces el fin de semana que viene?*

■ *¿Adónde vas a ir de vacaciones en Semana Santa?*

■ *Voy de camping con unos amigos, ¿y tú?*

■ *Pienso ir a Perú.*

G de Gramática

■ **To talk about future plans:**

• Verb in present tense:
¿Qué haces esta Semana Santa / este verano?
En Semana Santa voy a Buenos Aires. (At Easter I'm going to Buenos Aires.)
Este verano voy a ir a Colombia. (This summer, I'm going to Colombia.)

• Present of **ir** + **a** + **infinitive** (to be going to + infinitive) of the verb:
¿Qué vais a hacer el mes que viene? (What are you going to do next month?)
El mes que viene vamos a visitar a Enrique (Next month we're going to visit Enrique.)

■ **To talk about intentions**

• Present of **pensar** (**e**>**ie**) + **infinitive** (to be thinking of + gerund):
¿Qué piensas hacer la semana que viene? (What are you thinking of doing next week?)
La semana que viene pienso ir a pasar unos días en casa de mis padres. (Next week I'm thinking of going to my parents' house for a few days.)

■ **To talk about wishes for the future**

• Present of **querer** (**e**>**ie**) + **infinitive** (to want + infinitive):
El año próximo quiero ir a Guatemala. (Next year I want to go to Guatemala.)

The following time expressions will make it clear that the time reference is to the future:

mañana / pasado mañana (tomorrow / the day after tomorrow)
esta mañana / tarde / noche (this morning / afternoon / tonight)
el año / el mes / la semana ... que viene (next (in the coming) year / month / week)
el año / el mes / la semana próximo(a) (next year / month / week)
luego / más tarde (later)
dentro de una semana / un mes / un año (in a week's / month's / year's time)

■ **To answer questions about future plans and intentions:**

¿Qué vas a hacer el próximo fin de semana? (What are you going to do next weekend?)
Voy a ir a ... / No sé. (I am going to go to ... / I don't know.)
¿Piensas ir de vacaciones al extranjero el verano que viene? (Are you thinking of going on holiday abroad next summer?)
Sí, voy a ir a ... / Sí, pienso ir a ... / No, me voy a quedar en casa. / No sé.
(Yes, I'm going to (go to) ... / Yes, I thinking of going to ... / No, I'm going to stay at home. / I don't know.)

B Answer the following questions using *ir* + *a* + infinitive or *pensar* + infinitive.

1 ¿Qué piensas hacer el fin de semana que viene?
2 ¿Vas a salir esta noche?
3 ¿Cuándo vas a ir de compras?
4 El viernes por la noche ¿vas a venir al cine con nosotros?
5 ¿Piensas ir a España el año que viene?

C Say five things that you are planning to do next year. Find out what the people in your group are planning to do.

Apologising and making an excuse

<u>A</u> A friend of yours has sent you an e-mail announcing his visit.
Read it and then answer the questions.

1 ¿De dónde es Miguel Ángel?
2 ¿Cuántos días va a estar Miguel Ángel en Escocia?
3 ¿Qué días piensa Miguel Ángel quedarse en casa de su amigo
   Mike?
4 ¿Qué día piensa volver a España?

De: mikesm@hotmail.com
Para: miguelro@hotmail.com
Asunto: visita a Escocia

Hola Mike:
El martes en dos semanas voy a ir a Glasgow a trabajar y el fin de semana
pienso ir a verte. Pienso llegar a tu casa el sábado por la mañana y quiero
quedarme en tu casa hasta el martes al mediodía. El martes por la tarde
tengo que regresar a Glasgow y el jueves tengo que volver a Bilbao. ¿Te va
bien? Espero que sí.

Un abrazo muy fuerte,
Miguel Ángel

<u>B</u> Read Mike's reply to Miguel Ángel's e-mail and answer the
questions.

1 ¿Dónde va a estar Mike el fin de semana que Miguel Ángel
   quiere visitarlo?
2 ¿Por qué?
3 ¿Dónde va a estar Mike el lunes por la mañana?
4 Miguel Ángel, ¿va a ver a Mike?

From: miguelro@hotmail.com
To: mikesm@hotmail.com
Subject: Re:visita a Escocia

Querido Miguel Ángel:
Lo siento mucho pero es que el fin de semana que tú piensas venir a mi casa yo no voy a
estar. Ese fin de semana es el cumpleaños de mi suegro y la familia y yo, vamos a ir a
pasar el fin de semana a un hotel en el noroeste de Escocia. Volvemos el domingo por la
noche pero el lunes por la mañana yo tengo que ir a Londres. ¿Piensas volver a Escocia
pronto?

Un abrazo,
Mike

G de Gramática

C Read the second e-mail again. What expression is used by Mike
to apologise and explain why he is not going to be able to see
Miguel Ángel?

D With a partner, respond to the following questions by apologising
and making an excuse.

  1 ¿Vais a venir al cumpleaños de Teresa el sábado? (tener otro
cumpleaños)

  2 El próximo fin de semana ¿vienes de camping con nosotros? (ir
a casa de mis abuelos)

  3 Oye Juan, esta tarde ¿vienes a ver un vídeo a casa? (ir a jugar
un partido de fútbol)

  4 Luisa, esta noche vamos al cine, ¿vienes? (tener que trabajar)

  5 Sra. Moreno, ¿viene mañana a la excursión? (tener que dar
clase)

  6 Sr. Fuentes, ¿viene esta tarde a la conferencia? (tener que ver a
unos clientes)

4   The Spanish and their free time

A Read the following table out loud and then answer the questions.

¿En qué suele emplear, en general, su tiempo libre?			
	% (tanto por ciento)		%
Estar con la familia	76	Hacer deporte	32
Ver la televisión	69	Ir al cine	27
Estar con amigos/as	54	Salir con mi novia/o	18
Leer libros, revistas	45	Hacer trabajos manuales	18
Oír la radio	43	Ir a bailar	17
Escuchar música	42	Ir al teatro	8
Salir al campo, ir de excursión	40	Tocar un instrumento musical	4
Ver deporte	33	Ir a reuniones políticas	2

source http://www.cis es/boletin/10/est2.html. (Adapted)

B From what you have just read, say if the following statements are *verdaderos* or *falsos*.

1 Muchos españoles suelen ir al cine en su tiempo libre.
2 No muchos españoles hacen trabajos manuales en su tiempo libre.
3 La mayoría de los españoles pasan parte de su tiempo libre con la familia.
4 Casi ningún español suele hacer deporte en su tiempo libre.
5 Algunos españoles van a bailar en su tiempo libre.
6 Pocos españoles tocan un instrumento musical.
7 Muy pocos españoles van de excursión.
8 Todos los españoles ven la televisión.

C Look at the previous sentences and write sentences that reflect the findings of the study.

> **Example:** Ir a reuniones políticas 2 %
> Casi ningún español va a reuniones políticas en su tiempo libre.

1 Salir con mi novia/o   18%
2 Oír la radio   43%
3 Ver deporte   33%
4 Ir al teatro   8%
5 Ver la televisión   69%

D Say five things that you usually do during the weekends using *soler* + infinitive.

> **Example:** Los fines de semana *suelo ir* de excursión.

G de Gramática

■ Habitual actions in the present

The verb *soler* 'to usually' (do, go etc.) is a radical changing verb (*o>ue*) which can be used to ask for and give information about usual or habitual actions. *Soler* is followed by an infinitive.

> *¿En qué* **suele emplear**, en general, su tiempo libre?
> (How do you usually spend your free time?)
> *Los fines de semana* **suelo ir** *de excursión.* (At the weekend, I usually go out for the day.)

■ To refer to a whole or part of a whole, use the following quantifiers:

Todos/as los / las	No muchos/as
Casi todos/as los / las	Pocos/as
La mayoría de los / las	Muy pocos/as
Muchos/as	Casi ningún/ninguna
Algunos/as	Ningún/ninguna

Casi todos los españoles pasan parte de su tiempo libre con la familia. (Nearly all Spaniards spend part of their free time with their family.)
No muchos españoles suelen ir al teatro. (Not many Spaniards go to the theatre.)

Consolidation

A Write down the questions to the following answers:

1 En el mes de julio pienso ir al pueblo de mis abuelos.
2 Este sábado vamos a ir a un concierto de rock.
3 No sé qué voy a hacer el fin de semana.
4 Estas vacaciones voy a la costa.
5 Hoy después de trabajar voy a ir al cine con Jesús.
6 El fin de semana que viene vamos de camping.

B These days you are very busy, but your friends keep inviting you to do things with them and you keep giving them excuses.

1 ¿Vienes al partido esta tarde? Lo siento pero es que . . .
2 Este domingo vamos a comer fuera, ¿vienes?
3 ¿Vienes al gimnasio después de clase?
4 El mes que viene pensamos ir a pasar unos días en la montaña, ¿vienes?

C Using some of the following expressions, name six activities that people in your country, town or village do in their free time.

Casi todos/as los / las
Muchos/as
Algunos/as
Pocos/as
Muy pocos/as
Casi ningún/(a)

In class or at home

A Read the following statements. Rewrite them in the first person plural with a contrasting meaning. Revise the expressions of frequency at the start of this unit if you need to.

Example: Los fines de semana siempre me levanto a las siete de la mañana.
Los fines de semana **nunca nos levantamos** a las siete de la mañana.

¿Qué hacéis en vuestro tiempo libre?

1 Los domingos duermo hasta las once de la mañana.
2 Hago deporte de vez en cuando.
3 No salgo con mis amigos nunca.
4 A menudo voy de compras.
5 Veo la televisión de vez en cuando.
6 Los fines de semana a menudo voy de excursión.
7 Voy de copas pocas veces.
8 Voy de compras muchas veces.
9 Navego por Internet todas las noches.
10 Casi nunca leo.

B Match the questions on the left with their answers on the right:

1 Despúes de clase, ¿vamos al cine?

2 ¿Venís este fin de semana a la playa?

3 Sr. Fuertes, ¿va a venir a la fiesta?

4 Paco, ¿vamos de copas el sábado por la noche?

5 Sres Jiménez, ¿vienen a la cena?

6 Esta tarde, ¿vamos de compras?

a Lo sentimos pero es que esta noche tenemos otro compromiso.

b Lo siento pero es que este sábado voy a ver a mi novia.

c Lo sentimos mucho pero es que este fin de semana tenemos que terminar un trabajo.

d Lo siento pero tengo que trabajar.

e Lo siento mucho pero no puedo; es que tengo que cenar con un amigo.

f Lo siento mucho pero es que esta noche tengo otro compromiso.

C Write the questions to the following answers. Use *usted / ustedes*.

Example: En mayo vamos a Nicaragua.
¿Qué van a hacer ustedes en mayo?

1 Este domingo voy a quedarme en casa.
2 La semana que viene pensamos ir al teatro.
3 El lunes que viene vamos a ver un partido de tenis.
4 Mañana por la noche vamos a una discoteca.
5 El mes próximo voy a visitar a la familia de mi mujer.
6 En enero vamos a Argentina.

El tiempo y el clima

Weather and climate

<table>
<tr><td>

■ Expresiones esenciales

¿En qué estación estamos?

Estamos en invierno / primavera . . .

El verano empieza / termina

¿Qué tiempo hace? ¿Cómo está el tiempo?

Hace frío / calor / Llueve / Nieva

Hay nubes / niebla

El tiempo está frío / lluvioso / soleado

¿Cómo es el tiempo / el clima en . . . ?

El tiempo / el clima es caluroso / frío

Tener frío / calor

Si llueve, voy / vamos a . . .

</td><td>

■ Essential expressions

What season are we in?

We're in summer / spring . . .

Summer starts / finishes

What's the weather like?

It's cold / hot./ It's raining / It's snowing

It's cloudy / foggy

It's cold / rainy / sunny

What's the weather / climate like in . . . ?

The weather / climate is hot / cold

To feel cold / hot

If it rains, I'm / we're going to . . .

</td></tr>
</table>

■ ¿En qué estación estamos?

■ Estamos en invierno.

1 **Seasons of the year**

a

b

c

d

G de Gramática

■ Las estaciones del año

- All the seasons of the year are masculine except *la primavera* (spring).

- The names of the seasons are usually introduced by an article: *El invierno es frío.* (Winter is cold.)

A Match the name of the seasons to the photographs.

la primavera   el invierno   el otoño   el verano

B Complete the following sentences. Work with a partner.

1 ¿_____ estación del año estamos? _____.

2 El verano en Argentina empieza _____ y termina _____.

3 La primavera en España empieza _____ y termina _____.

4 Las hojas de los árboles caen en _____.

5 Las flores nacen en _____.

Gustos y otras cosas

unidad 6

174

C Read the following text about the northern and southern hemispheres and answer the questions.

El globo terrestre se divide de manera ficticia según la posición de línea del ecuador terrestre o de un meridiano en el hemisferio norte o boreal y el hemisferio sur o austral.

El hemisferio boreal (norte o septentrional) comprende el polo ártico o boreal y las regiones y océanos que lo rodean. El hemisferio austral (sur o meridional) comprende el polo antártico o austral y las regiones y océanos que lo rodean.

Desde el punto de vista climático las diferencias entre este hemisferio y el austral son claras: las estaciones se distribuyen de manera opuesta de forma que el verano boreal corresponde con el invierno austral. Así cuando en Europa es verano, en países del hemisferio sur como Chile es invierno.

1 Menciona tres países situados en el hemisferio norte y tres situados en el hemisferio sur.

2 Cuando es primavera en España es _____ en Uruguay.

3 Menciona los meses que se corresponden con el otoño en el hemisferio norte y en el hemisferio sur.

4 Menciona los meses que se corresponden con el verano en el hemisferio norte y en el hemisferio sur.

The weather

A Read the following expressions.

hace viento y frío = hace (muy) mal tiempo
hace sol y calor = hace (muy) buen tiempo

¿Qué tiempo hace?	
Nouns	
el calor	hace calor
el frío	hace (mucho) frío
el sol	hace (bastante) sol
el viento	hace (poco) viento
la lluvia	llueve (mucho)
la nieve	nieva (bastante) (poco)
la niebla	hay (mucha) niebla
las nubes	hay (pocas) nubes

B Using the expressions you have just learnt, describe today's weather.

C Below are some more expressions used to describe the weather. Match the expressions in the left-hand column with those on the right.

¿Qué tiempo hace?	¿Cómo está el tiempo? El tiempo está (muy / bastante)
Llueve	bueno
Hay niebla	caluroso
Hay nubes	nublado
Hace sol	lluvioso
Hace viento	malo
Hace calor	nuboso / cubierto
Hace frío	soleado / despejado
Hace buen tiempo	ventoso
Hace mal tiempo	frío

G de Grámatica

■ *Muy, mucho* **when referring to the weather**
- *Muy* + **adjective**: *El tiempo está muy soleado.* (The weather is very sunny.)
- *Mucho/a/os/as* + **noun**: *Hace mucho sol.* (It is very sunny.)
- **Verb** + *mucho*: *Llueve mucho.* (It rains a lot.)

D Work with a partner to describe what the weather is like in some of the following cities:

Bogotá	Caracas	Madrid	Managua	Santiago de Chile
13°C	32°C	11°C	25°C	12°C

Example: – ¿Qué tiempo hace en Bogotá?
  – Hace buen tiempo. Hace sol y está despejado.
  – ¿Hace frío?
  – Sí, un poco.
  – ¿Cuántos grados hace?
  – Hace trece grados centígrados / Celsius

G de Gramática

■ Describing the weather

• *¿Qué tiempo hace?* (What's the weather like?)

Note that weather expressions with *haber* and *hacer* are equivalent to in English: 'to be + adjective'.

• Using the verb **hacer** in the third person singular + **noun** (*frío* 'cold', *calor* 'heat', *sol* 'sun'):
  Esta mañana ha hecho frío pero ahora hace calor. (This morning it was cold but now it's warm.)
  Hace buen / mal tiempo. BUT *Hace bueno / malo.* (The weather is good / bad.)
• Using the verb **haber** in the third person singular + **noun** (*nubes* 'clouds', *niebla* 'fog'):
  Hay nubes. (It is cloudy.)
  Hay niebla. (It is foggy.)
• Radical-changing verbs **llover (o>ue)** 'to rain' and **nevar (e>ie)** 'to snow':
  Llueve. (It's raining.)   *Hoy ha llovido mucho.* (Today it has rained a lot.)
  Nieva. (It's snowing.)   *Esta tarde ha nevado.* (This afternoon it has snowed.)

Note that all the above verbs are used only in the third person singular forms when describing the weather.

The weather and the climate

A Read the following expressions and explain why you think different verbs are used. Then read the grammar section about weather expressions with *estar* and *ser*.

1 Aquí en invierno el tiempo <u>es</u> bueno pero este invierno <u>está</u> malo, llueve mucho y hace frío.
2 Aquí el tiempo en verano <u>es</u> caluroso pero este verano <u>está</u> frío.

Gustos y otras cosas
unidad 6

■ *Estar* and *ser* with weather expressions

- *Estar* is used to describe the weather at a particular time. The state or condition is regarded as temporary.

  ¿Cómo está el tiempo hoy? (What's the weather like today?)

  Está frío. (It's cold.)

- *Ser* is used if talking about the climate or the weather in general terms:

  ¿Cómo es el tiempo / el clima? (What is the weather like ([generally]?)

  ¿Cómo es el tiempo en Madrid en invierno? (What's the weather like in Madrid in winter?)

  Es muy frío pero llueve poco. (It's very cold but it doesn't rain much.)

- *Ser versus estar*

  Aquí el tiempo en verano __es__ caluroso pero este verano __está__ frío.

  (Here the weather in summer is warm but this summer it's cold.)

  Ser is used to describe the climate, what the weather is like in general terms every summer.

  Estar is used to describe what the weather is like at a particular time: e.g. this summer.

- *Estar* + **present participle** is used to refer to an action which is perceived as ongoing or in progress.

  Está lloviendo. (It is raining.)

  Está nevando. (It is snowing.)

  Está haciendo sol / frío. (It is sunny / cold.)

- Expressions to describe how one is feeling regarding temperature:

Tener frío	(to be cold)	Tengo frío.	(I am cold.)
Tener calor	(to be warm, hot)	Tengo calor.	(I am warm, hot.)
Estar bien	(to be neither hot or cold)	Estoy bien.	(I'm fine / comfortable.)

B Complete the following sentences with *estar*, *hacer* or *ser* in the present or perfect tense.

  1 Hoy _____ mucho frío. _____ 2ºC.

  2 Esta mañana _____ cubierto pero ahora _____ despejado.

  3 Aquí en primavera el tiempo _____ bueno, _____ bastante calor.

  4 En estos momentos _____ nevando.

  5 Esta mañana _____ nublado pero ahora _____ sol.

  6 El verano en Sevilla _____ muy caluroso.

  7 Estos días _____ haciendo sol pero _____ mucho frío.

  8 Hoy _____ 20 grados bajo cero.

C *¿Tienen frío o calor? ¿Están bien?* Say how the people in the photograph are feeling.

■ **The climate in Spain and Hispano-America**

Spain

Spain is a large country and the climate varies from one region to another. So, for example, summers are much cooler in the north than in the south where they can get very hot. Winters on the Mediterranean coast are much warmer than inland. Southern Spain is dry, whereas Northern and Northwest Spain are wet.

Hispano-America

It is very difficult to generalise about the climate in Hispano-America but it could be said that in many places except Chile, Uruguay and Argentina, the weather is tropical or subtropical and that there are only two seasons – dry and rainy. It is mostly hot except in the high mountains, where it tends to be warm during the day and very cold at night. In Argentina, Chile and Uruguay there are four seasons.

D 🎧 Read the culture box and then listen to *Luis* and *Nancy* talking about the weather in their cities and fill in the missing words.

1 Luis, Madrid

Madrid tiene un clima _____. Los inviernos son _____ y los _____ muy calurosos. En otoño _____ bastante y en invierno _____. La temperatura media anual es de _____.

2 Nancy, La Habana

La Habana tiene un clima _____. El año tiene dos estaciones, la época _____ de _____ a octubre y la época seca de noviembre a _____. El mes más _____ es agosto, con una temperatura media de _____ y el mes más frío febrero con 21°. En cuanto a las precipitaciones, los meses más _____ son febrero y marzo con 46 mm (milímetros) y el más húmedo octubre con _____ mm.

E Read the culture box again and answer the following questions.

1 ¿Cuál de las dos ciudades tiene el clima más variable?
2 ¿En qué mes nieva en Madrid?
3 ¿Cuál es el mes menos caluroso en La Habana?
4 ¿Y el más lluvioso?
5 Las precipitaciones son el agua que cae de las nubes y pueden caer en forma líquida o sólida. Cuando cae en forma líquida _____ y cuando cae en forma sólida _____.

4 The weather and free time

A Many of the activities we do or plan to do depend on the weather. What will you do, for example, if it rains (*si llueve . . .*)? Work with your partner and link the phrases in the left-hand column with a phrase from the right-hand column.

1 (tú) Si llueve
2 (ellos) Si el tiempo está lluvioso
3 (usted) Si nieva mucho

4 (vosotros) Si hace mucho viento
5 (él) Si está despejado
6 (nosotros) Si hace mucho calor
7 (yo) Si el tiempo está malo
8 (nosotros) Si hace mucho frío
9 (ellos) Si hace sol

a va a jugar al fútbol
b no vamos a la playa
c este fin de semana van a ir a la montaña
d vamos a la playa
e vas al cine
f no salís en barco
g me quedo en casa
h no van de camping
i no va de excursión

B Read the mini-dialogue and then ask people in your class what they are going to do this weekend.

■ ¿Qué vas a hacer este fin de semana?

G de Gramática

■ Expressing conditions and their consequences

In Spanish, as in English, conditions are expressed by conditional sentences. A conditional sentence is made up of a main clause and a subordinate clause. The main clause expresses the condition for the fulfilment of the action expressed in the subordinate clause. In Spanish, as in English, a condition is expressed by using clauses introduced by **si** : ('if-clauses'). The following examples use the first type of conditional which you've met so far, where, if the condition is fulfilled, the outcome is certain.

Subordinate clause	Main clause
Si + present indicative +	present indicative
Si llueve *If it rains*	no voy a la playa *I'm not going to the beach*
Si llegas pronto *If you arrive early*	vamos al cine *we'll go to the cinema*

Or the other way round: *No voy a la playa si llueve.*

■ No sé, depende del tiempo. Si hace sol, voy a ir a la playa, pero si llueve, me quedo en casa. ¿Y tú?

Consolidation

A Tell your partner what your favourite season of the year is and describe what the weather is like.

B Choose a place that you know well and describe its climate.

C Complete the following sentences:
  1 Si deja de llover . . .
  2 Si nuestros amigos nos llaman . . . .
  3 Si salgo pronto de trabajar . . .
  4 Si la semana que viene el tiempo está bueno . . . (nosotros)
  5 Si venís a mi país . . .

D Tell your partner what you've done this weekend.

  Example: Este fin de semana he jugado al fútbol.

In class or at home

A Complete the information about the seasons of the year in the Northern Hemisphere.

  1 _____ empieza el 21 de marzo y acaba _____
  2 _____ empieza el 21 de junio y termina _____
  3 _____ comienza el 21 de se(p)tiembre y acaba _____
  4 _____ comienza el 21 de diciembre y termina _____

B Read the weather expressions in the column on the left and write their equivalents in the column on the right.

¿Qué tiempo hace?	¿Cómo está el tiempo?
Llueve	El tiempo está lluvioso
Hay niebla	
Hay nubes	
Hace sol	
Hace viento	
Hace calor	
Hace frío	
Hace buen tiempo	
Hace mal tiempo	

C Write sentences following the model. Write down the temperatures in full and say how you're feeling about the temperature.

Example: 35°C

Hoy hace mucho calor, hace treinta y cinco grados centígrados. Tengo calor.

a 5°C
b 28°C
c −10°C
d 24°C
e −17°C

D Look at the map of Spain and say what the weather is like in some of the places shown.

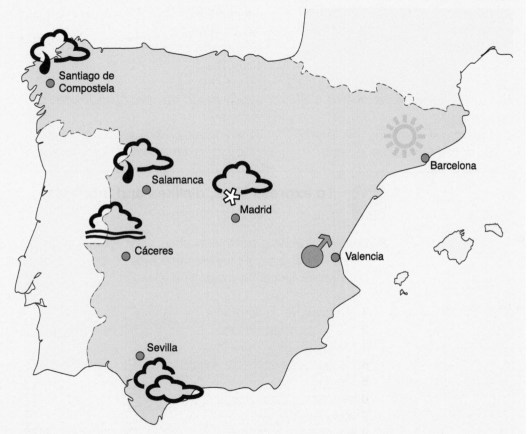

Example: En Santiago llueve. El tiempo está lluvioso.

a Barcelona
b Cáceres
c Madrid
d Salamanca
e Sevilla
f Valencia

Gustos e intereses

Tastes and interests

■ **Expresiones esenciales**	■ **Essential expressions**
¿Qué te / le gusta hacer en tu / su tiempo libre?	What do you like doing in your free time?
Me gusta ver la televisión / leer	I like watching television / reading
Me gusta el tenis / la ópera	I like tennis / opera
Me gustan los deportes	I like sport
¿Te / le gusta / interesa . . . ?	Do you like / are you interested in . . . ?
(No) me gusta / interesa / aprender español / el teatro	I'm (don't) like / I'm not interested in learning Spanish / the theatre
(No) me gustan / interesan los idiomas	I'm (don't) like / I'm not interested in languages
A mí también	So am I / Me too
A mí tampoco	Neither am I / Nor am I
A mí sí	I do / Yes
A mí no	I don't / No
¿Qué te / le gusta más el invierno o el verano?	Which do you like more / better: winter or summer?
¿Qué prefiere(s) el invierno o el verano?	Which do you prefer: winter or summer?
Me gusta más / prefiero el invierno	I like winter more / better / I prefer winter

To express likes, dislikes and interests

■ ¿Qué te gusta hacer en tu tiempo libre?

■ Me gusta hacer deporte.

A Read the following statements about what you like to do in *tu / su tiempo libre* and say if they are *verdaderos* or *falsos*. If false, write a negative sentence: *No me gusta la televisión.*

	Verdadero	Falso
1 Me gusta ver la televisión.	☐	☐
2 Me gusta hacer deporte.	☐	☐
3 Me gusta leer.	☐	☐
4 Me gusta salir con mis amigos.	☐	☐
5 Me gusta bailar.	☐	☐
6 Me gusta ir de compras.	☐	☐
7 Me gusta dormir.	☐	☐
8 Me gusta escuchar música.	☐	☐

B Read what your partner likes to do and tell the rest of the group.

> **Example:** A Peter le gusta ver la televisión, le gusta salir con sus amigos y le gusta escuchar música.

C Look at the sentences in A and write the Spanish equivalent of the English expression '*I like*', then read the grammar section.

G de Gramática

■ To express likes and dislikes: *gustar* and other verbs

Spanish does not have a direct equivalent of the verb 'to like'. The verb **gustar**, which literally means 'to please', is the most commonly used verb to express likes and dislikes. The Spanish equivalent of the sentence 'I like tennis' is *Me gusta el tenis,* which in English means: 'tennis pleases me' (literally, tennis is pleasing to me). So in Spanish, unlike English, the person to whom something is pleasing is shown by an indirect object pronoun and the thing which is pleasing is the subject of the verb:

The indirect object pronouns (listed below) stand for the indirect object, i.e. the person or object that benefits or loses as the result of an action.

Indirect object prepositional phrase: a + noun or pronoun. not essential, but used for clarification or emphasis.	Indirect object pronoun. The indirect object pronoun is essential	Verb Gustar does not literally mean to like, but rather to please. Gustar is predominantly used in the third person singular or plural.	Subject	Examples
(a mí)	(no) **me**			(A mí) **me** gusta el cine
(a ti)	(no) **te**	**gusta**	singular noun /	(A ti) **te** gusta el cine
(a usted)	(no) **le**		infinitive	(A usted) no **le** gusta el fútbol
(a él / a ella; a Carlos)	(no) **le**			(A ella) **le** gusta nadar
(a nosotros(as))	(no) **nos**			(A nosotros) no **nos** gustan los deportes
(a vosotros(as))	(no) **os**			(A vosotros) **os** gusta la paella
(a ustedes)	(no) **les**	**gustan**	plural noun	(A ustedes) **les** gustan los aviones
(a ellos / a ellas, a Mary y a Juan)	(no) **les**			(A Pedro y a Marta) no **les** gusta viajar

Other verbs similar to *gustar* are: **agradar** (to please); **apetecer** (*to fancy*); **desagradar** (to dislike); **encantar** (to love, to enjoy); **horrorizar** (to hate / not to be able to stand); **interesar** (to interest).

■ To express interest

The verb *interesar* is used; again predominantly in the third person:
A mi hija le interesan los libros de aventuras. (My daughter is interested in adventure stories.) Literally: To my daughter adventure stories are interesting (to her).

D Complete the following sentences with *gusta, gustan* or *interesa, interesan*.

1 Me _____ vivir en el campo. (gustar)
2 ¿Te _____ las discotecas? (gustar)
3 A Pedro le _____ la música clásica. (interesar)
4 A Pablo y a mí, nos _____ salir de copas. (gustar)
5 A nosotros, nos _____ los programas de informática. (interesar)
6 ¿No os _____ viajar? (gustar)
7 No me _____ tus problemas. (interesar)
8 A ellas les _____ las ciudades grandes. (gustar)
9 No nos _____ ir de compras. (gustar).
10 ¿A ustedes les _____ los idiomas? (interesar)
11 Les _____ la comida china. (gustar)
12 No os _____ el proyecto. (interesar)

Gustos e intereses

183

E Make sentences by linking appropriate phrases between the boxes.

A ti	os gustan	el cine nada
A sus alumnos	no les gusta	los animales
A ti y a mí	me gusta	las mismas cosas
A mí	les gustan	los idiomas
A Carmen y Elena	no te gusta	el fútbol
A vosotros	nos gustan	la clase de las nueve

F Ask people in your group about their likes, dislikes and interests.

- ¿Te gusta / interesa la ópera?

- la música: clásica, pop, rock, jazz, punk, ópera . . .
- el deporte: tenis, golf, fútbol, gimnasia . . .
- el cine: cómico, de ciencia-ficción, de guerra, de aventuras . . .
- la literatura: novela, poesía, teatro, biografías . . .
- viajar, estudiar, levantarse temprano
- las matemáticas, las ciencias, las artes

2 To express degrees of liking and disliking

A Study the expressions below and then listen to Isabel talking about her likes, dislikes and interests, then tick the appropriate box in the grid.

me encanta/n		me horroriza/n	
me gusta/n me interesa/n	muchísimo mucho bastante un poco poco	no me gusta/n no me interesa/n	mucho nada

	Le encanta	Le gusta muchísimo	Le gusta bastante	Le interesan	No le gusta mucho	Le horroriza
ir al cine						
leer						
los libros de historia						
quedarse en casa						
salir de copas						
ver la televisión						

Gustos y otras cosas

unidad 6

184

B Express your likes, dislikes and interests regarding the topics on the previous page. Use some of the expressions you have just learnt. Then ask your partner about his/her likes and dislikes and compare your answers. This time, use *usted*.

> **Example:** Me encanta viajar / Me interesa la música / No me gusta nada bailar, ¿y a usted?

3 To express agreement (*acuerdo*) and disagreement (*desacuerdo*)

A Study the following information.

- ¿Le gusta viajar?

  Sí, me encanta/n
  Sí, me gusta/n
  Mucho/bastante/un poco
  No, no me gusta/n mucho nada
- ¿te gustan los deportes?

  Me horroriza/n

- ¿Y a ti / a usted?

Acuerdo	**Desacuerdo**
A mí también	A mí no
A mí tampoco	A mí sí

B Respond to the following statements and then share the information with the rest of the group.

	Agreement	Disagreement
Me gusta vivir en el campo.	A mí también.	A mí no.
Me interesan los idiomas.		
No me interesa la música pop.		
No me gusta nada el tabaco.		
Me horrorizan los lunes.		
No me gusta trabajar.		
Me encanta el chocolate.		

G de Gramática

■ To express agreement and disagreement

- **To express agreement**

  También (also, too) is used in affirmative phrases:
  Me gusta bailar. (I like dancing.)
  A mí también. (Me too.)

  Tampoco (not … either) is used in negative phrases:
  A Carlos no le gustan los aviones. (Carlos doesn't like aeroplanes.)
  A María tampoco. (Neither does María.)

- **To express disagreement**

  Sí is used to contradict negative phrases: *No me gustan las películas románticas.* (I don't like romantic films.)
  A mí sí. (I do.)

  No is used to contradict affirmative phrases:
  Nos gusta la casa de Pedro. (We like Pedro's house.)
  A mí no. (I don't.)

C Translate the following mini-dialogues into Spanish.

1 We like golf very much; do you? (*sing, formal*)
Yes, I do, too.

2 Do you (*plural, familiar*) like this village?
Yes, we like it very much.

3 I don't like coffee at all; do you? (*sing. familiar*)
No, I don't either.

4 Ricardo and Elena are interested in modern art; what about Laura?
She is, too.

5 They love Indian food; what about you (*sing. formal*)?
I do, too.

6 Laura doesn't like getting up early in the morning; what about you
(*sing. familiar*)?
I don't either.

Contrasting opinions using *pues* and *pero*

A The words **pues** (well) or **pero** (but) can be used to contrast
opinions in the following way:

■ *¿Te gusta leer?*   ■ *Sí, mucho.*

■ *Pues a mí, no mucho.*   ■ *A Luis, le interesa la
                              política pero a mí no
                              me interesa mucho.*

B Chain reaction. Respond to the following, depending on what
people in your group say:

Example:

Student A	Student B	Student C
¿Te gusta bailar?	Sí, muchísimo	Pues a mí no.
	No, nada	Pues a mí sí / mucho.

Student D
A Mike (Student B) le gusta bailar pero a mí no me gusta nada. A Mike no le gusta bailar pero a mí me gusta mucho.

1 ¿Te gusta la comida mexicana?   **3** ¿Te interesa la moda?
2 ¿Te gustan los coches deportivos?   **4** ¿Te interesa conocer
                                                gente?

5 Saying what you think of something

G de Gramática

■ Expressing opinions and preferences

- To express an opinion use **me / te / le / nos / os / les parece(n)** + **adjective / adverb**

  The verb *parecer* (to appear, seem) works in the same way as *gustar*.

  ¿Qué te / le parece la música clásica? (What do you think of classical music? Literally, 'how does classical music appear to you?')

  La música clásica me parece interesante. (I think classical music is interesting.)

Tu trabajo no nos parece bien. (We don't think much of your work.)

- To express preference you can use either **gustar** followed by **más** or the verb **preferir** (to prefer):

  ¿Qué te / le gusta más el invierno o el verano? (Which do you like more: winter or summer?)

  Me gusta más el verano. (I like summer more.)

  ¿Qué prefiere(s) el invierno o el verano? (which do you prefer winter or summer?)

  Prefiero el verano. (I prefer summer.)

A Link up the following:

- ¿Qué te / le parecen los cómics?
- Me gustan mucho, me parecen divertidos.

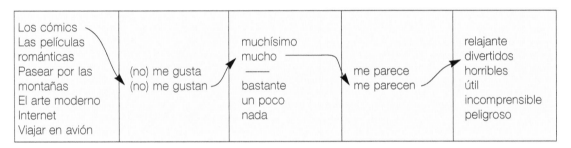

B Ask your partner the following questions:

1 ¿Qué te gusta más venir a clase por la mañana o por la tarde?
2 ¿Qué prefieres las ciudades grandes o las ciudades pequeñas?
3 ¿Qué te gusta más el cine o la televisión?
4 ¿Qué le gustan más los colores claros o los colores oscuros?
5 ¿Qué prefieres hacer deporte o ver deporte?

Consolidation

A Write three things or activities *que te gustan mucho* and three *que no te gustan nada* and justify your opinions.

- ■ Me gusta mucho ver vídeos. Me parece relajante.
- ■ No me gustan nada las serpientes. Me parecen peligrosas.

B Now, compare your likes and dislikes with those of your partner and tell the group about your findings.

– *A Laura y a mí nos gusta mucho ver vídeos. Nos parece relajante. A Laura le gustan las serpientes pero a mí no, a ella le parecen bonitas pero a mí me parecen peligrosas.*

In class or at home

A Complete the following sentences with *gusta, gustan* or *interesa, interesan*.

1 A mí, _____ los perros mucho pero no _____ los gatos. (gustar)
2 ¿A ti _____ el golf? A mí no _____ nada. (gustar)
3 ¿A Luisa _____ los idiomas? (interesar)
4 A Pablo y a mí, _____ la arqueología pero a Pepe no _____ mucho. (interesar)
5 A vosotros, ¿_____ el cine latinoamericano? (gustar)
6 No _____ nada correr. (gustar / nosotros)
7 No _____ sus ideas. (interesar / yo).
8 ¿A ellas, _____ las matemáticas? (interesar)
9 _____ salir por la noche. (gustar / nosotros)
10 ¿A ustedes _____ el piso? (gustar)
11 A su madre no _____ la ópera. (gustar)
12 A la profesora _____ la gramática. (interesar)

B Read the text and complete it with the correct parts of *gustar, parecer* or *preferir*.

¡Qué diferentes somos!

A mi marido y a mí no nos gustan las mismas cosas. A mí _____ mucho ir al cine, _____ todas las películas, especialmente las románticas pero a mi marido no _____ ir al cine, él _____ ver películas en la televisión. También _____ muchísimo hacer deporte, _____ la natación, el tenis y el baloncesto pero a mi marido no _____ nada hacer deporte, _____ aburrido y cansado. A mí _____ consultar Internet porque _____ útil pero a mi marido, Internet no le _____ nada. Él _____ consultar libros. A mí _____ mandar correos electrónicos a mis amigos pero mi marido _____ escribir cartas.

C Read the information below and complete the dialogues.

Nombre: Natalia
Le gusta: ver la televisión, el rugby, salir de copas
No le gusta: leer, la música clásica

Nombre: Lionel
Le gusta: ver la televisión, el béisbol, leer
No le gusta: el rugby, el cine, el rock

Nombre: Emilia
Le gusta: leer, el cine, la música clásica
No le gusta: el rock, ver la televisión, el rugby

Example: Lionel: ¿Te gusta ver la televisión?
Natalia: Sí, ¿y a ti?
Lionel: A mí también.

1
Lionel: ¿Te gusta ver la televisión?
Emilia: No, ¿y a ti?
Lionel: _____

2
Natalia: ¿Te gusta leer?
Lionel: _____
Natalia: _____

3
Emilia: ¿Te gusta leer?
Lionel: _____
Emilia: _____

4
Emilia: ¿Te gusta la música clásica?
Natalia: _____
Emilia: _____

5
Natalia: ¿Te gusta el rugby?
Emilia: _____
Natalia: _____

De viaje
Travelling

<table>
<tr><td>■ **Expresiones Esenciales**</td><td>■ **Essential Expressions**</td></tr>
<tr><td>¿Viaja(s) a menudo?</td><td>*Do you travel often?*</td></tr>
<tr><td>¿Le / Te gusta viajar?</td><td>*Do you like travelling?*</td></tr>
<tr><td>¿Ha(s) estado alguna vez en . . . ?</td><td>*Have you ever stayed in / been to . . . ?*</td></tr>
<tr><td>¿Ha(s) ido alguna vez a . . . ?</td><td>*Have you ever been to . . . ?*</td></tr>
<tr><td>Sí, una vez / muchas veces / nunca</td><td>*Yes, once / many times / never*</td></tr>
<tr><td>No, nunca, pero me gustaría</td><td>*No, but I'd like to*</td></tr>
<tr><td>¿Le / Te gustaría ir a . . . / viajar en . . . ?</td><td>*Would you like to / go to . . . / travel in . . . ?*</td></tr>
<tr><td>Sí, me gustaría mucho</td><td>*Yes, I'd really like to*</td></tr>
<tr><td>No, no me gustaría</td><td>*No, I wouldn't like to*</td></tr>
</table>

 Talking about travelling

A Read this questionnaire about holiday travel and tick the responses which apply to you.

Encuesta: viajar durante las vacaciones

	Tú		Tu compañero(a)		Sra Mascato	
¿Viaja a menudo?	sí	☐	sí	☐	sí	☐
	no mucho	☐	no mucho	☐	no mucho	☐
	no	☐	no	☐	no	☐
¿Le gusta viajar . . . ?	solo(a)	☐	solo(a)	☐	solo(a)	☐
	con la familia	☐	con la familia	☐	con la familia	☐
	con amigos	☐	con amigos	☐	con amigos	☐
¿Le gusta viajar . . . ?	en coche	☐	en coche	☐	en coche	☐
	en tren	☐	en tren	☐	en tren	☐
	en avión	☐	en avión	☐	en avión	☐
	en barco	☐	en barco	☐	en barco	☐
¿Le gusta viajar por . . . ?	países exóticos	☐	países exóticos	☐	países exóticos	☐
	países cercanos	☐	países cercanos	☐	países cercanos	☐
	su país	☐	su país	☐	su país	☐
¿Prefiere . . . ?	la playa	☐	la playa	☐	la playa	☐
	la montaña	☐	la montaña	☐	la montaña	☐
	el campo	☐	el campo	☐	el campo	☐
	la ciudad	☐	la ciudad	☐	la ciudad	☐
¿Prefiere alojarse en . . . ?	hoteles	☐	hoteles	☐	hoteles	☐
	campings	☐	campings	☐	campings	☐
	apartamentos	☐	apartamentos	☐	apartamentos	☐
¿Viaja porque le interesa . . . ?	la naturaleza	☐	la naturaleza	☐	la naturaleza	☐
	otras culturas	☐	otras culturas	☐	otras culturas	☐
	museos y monumentos	☐	museos y monumentos	☐	museos y monumentos	☐

Gustos y otras cosas

¿Le gusta viajar en . . . ?	verano	☐	verano	☐	verano	☐
	primavera	☐	primavera	☐	primavera	☐
	otoño	☐	otoño	☐	otoño	☐
	invierno	☐	invierno	☐	invierno	☐
¿Le gustan los viajes organizados?	sí	☐	sí	☐	sí	☐
	no	☐	no	☐	no	☐

B Now compare your answers with your partner's and give a brief summary to the rest of the group of the main differences between your partner and you.

■ Melanie prefiere ir a la montaña pero yo prefiero ir a la playa.

■ A Paul le gusta viajar solo pero a mí me gusta viajar con amigos.

C  Now listen as señora Mascato answers this questionnaire and tick the answers she gives.

2 Say what you have done or have not done

A Read the following mini-dialogue and then find out if people in your group have done some of the following.

– ¿Has estado alguna vez en Cuba?
– Sí, yo he estado una vez.
– No, yo no he estado nunca.
– Pues, yo he estado muchas veces.

1 ¿Has estado alguna vez en Alaska?
2 ¿Has estado alguna vez en Sudamérica? ¿Dónde?
3 ¿Has viajado alguna vez en barco? ¿Adónde has ido?
4 ¿Has subido alguna vez una montaña? ¿Cuál?
5 ¿Has ido alguna vez en helicóptero?

B Think about three special things you have done and find people in your group who have also done some of them. Then present your findings to the group.

Example: Mary y yo hemos estado en Japón varias veces pero nadie ha ido a China.

G de Gramática

■ **The perfect tense**

• The perfect tense can be used to refer to past events without specifying a time:
¿Habéis ido alguna vez a Bogotá? (Have you ever been to Bogotá?)
Sí, yo he ido muchas veces. (Yes, I've been lots of times.)
Pues, yo no he ido nunca. (Well, I've never been.)

• Very often expressions of frequency are used:
muchas veces (lots of times);
varias veces (a few times);
alguna vez (some time; ever);
cuatro veces (four times);
una vez (once);
casi nunca (hardly ever);
nunca (never)

De viaje

191

3 Means of transport

<u>A</u> Try to recall all the types of transport that you already know in Spanish.

<u>B</u> Read the following list of vehicles. First write the definite article next to each of them and then match them to the picture.

autocar
autobús
avión
barco
bicicleta
camión
coche
globo
helicóptero
motocicleta
metro
camión cisterna
tren

<u>C</u> Tell your partner which means of transport you prefer and why.

Example: Para desplazarme por la ciudad prefiero el metro
porque es muy rápido.
Para desplazarme por la ciudad prefiero el autobús.
No es muy cómodo pero es barato.

1 Para hacer viajes cortos . . .
2 Para hacer viajes largos . . .
3 Para desplazarme por mi pueblo / por la ciudad . . .
4 Para llevar objetos grandes de un lugar a otro . . .
5 Para ir a trabajar . . .
6 Para . . .

<u>D</u> Read the text below and then classify the vehicles from Ex. A under the following headings:

Transporte terrestre; Transporte marítimo; Transporte aéreo

En la actualidad existe una gran diversidad de medios de transporte, capaces de recorrer la superficie de la tierra, surcar los aires, desplazarse por el agua, e incluso salir al espacio exterior.

Los medios de transporte se clasifican según la vía de comunicación que utilizan para desplazarse. Así distinguimos: el transporte terrestre, el transporte marítimo y el transporte aéreo.

Gustos y otras cosas

unidad 6

4 Transport infrastructure

A Match the phrases in the left-hand column with those on the right.

1 los coches circulan por   **a** los puertos
2 los aviones despegan de   **b** las estaciones
3 los barcos llegan a   **c** las carreteras
4 los trenes salen de   **d** los aeropuertos

B Read the text below and then say if the following statements are *verdaderos* or *falsos*.

1 Las personas tienen acceso a las autopistas.
2 Las bicicletas circulan por las carreteras pero no circulan por las autopistas.
3 Los trenes circulan por las vías férreas.
4 La mercancía de un barco se descarga en los puertos.
5 Los aeropuertos están en el centro de las ciudades.

Infraestructuras

Para que los vehículos de transporte puedan desplazarse de un lugar a otro necesitan infraestructuras. Cada sistema de transporte utiliza infraestructuras propias.

Transporte terrestre

Para el transporte terrestre se utilizan vías urbanas o interurbanas, que permiten que los vehículos circulen con seguridad. Las vías interurbanas son las carreteras, las autovías y las autopistas.

A diferencia de las carreteras, el trazado de autopistas y autovías se hace de manera que las curvas y las pendientes se salvan con facilidad. El acceso de personas o animales está prohibido para evitar las posibilidad de accidentes. Y además tienen un número determinado de entradas y salidas.

La circulación de trenes requiere la construcción del tendido ferroviario (vías férreas). Por otra parte, la carga y descarga de mercancías y pasajeros exige la construcción de estaciones.

Transporte marítimo

Los barcos no necesitan la construcción de vías de navegación pero necesitan instalaciones para carga y descarga de mercancía y pasajeros. Estas instalaciones se conocen con el nombre de puertos.

Transporte aéreo

Los aviones necesitan aterrizar y despegar en instalaciones específicas conocidas como aeropuertos. Suelen situarse a las afueras de las grandes ciudades por la gran superficie que necesitan para sus pistas y por el ruido que producen los motores de los aviones. Las terminales de los aeropuertos disponen de servicios para el transporte de mercancías y pasajeros.

Source: Tecnología ESO1er vido, Rodeira Group Edebé (adapted)

C Imagine you have to go from Barcelona to Málaga. Discuss with your partner the pros and cons of the different means of getting there and say which you prefer.

De viaje

5 **Saying what you would or wouldn't like to do**

■ ¿Has estado alguna
vez en Colombia?

■ ¿Te gustaría pasar estas
vacaciones en Madrid?

■ No, pero me
gustaría ir.

■ No, no me gustaría, no me
gustan las ciudades grandes.

G de Gramática

■ Saying what you would or would not like to do

What one would or would not like to do is expressed by the construction: **indirect object
pronoun** + *gustaría* + **(infinitive):**

¿Te gustaría venir de vacaciones con nosotros? (Would you like to come on holiday with us?)

Sí, mucho. (Yes, very much.)

¿Has estado alguna vez en Cuba? (Have you ever been to Cuba?)

No, pero me gustaría ir. (No, but I'd like to go.)

No me gustaría tener que ir en avión. (I wouldn't like to have to fly.)

The form *gustaría* is the conditional tense of *gustar*. You will study this tense at a later stage.

A First write the verbs in brackets in the appropriate form of the perfect tense.
Then link each question to its answer.

1 ¿_____ (estar / tus padres)
alguna vez en Perú?

2 ¿_____ (visitar / ustedes) algún
museo español?

3 ¿_____ (hacer / tú) alguna vez
paracaidismo?

4 ¿_____(fumar / tú) alguna vez?

5 ¿_____ (probar / usted) el
tequila?

6 ¿_____ (escribir / tú) alguna
poesía?

7 ¿_____ (correr / tú) alguna vez
en un maratón?

8 ¿_____ (ir / vosotros) a
Centroamérica?

a No, pero no me gustaría; no me gusta
correr.

b Sí una vez, pero no me gustaría volver
a tomarlo; es muy fuerte.

c No, nunca; me gustaría pero me parece
difícil.

d No, y no me gustaría; me parece un
deporte peligroso.

e No, pero les gustaría ir.

f No, nunca, pero nos gustaría mucho.

g No, nunca, y no me gustaría hacerlo
porque es malo para la salud.

h Sí, una vez, pero nos gustaría volver.

B Now ask your partner the questions in Ex.A.

C In groups of four, try to organise a week's holiday which accommodates everybody's wishes.

> **Example:** A mí me gustaría ir a la playa porque me gusta nadar.
> Pues a mí me gustaría ir a la montaña.
> Podemos ir tres o cuatro días a la playa y el resto a la
> montaña. ¿Qué os parece?

Consolidation

A Complete the following information.

1 Los pasajeros de un avión llegan a _____ de los aeropuertos.
2 Los pasajeros de un tren toman el tren en _____.
3 Los coches circulan por _____, _____, _____.
4 Los barcos salen de _____.

B Think of three holiday activities and ask your partner if he/she has ever done them.

C Complete the sentences, following the model.

> **Example:** Me gustan las capitales grandes. *Me gustaría ir a México D. F.*
> No nos gustan los barcos. *No nos gustaría hacer un crucero.*

1 Me gustan los países exóticos. _____
2 No nos gusta el campo. _____
3 No me gusta tomar el sol. _____
4 Nos gustan las grandes montañas. _____
5 Me gusta viajar. _____

In class or at home

A Read the text in which la señora Mascato talks about how she likes to travel. Then rewrite the text in the third person. Your text should start: *A la señora Mascato le gusta viajar mucho y . . .*

A mí me gusta viajar mucho y viajo a menudo. Me gusta viajar con mis amigos. Siempre que puedo, viajo en avión. Viajo porque me interesan otras culturas. Me gusta ir a países exóticos. Me encanta visitar ciudades. La verdad es que prefiero las ciudades al campo. Siempre me alojo en hoteles y nunca he viajado en viajes organizados. Mi estación preferida para viajar es el otoño porque hay menos gente.

B Write the questions which correspond to the following answers.

1 No, no he viajado nunca por Argentina.
2 No, nunca hemos ido en globo.
3 Sí, Paco y María han estado una vez en Costa Rica.
4 No, no he viajado nunca en avión.
5 No, no hemos visitado nunca el Museo Picasso de Barcelona.
6 Sí, los señores Baltar han ido una vez a España.

C Organise your next holiday. Write sentences, following the model.

> **Example:** marido / otras culturas / visitar Europa
> A mí marido le gustan otras culturas. Le gustaría visitar Europa.

1 Yo / el sol / ir a la playa
2 Mi hija / salir de noche / ir a un lugar turístico
3 Mi hijo / aventura / ir a un país exótico
4 Mis padres / tranquilidad / ir a un hotel de lujo
5 Mis mejores amigos / la montaña / vistar los Pirineos en España

De viaje

195

Acércate al mundo del español

A Here are some of the findings of a survey, carried out by the Spanish newspaper *El Mundo,* about the typical Spaniard. Read it out loud and then answer the questions below.

¿Es usted el típico español medio?

Por Silvia Nieto

Edad. Es treintañero por los pelos. El español medio tiene 38,8 años (40,1 las mujeres y 37,4 los hombres).

Tiempo libre. Primero la familia, la tele, y despúes los amigos.

Teleadicto. Y desde pequeñito. El español medio pasa delante del televisor el 70% de su tiempo libre. Para ser más concretos, dedica 1.250 horas anuales a ver la televisión, frente a las cuatro que pasa en el cine o las 17 que le concede al visionado de vídeos.

Ordenadores e Internet. El 64% no usa jamás un PC y un 75% no ha visto Internet ni en pintura.

Vacaciones. 27, 7 días de vacaciones al año tiene el estresado habitante de un país cuya fuente principal de ingresos es el turismo. El 72% los toma todos juntos y el 71% fuera de su residencia (pero, eso sí, en un lugar fijo, preferentemente junto al mar).

Viajes. Al español medio le gusta mucho viajar (66%), lo hace siempre que puede y con la familia y amigos antes que solo. Es alérgico a los viajes organizados (un 72% opta por organizarse a su manera) y, en vacaciones, prefiere estar tranquilo y "no hacer nada" (55%). Eso sí: si hay fiesta en el pueblo, no lo duda: a un 66% le gustan las fiestas y bailes populares.

Deportes. El 60% de los adultos no practica actividades físicas que alcancen el mínimo recomendado, y uno de cada cuatro, sobre todo las mujeres, no realiza actividad física de ningún tipo.

Source,
htt://www.elmundo.es/magazine/2003/172 104221322.html (Adapted)

B Say if the following statements are *verdaderas* or *falsas*. If false, give the right answer.

El español medio:

1 Pasa mucho tiempo con la familia.
2 Es activo y ve poco la televisión.
3 Va a menudo al cine.
4 No le interesa Internet.
5 Reparte las vacaciones a lo largo del año.
6 Le gusta pasar sus vacaciones en distintos lugares cada año.
7 Le gusta la playa.
8 Le encantan los viajes organizados y las vacaciones activas.
9 Casi no practica deporte.

C Compare the typical person of your country with the typical Spaniard.

Example: La gente de mi país practica más deporte que los españoles.

Essential vocabulary

Actividades del tiempo libre / *Leisure activities*

estar con la familia	*to spend time with family*
estar con amigos/as	*to spend time with friends*
escuchar música	*to listen to music*
hacer deporte	*to do sport*
hacer yoga	*to do yoga*
hacer trabajos manuales	*to do crafts*
ir a bailar	*to go dancing*
ir al teatro	*to go to the theatre*
ir al cine	*to go to the cinema*
ir de compras	*to go shopping*
ir de paseo	*to go for a stroll*
ir de camping	*to go camping*
ir de copas	*to go out for a drink*
ir de excursión	*to go on an excursion*
navegar por internet	*to surf the net*
leer	*to read*
oír la radio	*to listen to the radio*
salir con amigos	*to go out with friends*
ver deporte	*to watch sport*
ver la televisión	*to watch television*
ver un vídeo	*to watch a video*
soler	*to usually . . .*

Expresiones temporales / *Time expressions*

el año / mes próximo / la semana próxima / que viene	*next / coming year / month / week . . .*
luego / más tarde	*later*
dentro de una semana / un mes / año	*in a week's / month's / year's time*

Cuantificadores / *Quantifiers*

todos/as los/las	*every . . .*
casi todos/as los/las	*almost every . . .*
casi nunca	*almost never / hardly ever*
casi ningún/ninguna	*almost no . . . / hardly any*
la mayoría de los/las	*most . . .*
muchas veces	*many times*
algunos/as	*some . . .*
no muchos/as	*not many*
pocos/as	*few*
pocas veces	*few times / rarely*
muy pocos/as	*very few*
ningún/ninguna	*none*

Las estaciones del año / *Seasons of the year*

otoño (m)	*Autumn*
invierno (m)	*Winter*
primavera (f)	*Spring*
verano (m)	*Summer*

El tiempo / *The weather*

clima (m)	*climate*
grados (m)	*degrees*
llueve	*it's raining / it rains*
nieva	*it's snowing / it snows*
hace calor (m)	*it's hot*
sol (m)	*sun*
frío (m)	*cold*
viento (m)	*wind*
lluvia (f)	*rain*
nieve (f)	*snow*
niebla (f)	*fog, mist*
nubes (f)	*clouds*

Verbos para expresar gustos, desagrado, preferencias e intereses / *Verbs to express likes, dislikes, preferences and interests*

gustar	*to like*
agradar	*to please*
apetecer	*to fancy*
encantar	*to love, to enjoy*
interesar	*to interest*
preferir	*to prefer*
desagradar	*to dislike*
horrorizar	*to hate / not to be able to stand*

Medios de transporte / *Means of transport*

autocar (m)	*coach*
avión (m)	*plane*
barco (m)	*boat, ship*
camión (m)	*lorry, truck*
globo (m)	*balloon*
helicóptero (m)	*helicopter*
petrolero (m)	*oil tanker*

Transporte / *Transport*

puerto (m)	*harbour, port*
carretera (f)	*road*
autovía (f)	*dual carriageway*
autopista (f)	*motorway*
pasajero/a	*passenger*
terminal (f)	*terminal*
pista (f)	*runway*
mercancía (f)	*goods*

Expresiones útiles / *Useful expressions*

pues	*well*
pero	*but*
también	*too*
tampoco	*neither*

Cuéntame qué pasó

 A ¿Qué hiciste?

What did you do?

■ **Expresiones esenciales**	■ **Essential expressions**
¿Qué hiciste / hizo ayer?	*What did you do yesterday?*
Me levanté / desayuné / trabajé	*I got up / had breakfast / worked*
Ayer por la tarde ¿jugaste / jugó al tenis?	*Did you play tennis yesterday afternoon?*
Yo también / Yo tampoco	*So did I / Neither did I*
Yo no / Yo sí	*I don't / (didn't) / I do / (did)*

1 **Referring to daily routine in the past**

A Look at the following verbs, make sure you know their meaning, then classify them according to their conjugation.

acostarse	asistir	cenar	comer	decidir
encontrarse	hablar	regresar	levantarse	empezar
tomar	trabajar			

First conjugation: acostarse . . .
Second conjugation: comer . . .
Third conjugation: asistir . . .

B Read the following extract about what Inés did yesterday and underline all the finite verbs in the text.

Ayer me levanté tarde, por eso tomé un taxi para llegar al trabajo a tiempo. Trabajé toda la mañana y a la hora de comer, comí con mi amiga Luisa. Después de comer regresé a la oficina, asistí a una reunión, empecé a escribir unos documentos y a las ocho de la tarde decidí ir al gimnasio. A la salida del gimnasio me encontré con Paco, hablamos un rato y después regresé a casa, cené y a las once de la noche me acosté.

C Read the text again and link the infinitives listed in Ex. A to the conjugated forms that appear in the text.

Example: acostarse – me acosté

D Now read the grammar section below.

G de Gramática

■ Preterite tense

The preterite is generally rendered in English by the simple past tense: 'I got up'; 'I worked'. In Spanish, as in English, it expresses a completed past action viewed as over and done with.

■ Formation of the preterite

Regular verbs

	hablar (*to speak*)	comer (*to eat*)	decidir (*to decide*)	levantarse (reflexive) (*to get up*)
yo	habl**é**	com**í**	decid**í**	**me** levant**é**
tú	habl**aste**	com**iste**	decid**iste**	**te** levant**aste**
usted	habl**ó**	com**ió**	decid**ió**	**se** levant**ó**
él / ella	habl**ó**	com**ió**	decid**ió**	**se** levant**ó**
nosotros(as)	habl**amos**	com**imos**	decid**imos**	**nos** levant**amos**
vosotros(as)	habl**asteis**	com**isteis**	decid**isteis**	**os** levant**asteis**
ustedes	habl**aron**	com**ieron**	decid**ieron**	**se** levant**aron**
ellos(as)	habl**aron**	com**ieron**	decid**ieron**	**se** levant**aron**

- Note that the endings for *-er* and *-ir* verbs are the same.
- Note that the first and third persons singular have a written accent so that the stress is shifted to the end of the word.
- The first-person plural of *-ar* and *-ir* verbs is identical to the present tense forms. Context normally helps to determine the meaning:
  Ayer hablamos con tu jefe. (Yesterday we spoke to your boss.)
  Hoy hablamos con tu jefe. (Today we're speaking to your boss.)

■ Usage

- **To indicate an event which is past and complete**
  Ayer me levanté tarde. (Yesterday I got up late.)
  El otro día Juan y Lupita vendieron su piso. (The other day Juan and Lupita sold their flat.)
  Some common adverbial phrases that accompany the preterite are:

ayer	(yesterday)
anteayer	(the day before yesterday)
anoche	(last night)

el otro día	(the other day)
hace dos días, años	(two days / years ago)
la semana pasada	(last week)
el año pasado	(last year)
durante tres siglos	(for three centuries)
en 1936	(in 1936)

- **For narrative events or a series of events that follow one another**
  Regresé a casa, cené y a las once de la noche me acosté. (I went home, had dinner and at eleven o'clock went to bed.)

- **To indicate the beginning of a state or action**
  Empecé a escribir unos documentos. (I started to write some documents.)
  Mi padre empezó a cantar ópera a los seis años. (My father started to sing opera at the age of six.)
  Mi hermana pequeña caminó a los diez meses. (My little sister started walking at ten months.)

E Look again at the diary extract in Ex.B and answer the following questions:

1 ¿Qué empezó a hacer por la tarde?
2 Inés, ¿comió sola?
3 ¿Por qué tomó Inés un taxi por la mañana?
4 ¿Cuándo y dónde se encontró con Paco?
5 ¿Dónde cenó?

F Rewrite the text in the third person singular: *Ayer Inés se levantó tarde, por eso ...*

2 What did you do yesterday?

A *¿Qué hiciste ayer?* Did you do any of the things listed below? Say in Spanish what you did.

Levantarse pronto   Practicar yoga
Desayunar en casa   Cenar con los amigos
Asistir a clase   Estudiar
Trabajar   Leer
Jugar al tenis   Acostarse tarde

B Some of the verbs listed above (*jugar*, *practicar* and *leer*) undergo some spelling changes in the preterite. This is to maintain a consistent sound in their pronunciation. Read the grammar section below to find out how to write them.

G de Gramática

■ **Spelling changes in the Preterite**

Verbs that undergo a spelling change in the first person singular
- Verbs ending in:
  -gar: jugar (to play); **llegar** (to arrive) change **g** to **gu**   **yo jugué** (but *tú jugaste* etc.)
  -car: buscar (to look for); **practicar** (to practise), change **c** to **qu**   **yo busqué** (but *tú buscaste* etc.)
  -zar: almorzar (to have lunch); **empezar** (to start), change **z** to **c**   **yo almorcé** (but *tú almorzaste* etc.)
  before **é** in the first-person singular of the preterite.

Verbs that undergo an spelling change in the third person: *i > y*
- Verbs whose stem ends in a strong vowel change the unstressed *i* of the preterite ending to **y** in the second (polite) and the third person singular and plural of the preterite.
  leer (to read) = *usted / él / ella leyó   ustedes / ellos(as) leyeron*
  oír (to hear) = *usted / él / ella oyó   ustedes / ellos(as) oyeron*

C Read the mini-dialogues and ask your partner if he/she did any of the things listed in Ex.A.
  – *¿Te levantaste pronto ayer?*
  – *Sí, me levanté a las siete, ¿y tú?*
  – *Yo también.*
  – *Pues yo no, yo me levanté a las diez.*

D  Listen to Gabriel, Lola and Roberto talking about what they did yesterday and complete the chart. Check your answers with your partner. Note that *¿Qué hizo ...?* means 'What did he/she do ...?'

	Gabriel	Lola	Roberto
1 ¿A qué hora se levantó?			
2 ¿Dónde desayunó?			
3 ¿Qué hizo por la mañana?			
4 ¿Dónde comió?			
5 ¿Con quién?			
6 ¿Qué hizo por la tarde?			
7 ¿Qué hizo a las nueve de la noche?			
8 ¿A qué hora se acostó?			
9 ¿A qué se dedica?			

Practising the preterite

A Read the grammar section about the preterite of radical-changing verbs and then do Ex.B and C.

B Let's conjugate. Your tutor chooses student A to start conjugating one of the verbs in the table, e.g. *aparcar, yo*. Student A conjugates it and then chooses another verb, e.g. *cerrar, ellas,* for student B to conjugate, and so on.

G de Gramática

■ Preterite of radical-changing verbs

- *-ar* and *-er* verbs which change their stems in the present indicative are regular in the preterite.

  *Ayer ce**rré** tarde pero hoy ci**e**rro temprano.* (Yesterday I closed late but today I'm closing early.)
  *La semana pasada Paco v**o**lvió sin dinero pero hoy v**ue**lve con él.* (Last week Paco came back without money but today he's coming back with it.)

- *-ir* radical-changing verbs change *e* to *i* or *o* to *u* in the third person singular and plural in the preterite.
  vestirse *(me vestí, te vestiste, se v**i**stió, nos vestimos, os vestisteis, se v**i**stieron)*

  dormir *(dormí, dormiste, d**u**rmió, dormimos, dormisteis, d**u**rmieron)*

  *El otro día mi amigo me p**i**dió ayuda.* (The other day my friend asked me for help.)
  *Ayer los niños d**u**rmieron muy bien.* (Yesterday the children slept very well.)

		Preterite		
	Infinitive	-ar	-er	-ir
yo	llegar / comer / partir			
tú	estudiar / / beber / vivir			
usted / él / ella	hablar / leer / vestirse			
nosotros(as)	jugar / entender / recibir			
vosotros(as)	comprar / vender / salir			
ustedes / ellos / ellas	cerrar / aprender / divertirse			

<u>C</u> Write the verbs in brackets in the preterite and answer the questions, following the model. Use the first verb for your answer in each case.

Example: Question: *¿Se lo pediste* (pedir, tú) *o se lo cogiste* (coger, tú)?
Answer: *Se lo pedí.*

1 ¿ _____ (divertirse, vosotros) u _____ (aburrirse, vosotros) en la fiesta?

2 ¿Cómo _____ (dormir) el niño bien o mal?

3 ¿Le_____ (pedir, tú) el ordenador o te lo _____ (regalar) él?

4 ¿ _____ (repetir, ella) el ejercicio o lo _____ (entregar) sin cambiar?

5 ¿_____ (vestirse, ella) de rojo o de azul?

6 ¿_____ (seguir, vosotros) despiertos u _____ (dormirse, vosotros)?

Consolidation

<u>A</u> Work with a partner. Complete the following dialogues, putting the verbs given into the preterite. Then practise the dialogues.

1 – *¿A qué hora _____ a casa anoche? (llegar, vosotros)*
Yo _____ a las nueve y Carlos _____ a las once y media.

2 – *Oye, la semana pasada ¿_____ la cuenta del teléfono? (pagar, tú)*
Sí, sí claro, la _____ el martes pasado.

3 – *Sr. Romero, el mes pasado _____ su documentación, ¿verdad? (entregar)*
Sí, _____ todos los papeles el día ocho.

4 – *¿Qué tal el partido de ayer?*
Muy bien, _____ cinco goles (meter, nosotros).

5 – *¿_____ mucho ayer? (estudiar, vosotros)*
No mucho, unas dos horas.

<u>B</u> Think of four activities that you did yesterday such as *trabajar, estudiar, comer en un restaurante, practicar un deporte*, then ask your partner if he/she did them, too. Use the mini-dialogues as models.

– *Ayer por la tarde, ¿jugaste al tenis?*
– *Sí, ¿y tú? / No, ¿y tú?*
– *Yo también. / Yo tampoco.*

– *Ayer por la tarde, ¿estudiaste español?*
– *Sí, ¿y tú? / No, ¿y tú?*
– *Yo no. / Yo sí.*

In class or at home

A Change the verbs of the following sentences from the present tense to the preterite:

1 Pedro y Elena viven en Buenos Aires.
2 Las tiendas cierran a las cinco pero esta tienda no cierra hasta las diez de la noche.
3 Paco llega a las diez y yo llego a la una.
4 Usted gana mucho dinero.
5 Los niños juegan al baloncesto en el colegio.
6 ¿Entiendes el problema?
7 Llegáis a tiempo para comer.
8 Compramos los regalos.
9 Julio se viste rápidamente.
10 Realizo mis sueños.

B First rewrite the verbs in the sentences below in the preterite and then replace the words in bold (direct objects) with the correct direct object pronouns.

Example: Compro **el pan**.
Compré el pan.
Lo compré.

1 Cierro **las puertas**.
2 Visitamos **a Pedro**.
3 Comprendemos **la lección**.
4 Pablo y Margarita pintan **el piso**.
5 Buscáis **a vuestras amigas**.
6 Los estudiantes ganan **el partido**.
7 Elimináis **los insectos**.
8 Saludan **a su profesora**.
9 Usted firma **el acuerdo**.
10 Compráis **la casa**.

C Rewrite the verbs in the following sentences in the preterite. Then replace the words in bold (indirect objects) with the correct indirect object pronouns and the words in italics (direct objects) with the correct direct object pronouns. Follow the example given.

Example: Envío *el telegrama* **a su padre**.
Envié *el telegrama* **a su padre**.
Le envié *el telegrama*.
Se *lo* envié.

1 Entrego *los deberes* **a los estudiantes**.
2 Explican *el asunto* **al ministro**.
3 Regalamos *un vestido* **a nuestra prima**.
4 Mandan *un paquete* **a mí**.
5 Escribo *una carta* **a mis tías**.
6 El jefe paga **a vosotros** *la cena*.
7 Prestan *dinero* **a ti**.
8 Usted compra *lotería* **a nosotros**.
9 Mike enseña *inglés* **a ellas**.
10 Arreglo *el coche* **a vosotras**.

D Write the questions which correspond to the following answers:

1 Ayer trabajamos con gente inglesa.
2 El tren llegó a las cinco de la tarde.
3 (El lunes pasado) salí con tu novia.
4 Compré el coche el mes pasado.
5 El avión aterrizó en Roma.
6 Compramos cinco vestidos de verano.
7 La semana pasada vendieron siete pisos.
8 Escogí el sofá azul.
9 (Escogí) el azul.
10 Ayer repasé los pronombres demostrativos.

B ¿Qué tal las vacaciones?

How were your holidays?

■ **Expresiones esenciales**	■ **Essential expressions**
¿Qué hiciste / hizo el verano pasado?	*What did you do last summer?*
¿Adónde fuiste / fue el verano pasado?	*Where did you go last summer?*
Fui a . . .	*I went to . . .*
Estuve en . . .	*I was in . . .*
¿Cuánto tiempo estuviste / estuvo de vacaciones?	*How long were you on holiday for?*
Un mes / 10 días	*A month / 10 days*
¿Con quién pasaste / pasó las vacaciones?	*Who did you spend the holidays with?*
Las pasé con . . .	*I spent them with . . .*
¿Qué tiempo hizo?	*What was the weather like?*
Hizo frío / calor	*It was cold / hot*
¿Cómo lo pasaste / lo pasó?	*What was it like / How was it?*
Bien, mal	*Fine / awful*

Saying what you did yesterday

A Read about what Federico and Susana did yesterday evening.

1 Underline all the verbs that appear in the text and match them with their infinitive forms: *estar; ir; regresar; ver.*

2 Three of the verbs listed are irregular. Identify them and then read the grammar section opposite to find out how to conjugate them.

> Ayer mi mujer y yo fuimos a cenar a un restaurante mexicano. Después de cenar, fuimos al cine. Vimos una película muy divertida. Al terminar la película, fuimos a tomar unas copas, estuvimos un rato en un bar de unos amigos y sobre las doce de la noche regresamos a casa.

B Tell your partner what Federico and Susana did yesterday evening.

C Complete the sentences with one of the verbs below in the appropriate form of the preterite:

estar(2); hacer(2); ir; ser; ver(2); poder(2); querer

1 Carlota, Begoña y yo _____ a Madrid la semana pasada.

2 Lionel _____ en México hace seis meses.

3 Ayer nosotros _____ una película horrible en el cine.

4 Anoche no _____ frío.

5 Tu abuela, ¿_____ la abogada de mi padre?

6 El fin de semana pasado Julián y yo _____ la cena.

7 La semana pasada mi hermana _____ en Londres.

8 Señor Ferrán ¿_____ al director ayer?

9 El año pasado mi familia no _____ ir de vacaciones.

10 Yo _____ arreglar el coche pero no _____.

G de Gramática

■ Irregular forms of the preterite: *dar, ir / ser, ver*

The verbs *dar*, *ir* and *ser* are totally irregular. *Ver* has no accents.

	dar (to give)	ir & ser (to go & to be)	ver (to watch / to see)
yo	di	fui	vi
tú	diste	fuiste	viste
usted	dio	fue	vio
él / ella	dio	fue	vio
nosotros(as)	dimos	fuimos	vimos
vosotros(as)	disteis	fuisteis	visteis
ustedes	dieron	fueron	vieron
ellos(as)	dieron	fueron	vieron

Note that *ser* and *ir* have identical preterite forms; however, there is no confusion as to their meaning because the context makes it clear.

> *Ayer fui al cine.* (Yesterday I went to the cinema.)
>
> *Fui albañil antes de ser arquitecto.* (I was a bricklayer before becoming an architect.)

More irregular forms of the preterite

Most of the other irregular verbs have irregular stems but regular endings:

Infinitive	stem	endings	
estar (*to be*)	estuv-	-e	(yo)
hacer (*to do / to make*)	hic-	-iste	(tú)
poder (*to be able to*)	pud-	-o	(usted/él/ella)
poner (*to put / to set*)	pus-	-imos	(nosotros/(as))
querer (*to want / to love*)	quis-	-isteis	(vosotros/(as))
saber (*to know*)	sup-	-ieron	(ustedes/ellos/(as))
tener (*to have*)	tuv-		
venir (*to come*)	vin-		

Note that the third person of *hacer* is *hizo*.

The preterite of the impersonal *hay* (there is / are) is *hubo* (there was / were).

The preterite of *decir* (to say) is; *dije: dijiste, dijo, dijimos, dijisteis, dij**eron***

D Listen to three people talking about their holidays. Complete the information. *¿Qué hizo / hiciste el verano pasado?*

	Dónde	Cuándo	Duración	Alojamiento	Actividades
Flora					
Ernesto					
Carlos					

E Listen again to the recording in Ex.D and identify who is being addressed as *usted*.

2   How was your weekend?

A Say if you did any of the activities listed last weekend.

- **a** dormir la siesta
- **b** hacer deporte
- **c** hacer yoga
- **d** ir a bailar
- **e** ir al cine
- **f** ir de camping
- **g** ir de compras
- **h** ir de copas
- **i** ir de paseo / pasear
- **j** jugar al baloncesto
- **k** navegar por Internet
- **l** quedarse en casa
- **m** estar con los amigos
- **n** ver la televisión

■ *El sabádo no hice nada pero el domingo fui de excursión.*

B Find out what your partner did last weekend. List three things he/she did and three things he/she didn't do.

C *El cumpleaños del marido de María*. Write sentences about María's husband's birthday party using the preterite tense. Write the missing definite articles and the times in full. The words are given in the right order:

Example: sábado pasado / pasar (nosotros) / noche en casa de María

El sábado pasado pasamos la noche en casa de María.

1 sábado pasado / María / celebrar / cumpleaños de su marido
2 fiesta / comenzar / 7 p.m.
3 marido de María / recibir / muchos regalos
4 invitados / beberse / toda / cerveza
5 padre de María / aburrirse / en / fiesta
6 Yo bailar / todo tiempo
7 Pablo / perder / llaves de coche
8 Pedro y yo / llevar / a Pablo / a su casa / 2 a.m.
9 María / limpiar / casa / por noche antes de acostarse
10 domingo / María / dormir / todo día

3 How were the holidays?

A Read the information and tick the boxes that apply to you.

1 ¿Adónde fuiste el verano pasado?
a la playa ☐   a la montaña ☐ al extranjero ☐   al pueblo ☐
a la ciudad ☐

2 ¿Con quién pasaste las vacaciones?
con la familia ☐   con los amigos ☐   solo(a) ☐

3 ¿Cuándo fuiste de vacaciones?
en junio ☐   en julio ☐   en agosto ☐   en se(p)tiembre ☐

4 ¿Cuánto tiempo estuviste de vacaciones?
10 días ☐   dos semanas ☐   tres semanas ☐   un mes ☐

5 ¿En dónde estuviste?
en un hotel ☐   en un camping ☐   en casa de amigos ☐
en casa de la familia ☐

6 ¿Cómo fuiste?
en coche ☐   en tren ☐   en avión ☐   en barco ☐

7 ¿Qué hiciste?
descansar ☐   nadar ☐   leer ☐   ir a conciertos ☐
hacer excursiones ☐   tomar el sol ☐   salir ☐   ir a fiestas ☐
practicar deporte ☐   pasear ☐   visitar museos ☐

8 ¿Cómo lo pasaste?
Muy bien ☐   bien ☐   normal ☐   regular ☐   mal ☐   muy mal ☐

9 ¿Cómo fueron tus vacaciones?
divertidas ☐   aburridas ☐   activas ☐   tranquilas ☐

10 ¿Qué tiempo hizo?
Hacer frío ☐   hacer calor ☐   llover ☐   nevar ☐

B Rewrite all the possible questions from the previous exercise, using *usted*.

C Now tell your partner about your summer holidays. Take turns.

D Read the postcard and say if the following statements are *verdaderos* or *falsos*. If false, give the correct information.

1 Emilia estuvo en Costa Rica hace unos meses.

2 Estuvo en Costa Rica dos semanas.

3 Viajó con su novio.

4 Costa Rica le pareció preciosa.

5 Emilia va a telefonear a Clara inmediatamente.

Hola Clara:

¿Cómo estás? Yo bien. Acabo de llegar de vacaciones. Estuve en Costa Rica quince días. ¡Qué país tan bonito! Me lo pasé muy bien. Hice muchas excursiones, fui a lugares increíbles. Fui sola pero conocí a gente muy interesante y simpática. Pienso volver el año que viene porque además conocí a un chico simpatiquísimo. . De verdad, Costa Rica me gustó mucho. Te llamo la semana que viene y te cuento. Ahora tengo que irme.

Un abrazo

Emilia

Clara Rosado Agrafojo
c/Río Largo No 21 3D
12301 Sevilla

4 ¿Me he levantado o me levanté?

A Read the following dialogue at the same time as you listen to it.

Julia:	Hola, Álvaro. ¡Cuánto tiempo sin verte! ¿Cómo estás?
Álvaro:	Bien, bien, gracias, ¿y tú?
Julia:	Bien, todavía un poco dormida. Hoy me he levantado a las diez y todavía no me he despertado.
Álvaro:	¡Qué suerte! Yo hoy me he levantado a las siete de la mañana y ayer me levanté a las cinco de la mañana para terminar un trabajo que tengo que entregar mañana.
Julia:	¡Vaya! Oye, ¿tienes tiempo de tomar un café?
Álvaro:	No, lo siento, otro día, es que hoy tengo prisa.
Julia:	No importa. Lo tomamos otro día.

1 Which tenses does Álvaro use in the following expressions? *hoy me he levantado* and *ayer me levanté*?

2 Which of them refers to:

   a an action in the past which is completed, but considered to be in a time frame which is still not finished?

   b an action in the past which is completed, but considered to be in a time frame which has finished?

B With a partner, complete the following dialogues. Write the verbs either in the preterite or perfect tense.

1 – Esta mañana le he comprado un regalo a Sofía.

   – Yo lo _____ ayer.

2 – ¿ _____ al tenis hoy por la mañana?

   – No, hoy no hemos jugado. _____ ayer por la tarde.

3 – Este mes he gastado mucho dinero.

   – Pues yo, este mes no, pero el mes pasado _____ muchísimo.

4 – ¿Has encontrado el libro?

   – Sí, gracias, lo _____ anoche.

5 – ¿Dónde _____ estas vacaciones?

   – Las he pasado en casa de mis padres.

G de Gramática

■ Preterite versus perfect tense

Both tenses refer to past and completed events. However, the perfect tense is used to refer to events or actions that have happened in a period of time that includes the present (*hoy, esta semana, este año* …) and the preterite is used to refer to events or actions in the past that took place in a period of time that is considered finished (*ayer, la semana pasada* …). However, in many regions of the Spanish-speaking world, the preterite is more commonly used than the perfect tense.

Esta semana he ido al médico dos veces. (This week, I've been to the doctor twice.)

but

La semana pasada fui al médico dos veces. (Last week, I went to the doctor twice.)

C Complete the following information. Follow the model.

Example: Esta semana he estado en Italia.
La semana pasada estuve en Italia.

1 Este mes he comido dos veces en este restaurante.
2 Este verano hemos trabajado en Nueva York.
3 Hoy he hablado con tu hermana.
4 ¿Habéis viajado por Nueva Zelanda este invierno?
5 Esta semana ellos han practicado mucho deporte.
6 Usted ¿ha leído el informe esta semana?
7 Este mes no has ganado dinero.
8 Estas vacaciones los niños han dormido mucho.

D Expressing personal feelings. The following expressions are used in the dialogue between Julia and Álvaro (Ex. A).

¡Cuánto tiempo sin verte!
¡Qué suerte!
¡Vaya!
Lo siento; es que . . .
No importa

Say what feelings they express and then use some of them to respond to the following situations:

1 A friend of yours has passed an exam which you still haven't taken.
2 You happen to meet a friend whom you haven't seen for a year.
3 A friend tells you she has just had a minor accident in her car.
4 Your friend asks you to go with him to the cinema, but you cannot go.
5 Your friend apologises for forgetting your birthday.

Saying what had or hadn't happened when something else took place

A Read the grammar section and complete the following sentences with an appropriate form of the verb in brackets:

G de Gramática

■ **Pluperfect tense**

To refer to a past event that had happened before another past event or situation, Spanish and English both use the pluperfect tense.

Formation of the Pluperfect

The Pluperfect is formed with the imperfect tense of *haber* + a past participle:

Habíamos llegado. (We had arrived.)

We will be looking at the imperfect tense in more detail later in this unit. For now, just learn the imperfect endings of *haber*:

Imperfect of *haber* +	Past participle
yo había estudiado	I had studied
tú habías estudiado (informal)	You had studied
usted había estudiado (formal)	You had studied
él/ella había estudiado	He/She had studied
él/ella había estudiado	He/She had studied
nosotros(as) habíamos estudiado	We had studied
vosotros(as) habíais estudiado (informal)	You had studied
ustedes habían estudiado (formal)	They had studied
ellos(as) habían estudiado	They had studied

Note the adverb *ya* (already) often goes before the Pluperfect tense to emphasise the idea that something had already taken place when something else happened. ***Todavía no*** and ***aún no*** (not yet) are often used to indicate that the action had not yet taken place.

Example: Me contó que tú lo *habías* pasado muy bien en Cuba (pasar)

1 Ayer Pedro me dijo que _____ a su novia. (dejar)
2 Cuando empezó a llover nosotros ya _____ a casa.(llegar)
3 Cuando nació mi hijo, aún no _____ a vivir a Chile. (irse, nosotros)
4 Cuando llegué al aeropuerto, el avión todavía no _____. (aterrizar)
5 La semana pasada ya _____ el billete, cuando Juan me llamó. (comprar)

Consolidation

A Work with three or four people and talk about your most recent holiday.

B Think of four places and ask your partner if he/she has been there. Follow the examples.

– ¿Has estado alguna vez en . . .?
– Sí.
– ¿Cuándo?
– Pues estuve allí hace un año.
– ¿Te gustó?
– ¡Oh! Sí, es un lugar precioso . . .

– ¿Has estado alguna vez en . . .?
– No, no he estado nunca. ¿Y tú?
– Yo, sí estuve allí el año pasado
– ¿Te gustó?
– No, mucho. Es un sitio . . .

In class or at home

A Write the questions which correspond to the following answers.

1 El año pasado fui de vacaciones a Argentina.
2 Fui (a Argentina) con mis mejores amigos.
3 Fuimos en enero.
4 Estuvimos tres semanas.
5 Nos alojamos en hoteles.
6 Fuimos en avión.
7 Hicimos muchas cosas: fuimos a fiestas, hicimos excursiones . . .
8 Lo pasamos muy bien.
9 Hizo bastante calor.

B Read the text and write in the missing verbs from the list below, in the preterite. Make sure you understand the meaning of the verbs before you start writing.

ir	hacer(2)	viajar	llover	visitar	tener	venir	pasar
salir	estar	andar	ser	llevar	poder	irse	

Mis amigos Mary y Paul _____ (1) a visitarme el verano pasado a España. _____ (2) en mi casa quince días. Esas dos semanas _____ (3 nosotros) mucho, yo les _____ (4) a muchos sitios interesantes _____ (5 nosotros) museos, parques, iglesias y muchos otros lugares. También _____ (6) tiempo para disfrutar de la playa. El tiempo _____ (7) muy bueno, _____ (8) mucho calor y no _____ (9). _____ (10 nosotros) casi todas las noches y además ellos _____ (11) practicar su español. Después de estar en mi casa ellos _____ (12) unos días de viaje solos. _____ (13 ellos) a la montaña, _____ (14) muchas caminatas, _____ (15) muchos kilómetros. Lo _____ (16 ellos) muy bien.

C Rewrite the verbs in the following sentences in the preterite. Then replace the words in bold and italics with the correct object pronouns. Follow the example.

Example: Os revelan **las fotos** muy pronto.
   Os **las** *revelaron muy pronto.*

1 Explicamos **la situación** *a los vecinos.*
2 Compro **un libro** *a mi amigo.*
3 No te doy **el coche**.
4 Los profesores comunican **el resultado** *a sus padres.*
5 Os envían **la factura** por correo.
6 Sus tíos le prometen **un premio**.
7 Les como **el flan**.
8 Tenemos que pagar **la cuenta**.
9 ¿Te mando **el dinero**?
10 Vais a dar **caramelos** *a los niños.*

D Complete the dialogues. Write the verbs in either the preterite or the perfect tense.

1 – *Esta mañana he recibido las notas de los exámenes.*
   – *Nosotros las _____ ayer.*
2 – *Hoy _____ (nosotros) en casa de Marta.*
   – *Yo estuve la semana pasada.*
3 – *¡Estoy cansadísima! He trabajado muchísimo.*
   – *Pues yo estoy bien, ayer _____ al gimnasio y hoy estoy muy relajado.*
4 – *Luis _____ la traducción hoy por la mañana.*
   – *¿De verdad? Nosotras la _____ la semana pasada.*
5 – *Este año los directores _____ las cosas bien.*
   – *Pues el año pasado las _____ mal.*

E Complete the sentences with the appropriate form of the pluperfect:

1 Llegué pronto pero Javier todavía no _____. (llegar)
2 Cuando apareció Manuel, la cena ya _____. (terminar)
3 Cuando bajamos a la playa, el sol aún no _____. (ocultarse)
4 Elena me comentó que Juana ya _____ problemas en el trabajo antes. (tener)
5 No fui al cine porque ya _____ la película. (ver)

La vida de uno

Your life

■ **Expresiones esenciales**

¿Cuándo naciste / nació?
Nací el . . .
¿Dónde naciste / nació?
Nací en . . .
¿Cuándo empezaste a trabajar?
Empecé . . .
¿Cuándo te casaste / se casó?
Me casé el . . .
¿Cuándo nació tu / su primer hijo?
Paco trabajó en Barcelona desde / de
1995 hasta / a 2002
Empezó a las diez y al cabo de dos
horas terminó
Empezó a las diez y dos horas después
terminó
Por poco me caigo

■ **Essential expressions**

When were you born?
I was born on the . . .
Where were you born?
I was born in . . .
When did you start working?
I started . . .
When did you get married?
I got married on the . . .
When was your first child born?
Paco worked in Barcelona from 1995–2002

He started at ten o'clock and, after two hours,
he finished
He started at ten and two hours later he finished

I nearly fell over

 Finding out about someone's life

A Read the information below and then link the questions in the
column on the left with their answers in the column on the right.

1 ¿Cuándo naciste?
2 ¿Dónde naciste?
3 ¿Viviste siempre en
 Guadalajara?
4 ¿Cuándo empezaste a
 estudiar en la universidad?
5 ¿Estás casado?
6 ¿Cuándo te casaste?
7 ¿Tienes hijos?
8 ¿Cuándo nació tu primer
 hijo?

a Me casé hace cuatro años.
b Sí, tengo dos.
c Nació hace tres años.
d Sí.
e Nací en 1976.
f El año pasado.
g Nací en Guadalajara, México.
h No, viví en Guadalajara los
 primeros ocho años de mi vida,
 después mi familia y yo, nos
 fuimos a vivir a México capital.

B Say if the person being questioned above is a man or a woman.
Give reasons for your answer.

C Ask your partner about his/her life, use Ex.1A as a model, but this
time address your partner using *usted*.

Cuéntame qué pasó

unidad 7

212

D Listen to the recording and choose the right answer.

1
a Elías y Dolores son de Uruguay.
b Elías y Dolores son españoles.
c Elías es argentino y Dolores es uruguaya.

2
a Elías y Dolores viven en Montevideo.
b Elías y Dolores viven en Madrid.
c Elías y Dolores viven en Buenos Aires.

3
a Elías y Dolores llegaron a Madrid en 1995.
b Elías llegó a Madrid en 1995 y Dolores en 1996.

4
a Elías es fotógrafo.
b Elías es periodista.
c Elías es escultor.

5
a Elías tiene novia.
b Elías no tiene novia.

G de Gramática

■ **Years and definite article**

The definite article is not used when the years 1101 to 1999 are written out in full.
Elías y Dolores llegaron a Madrid en 1995

However, the article MUST be used when the first two digits are omitted:
Elías y Dolores llegaron a Madrid en el 95

From the year 2000 the use of the article is optional.
Elías y Dolores llegaron a Madrid en 2000 / en el 2000

2 Locating events in time

A Study the information in the grammar section 'Locating events in time' on p.214.

B Say how long ago things happened. Change the sentences, following the example.

Example: Se fue en 2003 a Australia.
Se fue *hace x años* a Australia.
Hace x años que se fue a Australia.

1 Mike empezó a aprender español en el 2004.
2 En 1999 compramos una casa en la playa.
3 Patricia y Miguel se divorciaron en el 2000.
4 Mi primer nieto nació en 1998.
5 El verano pasado mi marido cambió de trabajo.

■ Locating events in time

	Time expressions	Examples
Para situar los hechos en el pasado Locating events in the past	**hace dos días / semanas / meses** two days / weeks / months ago **en + año / en + tiempo** in + year **a los x años** at the age of x / at x years old	Me casé **hace cuatro años** / Hace cuatro años que me casé I got married 4 years ago. Nací **en 1976** I was born in 1976. Fui a vivir a México **a los ocho años.** At the age of eight I went to live in Mexico.
Para relacionar dos momentos del pasado Linking two moments in the past	**al cabo de x tiempo** at the end of x time **después de x tiempo** after x time	Llegaron en 2000 y, **al cabo de cuatro años** regresaron a su país. They arrived in 2000 and, at the end of four years, they returned to their own country Se casaron en marzo de 2003 y, **después de unos meses / de dos años** se divorciaron. They got married in March 2003 and, after a few months / 2 years they got divorced.
Para representar límites temporales en el pasado Defining time parameters	**desde ... hasta** from ... until **de ... a** from ... to	Vivió en Madrid **desde** los 23 **hasta** los 30 años. He/she lived in Madrid from the age of 23 to 30. Vivió en Madrid **desde** 1941 **hasta** 1945. He/she lived in Madrid from 1941 until 1945. Fue presidente **de** 1960 **a** 1963. He/she was president from 1960 to 1963.
Para referirse al inicio / final de una actividad. Referring to the start / end of an activity	**comenzar a / empezar a** to start / begin to **iniciar** to start / begin **terminar en** to end / finish in	Comenzó a / empezó a pintar **en 1986.** He/she started to paint in 1986. **Inició** sus estudios **el año pasado.** He/she began her / his studies last year. **Terminé** mis estudios **en 1999.** I finished / completed my studies in 1999.
Para presentar un suceso como paralelo a otro en el pasado. Presenting simultaneous / parallel events in the past.	**Cuando** + preterite + phrase When + preterite + phrase Phrase + **cuando** + preterite Phrase + when + preterite	**Cuando** cumplí ocho años, me fui a México capital. When I was eight years old, I left for Mexico City. Me fui a México capital, **cuando** cumplí ocho años. I left for Mexico City when I was eight years old.

C Change the sentences, following the example

Example: Paco trabajó en Barcelona siete años (1995–2002)
Paco trabajó en Barcelona desde 1995 hasta 2002.
Paco trabajó en Barcelona de 1995 a 2002.

1 Carmen representó esta obra de teatro cuatro años (2000–2004).

2 Mis padres vivieron en Cuba dos años (1976–1978).

3 El señor Román fue director de esta compañía durante quince años (1980–1995).

4 Estudié chino durante diez años (1990–2000).

5 Los señores del primer piso vivieron en los Estados Unidos nueve años (1996–2005).

D Change the sentences, following the example. Explain to your partner what happened.

Example: Empecé el examen a las diez y a las doce lo terminé.
Empezó el examen a las diez y *al cabo de dos horas* lo *terminó.*
Empezó el examen a las diez y *dos horas después* lo *terminó.*

1 Mi marido y yo nos conocimos en 1991 y en 1993 nos casamos.
2 Comencé a escribir mi segunda novela el 6 de enero de 2004 y en junio de 2005 la terminé.
3 En 1997 nos fuimos a vivir a Santiago de Chile y en 2004 regresamos a Buenos Aires.
4 Mi tío Francisco se casó con su tercera mujer en marzo de 2002 y en se(p)tiembre de 2002 se divorció.
5 El partido de tenis empezó a las cuatro y a las cinco terminó.

E Change the sentences, following the example. Write the verbs in the preterite and add all the necessary elements (prepositions, possessives, articles) for the sentences to make sense.

Example: Cumplir / ocho años, irme / México capital
Cuando cumplí ocho años, me fui a México capital.
Me fui a México capital, cuando cumplí ocho años.

1 Ir (yo) / España, aprender / español
2 Pablo / terminar / estudios, viajar / mundo
3 Recibir (vosotros) / correo electrónico, mandar / material ¿verdad?
4 Abrir (nosotros) / cuenta / banco, llegar / Nueva York
5 Carlota / comprar / piso, empezar / trabajar

F Taking into account the information given in Ex.A on p.212 answer the following questions:

1 ¿Hasta que año vivió en Guadalajara?
2 ¿De qué año a qué año vivió en Guadalajara?
3 ¿Cuándo se fue a México capital?
4 ¿En qué año inició sus estudios universitarios?
5 ¿En qué año se casó?
6 ¿Cuántos años hace que se casó?
7 ¿Cuándo nació su primer hijo?
8 ¿Cuántos años lleva viviendo en México capital?
9 ¿Desde qué año vive en México capital?
10 ¿Cuántos años tiene?

3 Referring to the life and work of famous people

A Read about the life and work of one of the most famous painters of all time and complete the account by putting the verbs in brackets in the appropriate form of the preterite.

el taller *workshop*

el maestro *master*

éxito *success*

Los encargos *commissions*

el cortesano *courtier*

Diego Rodríguez de Silva y Velázquez, pintor español, _____ (1 nacer) en Sevilla en 1599. A los 11 años _____ (2 empezar) su formación como pintor en el taller de Francisco Pacheco donde _____ (3 permanecer) hasta 1617. Al año siguiente, con 19 años _____(4 casarse) con Juana Pacheco, hija del maestro, con quien _____ (5 tener) dos hijas. Entre 1617 y 1623 _____ (6 pintar) obras de bastante éxito, en esa época sus obras _____ (7 estar) influidas por el estilo del pintor italiano Caravaggio. En 1623 _____ (8 trasladarse) a Madrid, allí _____ (9 obtener) el título de Pintor del Rey Felipe IV. A partir de ese momento, _____ (10 iniciar) su ascenso en la Corte española. En esos años _____ (11 conocer) a Rubens, quien _____ (12 pasar) una temporada en Madrid. En 1629 _____ (13 viajar) a Italia. Allí _____ (14 estudiar) las obras de Tiziano, Tintoretto, Miguel Ángel, Rafael y Leonardo da Vinci. En Italia _____ (15 pintar) entre otros *La fragua de Vulcano*. _____ (16 regresar) a Madrid en 1631 y durante la década de 1630 _____ (17 recibir) numerosos encargos. _____ (18 pintar) retratos como *La dama del abanico*, obras mitológicas como *La Venus del espejo* o escenas religiosas como *el Cristo crucificado*. Velázquez _____ (19 desarrollar) además una importante labor como cortesano que le _____ (20 restar) tiempo para dedicarse a la pintura. En 1649 _____ (21 regresar) a Italia. Allí _____ (22 triunfar) como pintor. Al cabo de dos años _____ (23 volver) a Madrid. En los últimos años de su vida _____ (24 pintar) grandes obras como *Las hilanderas* o *Las meninas*. Velázquez _____ (25 morir) el 6 de agosto de 1660, a la edad de 61 años.

Source: http.//www/arthistoria.com/historia/personajes/3652.html (Adapted)

B Read the text again and underline all the time expressions. Then choose four of these expressions and write four sentences that relate to your own life. Share this information with your partner.

Example: durante la década de 1630
Durante la década de 1990 trabajé en varios países.

C Read the text again and fill in the information.

Nombre:	
Apellidos:	
Profesión:	
Nacionalidad:	
Fecha de nacimiento:	
Lugar de nacimiento:	
Año de entrada en el taller de Francisco Pacheco:	
Año de su boda:	
Nombre de su mujer:	
Nº de hijos:	
Fecha de traslado a Madrid:	
Cargo ejercido:	
Viajes a Italia:	
Obras relevantes:	
Fecha de su muerte:	

D If you want to know more about the life and work of Velázquez, you will find a lot of information on the Internet. You could share the information you find with the people in your group next time you see them.

E Now you and your partner think of a famous person from your country, but do not disclose his/her name. Write a summary of his/her life, then read it to two other people in your group and see if they can guess who you are talking about.

C de Cultura

■ Spain: a cultural melting pot

Before evolving into the country we know today, Spain has been through many stages in her history, including having been invaded and conquered by many peoples: Swedes, Vandals, Alani, Romans, Visigoths, Arabs … It was not until 1492 when Granada, the last Muslim kingdom, was reclaimed, that Spain began to become what she is today. Despite the inevitable tensions and problems that they brought, the invading peoples also left their mark on every aspect of Spanish society and culture: language, architecture, literature, sciences, agriculture and the judiciary.

Narrating historical events

A Read the text, underline all the finite verbs and identify the tense used; make sure you understand all the words and expressions.

En abril del 711 Tariq desembarca en Gibraltar con un ejército de unos 7.000 hombres. Semanas más tarde se enfrenta victorioso a las tropas del rey visigodo Rodrigo. Así comienza la invasión de la Península Ibérica por los musulmanes. En sólo siete años, con un ejército reducido, los musulmanes ocupan toda la Península, excepto la parte más montañosa del Noroeste, y sustituyen al Estado visigodo. La España musulmana recibe el nombre de Al-Ándalus. Los musulmanes permanecen en la Península ocho siglos, hasta 1492, año en que la ofensiva cristiana obtiene su triunfo definitivo al reconquistar los reyes Católicos, Isabel y Fernando, Granada, el último reino musulmán.

B Rewrite all the verbs in the text in the preterite.

C Say if the following statements are *verdaderos* or *falsos*. If false, correct them.

	V	F
1 Los musulmanes llegan a la Península Ibérica en el siglo nueve.		
2 El Noroeste de la Península se rinde inmediatamente.		
3 Los musulmanes vencen a los visigodos.		
4 Los mulsumanes tardan más de diez años en ocupar la Península.		
5 Los cristianos derrotan definitivamente a los musulmanes ocho siglos después de su llegada.		

G de Gramática

■ **Referring to historical events**

To make the narration of past events more vivid, the present tense is sometimes used instead of the preterite. When the present is used in this way, it is known as the 'historic present'. This use of the present tense is more common in Spanish than in English.

En abril del 711 Tariq desembarca en Gibraltar. (In April 711, Tariq disembarked in Gibraltar.)

Cristóbal Colón descubre América en 1492. (Christopher Columbus discovered America in 1492.)

Diego Rodríguez de Silva y Velázquez nace en Sevilla en 1599. (Diego Rodriguez de Silva y Velázquez was born in Seville in 1599.)

D Write sentences using the historic present.

  1 Guerra Civil española / 18 julio 1936 / 1 abril 1939
    (comenzar / terminar)
  2 Gabriela Mistral / escritora chilena / Premio Nobel de
    Literatura 1945 (ganar)
  3 Hernán Cortés / México / 1519 (llegar)
  4 Santiago Ramón y Cajal / científico español / Premio
    Nobel de Medicina 1906 (obtener)
  5 Picasso / Guernica / 1937 (pintar)
  6 Revolución Cubana / 1959 (tener lugar)

Referring to events that almost (por poco) happened

G de Gramática

■ **Referring to events that almost happened**

To describe something that almost happened, the expression ***por poco*** with the verb in the historic present is used in everyday speech.

Ayer por poco tengo un accidente de coche.
(Yesterday, I nearly had a car accident.)

A Read the mini dialogues and answer the questions.

  ■ ¿Qué tal ayer,
    Marisa?.

  ■ Bien, pero por poco
    tengo un accidente
    de coche.

  1 Has Marisa had a car accident or not?
  2 What tense is the verb in?
  3 Is Marisa refering to a present or past event?

B Now practise with your partner, following the example. Take turns.

  Example: – Laura ¿llegaste a tiempo a la estación?
           (perder el tren)
         – Sí, pero por poco pierdo el tren.

  1 – ¿Qué tal?   **3** – ¿Qué tal el viaje?
    – Bien, (caerse en la calle)   – Bien, (no llegar al aeropuerto)
  2 – ¿Entregaste el trabajo a tiempo? **4** – ¿Estás bien?
    – Sí, (no terminarlo)   – Sí, (romperse el brazo el lunes pasado)

C Now think of three things which almost happened to you this week and tell your partner.

Consolidation

A Read the following information about the Hispano-American writer Gabriel García Márquez and then write a summary of his life using the verbs in the preterite. Use some of the following expressions: *en 19 . . .*, *a los x años*; *al cabo de . . .*, etc.

Nombre: Gabriel
Apellidos: García Márquez
Profesión: escritor y periodista
Nacionalidad: colombiana
Fecha de nacimiento: 1928
Lugar de nacimiento: Aracataca, Colombia
Estudios universitarios: Derecho y periodismo en la Universidad Nacional de Colombia.
Primera obra publicada: *La hojarasca* (1955)
Obra más famosa: *Cien años de soledad* (1967)
Premios recibidos: 1965 Premio Nacional (Colombia); 1972 Premio Internacional Rómulo Gallegos, 1982 Premio Nobel de Literatura

B Answer the following questions.

1 ¿Cuántos años hace que García Márquez publicó *Cien años de soledad*?
2 ¿A qué edad recibió el Premio Nobel de Literatura?
3 Desde su primera publicación, ¿al cabo de cuántos años publicó su obra más importante?
4 ¿Conoces alguna obra de García Márquez? ¿Cuál?

C Work with your partner. Think about an important historical event in your country's past and give a brief summary of it, using the historic present.

In class or at home

A Read the outline of the life of the Spanish painter Francisco de Goya y Lucientes. Use the dictionary to find out the meaning of the words you don't know, then write a summary of his life. Write a sentence for each date and write all the dates in words. Use the preterite tense.

Your summary could start:

Goya *nació* en Fuendetodos, España, en *mil setecientos cuarenta y ocho*. A los *veintidós años . . .*

1748	Goya nace en Fuendetodos, España.
1770	Se va a Roma donde pinta algunas obras.
al cabo de un año, en 1771	Regresa a Zaragoza.
entre 1773–1792	Trabaja en la Fábrica de Tapices donde pinta sus obras más alegres.

1792	Sufre una crisis profunda. En este momento se queda sordo.
De 1792 a 1808	Pinta retratos de aristócratas en los que representa aspectos negativos de los personajes.
1808	Napoleón invade la Península.
entre 1808–1814	Tiene lugar la Guerra de la Independencia. En esa época Goya pinta *Los fusilamientos de la Moncloa.*
1814	Napoleón pierde la guerra y se restituye la monarquía absoluta.
1808–1820	Goya pinta sus *pinturas negras*, obras llenas de horror y brutalidad.
desde 1820 hasta 1828	Goya vive en Francia donde muere en 1828.

B Look at the information about Goya's life and answer the following questions.

1 ¿En qué siglo nació Goya?
2 ¿A qué edad se quedó sordo?
3 ¿A principios de qué siglo invadió España Napoleón?
4 ¿Cuántos años duró la Guerra de la Independencia?
5 ¿De qué año a qué año vivió Goya en Francia?

C If you are interested in the life and work of Goya, go to the Internet to find out more. You can tell the members of your group about him next time you see them in class. You may be interested to know that many of Goya's paintings, as well as works by Velázquez, are in the Museo del Prado in Madrid.

D Read the text about the Mayas, who lived in the Yucatán in Mexico, and in Guatemala. Rewrite it, using the historic present and answer the questions below.

La civilización maya alcanzó su mayor desarrollo en el siglo V y empezó su decadencia a partir del siglo X. Los mayas alcanzaron un gran desarrollo científico, sobre todo en las matemáticas y astronomía, que en algunos aspectos superó los conocimientos europeos de la época. La civilización maya fue clasista y esclavista. Los españoles conquistaron Guatemala en 1525 y Yucatán en 1536.

1 ¿Cuándo alcanza la civilización maya su apogeo?
2 ¿En qué siglo llegan los españoles?

Recuerdos del pasado
Memories

■ **Expresiones esenciales**	■ **Essential expressions**
Es que estaba . . .	*You see, I was . . .*
Luisa iba todos los días a la piscina	*Luisa used to go to the pool every day*
Hacía un día frío	*It was a cold day*
Era una mujer bella y agradable	*She was a beautiful and pleasant woman*
Antes había . . . ahora hay	*Formerly, there used to be . . . and now there is*
Yo acababa de salir cuando sonó el teléfono	*I had just left when the phone rang*
Mi madre siempre cantaba mientras cocinaba	*My mother always used to sing while she was cooking*
María salía cuando Eduardo llegó / María estaba saliendo cuando Eduardo llegó	*María was leaving / going out when Eduardo arrived*

 Referring to the past

A Read the mini-dialogues and answer the questions below.

■ ¿Y tu marido?   ■ ¿Qué tal el sábado pasado?   ■ ¿Por qué no viniste a clase ayer?

■ Tenía trabajo y no pudo venir.   ■ Normal. Estuvimos en casa. Es que llovía y hacía frío . . .   ■ Es que estaba cansadísima.

1 Identify the phrases in the mini-dialogues that describe situations in the past.
2 Identify the phrases in the mini-dialogues that tell us about what happened.
3 Read the grammar section.
4 Practise these mini-dialogues with your partner. Give different answers.

G de Gramática

■ **The Imperfect tense**

So far you have studied and practised how to refer to the past, using three tenses: the perfect (*Esta mañana no he desayunado*), the preterite (*Ayer fuimos al cine*), the pluperfect (*Juan había salido cuando llamé*). Now you are going to learn another past tense: the imperfect (*comía*).

Spanish verbs not only explain the time in which the action takes place (present, past or future), but they also express whether the action is finished or not. So the forms *comí / he*

comido and *comía* all express past time but *comí / he comido* present the action as finished whereas *comía* presents it as not finished, i.e. it does not make any reference to the end of the action.

English does not have an imperfect tense as such, but uses the forms '*I used to eat*', '*I was eating*', '*I would* (habitually) *eat*' to express incomplete action in the past. These are almost always rendered in Spanish by the imperfect.

Cuéntame qué pasó

unidad 7

222

◼ Formation of the imperfect tense

Regular verbs

	hablar (to speak)	comer (to eat)	recibir (to receive)	levantarse (reflexive) (to get up)
yo	hablaba	comía	recibía	me levantaba
tú	hablabas	comías	recibías	te levantabas
usted	hablaba	comía	recibía	se levantaba
él / ella	hablaba	comía	recibía	se levantaba
nosotros(as)	hablábamos	comíamos	recibíamos	nos levantábamos
vosotros(as)	hablabais	comíais	recibíais	os levantabais
ustedes	hablaban	comían	recibían	se levantaban
ellos(as)	hablaban	comían	recibían	se levantaban

- Note that the endings for the **–er** and **–ir** verbs are the same.

Irregular verbs

There are only three irregular verbs in the imperfect tense. They are **ir** (to go), **ser** (to be), **ver** (to see).

	ir	ser	ver
yo	iba	era	veía
tú	ibas	eras	veías
usted	iba	era	veía
él / ella	iba	era	veía
nosotros(as)	íbamos	éramos	veíamos
vosotros(as)	ibais	erais	veíais
ustedes	iban	eran	veían
ellos(as)	iban	eran	veían

- Note the imperfect tenses of **haber** and **hacer** (impersonal): **había** (there was / there were) and **hacía** (it was):
  *Había mucha gente en la fiesta. (*There were a lot of people at the party.)
  *Antes siempre **hacía** mucho frío en el mes de enero.* (Formerly, it always used to be very cold in January.)

◼ Usage

The imperfect tense is used to describe an event in the past. Thus it describes ongoing or habitual activity, as well as background scenes, landscapes and moods against which action takes place. Look at the following examples:

- **Description in the past**:
  ***Era** un día soleado pero **hacía** frío.* (It was a sunny day, but it was cold.)
  *Mi profesor de filosofía **era** muy atractivo.* (My philosophy teacher was very good-looking.)

- **Description of a past situation, interrupted by the main action, which is in the preterite:**
  ***Salía** del banco cuando le robaron.* (He was coming out of the bank when he was robbed.)
  ***Estaba preparando** la cena cuando sonó el teléfono.* (I was cooking supper when the phone rang.)

- **Reference to a past event which immediately precedes another. In this case, the imperfect of *acabar* + infinitive is used:**
  ***Acababa de salir** del banco cuando le robaron.* (He had just left the bank when he was robbed.)

- **Description of two simultaneous open-ended activities in the past, using *mientras*:**
  *Mi madre siempre **cantaba** mientras **cocinaba**.* (My mother always used to sing while she was cooking.)

- **Description of an ongoing activity in the past:**
  *Entonces yo **vivía** en Singapur.* (At that time, I was living in Singapore.)

- **Description of an habitual activity in the past:**
  *Luisa **iba** todos los días a la piscina.* (Every day, Luisa used to / would go to the swimming pool.)

  Some common adverbial expressions which indicate duration, repetition and frequency and thus require the use of the imperfect tense are:

siempre	(always)	*de vez en cuando*	(sometimes, from time to time)
con frecuencia/frecuentemente	(frequently)	*muchas veces*	(often)
a menudo	(often)	*cada año / día / mes*	(every year / day / month)
a veces	(sometimes)	*todos los días / lunes*	(every day / every Monday)

- **Description of ongoing physical, mental, or emotional state in the past:**
  Estaban muy cansados. (They were very tired.)
  Estaban muy contentos. (They were very happy.)
  Quería mucho a su madre. (He adored his mother.)

- **Reference to time and age in the past:**
  Era la una. / Eran las dos. (It was one o'clock. / It was two o'clock.)
  Irene tenía 18 años. (Irene was 18 years old.)

- **Polite enquiries:**
  ¿Qué deseaba? (What would you like?)
  Quería un kilo de fresas. (I'd like a kilo of strawberries.)

B Rewrite the following sentences in the plural and the past. Write the time, using the 12-hour clock.

Example: Tú vas siempre al cine los viernes a las 7 (p.m.)
Vosotros ibais siempre al cine los viernes *a las siete de la tarde.*

1 Mi tía va al médico todos los martes a las 10:45 (a.m.).
2 La clase es muy fría y pequeña.
3 Tu abuelo cena siempre tortilla de patatas.
4 La azafata siempre pide el pasaporte al pasajero cuando éste entra en el avión.
5 Ella siempre hace ejercicio a las 8:15 (a.m.).
6 Mi hijo escucha música mientras estudia.
7 El profesor me dice que tengo que estudiar más.
8 Este restaurante cierra el lunes por la noche.
9 El programa de radio de las 9:50 (p.m.) es interesante.
10 Tú eres un chico alegre y despreocupado.

<u>**C**</u> Talk about habitual actions in the past. Complete the sentences with the appropriate form of the verb in the imperfect.

Example: Antes, hace x años, no *había* (haber) móviles. Ahora todo el mundo tiene uno.

1 Antes, hace x años, _____ (ir) al colegio todos los días. Ahora trabajo.

2 Ahora aquí casi no nieva, antes _____ mucho.

3 Ahora casi no veo la televisión, antes la _____ muchísimo.

4 Antes los jóvenes _____ poco, ahora viajan con frecuencia.

5 De pequeña, siempre _____ (pasar) los veranos en casa de mis abuelos.

6 Ahora no esquío, pero antes mi marido y yo _____ todos los inviernos.

<u>**D**</u> Now think of five things which you used to do, which you don't do now and tell your partner about them.

<u>**E**</u> Listen to Sr Reinosa giving an account of what he used to do before and what he does now and complete the grid.

	antes	ahora
vivir en . . .	vivíamos en Londres	
tener un . . .		
trabajar . . .		
ir de . . .		
gustar . . .		
nuestros hijos ir a . . .		

	antes	ahora
llevar a . . .		
en Navidades . . .		
mis hijos . . .		
vivir en . . .		
tener un . . .		
tener más . . .		

<u>**F**</u> Think of five things you were doing when the following events took place.

Example: cuando llamaron a la puerta
Estaba comiendo cuando llamaron a la puerta.

1 cuando sonó el teléfono
2 cuando llegó mi tía
3 cuando me encontré con mi jefe
4 cuando la profesora me preguntó
5 cuando oí la sirena de la ambulancia

2 Describing something in the past

A Before reading the text about the Inca civilisation, say what you know about it.

B Find out the meaning of the following words:

meridional   la llegada   el desarrollo   un culto obligatorio
descender   la artesanía   cultivar   el maíz   el algodón
el calendario

C Read the following extract about the Inca civilisation. Identify all the verbs in the imperfect and preterite and write down their infinitive forms.

Los incas formaban el mayor imperio de la América meridional a la llegada de los españoles. El Imperio incaico, que alcanzó su máximo desarrollo entre 1450 y 1550, se extendía desde el río Ancasmayo en Colombia hasta el río Maula, en Chile, a lo largo de 4.000 kilómetros. La llegada de los españoles en 1531 con Francisco Pizarro al frente, interrumpió su expansión.

El emperador, la máxima autoridad, era el Inca, que creían que era hijo del Sol. La capital del Imperio era Cuzco. Los incas tenían un aparato administrativo muy eficiente, una lengua oficial, el quechua, y un culto obligatorio, el del dios del Sol. La base de la organización social era el ayllu o conjunto de familias que

descendían de un mismo individuo. La propiedad de las tierras y el ganado era colectiva. La agricultura, la ganadería y la artesanía estaban muy desarrolladas. Eran capaces de lograr cosechas por encima de los 3.000 metros de altitud. Cultivaban patatas, maíz, cacao, papayas, algodón. Criaban llamas, vicuñas y alpacas.

Su desarrollo cultural y científico era inferior al de los mayas, no conocían la escritura pero usaban el calendario y conocían un sistema decimal para contar, semejante al ábaco, llamado quipu.

Eran buenos constructores: Templo del Sol en Cuzco, fortaleza de Sacsahuamán, al norte de Cuzco, conjunto arquitectónico de Machu Picchu.

Source: Guía escolar Vox, historia (Adapted)

D Answer the following questions:

1 ¿Qué extensión tenía el Imperio Inca?
2 ¿Quién gobernaba el Imperio Inca?
3 ¿A qué dios adoraban?
4 ¿Qué ganado criaban?
5 ¿Qué usaban para escribir?

E Give an oral summary in Spanish of what you have just read about the Incas.

3 Imperfect versus preterite

Read the following sections and complete the exercises.

A Habitual or completed action? Read the paragraph below and
write the verbs in brackets in the appropriate tenses, following the
examples.

Example: Íbamos a la montaña todos los veranos.
(*We used to go to the mountains every summer.*)
Fuimos a la montaña el año pasado.
(*We went to the mountains last year.*)

El año pasado, los lunes yo _____ (1 salir) siempre de clase de
inglés a las ocho de la tarde, _____ (2 ir) a tomar un vino con
mis amigos y _____ (3 regresar) a casa sobre las once de la
noche. Pero aquel lunes _____ (4 terminar) las clases más
temprano y _____ (5 marcharse) directamente a casa. Cuando
_____ (6 llegar), _____ (7 encontrarse) con la vecina del cuarto.
_____ (8 hablar, nosotros) un rato y después la _____ (9 invitar)
a tomar un café. Al cabo de dos meses de conocerla _____
(10 hacerse) novios y pensamos casarnos el año próximo.

B Description or narration? Complete the story using the appropriate
tenses of the verbs in brackets, following the examples.

Example: Era un día oscuro y hacía frío.
(*It was a dark day and it was cold.*)
Los chicos se burlaban de la chica que lloraba.
(*The boys were making fun of the girl who was crying.*)
Fui al centro, compré unas camisas y volví a casa.
(*I went to town, bought some shirts and returned home.*)

_____ (1 ser) una noche oscura y fría. _____(2 llover) mucho. Al
fondo _____ (3 verse) una casa de estilo colonial, vieja y
abandonada. Pedro _____ (4 salir) del coche y
_____ (5 dirigirse) hacia ella. La puerta de la casa
_____ (6 estar) abierta y _____ (7 haber) luz en el
primer piso. Pedro _____ (8 llamar) dos veces y de repente
_____ (9 aparecer) un hombre. Este hombre _____
(10 ser) bajo y fuerte. _____ (11 tener) un aspecto extraño.
Pedro casi no _____ (12 poder) hablar porque
_____ (13 tener) miedo.

Consolidation

A In groups of four or five, write an ending to the story you have just read. Your tutor will provide you with any additional words and expressions you may need.

B On the left is a summary of uses of the preterite and the imperfect. Read them and link them with the example on the right.

1 To indicate that an event is over and finished.

a Mis padres iban todos los años a Madrid.

2 To indicate states or actions which continued in the past for an unspecified period of time, or events whose beginning or end is not specified.

b Ella era una mujer bella y muy agradable.

3 To narrate actions that occurred in the past.

c Octavio Paz, escritor mexicano, ganó el Premio Nobel de literatura en 1995.

4 For events that lasted for a specific period of time and then ended.

d Un hombre llegó al banco, sacó una pistola, pidió el dinero y se fue.

5 To describe people, characteristics, settings and situations when narrating in the past.

e Cuando yo tenía cinco años, mi padre trabajaba en Estados Unidos.

6 To refer to habitual actions in the past.

f La fiesta duró cinco horas.

In class or at home

A Say what had just occured when something else happened. Link the phrases on the left with the ones on the right to make complete sentences.

1 Acababa de hacer la cena
2 Acabábamos de arreglar el coche
3 Acababan de llegar a casa
4 Acababa de levantarme
5 Acababas de comprar un piso
6 Acababa de terminar la carrera
7 Acababais de salir
8 Acababa de llamar tu madre

a cuando saliste.
b cuando perdiste el trabajo, ¿verdad?
c cuando encontré trabajo.
d cuando tuvo lugar la explosión ¿verdad?
e cuando tuvimos el accidente.
f cuando les comunicaron la noticia.
g cuando sonó el despertador.
h cuando llegaron los invitados.

B Complete the sentences with the verbs in brackets in either the preterite or imperfect.

  1 En casa de mi abuelo _____ (comer) siempre comida mexicana.

  2 _____ (*estar* + gerund *ver, yo*) la televisión cuando alguien _____ (llamar) a la puerta, _____ (levantarse), _____ (abrir) la puerta pero no _____ (haber) nadie.

  3 Paco _____ (pasear) tranquilamente cuando _____ (oír) la explosión.

  4 Marta _____ (ir) todos los fines de semana a casa de sus abuelos pero ese fin de semana no _____ (poder) ir porque su abuela _____ (ponerse) enferma.

  5 Ayer _____ (hacer) un día horrible, _____ (llover) tanto que _____ (decidir, yo) quedarme en casa. _____ (ver) la televisión un rato y mientras _____ (preparar) la cena _____ (terminar) los ejercicios de latín.

  6 Luis _____ (trabajar) habitualmente por las mañanas; pero durante dos meses _____ (tener) que trabajar en el turno de la noche.

  7 Mi tío Manolo siempre _____ (volver) a casa en el mes de mayo.

  8 Mientras _____ (esperar, nosotros) por ti _____ (comprar, nosotros) el regalo para Paz.

  9 ¿_____ (ir, vosotros) al cine ayer?

 10 Vuestro abuelo _____ (ser) un señor muy simpático, siempre _____ (estar) de buen humor.

C Read the summary of the biography of the great Spanish dancer Antonio Gades and rewrite all the verbs in the past.

Antonio Gades, uno de los mejores bailarines de flamenco de todos los tiempos nace en Elda (Alicante) el 6 de noviembre de 1936. Nada más comenzar la guerra civil se marcha con su familia a Madrid, donde el padre está combatiendo las fuerzas fascistas.

Gades abandona el colegio a los 11 años y se pone a trabajar. Empieza a bailar por necesidad. Su primera maestra, Pilar López, descubre su talento y lo forma. Después de 9 años con Pilar López, abandona la compañía y empieza su carrera hacia el éxito. Gades lleva espectáculos como *Bodas de sangre, Carmen* y *El amor brujo* por todos los escenarios del mundo.

Gades es un hombre comprometido con su arte y con la sociedad. Siempre dice lo que piensa. Gades muere en Madrid el 20 de julio de 2004.

Acércate al mundo del español
Un mundo de creadores

A Do you know or have you heard of any Spanish or Hispano-American artists: *escritores, pintores, escultores, directores de cine, actores, actrices, cantantes, fotógrafos . . . ?*

Spain and Hispano-America are homes to great creators: Cervantes, García Lorca, Borges, García Márquez, Isabel Allende, Velázquez, Goya, Picasso, Dalí, Diego Rivera, Frida Kahlo, Plácido Domingo, Monserrat Caballé etc.

One of the best-known painters is the Mexican, Frida Kahlo. Read a summary about her life and work and then do the activities.

B Write Kahlo a chronology of the life of Frida Kahlo.
1907: Nace en Coyoacán (Ciudad de México)

C Look at the self-portrait of Frida and describe it. Include also some features of her character as you imagine it to have been.

D Go to the Internet and find out more about her and/or any of the other artists mentioned above.

Frida Kahlo
(1907–1954).

Frida Kahlo, pintora mexicana, nació en la Ciudad de México, en el distrito de Coyoacán en 1907. Su vida estuvo marcada por la enfermedad y el dolor. A los ocho años tuvo poliomielitis y en 1925 sufrió un terrible accidente de autobús que la mantuvo en la cama durante varios meses. Durante esos meses se dedicó a pintar y empezó a retratarse a sí misma porque como ella misma dice: "me retrato a mí misma porque paso mucho tiempo sola y porque soy el motivo que mejor conozco". En 1928 conoció al pintor mexicano, Diego Rivera, con quién se casó en 1929. Diego y Frida tuvieron una relación difícil y en 1935 se separaron y ella se fue a España. En 1937 tuvo una relación amorosa con el revolucionario y político ruso León Troski. En 1938 tuvo lugar su primera exposición en Nueva York y en 1939 en París donde conoció entre otros a Picasso, Miró y Kandinski. Ese año Diego y Frida se divorciaron pero siguieron en contacto. La salud de Frida empeoró, Diego se mantuvo a su lado y en 1940 se casaron otra vez. Frida siguió pintando hasta el final de su vida en 1954.

La obra de Frida está marcada por su vida. En ella expresa su dolor físico, su sufrimiento por los problemas con Diego Rivera así como su enorme tristeza por no poder tener hijos.

Essential vocabulary

Expresiones temporales que pueden acompañar el pretérito indefinido

ayer
anteayer
anoche
el otro día
hace dos días/años
la semana pasada
el año pasado
durante tres siglos
en 1936
en + año / en + tiempo
a los x años

al cabo de + tiempo
después de + tiempo
desde . . . hasta
de . . . a

Expresiones temporales que pueden acompañar el imperfecto

siempre
con frecuencia
frecuentemente
a menudo
a veces
de vez en cuando

muchas veces
cada año / día / mes
todos los días / lunes

Para expresar emociones

¡Cuánto tiempo sin verte!

¡Qué suerte!
Lo siento, es que . . .
No importa

Time expressions that can accompany the simple past

yesterday
the day before yesterday
last night
the other day
two days / years ago
last week
last year
for three centuries
in 1936
in + year
at the age of x /
   at x years old
at the end of + time
after + time
from . . . until
from . . . to

Time expressions that can accompany the imperfect

always
frequently
frequently
often
sometimes
sometimes, from time to
time
many times
every year / day / month
every day / Monday

To express personal feeling

It's been so long
   (since I've seen you)!
What luck!
I am sorry that . . .
It doesn't matter

Verbos

nacer
morir(se)
comenzar a/
   empezar a
iniciar
terminar
desarrollar

Mundo de la pintura

comisión (f)
escena (f) religiosa
maestro (m)
obra (m) mitológica
pintor (m)
pintura (f)
retrato (m)

Para hablar de los Incas u otras civilizaciones

ábaco (m)
agricultura (f)
algodón (m)
alpaca (f)
artesanía (f)
cacao (m)
calendario (m)
constructor (m)
culto (m)
emperador (m)
escritura (f)
expansión (f)
ganadería (f)
ganado (m)
imperio (m)
incas (m)
llama (f)
maíz (m)
papaya (f)
propiedad (m)
quechua (m)
sistema (m) decimal
tierra (f)
vicuña (f)

Verbs

to be born
to die
to start / begin to

to start / begin . . .
to end/finish
to develop

World of painting

commission
religious scene
master
mythological work
painter
painting / work
portrait

To talk about the Incas and other past civilisations

abacus
agriculture
cotton
alpaca
craftmanship / handicrafts
cocoa
calendar
builder
cult
emperor
writing
expansion
cattle raising
cattle
empire
Incas
llama
corn
papaya
property
Quechuan
decimal system
land
vicuna (small Andean
   camel)

essential vocabulary

¡Olé!

 ¡Baila conmigo!

Dance with me!

■ **Expresiones Esenciales**

¿Puedo abrir la ventana?
Sí, ábrela / ábrala (*informal / polite*)
No, no la abras / la abra; yo tengo frío
Ven conmigo (*informal*)
Va contigo
Habla consigo mismo(a)
Lo hacemos entre tú y yo
Según tú, nadie trabaja bien

■ **Essential Expressions**

Can I open the window?
Yes, open it
No, don't open it; I'm cold
Come with me
He/she goes / is going with you
He/she talks / is talking to him / herself
We're doing it between the two of us
According to you, nobody is working well

---

 1 **Giving and refusing permission**

A Read the following two mini-dialogues and try to work out who is being addressed as *tú* and who as *usted*. Note the expressions used to give permission and to refuse permission in each case. Now read the grammar section on the next page.

1 – *¿Puedo abrir la ventana?*
  – *Sí, ábrela.*
  – *No, no la abras; yo tengo frío.*

2 – *¿Puedo abrir la ventana?*
  – *Sí, ábrala.*
  – *No, no la abra; yo tengo frío.*

B Complete the following instructions using the verbs in brackets. The subject pronouns indicate which form of the imperative to use.

1 ¡ _____ la puerta! (cerrar – tú)
2 ¡ _____ la ventana! (cerrar – usted)
3 ¡ _____ las patatas! (comer – vosotros)
4 ¡ _____ las verduras! (comer – ustedes)
5 ¡ _____ en seguida! (acostarse – usted)
6 ¡ _____ los dientes! (lavarse – ustedes)
7 ¡ _____ los deberes! (terminar – tú)
8 ¡ _____ la carta! (escribir – vosotros)

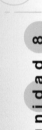

Polite imperatives

In the first mini-dialogue, the expression used by the speaker to give permission is *Sí*, *ábrela* (Yes, open it). This is the **informal imperative**, used when addressing people as *tú* and *vosotros*, which you learnt in Unit 5, p 151.

In the second mini-dialogue, the expression used by the speaker to give permission is *Sí*, *ábrala* (Yes, open it). This is the **polite imperative**, which is formed in Spanish with a tense called the **Present Subjunctive**. (For a definition of 'subjunctive mood' see the grammar glossary on p.296.)

The use of the subjunctive is very common in Spanish: one of its most important uses is that in the third person singular and plural (*usted* and *ustedes*) it provides the polite positive imperative - to give permission, orders, instructions and advice.

The Present Subjunctive

To conjugate the present subjunctive, you take the present indicative and make the following changes:

• *-ar* verbs change the *-o* or *-a* of the present indicative ending to *-e*.

• *-er* and *–ir* verbs change the *-o* or *-e* of the present indicative ending to *-a*.

Here is a table of the present subjunctive of regular verbs:

	hablar	comer	abrir	levantarse (reflexive)
	(to speak)	*(to eat)*	*(to open)*	*(to get up)*
(yo)	hable	coma	abra	me levante
(tú)	hables	comas	abras	te levantes
(usted)	hable	coma	abra	se levante
(él/ella)	hable	coma	abra	se levante
(nosotros(as))	hablemos	comamos	abramos	nos levantemos
(vosotros(as))	habléis	comáis	abráis	os levantéis
(ustedes)	hablen	coman	abran	se levanten
(ellos(as))	hablen	coman	abran	se levanten

Negative Imperatives

The expressions *No la* **abras** (first mini-dialogue) and *No la* **abra** (second mini-dialogue) are used by the speaker to say 'Don't open'. In both sentences the verbs appear in the Present Subjunctive. This is because the Present Subjunctive provides the negative forms of both the polite and the informal imperatives. The informal negative imperative uses the second person (*tú* and *vosotros*) forms of the verb: **no abras, no abráis.**

The following table gives you all four forms of the imperatives of hablar and abrir:

	Positive Imperative		Negative Imperative	
tú	habla	abre	no hables	no abras
usted	hable	abra	no hable	no abra
vosotros(as)	hablad	abrid	no habléis	no abráis
ustedes	hablen	abran	no hablen	no abran

Note that in Hispano-America and the Canary Islands, the *vosotros* form of the imperative is not used; the *ustedes* form is used instead.

Position of object pronouns

As you will remember, object pronouns and reflexive pronouns with the informal imperative are added on to the end of the word:

ábrela, cómelo, levántate, etc.

The same thing happens with the polite imperative:

ábrala, cómalo, levántese

But with negative imperatives (both polite and informal) the object pronoun precedes the verb:

Informal: *no la abras, no lo comas, no te levantes*

Polite: *no la abra, no lo coma, no se levante*

C Write the negative imperative of the following.

	tú	usted	vosotros	ustedes
Habla ahora	**no hables**	**no hable**	**no habléis**	**no hablen**
1 Come más				
2 Escribe rápido				
3 Vende caro				
4 Compra poco				
5 Reparte con ella				
6 Limpia con cuidado				
7 Arréglate				
8 Mírate al espejo				
9 Sube por las escaleras				

D Complete the mini-dialogues and then practise them with two other people in your group.

Example: – ¿Puedo llevar vuestro coche?
– Sí, llévalo.
– No, no lo lleves, lo necesito yo.

1 – ¿Puedo tomar una Coca-Cola?
– Sí, _____
– No, no _____, es la última que me queda.

2 – ¿Puedo limpiar el salón ahora?
– Sí, _____.
– No, no _____; límpialo más tarde.

3 – ¿Podemos comprar un helado?
– Sí, _____.
– No, no _____; vamos a comer en diez minutos.

4 – ¿Podemos escuchar música?
– Sí, _____.
– No, no _____; yo quiero ver la tele.

5 – Puedo fumar?
– Sí, _____.
– No, no _____; no soporto el tabaco.

6 – ¿Podemos preparar la cena?
– Sí, _____.
– No, no _____; vamos a cenar fuera

E Can you say the following in Spanish using the polite *usted* form?

1 Don't wait for me!
2 Don't talk now please!
3 Don't give it to them.
4 Don't sit down! (*sentarse*)
5 Don't take this train; take the next.

2 Prepositions

A Write down the missing prepositions in the following sentences.

1 Mi mejor amigo es _____ Japón.
2 Yo nací _____ Canadá.
3 Los Picos de Europa están _____ el norte de España.
4 Ese reloj no es _____ oro.

5 Ellos vivieron en Australia _____ 1999 _____ 2004.

6 Mañana vamos _____ viaje.

7 La semana que viene van _____ ir _____ Lima.

8 Antes siempre iba _____ pie al trabajo; ahora voy _____ metro.

9 El dinero estaba _____ la mesa.

10 Este tren pasa _____ Sevilla.

11 Este regalo es _____ tu hermana.

12 El CD lo tengo _____ el salón.

13 Juan llegó _____ las diez _____ la mañana.

14 Mañana _____ la tarde usted va _____ Barcelona, ¿verdad?

15 ¿Habéis estado _____ Colombia?

16 ¿Conoces _____ mi padre?

B Now read the grammar section.

G de Gramática

■ Prepositions

In Unit 3 (prepositions and prepositional phrases to express location), Unit 5 (*por* and *para*, personal *a*) and Unit 7 (time expressions with *a, de, desde, hasta*) you studied in detail some prepositions and prepositional phrases. You have also learnt many expressions which require specific prepositions: *ser de España, ser de plástico, a las diez, ir al cine, estar en el norte*, etc. Here is a comprehensive list of single-word prepositions.

a (to, at)	*de* (of, from)	*hacia* (towards)	*según* (depending on, according to)
ante (before)	*desde* (since, from)	*hasta* (until, as far as)	*sin* (without)
bajo (under, beneath, below)	*durante* (during, for)	*mediante* (by means of)	*sobre* (on, about, concerning)
con (with)	*en* (in, on, inside, by, at)	*para* (for, in order to)	*tras* (behind, after)
contra (against)	*entre* (between, among)	*por* (by, through, for)	

Note that only the most common translations are given.

Remember that the masculine singular article used after *de* must contract thus: *de* + *el* = *del* and that the same rule applies after *a*: *a* + *el* = *al*.

■ Prepositional pronouns

There is a group of pronouns which, as in English, can be used after prepositions. You have already met some of them when studying how to express likes and dislikes:

a mí me gusta el chocolate. (I like chocolate.); *a ti te gusta el cine* (you like the cinema).

Here is a complete list with examples of their use:

	Examples
mí (*me*)	Cómpralo **para mí**. (*Buy it for me.*)
ti (*you*)	Lo hice **sin ti**. (*I did it without you.*)
usted (*you*)	Voy **con usted**. (*I go / I am going with you.*)
él / ella (*him, it / her / it*)	No trabajes **por ella**. (*Don't do the work for her.*)
nosotros(as) (*us*)	Juan venía **hacia nosotros**. (*Juan was coming towards us.*)
vosotros(as) (*you*)	Os doy el dinero **a vosotros**. (*I give the money to you.*)
ustedes (*you*)	Todo depende **de usted**. (*Everything depends on you.*)
ellos(as) (*them*)	No te pongas **contra ellos**. (*Don't set yourself / go against them.*)

C Read the grammar section on the next page and then rewrite the
following sentences in the singular.

Example: Comed con nosotros.
           Come conmigo.

   1 Venid con nosotros.
   2 No bailéis con ellas.
   3 ¿Lo hacemos con vosotros?
   4 No habléis con vosotros mismos.
   5 Según vosotros, todo estaba bien, ¿verdad?
   6 Con ustedes, no podemos hablar.
   7 Entre nosotros y vosotros vamos a solucionar el problema.
   8 ¿No fuisteis con ellos?
   9 Antes ellos siempre viajaban con nosotros, ahora viajan solos.
   10 No me gusta trabajar con vosotros.

3   ## Finding out and talking about traditional and popular music: *el flamenco*

A Read the text about *El flamenco* and fill in the missing prepositions in the first part.

El flamenco

El flamenco es _____ (1) duda la música popular española más conocida dentro y fuera _____ (2) España. El flamenco es cante, es música instrumental – principalmente guitarra – y es baile. El flamenco es la interpretación personal _____ (3) un artista – cantaor, guitarrista, bailaor –; pero también tradición, música transmitida _____ (4) generación _____ (5) generación, música popular, folclore. En su origen es música _____ (6) un pueblo, expresión _____ (7) el pueblo gitano, y _____ (8) un lugar, Andalucía. El flamenco es un arte profundo – cante jondo (hondo) –, fundamentalmente trágico, que nos habla _____ (9) las realidades universales: amor, celos, muerte, dolor, penas; los sentimientos más fuertes _____ (10) la vida humana.

El flamenco nace _____ (11) las comunidades gitanas asentadas _____ (12) la zona occidental andaluza. Los gitanos llegaron _____ (13) España _____ (14) el siglo XV procedentes _____ (15) la India _____ (16) recorrer toda Europa. Trajeron su lengua, el caló; su oficio: la herrería; sus costumbres. El flamenco nació _____ (17) algún momento _____ (18) la llegada de los gitanos _____ (19) España y las primeras noticias que _____ (20) él tenemos, a mediados _____ (21) el siglo XVIII.

El origen del flamenco tal como hemos dicho es gitano, pero a lo largo de la historia y en la actualidad encontramos artistas flamencos tanto gitanos como payos (el nombre que les dan los gitanos a las personas no gitanas). Los cantes son variados, pertenecen a distintos tipos o palos. Algunos son más trágicos, dramáticos, dolorosos, íntimos, otros son más alegres y vivos. Las letras son breves, directas y sin adornos:

El día que tú naciste
el sol se vistió de limpio
y hubo en el cielo una juerga
que bailó hasta Jesucristo.

El baile es la parte más espectacular del flamenco, los bailes son tan variados como los cantes. La guitarra es hoy tanto acompañamiento del cante o baile como instrumento solista. Las tradicionales voces de *ole* u *olé* las dicen los participantes en una reunión o espectáculo flamenco para animar al artista.

Source: http://www.inicia.es/de/trivioech/cultura_flamenco.htm (Adapted)

B Find in the text words that match the following definitions.

    1 La persona que canta flamenco
    2 La persona que toca la guitarra
    3 La persona que baila flamenco
    4 La lengua de los gitanos españoles
    5 El oficio de forjar el hierro
    6 Tipo de cante o baile

C Read the text again and complete the information.

Perfil del pueblo gitano en España	**El flamenco**
Fecha de llegada a España:	Definición del flamenco:
Procedencia:	Lugar de origen:
Lengua:	Fecha de nacimiento:
Oficio tradicional:	Tipos de cante y de baile:
Lugar de asentamiento en España:	Expresión más espectacular del flamenco:
	Función de la guitarra:

D Write a brief summary in your own words of what you have just learnt about *el flamenco*.

E Apart from *el flamenco*, can you name any other popular music or dance from a Hispanic country?

G de Gramática

Note that the prepositional pronouns are the same as the subject pronouns except for the first and second person singular (*mí* and *ti*). *Mí* has an accent to differentiate it from *mi* meaning 'my'. The same applies to *sí* where the accent differentiates it from *si* meaning 'if'.

Exceptions

- The preposition **con** (with) + **mí, ti, or sí** (reflexive pronouns which can be followed by **mismo / a**) forms a single word: **conmigo / contigo / consigo**. With the other pronouns, it is used in the same way as with other prepositions: con usted, con nosotros, con vosotros ...
  Ven conmigo. (Come with me.)
  Los estudiantes no fueron contigo. (The students did not go with you.)
  Nunca salimos con ellos. (We never go out with them.)

- Prepositions **entre** (between, among) and **según** (according to, depending on)
  With these prepositions, **yo** and **tú** are used instead of *mí, ti*
  Lo hacemos entre tú y yo. (We're doing it between us.)
  Según tú, nadie trabaja bien. (According to you, nobody works well.)

Consolidation

A Write in the missing prepositions. Note that in some cases more than one preposition is correct.

1 Antes mi familia y yo siempre íbamos ____ viaje en verano.
2 Hazlo ____ cuidado.
3 Esto es ____ ti, es tu regalo ____ cumpleaños.
4 Ayer estuvimos ____ el museo del pueblo.
5 El pasaporte está ____ el cajón ____ la derecha.
6 ¿Mañana ____ la noche vais ____ salir ____ los señores Gil?
7 Este autobús pasa ____ tu calle.
8 Los paquetes no llegan ____ el jueves.
9 Me horroriza viajar ____ avión.
10 No nos ve ____ hace cuatro años.
11 ____ el informe de la policía, el robo lo hicieron cuatro personas.
12 La conferencia es ____ el cambio climático.
13 El trabajo lo hicieron ____ Pedro y Carmen.
14 Se apoyó ____ la pared ____ no caerse.
15 Hoy hace una temperatura ____ −5ºC

In class or at home

A Complete the mini-dialogues.

Example: – ¿Puedo invitar a cenar a María?
            – No, no la invites, no me apetece verla.
            – Sí, invítala.

1 – ¿Puedo consultar tu diccionario?
  – Sí, _____.
  – No, no _____, lo necesito yo.

2 – ¿Os puedo tomar una foto?
  – Sí, _____.
  – No, no _____, estoy feísima.

3 – ¿Podemos abrir los regalos?
  – Sí, _____.
  – No, no _____, esperad hasta la noche.

4 – ¿Puedo tirar estos papeles?
  – Sí _____
  – No, no _____, son importantes.

5 – ¿Podemos comprar una pizza para cenar?
  – Sí _____.
  – No, no _____, ya he hecho la cena.

B Read the text about *el tango*.
Note all the words which belong to the same semantic field.

Música y baile		Perfil de una población
nouns	verbs	
el tango	bailar	blancos

C Say if the following statements are *verdaderos* or *falsos*. If false, give the right answer.

a El tango surgió hacia 1880.

b La población negra bailaba el vals y las polkas.

c Los negros bailaban el candombe de dos en dos pero sin unirse.

d La población de Buenos Aires a finales del siglo XIX era muy variada.

e Casi todo el mundo tenía dinero en Buenos Aires. La gente vivía bien.

f Todo el mundo hablaba español.

g Casi todos los habitantes de Buenos Aires eran hombres.

h El tango nace en lugares pobres.

i Muchas de las mujeres que trabajaban en los bares eran prostitutas

j El tango era un baile socialmente aceptado.

El tango

El tango nació a finales del siglo XIX en Buenos Aires, Argentina. En principio no era más que una determinada manera de bailar la música. La sociedad donde nace el tango escuchaba y bailaba habaneras, polkas, mazurcas y algún vals, por lo que respecta a los blancos, mientras que los negros, un 25% de la población de Buenos Aires en el siglo XIX, se movían al ritmo del candombe, una forma de danza en la que la pareja no se enlazaba y bailaba de una manera más marcada por la percusión que por la melodía.

Musicalmente, el tango entronca en su genealogía con la habanera hispano-cubana. Inicialmente, el tango es interpretado por modestos grupos que cuentan sólo con violín, flauta y guitarra. El instrumento mítico, el bandoneón, instrumento parecido al acordeón pero más grande y con teclado a ambos lados, no llega al tango hasta un par de décadas después de su nacimiento, en 1900 aproximadamente, y poco a poco sustituye a la flauta.

El escenario de su nacimiento, la ciudad de Buenos Aires, era a finales del XIX una ciudad en expansión con un enorme crecimiento demográfico sustentado sobre todo en la emigración que procedía de multitud de países. Había españoles e italianos y también alemanes, húngaros, eslavos, árabes, judíos ...Todos ellos componían una gran masa obrera desarraigada, pobre, con escasas posibilidades de comunicación debido a la barrera lingüística y mayoritariamente masculina, ya que eran fundamentalmente hombres en busca de fortuna, hasta el punto de que la composición natural de la población de Buenos Aires quedó totalmente descompensada, de modo que el 70% de los habitantes eran hombres.

En este ambiente, se comienza a bailar en tugurios (bares de mala fama) y lupanares (prostíbulos) el nuevo ritmo que se asocia así desde su inicio al ambiente prostibulario, ya que eran sólo prostitutas y 'camareras' las únicas mujeres presentes. Puesto que se trataba de mujeres dedicadas en alma y, sobre todo, en cuerpo a sus accidentales acompañantes, el tango se comenzó a bailar de un modo muy 'corporal', provocador, cercano, explícito ... de un modo socialmente poco aceptable.

Source: http://www.esto.es/tengo/Historia/historia.hmt (Adapted)

D Write a summary of what you have learnt about *el tango* and prepare a brief presentation for your next class.

B ¡Siga por ahí!

Carry on that way!

<table>
<tr><td>■ **Expresiones esenciales**</td><td>■ **Essential expressions**</td></tr>
<tr><td>¿Sabes dónde hay...?</td><td>*Do you know where there is a ...?*</td></tr>
<tr><td>Sí, sigue todo recto hasta el final de la calle</td><td>*Yes, carry straight on to the end of the street*</td></tr>
<tr><td>No vengas / no venga / no vengáis / no vengan (*informal / polite*)</td><td>*Don't come*</td></tr>
<tr><td>Pon / Ponga</td><td>*Put*</td></tr>
<tr><td>Odio / Detesto / Me espanta</td><td>*I hate / I can't stand*</td></tr>
<tr><td>¡Que aproveche! / ¡Buen provecho!</td><td>*Enjoy your meal!*</td></tr>
<tr><td>¡Qué rica / buena / mala!</td><td>*How delicious / nice / horrible!*</td></tr>
<tr><td>¡Qué tortilla!</td><td>*What an omelette!*</td></tr>
<tr><td>Las proteínas deben suponer</td><td>*Proteins should account for*</td></tr>
<tr><td>Hay que intentar consumir ...</td><td>*You should try to eat*</td></tr>
<tr><td>Te / le / os aconsejo / recomiendo / sugiero que comas ...</td><td>*I advise / recomend / suggest you to eat ...*</td></tr>
</table>

1 Giving directions, orders and advice

A Read these mini-dialogues, underline the verbs used to give instructions and say which verb form is being used, then practise them with your partner.

1 – *Mira, por favor, ¿sabes dónde hay una Oficina de Correos?*
– *Sí, sigue todo recto hasta el final de la calle, Correos es el edificio más moderno.*
– *Vale, gracias.*

2 – *Por favor, ¿la calle Buena Vista está cerca de aquí?*
– *¡Uf! Está un poco lejos, a unos diez minutos de aquí. Toma la primera calle a la derecha, camina unos cien metros y toma la calle de la izquierda, la calle que se llama Sol. La calle Sol es muy larga, vete hasta el final y después toma la calle de la derecha, esa es la calle Buena Vista.*
– *Muy bien, gracias.*

B Read the grammar section opposite and then practise the mini-dialogues again with your partner. This time use the polite form.

■ **Giving directions, orders and advice**

Present Subjunctive – irregular forms

In Unit 5, p. 151, you learnt the informal imperatives in their positive forms. In Section A of this unit, p.233, you learnt both the polite positive imperatives and the negative imperatives, using the forms of the Present Subjunctive. We looked mainly at the regular verbs. Some verbs, however, have irregular forms in the Present Subjunctive and also therefore have irregular imperatives.

■ **Irregular verbs in the present subjunctive**

Totally irregular verbs

1 Some of the most common irregular verbs are:

	ser	**haber**	**ir**	**saber**
(yo)	sea	haya	vaya	sepa
(tú)	seas	hayas	vayas	sepas
(usted)	sea	haya	vaya	sepa
(él / ella)	sea	haya	vaya	sepa
(nosotros(as))	seamos	hayamos	vayamos	sepamos
(vosotros(as))	seáis	hayáis	vayáis	sepáis
(ustedes)	sean	hayan	vayan	sepan
(ellos(as))	sean	hayan	vayan	sepan

2 *Dar* and *estar* are irregular in so far as they have a written accent on some of their endings:
Dar: d**é**, des, d**é**, demos, deis, den
Estar: est**é**, est**é**s, est**é**, estemos, est**é**is, est**é**n

3 Radical-changing verbs

● *-ar and -er types*
Remember that the present subjunctive has the same irregularities in the stem as the present indicative. The stem change affects all persons except the first and second person plural. (See Unit 4, p.107) The endings are, however, the same as for regular verbs in the Present Subjunctive:
Note that *jugar* (to play) with a stem vowel *u*, follows the same pattern as verbs with the stem vowel *o* plus a spelling change
g> gu: juegue, juegues, juegue, juguemos, juguéis, jueguen.

● *-ir* type
The same irregularities occur as in the present indicative but there are also changes in the stem of the first and second persons plural:

● *e>i* verbs, *pedir:* pid**a**mos, pid**á**is
● *o>ue* verbs, *dormir:* d**u**rmamos d**u**rm**á**is

G de Gramática

4 Irregular verbs in the first person singular

Verbs which have an irregular form in the first person singular of the present tense of the indicative use this same irregularity to form the stem of the present tense of the subjunctive mood.

	Present indicative	Present subjunctive
Hacer	Yo **hago**	haga, hagas, haga, hagamos, hagáis, hagan
Tener	Yo **tengo**	tenga, tengas, tenga, tengamos, tengáis, tengan
Salir	Yo **salgo**	salga, salgas, salga, salgamos, salgáis, salgan
Poner	Yo **pongo**	ponga, pongas, ponga, pongamos, pongáis, pongan
Venir	Yo **vengo**	venga, vengas, venga, vengamos, vengáis, vengan
Decir	Yo **digo**	diga, digas, diga, digamos, digáis, digan
Oír	Yo **oigo**	oiga, oigas, oiga, oigamos, oigáis, oigan
Conocer	Yo **conozco**	conozca, conozcas, conozca, conozcamos, conozcáis, conozcan
Ver	Yo **veo**	vea, veas, vea, veamos, veáis, vean

5 Some spelling-change verbs

- **-ar type:**

		Present indicative	Present subjunctive
-car: c>qu,	buscar:	busco	busque, busques, busque ...
-gar: g>gu,	llegar:	llego	llegue, llegues, llegue ...
-guar: gu>gü	averiguar:	averiguo	averigüe, averigües, averigüe ...

-er and -ir type:

		Present indicative	Present subjunctive
-ger / -gir: g>j	coger, elegir:	cojo / elijo	coja, cojas ... / elija, elijas ...
-guir: gu>g	distinguir:	distingo	distinga, distingas ...
-zar: z>c	amenazar:	amenazo	amenace, amenaces ...

__C__ Tell people what to do! Practise the positive imperative by completing the sentences. The verbs are given in brackets and the subject pronouns indicate which form of the imperative to use.

1 ¡_____ con nosotras! (bailar, vosotros)

2 ¡ _____ tranquilo! (dormir, tú)

3 ¡_____ hacia arriba! (mirar, vosotros)

4 ¡_____ el trabajo como le dije! (hacer, usted)

5 ¡_____ de protestar! (dejar, tú)

6 ¡_____ el trabajo bien! (hacer, vosotros)

7 ¡ _____ más dinero! (pedir, usted)

8 ¡_____ la ropa ahora mismo! (recojer, ustedes)

¡Olé!

unidad 8

242

D Tell people what not to do! Give the negative imperative of the following:

	tú	usted	vosotros	ustedes
Ven	no vengas	no venga	no vengáis	no vengan
1 Sal de ahí				
2 Haz la cama				
3 Pon la mesa				
4 Busca el dinero				
5 Dirige el grupo				
6 Elige				
7 Arréglate				
8 Mírate al espejo				
9 Sube por las escaleras				
10 Acuéstate pronto				

E Giving advice. Give two pieces of advice to your partner for each situation.

Example: Si quieres estar en forma, _____
Si quieres estar en forma, *no estés sentado todo el día; haz deporte*.

1 Si quieres estar en forma, _____
2 Si quieres tener menos estrés, _____
3 Si quieres dejar de fumar, _____
4 Si quieres dormir mejor, _____
5 Si quieres tener una dieta equilibrada, _____

Following instructions

A You are about to listen to an extract from a radio cookery programme, featuring a recipe for *tortilla española* (Spanish omelette),

1 Before listening, make sure you know the meaning of the following verbs:

batir	calentar (e>ie)
cortar	echar
freír	lavar
mezclar	mover (o>ue)
pelar	poner
sacar	usar

2 Match the pictures to the ingredients and utensils below:

aceite	cebollas	huevos	patatas	sal	plato
sartén	tenedor				

3 Complete the sentences with the appropriate noun from exercise 2.

Example: Lavar *las patatas*

a pelar _____

c batir _____

b cortar _____

d echar la _____

   y _____

e calentar _____

B 🔊 Now listen to the radio programme and say which form of the imperative is used by the speaker.

C Read the transcript below and write in the missing verbs from the list in Ex.A., as well as the ones listed below. Add the direct object pronouns.

mezclar   poner   mover   usar   sacar   servir

Tortilla de patatas

Ingredientes para seis personas
½ litro de aceite de oliva   8 huevos
1 kilo de patatas   1 cebolla de tamaño mediano
Sal

Preparación
_____ las patatas y después _____. _____ finas.
_____ la cebolla y _____ con las patatas.
_____ la sal.
_____ el aceite en la sartén a calentar.
_____ las patatas a freír.
_____ las patatas de vez en cuando.
_____ los huevos bien con un tenedor. No _____ la batidora eléctrica.
Una vez bien fritas las patatas y la cebolla, _____ el aceite.
Una vez sacado el aceite, _____ la mitad del huevo en la sartén y _____ con las patatas. Con un plato, dale la vuelta a la tortilla y _____ el resto del huevo. Con el mismo plato, _____ la tortilla de la sartén y _____ en un plato.
_____ caliente o fría.

D 🔊 Listen to the recording again and check your answers.

E Tell your partner how to make Spanish omelette. Address him/her using *usted*.

C de Cultura

■ **Greetings**
The expressions ¡*Que aproveche!* or ¡*Buen provecho!* (Enjoy your meal!) are very often used as a greeting when somebody comes into a place where people are eating. It doesn't matter if you know the people or not.

F Opinions differ! Look at the following dialogue:

Following the mini-dialogue ask your partner if he/she liked a particular meal you have just had in a restaurant. Here are some of the dishes you could use:

el pescado   la carne   la pasta   las verduras   el postre
la paella

■ ¿Te gustó la tortilla?

■ Sí. ¡Qué rica! Me gustó muchísimo.

■ Pues a mí no. ¡Qué tortilla tan mala! Lo siento pero me horrorizó.

3 Giving advice, making recommendations and suggestions

A Read the text about a balanced diet (*la dieta equilibrada*) on the next page and then the sentences that appear below. Choose the correct options, according to the information given in the text.

1 Según el texto:
  a todo el mundo debe alimentarse de la misma manera.
  b la dieta debe adaptarse a las necesidades de cada persona.

2 Una dieta equilibrada
  a debe contener todo tipo de nutrientes y alimentos.
  b debe contener sólo alimentos de origen vegetal.

3 En una dieta equilibrada
  a los hidratos de carbono deben aportar menos del 50% de calorías.
  b los hidratos de carbono deben aportar más del 50% de calorías.
  c las proteínas y grasas deben aportar más del 50% de calorías.

4 En una dieta equilibrada
  a hay que consumir más azúcar refinada y menos fruta, vegetales y granos enteros de cereales.

  b hay que consumir menos azúcar refinada y más fruta, vegetales y granos enteros de cereales.

5 En una dieta equilibrada
  a hay que consumir un porcentaje alto de grasas saturadas.
  b hay que consumir un porcentaje bajo de grasas saturadas.

6 Las proteínas deben proceder principalmente de
  a carnes como la carne de vaca o cordero.
  b carne como la del pollo o del pescado.

7 En una dieta equilibrada
  a hay que consumir mucha sal.
  b hay que controlar el consumo de sal.

8 En una dieta equilibrada
  a el consumo de bebidas alcohólicas puede ser alto.
  b el consumo de bebidas alcohólicas debe ser comedido.

G de Gramática

■ **To express dislike**

As you already know, the expression *me horroriza* means you dislike something enormously. You can also use the verbs *odiar, detestar* and *espantar.*

Odio / detesto el chocolate / la lluvia / los aviones. (I hate chocolate / rain / aeroplanes.)

Horrorizar and *espantar* work in the same way as gustar:

Me espanta el chocolate / la lluvia. (I can't stand chocolate / rain.)

Me espantan los aviones. (I can't stand aeroplanes.)

■ **To express your reactions**

- ***¡Qué* + adjective:** *¡Qué rica / buena / mala (está la tortilla)!* (How delicious / the omelette is!)
- ***¡Qué* + noun + *tan* + adjective:** *¡Qué tortilla tan buena / rica / mala!* (What a delicious / horrible omelette!)
- ***¡Qué* + noun *¡Qué tortilla!* (What an omelette!) The context and the intonation will make clear if the reaction is positive or negative.

¡Siga por ahí!

245

La dieta equilibrada

Es preferible hablar de dieta equilibrada y no de dieta ideal porque ésta no existe. La alimentación se debe adaptar a cada persona según sus características fisiológicas y condiciones de salud.

Una dieta equilibrada debe contener todos los grupos de alimentos y las cantidades suficientes de nutrientes para que el organismo pueda realizar todas sus funciones. El consumo de ellos no debe ser excesivo, pues esto conduce a desequilibrios, como puede ser niveles altos de colesterol o hipertensión.

La OMS (Organización Mundial de la Salud) ha establecido las siguientes proporciones:

- Los hidratos de carbono deben aportar al menos un 55-60% del aporte calórico total
- Las grasas no deben superar el 30% de las calorías totales ingeridas
- Las proteínas deben suponer el 15% restante en la dieta

Para conocer si tomamos una dieta adecuada podemos consultar las tablas que se editan en nuestro país, tablas de composición de los alimentos, y también podemos seguir las recomendaciones generales que da la Comisión de Nutrición del Senado de los EEUU:

- Seguir los porcentajes dichos anteriormente para cada nutriente, sin que se consuma más del 10% de azúcares dentro del consumo de los carbohidratos, reduciendo el azúcar refinada y aumentando la ingesta de frutas, vegetales y granos completos de cereales.
- La ingesta de grasas no debe superar el 30% y de éste, menos del 10% debe ser grasas saturadas. Hay que intentar consumir grasas monoinsaturadas.
- El aporte de proteínas debe provenir de las aves y pescados en detrimento de las carnes rojas y debe ser de 0,8gr / día.
- La fibra vegetal debe aportar al menos 22 gr/día. De éstas, el 50% debe corresponder a fibra soluble.
- La cantidad de calorías adecuada es de unas 40 kilocalorías por kilo de peso y día para cubrir las necesidades metabólicas de energía.
- Hay que evitar el exceso en el consumo de sal, como alimentos procesados y conservas de comidas preparadas. El aporte de sal no debe superar los 3 gr/día.
- Por último, el consumo de bebidas alcohólicas debe ser moderado.

Source:
http//www.elmundosalud.elmundo.es/elmundosalud/
especiales/dietas/b1.html (Adapted)

B Work with two other people in your group. Read the text again and note all the words which belong to the same semantic field.

Alimentos	Componentes de los alimentos
azúcar refinada	nutrientes

C Read the grammar section. Now look at the statements below and make recommendations following the example.

Example: Los hidratos de carbono *deben aportar* al menos un 55–60% del aporte calórico total.

La Comisión recomienda que los hidratos de carbono *aporten* al menos un 55-60% del aporte calórico total.

1 Las grasas *no deben superar* el 30% de las calorías totales ingeridas.
2 Las proteínas *deben suponer* el 15% restante en la dieta.
3 La ingesta de grasas *no debe superar* el 30%.
4 El aporte de proteínas *debe provenir* de las aves y pescados y debe ser de 0,8gr/día.
5 El consumo de bebidas alcohólicas *debe ser* moderado.

G de Gramática

■ Giving advice and recommendations

The following constructions can be used.

- **deber + infinitive**
  Las proteínas **deben suponer** el 15% restante en la dieta.
  (Proteins should account for 15% of the diet.)
  La ingesta de grasas no debe superar el 30%.
  (Fat intake should not exceed 30%.)

- **hay** (impersonal form of *haber)* que + infinitive
  Hay que intentar *consumir grasas monoinsaturadas.*
  (You should try to eat monounsaturated fats.)

Note that the same structures could be used to express obligation:

Debo terminar este trabajo esta tarde. (I should finish this work this afternoon.) Aquí hay que ponerse casco. (Hard hats should be worn here.)

- **Verbs of advice: aconsejar** ('to advise'), **recomendar** ('to recommend')', **sugerir** ('to suggest') ... + **que** + **subjunctive**
  Te aconsejo / recomiendo / sugiero que comas más vegetales y menos dulces. (I advise you to / suggest / recommend that you eat more vegetables and fewer sweet things.)

D You have a friend who has neither a good diet nor a very healthy lifestyle and is not in very good shape. Give him/her advice on how to change both diet and lifestyle using the different expressions in the example.

Su dieta	**Su estilo de vida**
come muchos dulces y poca fruta	nunca hace ejercicio
siempre bebe refrescos, nunca bebe agua	ve la televisión demasiadas horas
nunca come pescado	nunca va al campo
come demasiadas hamburguesas	fuma muchísimo
y nunca come vegetales	compra comida "basura"
bebe demasiada cerveza	

Example: Si quieres estar en forma, *come* menos dulces y más fruta.
Debes comer menos dulces y más fruta.
Te aconsejo que comas menos dulces y más fruta.
Hay que comer menos dulces y más fruta.

Consolidation

A Think of a dish you really like, write down the recipe and then share it with the people in your group. Your tutor will help you with the vocabulary.

B Work with your partner and create what you consider to be a balanced diet. When you have finished, compare your 'balanced diet' with the suggestions of the other people in your group.

In class or at home

A Rewrite the first mini-dialogue in the informal register and the second one in the polite register.

- *Mire, por favor ¿sabe dónde está el ayuntamiento?*
- *Sí, tome la primera calle a la izquierda, sígala hasta el final y allí está.*

- *Mira, por favor, ¿sabes si hay una tienda de música por aquí?*
- *Uhmm . . . Ah sí, sigue todo recto hasta el final y después toma la calle de la derecha.*

B Write the positive and negative imperatives of *tú, usted, vosotros, ustedes* in the following sentences. Replace the words in italics with the appropriate pronoun.

		tú	**usted**	**vosotros**	**ustedes**
1	Subir *el volumen*	*súbelo / no lo subas*			
2	Bajar *las persianas*				
3	Elegir *un regalo a Paco*				
4	Pedir *dinero al jefe*				
5	Averiguar *el resultado*				
6	Traer *los paquetes*				
7	Dar *el mensaje a Juan*				
8	Comprar *una casa a tus / sus hijas*				
9	Devolver *la camisa*				
10	Levantarse				

C Match the sentence halves in the column on the left with the ones on the right, then rewrite them in the plural form using *ustedes*.

1 Si quieres adelgazar,	**a** trabaja más, no dejes todo para última hora.
2 Si quieres hacer amigos,	**b** ponte crema, no bajes a la playa al mediodía.
3 Si no quieres aburrirte,	**c** sal más a menudo, no te quedes en casa siempre.
4 Si no quieres tener problemas,	**d** no comas tanto, camina todos los días.
5 Si no quieres quemarte al sol,	**e** no veas la tele todo el día, haz algo activo.

D Respond to the following:

Example: Una tortilla riquísima: ¡Qué rica! / ¡Qué tortilla tan buena! / ¡Qué tortilla!

1 Una paella saladísima   **3** Un libro interesantísimo
2 Un café malísimo   **4** Una película horrible

E Write down the opposite response to the ones given. Note that it could be more than one answer.

Example: ¡Me encanta viajar!
            ¡Odio viajar!

1 ¡Detesto la ópera!
2 ¡Me gusta muchísimo la cerveza!
3 ¡Me horrorizan las películas románticas!
4 ¡Me encantan las hamburguesas!
5 ¡Qué pescado tan rico!
6 ¡Qué bueno!

F Following the recommendations given in the article *La dieta equilibrada,* write a leaflet with about 10 recommendations (5 things one should eat and 5 things one shouldn't eat) for a balanced diet. Share the information with your group.

¿Qué pasará?

What will happen?

Expresiones Esenciales	**Essential Expressions**
Creo que estudiaré en . . .	*I think I'll study at . . .*
Me imagino que viviré con . . .	*I imagine that I'll live with . . .*
Supongo que me casaré	*I suppose that I'll get married*
Seguramente no seré . . .	*I certainly won't be . . .*
Probablemente viviré en . . .	*I'll probably live in . . .*
¡Ojalá tengas mucho éxito!	*I hope you'll be very successful!*
Espero tener mucho éxito	*I hope to be very successful*
Espero / Quiero / Deseo que tengas mucho éxito	*I hope that you are / want you to be very successful*
Creo que en el futuro viviremos / vamos a vivir en . . .	*I think that in the future we'll live in . . .*
No creo que en el futuro vivamos / vayamos a vivir en . . .	*I don't think that we'll live in . . . in the future*
No sé si / cuándo / cómo iré a Madrid	*I don't know if / when / how I'll get to Madrid*
Ellos no saben cuánto costará el arreglo	*They don't know how much the settlement will cost*
No sabemos dónde viviremos	*We don't know where we'll live*
No sé qué haré el año que viene	*I don't know what I'll do next year*

 Thinking about the future

A Read what Carlota, now 10, thinks her life will be like in 10 years' time and say which tense is used to refer to the future.

Ahora	**Dentro de 10 años**
– *Estudio en el colegio*	– *Estudiaré en la universidad*
– *Vivo con mis padres*	– *Viviré con mis amigas*
– *Viajo con mis padres*	– *Viajaré sola por todo el mundo*
– *No trabajo*	– *Trabajaré*
– *No tengo dinero*	– *Tendré dinero*

B Now read the grammar section and then say what Carlota's life will be like in 10 years' time. You could start by saying:

En diez años, Carlota estudiará en la universidad . . .

G de Gramática

Referring to the future

In Unit 6, section A (*El tiempo libre*) you learnt that the present tense of *pensar* + infinite, *querer* + infinitive and *ir a* + infinitive can be used to talk about future plans, intentions and wishes in relation to the present. Now you are going to learn how

- **To refer to future events:**

  Mañana hará sol. (Tomorrow it will be sunny.)

  En julio iremos a Argentina. (In July we're going to Argentina.)

- **To make predictions about future events:**

  Dentro de diez años estudiaré en la universidad. (In ten years' time I shall be studying at the university.)

  En diez años, los científicos encontrarán una cura para el sida. (Within ten years, scientists will find a cure for AIDS.)

Expressions used to make predictions about the future

Creer que		*Creo que viajaré mucho.* (I think that I'll travel a lot.)
Imaginarse que		*Me imagino que tendré hijos.* (I imagine that I'll have children.)
Suponer que	+ **future**	*Supongo que me casaré.* (I suppose that I'll get married.)
Seguramente (no)		*Seguramente no seré rico.* (I certainly won't be rich.)
Probablemente		*Probablemente viviré en el extranjero.* (I'll probably live abroad.)

Formation of the future tense

The future tense is formed by adding the future endings to the infinitive of the verb. The endings are the same for all verbs.

Regular verbs

	hablar (*to speak*)	comer (*to eat*)	vivir (*to live*)	levantarse (reflexive) (*to get up*)
(yo)	hablar**é**	comer**é**	vivir**é**	me levantar**é**
(tú)	hablar**ás**	comer**ás**	vivir**ás**	te levantar**ás**
(usted)	hablar**á**	comer**á**	vivir**á**	se levantar**á**
(él / ella)	hablar**á**	comer**á**	vivir**á**	se levantar**á**
(nosotros(as))	hablar**emos**	comer**emos**	vivir**emos**	nos levantar**emos**
(vosotros(as))	hablar**éis**	comer**éis**	vivir**éis**	os levantar**éis**
(ustedes)	hablar**án**	comer**án**	vivir**án**	se levantar**án**
(ellos(as))	hablar**án**	comer**án**	vivir**án**	se levantar**án**

Irregular verbs

Twelve verbs (and all the verbs that derive from them) have an irregular future stem. They have the same endings as regular verbs.

caber (*to fit, to be contained*)	**cabr-**	**-é**	querer (*to want, to love*)	**querr-**	**-é**
decir (*to say, to tell*)	**dir-**	**-ás**	saber (*to know*)	**sabr-**	**-ás**
haber (*to have*)	**habr-**	**-á**	salir (*to go out, to leave*)	**saldr-**	**-á**
hacer (*to do, to make*)	**har-**	**-emos**	tener (*to have*)	**tendr-**	**-emos**
poder (*to be able*)	**podr-**	**-éis**	valer (*to be worth*)	**valdr-**	**-éis**
poner (*to put*)	**pondr-** +	**-án**	venir (*to come*)	**vendr-**	**-án**

C Imagine your life in 10 years' time and then give 5 predictions using the expressions in the grammar section above. You could use some of the following:

terminar la carrera   retirarse   casarse

vivir en   publicar mi primer libro   hablar muchos idiomas

viajar por el mundo   cambiar de trabajo   comprar una casa . . .

2 Expressing hopes and wishes

A Read the speech bubbles, and work out what you think they mean.

- ■ Espero tener mucho éxito en mi nuevo trabajo.
- ■ Espero que tengas mucho éxito en tu nuevo trabajo.
- ■ ¡Ojalá tenga mucho éxito en su nuevo trabajo!

1 Underline the verbs and note how many there are in each sentence.

2 Why do you think in the first bubble the verb *tener* appears in the infinitive while in the second it appears in the second person of the present subjunctive?

3 Read the grammar section about how to express hopes and wishes.

G de Gramática

■ Expressing hopes and wishes

There are various ways to express hope. Here are some of them:

- **Ojalá** (loosely translates as 'I / let's hope (so) / with luck' – see below) + **present subjunctive** when the speaker considers his/her wish as something possible to achieve: *¡Ojalá tengas éxito!* (I hope you'll be successful.) *¡Ojalá no llueva mañana!* (With luck it won't rain tomorrow.)
- **Esperar que** (*to hope that*)
- **Querer que** (*to want*) + **present subjunctive** when the subject of the main clause is different from the subject of the subordinate clause

- **Desear que** (*to want / wish*)

(yo) espero / quiero / deseo que *(tú) tengas mucho éxito en tu nuevo trabajo* (I want you to be successful in your new job.)

Note: When the subject of both the main clause and subordinate clause is the same, the second verb is in the infinitive. *(Yo) espero tener éxito en mi nuevo trabajo*. (I hope to be successful in my new job.)

B Say what you hope will happen. Choose one verb from the list below for each sentence

encontrar   ganar   hacer   llegar   pasar   regresar

Example: ¡Ojalá no *haga* frío mañana!
(yo) _____
Espero que mañana no haga frío.

1 ¡Ojalá _____ (vosotros) el partido!   (nosotros) _____.
2 ¡Ojalá te lo _____ bien en la fiesta!   (yo) _____.
3 ¡Ojalá _____ (yo) pronto!   (yo) _____.
4 ¡Ojalá el avión _____ a tiempo!   (yo) _____.
5 ¡Ojalá _____ (tú) trabajo!   (yo) _____.

C de Cultura

C Here are some of Alejandro's wishes for the future. Can you rewrite them as if you were making them for him?

Example: En el futuro quiero vivir en una casa grande y confortable.
Quiero que vivas en una casa grande y confortable.

En el futuro:
1 deseo tener muchos hijos.
2 quiero viajar por todo el mundo.
3 espero encontrar un buen trabajo.
4 deseo vivir en el campo.
5 quiero conocer a gente interesante.
6 espero tener buena salud.

3 Expressing opinions and beliefs.

A Read the split statements about the world in the future (*el mundo en el futuro*) and match up the halves in the left-hand column with those on the right.

1 El ser humano	a podrán vivir en otros planetas.
2 La medicina	b desaparecerán.
3 Los seres humanos	c será uno de los grandes problemas de la humanidad.
4 Habrá	d dominarán la vida cotidiana.
5 Muchas especies de animales y plantas	e vivirá más años.
6 El ordenador e Internet	f grandes cambios climáticos.
7 La escasez de recursos naturales	g avanzará y se encontrarán curas para el cáncer y el sida.

B Now, read the speech bubbles.

- Yo creo que en el futuro viviremos hasta los 150 años.
- Pues yo no creo que vivamos tantos años.

1 Underline the expressions of opinion and then identify the verbs in the clauses introduced by *que*.

2 Read the grammar section.

G de Gramática

■ Expressing opinions and beliefs

- ***creer / pensar que*** (to believe / to think that) in affirmative form are followed by a verb in the indicative.

Yo **creo que** en el futuro **viviremos / vamos a vivir** hasta los 150 años.
Nosotros **pensamos que** en el futuro el clima **será / va a ser** inestable.

- ***no creer / no pensar que*** in the negative form is followed by a verb in the subjunctive.

Yo **no creo que** en el futuro **vivamos / vayamos a vivir** hasta los 150 años.
Nosotros **no pensamos que** en el futuro el clima **sea / vaya a ser** inestable.

Note that there are cases when the indicative is required after *no creer / no pensar*, but you will learn these cases at a later stage.

C Read the paragraph below, in which Alejandro expresses his vision of the future, and rewrite it expressing the opposite. Your paragraph could start: *Pues yo no creo que en el futuro haya / vaya a haber grandes cambios . . .*

> *Pues yo creo que en el futuro habrá grandes cambios. También creo que en pocos años nuestra vida cotidiana estará dominada por la tecnología. Pienso que las casas del futuro estarán llenas de cámaras y que todo el trabajo doméstico será hecho por robots. Pienso que los niños dejarán de ir al colegio y que se educarán en casa a través del ordenador. En cuanto al medio ambiente, creo que habrá grandes cambios climáticos pero no creo que vayan a desaparecer muchas especies animales.*

D Work with your partner. Read the sentences in exercise A (page 253) and express your agreement or disagreement with the facts stated.

Example: Yo creo que el ser humano *vivirá* más años.
Yo no creo que el ser humano *viva / vaya a vivir* más años.

Expressing lack of knowledge about future events or situations

A Read the mini-dialogues.

1 Make a note of the phrases used to express lack of knowledge about what will happen.
2 Underline expressions of hope or desire.
3 Practise the mini-dialogue with your partner.

– Yo creo que en el futuro viviremos hasta los 150 años.
– Pues yo no sé cuánto viviremos pero espero que en el futuro la calidad de vida sea buena.

– No sé dónde viviré dentro de diez años pero ojalá viva en un lugar agradable ¿Y tú?
– Yo tampoco sé pero me gustaría vivir en una gran ciudad.

■ **Expressing ignorance or uncertainty about the future**

Useful expressions:

	si		*No sé si iré a Madrid este año.*
	cuándo		*Paco no sabe cuándo terminará la carrera.*
No saber +	*cómo*	*+ future*	*Los científicos no saben cómo saldrá el experimento.*
	cuánto		*Ellos no saben cuánto costará el arreglo.*
	dónde		*No sabemos dónde viviremos.*
	qué		*No sé qué haré el año que viene.*

Note: Question words carry a written accent in indirect questions as well as direct questions.

B 🔊 Listen to Marta talking about her future and then complete the following sentences.

1 No sé _____ dentro de cinco años, pero espero _____ y _____.
2 No sé _____ en España o en el extranjero, pero me gustaría _____.
3 No sé _____, pero ojalá que mi novio y yo _____.
4 No sé _____, pero me gustaría _____.
5 No sé _____, pero espero _____.

C Now write similar sentences about how you see your life in the future. Share the information with your partner.

Consolidation

A Work with a partner. Think about how a typical day in your life might be in 50 years' time and discuss it with your partner. You could talk about work, family life, living space, hobbies, transport, etc. Let your imagination take over. Then read it to the rest of the group and compare your stories.

Your story could start like this:

Yo me levantaré a las siete de la mañana. Tomás, mi robot, me preparará el baño y el desayuno . . .

In class or at home

A Rewrite the following sentences in the negative.

1 Este año creo que iré de vacaciones a México.
2 Pedro y yo, pensamos que el jefe nos subirá el sueldo.
3 Los expertos creen que el problema de la escasez del agua tiene solución.
4 Nuestro abogado piensa que mañana firmaremos los papeles.
5 Pienso dejar de trabajar dentro de dos años.
6 Creéis que los ordenadores dominarán nuestra vida, ¿verdad?
7 Creo que en este siglo va a haber muchos terremotos.
8 Mi hermano pequeño piensa ser médico.

B Read the diary entry of 17-year-old Amalia in which she writes about how she sees her future, then rewrite it in the third person.

Querido diario
La semana que viene empezaré mi carrera universitaria. Voy a estudiar económicas. Es la primera vez que voy a vivir fuera de casa. No sé cómo será mi vida pero espero que todo vaya bien. Me imagino que haré muchos amigos. A mí me gustaría acabar la carrera y encontrar un buen trabajo, claro, pero primero viajaré por todo el mundo, iré a países exóticos. Supongo que algún día me casaré y tendré hijos pero eso no me preocupa por el momento. No sé dónde acabaré viviendo, pero sé que viviré en un lugar bonito y tranquilo. Espero tener suerte y ser feliz.

C Rewrite the following sentences as in the example.

Example: Dentro de diez años quiero retirarme / dejar de trabajar / volver a escribir **(si, gustar)**

*No sé **si** me retiraré dentro de diez años pero **me gustaría** dejar de trabajar y volver a escribir.*

1 Quiero terminar mis estudios / encontrar un buen trabajo / ganar dinero **(cuándo, esperar)**
2 Deseo casarme / conocer a un hombre interesante (**si, gustar**)
3 Quiero comprar una casa en el futuro / comprarla en una ciudad grande (**dónde, esperar**)
4 Quiero hacer el experimento / salir bien (**cómo, esperar**)

D ¡Espero que tengas mucho éxito!

I hope you are very successful!

■ Expresiones esenciales	■ Essential expressions
Cuando / Tan pronto como / En cuanto coma, te llamo	When / as soon as I've eaten, I'll call you
Antes de comer, te llamo	Before eating, I'll call you
Antes de que comas, te llamo	Before you eat, I'll call you
Te llamo después de comer	I'll call you after lunch
Te llamo después de que comas	I'll call you after you've eaten
No te llamo hasta que acabes de comer	I won't call you until you've finished eating
¿Para qué vas a Santiago de Chile la semana que viene?	Why are you going to Santiago de Chile next week?
Voy para asistir a una conferencia	I'm going (in order) to attend a conference
¿Sabes para qué me ha llamado Jorge?	Do you know why Jorge phoned me?
Sí, te ha llamado para que no te olvides de . . .	Yes, he called you so that you won't forget to . . .
Me molesta que / Es posible que / Es importante que Paco venga a trabajar aquí	It bothers me that Paco should come / It's possible that / It's important that Paco comes to work here
¿Tú / Usted, qué llevaría/s?	What would you wear?
Pues, yo que tú / usted / En tu / su lugar, llevaría . . .	Well, if I were you, I'd wear . . .

 Using time expressions to refer to the past, present and future

A Read the following sentences.

- **a** Cuando llegó a casa, hizo la cena. / Hizo la cena, cuando llegó a casa.
- **b** Cuando llega a casa, hace la cena. / Hace la cena, cuando llega a casa.
- **c** Cuando llegue a casa, hará la cena. / Hará la cena, cuando llegue a casa.
- **d** Cuando llegues a casa, haz la cena. / Haz la cena cuando llegues a casa.

1 Identify the *main clause* (a clause which has independent meaning) and the *subordinate clause* (a clause which depends on a main clause in order to have meaning). Underline the verbs and identify the tense and mood in each case.

2 Identify the sentences which refer to a past, present habitual or future action.

B Read the following sentences, complete the table below and then read the grammar section.

1 Cuando vayas a Colombia, visita el Museo del Oro de Bogotá.
2 Llamamos a Juan tan pronto como llegamos a Lima.
3 Tan pronto como acabe de comer, te llamo.
4 Después de que os fuisteis, nos acostamos.
5 En cuanto pueda, dejaré de trabajar.
6 Cuando nieva, siempre hay problemas de tráfico.
7 Hasta que no le compré un coche, no me dejó tranquilo.
8 Hasta que no le compre un coche, no me dejará tranquilo.
9 Abriré el regalo después de que mi marido llegue.
10 Vendimos la casa cuando regresamos a Chile.
11 Llegaremos al aeropuerto antes de que aterrice tu avión.
12 Recogí a los niños en cuanto pude.
13 Cuando paseaba por el parque, me encontré con tu marido.
14 Cuando tenga cuarenta años, seré famosa.

Time expressions which introduce the subordinate clause	Verbs in the indicative mood in the *subordinate clause* when the verb of the <u>main clause</u> refers to past or present (habitual) actions	Verbs in the subjunctive mood in the *subordinate clause* When the verb of the <u>main clause</u> refers to future actions
Cuando	*Cuando **llegó** a casa,* <u>**hizo** la cena</u> *Cuando **llega** a casa,* <u>**hace** la cena</u>	*Cuando **llegue** a casa,* <u>**hará** la cena</u>

G de Gramática

■ Using time expressions to refer to the past, present or future

Here are some common time expressions used to refer to past, present or future actions:

cuando (when)
tan pronto como (as soon as)
en cuanto (as soon as)
después (de) que (after)
hasta que (until)
antes (de) que (before)

These time expressions introduce a subordinate clause, e.g. *Cuando llegue al trabajo* (When I arrive at work) which is dependent on a main clause, e.g. *mandaré el documento* (I will send the document). For now, just try to understand the essential concept of main and subordinate clauses. At a later stage, you will be able to deepen your knowledge.

Subjunctive or indicative after time expressions

These time expressions are followed by verbs in either the indicative or the subjunctive mood, depending on whether the main clause refers to past, present or future actions or states.

• **The indicative mood** is always used after the above time expressions when the verb in the <u>main clause</u> refers to past or present (habitual) actions.

unidad 8
¡Olé!

Cuando era pequeño, <u>quería ser astronauta.</u> (When he was a little boy he wanted to be an astronaut.)

Siempre <u>*pagamos el alquiler*</u> *en cuanto cobramos.* (We always pay the rent as soon as we get paid.)

- **The subjunctive mood** is always required when the verb of the <u>main clause</u> refers to future actions or states.

  *Cuando **llegue** al trabajo, <u>mandaré el documento.</u>* (When I get to work, I'll send the document.)

  *Cuando **sea** mayor, <u>seré astronauta.</u>* (When I grow up, I am going to be an astronaut.)

  <u>*Pagaremos el alquiler*</u> *en cuanto **cobremos**.* (We'll pay the rent as soon as we get paid.)

  <u>*Lo haremos*</u> *antes de que **llegue** el jefe.* (We'll do it before the boss arrives.)

Note that ***antes de*** and ***después de*** take the infinitive when the subject of the main clause and the subordinate clause is the same.

(Yo) saldré después de comer. (I'll go out after I've eaten)

Salí después de comer. (I went out after I'd eaten.)

(Nosotros) lo haremos antes de llegar. (We'll do it before we arrive.)

C Read the sentences, then write the verbs in brackets in the appropriate tense and mood.

1 El año pasado cuando _____ de vacaciones, me olvidé de llevar mis medicinas, este año cuando _____ de vacaciones, no me _____ (ir (x2), olvidarse).

2 Tan pronto como lo _____ me di cuenta de que me había equivocado, por lo que tan pronto como _____ a casa esta tarde lo _____ otra vez (entregar, llegar, hacer).

3 _____ uno de los paquetes después de que (tú) _____, el otro lo _____ antes de que _____ (recoger(x2), irse, volver).

4 Siempre _____ su coche antes de _____ pero ayer no _____ tiempo y no _____ revisarlo hasta que _____ a su destino (revisar, viajar, tener, poder, llegar).

5 El mes pasado tan pronto como me _____ (ellos), _____ que pagar muchísimo por un arreglo del coche, así que el mes que viene cuando me _____, me _____ un coche nuevo. (pagar(x2), tener, comprar).

D Complete the following mini-dialogues and then practise them with your partner:

Example: Oye ¿ya has estado de vacaciones?
No, todavía no, pero cuando *esté,* voy a dormir todo el día, ¡estoy cansadísimo! (estar)

1 María ¿te ha llegado el dinero?
No, todavía no, pero tan pronto como me _____, voy a comprar el último libro de Carlos Fuentes y el CD de Valdés y El 'Cigala' 'Lágrimas negras'. (llegar)

2 Mire, por favor, ¿ya han recibido pantalones de la talla 46?
Lo siento, todavía no, pero no se preocupe, deme su teléfono y en cuanto los _____, la llamo. (recibir)

3 Julián, ¿has terminado el trabajo?
No, aún no, lo voy a terminar después de _____. (comer)

4 ¿Sabes si Pedro ha recogido el paquete? Es tarde y van a cerrar.
No sé, pero no te preocupes, seguro que lo recogerá antes de que _____. (cerrar)

5 Carmen, ¿hasta cuándo te quedarás en Edimburgo?
Hasta que _____ inglés bien. (aprender)

E Working with your partner, find out the following information. Give full answers.

Example: ¿Hasta cuándo estudiarás español?
Estudiaré español hasta que lo domine.

1 ¿Hasta cuándo estudiarás español?
2 ¿Hasta cuándo trabajarás / estudiarás?
3 ¿Qué harás cuando termines este curso?
4 ¿Qué harás hoy tan pronto como llegues a casa?
5 ¿Cuándo verás a tu mejor amigo?
6 ¿Qué harás cuando te retires?

2 Expressing purpose

A ¿*Para qué* ... ? Expressing purpose. Read the speech bubbles.

■ ¿Sabes para qué me ha llamado Jorge?

■ Sí, te ha llamado para que no te olvides de recogerlo a las ocho.

1 Underline the expressions used to ask and express purpose, then identify the mood and tense.
2 Now read the grammar section on the next page.

G de Gramática

- **¿Para qué** + verb in indicative?
  *¿Sabes **para qué me ha llamado Jorge?*** (Do you know why (=for what reason) Jorge phoned me?)
- The most common expression of purpose is **para que** + **verb in the subjunctive**:

*Sí, te ha llamado **para que no te olvides de** recogerlo a las ocho.*

- **Para** + **infinitive** is used when the subjects of the main and subordinate clauses are the same: *Voy **para asistir** a una conferencia.* (I'm going in order to attend a conference.)

B Rewrite the sentences following the example. Don't forget to add all the necessary elements (articles, prepositions, etc) for the sentences to make sense.

Example: Juan llamar para nosotros hablar trabajo él
Juan llama para que nosotros hablemos del trabajo con él.

1 Yo venir para yo ver abuela
2 Él comprar un coche hija para ella poder ir a trabajar
3 Yo mandar hijos Italia para ellos aprender italiano
4 Yo dejar fumar para tener buena salud
5 Nosotros reunirnos para resolver problema

C Practise the mini-dialogue in exercise A with your partner, then create three similar mini-dialogues and practise them.

3 Expressing emotional reactions, value judgments, need, possibility and probability

A Link the sentence halves in the column on the left with the appropriate ones in the column on the right.

1 Es importante	**a** que el avión se retrase.
2 Nos molesta	**b** que la reunión dure más de dos horas.
3 Es imposible	**c** que mandemos ese mensaje a nuestro cliente.
4 No es necesario	**d** que no vengas a la reunión.
5 No es aconsejable	**e** que lleguen a tiempo.
6 Es improbable	**f** que nunca lleguéis a tiempo.
7 Me gusta	**g** que el señor Gil no quiera venir.
8 No es lógico	**h** que me ayudéis.
9 Nos extraña	**i** que mi hijo haga los deberes a tiempo.
10 Es probable	**j** que aprendáis idiomas.

¡Espero que tengas mucho éxito!

G de Gramática

■ **Expressing emotional reactions, value judgments, need, possibility and probability**

- **Expressing emotional reactions**

  (No) verb in indicative + _que_ + verb in subjunctive

  Me extraña que . . . (it surprises me that ...)

  Me sorprende que . . . (it surprises me that ...)

  Me alegro de que . . . (I'm pleased that ...)

  Me extraña que no llame. (I'm surprised she doesn't call.)

  Siento / lamento que . . . (I'm sorry that ...)

  Me gusta que . . . (I like [the fact that] ...)

  Me molesta que . . . (It bothers me that ...)

- **Expressing value judgments**

  (no) ser + adjective + _que_ + verb in subjunctive

  ser importante que (it is important that)

  ser bueno / malo que (it is good / bad that)

  ser mejor / ser peor que (it is better / worse than)

  Es importante que acabes el curso. (It is important that you finish the course.)

  ser lógico que (it is logical that)

  ser aconsejable que (it is advisable that)

  ser difícil / fácil que (it is difficult / easy that)

- **Expressing need, possibility and probability**

  (no) ser + adjective + _que_ + verb in subjunctive

  ser probable / improbable que (it is likely / unlikely that) _Es improbable que él llegue mañana._

  ser posible / imposible que (it is possible / impossible that) _Es posible que recibamos el dinero pronto._

  ser necesario (it is necessary) _No es necesario que hagáis tanto ruido._

Tense agreement and the subjunctive

In this last unit of _En marcha,_ you are meeting many linguistic situations which require the use of the subjunctive and so far we have only been looking at instances in which the present subjunctive is required. For now, you should just be aware that the tense of the verb in the subordinate clause depends on the tense of the verb in the main clause. You will learn how the tense agreement works at a later stage .

4 Giving advice

A Before reading an extract from an article published in the Spanish newspaper _El País,_ addressed to graduates, about how to do well in a job interview, look at the Spanish nouns and write down their equivalents in English.

job selection process   job interview   letter of application   qualified person   salary references   availability   member of interview panel   interview   curriculum vitae company   post   department   interviewer

la entrevista laboral

el currículum

el titulado

el sueldo

la entrevista

el departamento

la empresa

la selección laboral

el seleccionador

Solicitar un trabajo
Applying for a job

la disponibilidad

el cargo

el entrevistador

las referencias

la carta de presentación

Now read the text and complete the information.

Carta de presentación
Debe ser . . .
Datos a incluir . . .

Currículum vitae
Debe ofrecer . . .
Debe incluir información
  sobre . . .
No debe incluir
  información . . .
Hay que evitar . . .

En la entrevista personal
el entrevistado
Debe informarse sobre . . .
Debe explicar . . .
Debe prestar atención a . . .
Debe resaltar . . .
Debe cuidar . . .

C Now explain, in your own words, the expressions in *italics*.

1 Cómo *salir airoso* de un proceso de selección laboral

2 Trátese *con mimo*

3 Debe ofrecer *una información concisa*

4 Una vez pasado *el primer eslabón*

5 Llevar un atuendo de estos que están '*de acuerdo con las normas sociales*'.

Cómo salir airoso de un proceso de selección laboral

C.M. Sevilla

Antes de llegar a la entrevista personal hay dos documentos a tener en cuenta: la carta de presentación y el currículum vitae. Círculo de Progreso, una empresa de información laboral y académica, indica algunos consejos para tener éxito en estos trámites.

• **Carta de presentación.** Es la primera información que la empresa tiene del titulado. Trátese con mimo. La carta debe responder a la pregunta, ¿por qué debo seguir leyendo?, que se formularán en la empresa. Debe ser personal y directa. Es en este documento y no en otro donde se incluirán los datos de carácter delicado (sueldo, referencias, disponibilidad).

• **'Currículum vitae'.** Debe ofrecer una información concisa sobre la potencialidad del titulado y, por supuesto, despertar el interés en el seleccionador para que concierte una futura entrevista. Huir de biografías o listados de actividades sin sentido. Círculo recomienda, 'aunque resulte obvio', cuidar la presentación y evitar errores ortográficos o de fechas, en primer lugar.
No buscar formatos muy complicados que puedan distraer la atención sobre el contenido, y enfatizar las posibilidades futuras sin cargar en exceso las acciones pasadas. El texto debe estar bien organizado, seguir una trayectoria lógica y debe evitar la inclusión de detalles que no dicen mucho. Siempre es mejor seleccionar los datos precisos de verdadero interés. A ser posible, el currículo no superará las dos hojas.

• **Entrevista personal.** Una vez pasado el primer eslabón –ya se ha captado el interés de la empresa, 'estamos en la fase crítica del proceso de selección'. Lo primero será asegurarse de quién es la persona que hará la entrevista: su cargo y departamento al que pertenece. No hay que tener miedo a explicar los méritos y los logros obtenidos en la trayectoria hasta el puesto al que se aspira. Prestar mucha atención a los gestos del entrevistador durante el encuentro, a sus posturas. Círculo de Progreso da como último consejo al titulado que destaque sus cualidades personales y que finalice la entrevista pensando en el próximo paso a dar.

Y la vestimenta: llevar un atuendo de estos que están 'de acuerdo con las normas sociales'.

Source: http / / www.elpais.es / p / d / 19990126 / sociedad / estudio / htm Adapted.

D Read the following sentences, identify the type of clauses shown in italics and say why you think the verbs in two of them are in the subjunctive while the other two are in the indicative. Read the grammar section on the next page and check your answer.

1 Esta empresa prefiere un candidato *que <u>sepa</u> español*.
2 Esta empresa prefiere al candidato *que <u>sabe</u> español*.
3 No buscar formatos muy complicados *que <u>puedan</u> distraer la atención sobre el contenido*.
4 La información *que <u>aparece</u> en el texto* debe estar bien organizada.

¡Espero que tengas mucho éxito!

G de Gramática

■ **Giving information in order to clarify, specify or identify**

As you have already seen in Unit 5, section D, on many occasions we need to give additional information in order to clarify, specify or identify, and one way to do this is by using **relative clauses** which work in a similar way to an adjective.

> *Esta empresa prefiere al candidato* (antecedent) ***que** sabe español.* (relative clause)
> (This company prefers **the** candidate who knows Spanish.)

The subjunctive in relative clauses

The subjunctive is used in relative clauses when the relative pronoun refers back to something (antecedent) which is unknown, non-existent, negative or indefinite. So in the sentence *Esta empresa prefiere un candidato **que** sepa español* ('This company prefers **a** candidate who knows Spanish.') the identity of *un candidato* (antecedent) is not known and so the subjunctive is required. Compare this example with the one above in which the identity of the candidate <u>is</u> known.

Note also that the personal *a* is not used in Spanish if the antecedent is an unknown, non-existent, negative or indefinite person.

Relative prounouns

• ***el que, la que, los que, las que*** (who, whom, which, that) are very often used after prepositions, and agree in gender and number with the noun to which they refer.

> *El departamento **al que** pertenece* (The department to which he belongs)
> *El puesto **al que** se aspira* (The post to which you aspire)
> *La calle **en la que** vivo está lejos* (The street in which / where I live is a long way away)

Relative adverb *donde* (where)

The adverb ***donde*** can be used as a relative adverb:

> *Es en <u>este documento</u> y no en otro <u>donde se incluirán los datos de carácter delicado.</u>*
>   antecedent   relative clause
> (It's in this document alone that the facts will be kept.)
> <u>*Villagarcía*</u>, <u>*donde veraneo*</u>, *es un lugar precioso.* (Villagarcía, where I spend the summer, is a lovely place.)
> antecedent   relative clause

E Work with a partner. Read the article in Ex.B again and try to find the eight relative clauses.

5 Asking for advice and saying what you would do

A Read the mini-dialogues and note what Emilia and the man in the second mini-dialogue are asking for. Then, read the grammar section and practise them with your partner. You can introduce some changes.

> – *Oye Emilia, mañana tengo una entrevista para un trabajo y no sé qué ponerme. ¿Tú, qué llevarías?*
> – *Pues, yo que tú, llevaría un traje de chaqueta oscuro.*

> – *Pues, yo, señor Márquez, la verdad es que esta temporada estoy cansadísimo, duermo mal y no me concentro. No sé qué hacer para encontrarme mejor ¿Qué haría usted en mi lugar?*
> – *Pues yo en su lugar, tomaría unos días de vacaciones.*

B Your partner will describe a situation to you and ask for your advice. Can you say what you would do in his/her situation? Follow the example given on the next page.

G de Gramática

■ **Asking for advice and saying what you would do**

You have already learnt different ways of asking for and giving advice. Now you are going to learn how to do it using the **Conditional Tense**.

Formation of the conditional tense

In English the conditional tense is formed by placing an auxiliary verb: 'would' before the verb: 'I <u>would wear</u> a suit if I were you', whereas in Spanish the conditional is formed by adding the endings of the imperfect tense of **-er** and **-ir** verbs (*-ía, -ías* . . .) to the infinitive of the verb: *Deberías dejar de fumar.* (You should give up smoking.)

Regular verbs

	hablar (*to speak*)	comer (*to eat*)	vivir (*to live*)	levantarse (reflexive) (*to get up*)
(yo)	hablaría	comería	viviría	**me** levantaría
(tú)	hablarías	comerías	vivirías	**te** levantarías
(usted)	hablaría	comería	viviría	**se** levantaría
(él/ella)	hablaría	comería	viviría	**se** levantaría
(nosotros(as))	hablaríamos	comeríamos	viviríamos	**nos** levantaríamos
(vosotros(as))	hablaríais	comeríais	viviríais	**os** levantaríais
(ustedes)	hablarían	comerían	vivirían	**se** levantarían
(ellos(as))	hablarían	comerían	vivirían	**se** levantarían

Irregular verbs

Twelve verbs (and all the verbs that derive from them) have an irregular conditional stem. They are the same verbs that are irregular in the future. They have the same endings as the regular verbs.

caber (*to fit, to be contained*)	**cabr-**	-ía	querer (*to want, to love*)	**querr-**	-ía
decir (*to say, to tell*)	**dir-**	-ías	saber (*to know*)	**sabr-**	-ías
haber (*to have*)	**habr-**	-ía	salir (*to go out, to leave*)	**saldr-**	-ía
hacer (*to do, to make*)	**har-**	-íamos	tener (*to have*)	**tendr-**	-íamos
poder (*to be able*)	**podr-**	-íais	valer (*to be worth*)	**valdr-**	-íais
poner (*to put*)	**pondr-**	-ían	venir (*to come*)	**vendr-**	-ían

Usage

- **Asking for advice**

  ¿(Tú) qué + verb in conditional (*en mi lugar*)?

  Oye Emilia, mañana tengo una entrevista para un trabajo y no sé qué ponerme. ¿Tú qué llevarías? (Look, Emilia, I've got an interview tomorrow and I don't know what to wear. What would you wear?)

- **Giving advice**

  Yo, en tu / su lugar; Yo que tú / usted; Yo   + conditional

  Pues, yo que tú, llevaría un traje de chaqueta oscuro. (If I were you, I'd wear a dark suit.)

Example: Tienes un examen de conducir y te sientes inseguro/a.

  – *Tengo un examen de conducir y me siento inseguro/a. No sé qué hacer. Tú, ¿qué harías en mi lugar?*

  – *Pues, yo en tu lugar practicaría más.*

1 Estás muy cansado/a, no puedes trabajar.

2 Tienes un(a) novio/a que siempre está de mal humor.

3 Te gusta mucho el español pero necesitas más práctica.

4 Tienes un trabajo horrible, el jefe es insoportable.

¡Espero que tengas mucho éxito!

Consolidation

A Now work with a partner. Taking into account what you have read in the article *Cómo salir airoso de un proceso de selección laboral*, you are going to write to a friend advising him or her on what to do or not to do when applying for a job. Use some of the following expressions:

1 Te aconsejo que escribas una carta de solicitud que . . .
2 Es importante que en ella . . .
3 Yo en tu lugar (no) incluiría . . .
4 En cuanto a tu currículum vitae es necesario que . . .
5 Creo que es mejor que . . .
6 En cuanto a su extensión, es recomendable que . . .
7 En la entrevista te aconsejo que . . .
8 En cuanto a la vestimenta, yo que tú . . .
9 Yo . . .

B Compare your letter with the letters of other people in your group.

In class or at home

A Read the sentences and write the verbs in brackets in the appropriate form.

1 Cuando _____ a Madrid, avísame (ir).
2 Lo hice, tan pronto como me lo _____ (pedir, ellos).
3 Antes de _____ de casa, pondré la alarma (salir).
4 Después de que _____ la actuación, vamos a tomar una copa (terminar, ellos).
5 En cuanto _____ el resultado, te lo digo (saber).
6 Cuando _____, nunca llevamos el móvil (viajar).
7 Hasta que no le _____ la razón, no paró de discutir (dar, nosotros).
8 Saldré después de que _____ con los niños (hablar).

B Read the sentences and write the verbs in brackets in the appropriate form. Write *que* or *para que* when necessary.

1 Es necesario que _____ pronto a Luis para _____ saber qué tiene que hacer (llamar, tú; poder).
2 Es aconsejable que tú _____ ejercicio todos los días para no _____ dolor de espalda (hacer, tener).
3 Es probable que _____ el trabajo por fax para _____ lo _____ a tiempo (mandar, nosotros; recibir, vosotros).
4 Es importante que lo _____ bien para _____ no _____ problemas (hacer, vosotros; haber).
5 Es mejor que vosotros _____ juntos para _____ el viaje _____ más barato (viajar, ser).
6 No es lógico que vosotros no _____ para _____ del problema (reunirse, hablar).

7 Es lógico que os _____ para _____ planificar todo (ver, yo; poder, nosotros).

8 Me alegro de que me _____ para _____ de los preparativos (llamar, él; planificar, nosotros).

C Read the sentences and write the verbs in the indicative or the subjunctive.

1 No encuentro el documento que _____ la información necesaria (tener).
2 No encuentro un documento que _____ la información necesaria (tener).
3 Buscamos un candidato que _____ trabajar independientemente (poder).
4 Quieren el coche que _____ ayer (ver).
5 Quieren un coche que _____ aire acondicionado (tener).

D Rewrite the sentences following the example. Use the relatives *que* or *donde*.

Example: Aquí tienes el dinero. Cobré este dinero ayer.
Aquí tienes el dinero que cobré ayer.

1 Vimos un vídeo. El vídeo nos gustó mucho.
2 Este es el gimnasio. Entreno todos los días en este gimnasio.
3 Este es el hotel. Vivimos en este hotel cinco años.
4 Ellos vieron el accidente. El accidente tuvo lugar en la autopista.
5 Compraron un coche. El coche era de segunda mano.
6 Este es el pueblo. Mi familia y yo veraneamos en este pueblo.

E Complete the following sentences with the appropriate relative pronouns: *el que, la que, los que, las que*.

1 La casa en _____ vivo es muy vieja.
2 El coche en _____ íbamos no era mío.
3 Las calles por _____ pasamos ayer son muy peligrosas.
4 La señora de _____ te hablé quiere trabajar con nosotros.
5 Los clientes para _____ trabajo no son muy agradables.

F Read the mini-dialogues and complete them.

1 – Me gusta todo, no sé qué comer, ¿ _____?
– Yo, en tu lugar _____ paella.

2 – Sr. Romero, el martes tengo que cenar con el jefe y no sé de qué hablarle.
¿_____, _____?
– Yo, que _____, _____ de golf.

3 – Oye, Lola, tengo que ir a una fiesta y no sé qué llevar. ¿ _____?
– Yo, _____ una botella de vino.

4 – José, odio mi trabajo pero necesito el dinero. No sé qué hacer. _____ ¿
_____?
– Yo, en _____, _____ otro trabajo.

Acércate al mundo del español
La música: el alma del pueblo

You have reached the end of *¡En marcha!*. We hope you have enjoyed learning Spanish with *¡En marcha!* as much as the author and everybody involved in its production have enjoyed creating it. We also hope that you will carry on learning more about Spanish and the Spanish-speaking world. But before saying *Hasta la vista*, read the text that follows.

A través de la música los pueblos expresan lo más íntimo de su alma y el mundo del español está lleno de ritmos que suenan y resuenan por todas partes. El sonido de la guitarra, las palmas, las voces, en los tablaos flamencos, en las calles de Andalucía; el sonido del bandoneón acompañando los bailarines de los tangos en Buenos Aires; la música que surge de los violines, el guitarrón, la guitarra, la vihuela y las trompetas de la música de Mariachi en México; los cuerpos moviéndose al son de una salsa en Puerto Rico o Nueva York; las voces y la música de la Nueva Trova Cubana y un largo etcétera. La música y las palabras nos dejan entrever el alma de la gente que la disfruta, la siente y la vive. La música nos hace llorar, reír, bailar, soñar. La música, en definitiva, expresa el alma del pueblo que la vive y la crea.

A Think about the music of where you are from and talk about it with people in your group.

B You can go on the Internet and find out more about the music, dances and songs of the Spanish-speaking world.

¡MUCHA SUERTE Y HASTA PRONTO!

Essential vocabulary

Verbos relacionados con cocinar / *Cookery terms*

batir	*to beat / whisk*
calentar (e>ie)	*to heat*
cortar	*to cut*
echar	*to throw*
freír	*to fry*
lavar	*to wash*
mezclar	*to mix*
mover (o>ue)	*to move*
pelar	*to peel*
poner	*to put*
sacar	*to take out*
usar	*to use*

Utensilios de cocina / *Kitchen utensils*

plato (m)	*plate*
sartén (f)	*frying pan*
tenedor (m)	*fork*

Alimentos / *Food*

aceite (m)	*oil*
alimentos (m) procesados	*processed food*
aves (f)	poultry
azúcar (m)	sugar
carne (f)	meat
carnes rojas	red meat
cebollas (f)	onions
dulces (m)	sweets / sweet things
fruta (f)	fruit
huevos (m)	eggs
pasta (f)	pasta
patatas (f)	potatoes
pescado (m)	fish
sal (f)	*salt*
vegetales (m)	*vegetables*
verduras (f)	*vegetables*

Componentes de los alimentos / *Food ingredients*

azúcares (m)	*sugars*
hidratos (m) de carbono	*carbohydrates*
grasas (f)	*fats*
nutrientes (m)	*nutrients*
proteínas (f)	*proteins*
fibra (f)	*fibre*

Solicitar un trabajo / *Applying for a job*

cargo (m)	*post / responsibility*
carta (f) de presentación	*letter of application*
currículo (m)	*curriculum vitae*
departamento (m)	*department*
disponibilidad (f)	*availability*
empresa (f)	*company*
entrevista (f)	*interview*
entrevista laboral (f)	*job interview*
entrevistador (m)	*interviewer*
referencias (f)	*references*
selección (f) laboral	*job selection process*
seleccionador (m)	*member of interview panel*
sueldo (m)	*salary*
titulado (m)	*graduate / qualified person*

Música y baile / *Music and dance*

artista (m+f)	*artist*
bailaor (m)	*flamenco dancer*
baile (m)	*dancing*
cantaor (m)	*flamenco singer*
cante (m)	*flamenco singing*
danza (f)	*dance*
flamenco (m)	*flamenco*
flauta (f)	*flute*
guitarra (f)	*guitar*
guitarrista (m+f)	*guitar player*
habanera (f)	*type of Cuban music*
instrumento (m)	*instrument*
mazurca (f)	*mazurka*
melodía (f)	*tune*
música (f)	*music*
percusión (f)	*percussion*
polka (f)	*polka*
tango (m)	*tango*
vals (m)	*waltz*
violín (m)	*violin*

Perfil de una población / *Peoples of the world*

húngaro (m)	*Hungarian*
eslavo (m)	*Slav*
árabe (m)	*Arab*
judío (m)	*Jew*

Role-play 1   En el aeropuerto

 Public Announcements

A 🔊 Listen to the recording and say which two of the following announcements are made:

1 'Atención señores pasajeros, el avión con destino a Mallorca va a salir con una hora de retraso.'

2 'Se ruega al señor García, pasajero del vuelo IB501 con destino a Santiago de Compostela, se presente en la Oficina de Información'.

3 'Última llamada para los señores pasajeros del vuelo IB765 con destino a Miami, por favor diríjanse inmediatamente a la puerta de salida número 2'.

4 'Se ruega a la señora García, pasajera del vuelo IB502 con destino a Santiago de Chile, se presente en la Oficina de Información'.

B Read the announcements again and look for the Spanish words or expressions equivalent to:

1 a male passenger
2 delay
3 departure gate
4 destination
5 last call

 En la aduana **(Customs)**

A Look at the drawings and match them to the following items.

> bolsa   bolso   libros   maleta
> máquina de afeitar   mochila
> paraguas   ropa zapatos

B 🔊 Listen to the dialogue between el señor García and *el funcionario de aduanas* (customs officer) and then answer the following questions in English.

1 Does el señor García have something to declare?
2 What pieces of luggage is he carrying?
3 Which item in his rucksack is he being questioned about?
4 Is he carrying an umbrella in his suitcase? If not, what has he got in it?

C Now look at the transcript of the dialogue in the Support Book and role-play a similar situation with your partner.

Role-play 2 En la cafetería del aeropuerto

Juan and Luisa are at Madrid–Barajas airport to collect their Mexican friends, Carlos and Lupita. The aeroplane from Mexico still hasn't arrived and, while they wait, they go and have a drink in the café.

A 🗣 Listen to the dialogue between Juan, Luisa and a waitress.

Camarera:	Buenos días, ¿qué quieren tomar?
Luisa:	_____
Juan:	Yo una cerveza fría.
Camarera:	¿Quieren alguna tapa?
Luisa:	_____
Camarera:	Tenemos calamares, ensaladilla, aceitunas, tortilla de patatas y queso.
Luisa:	_____
Juan:	Para mí, tortilla y queso.
Camarera:	Muy bien "Se anuncia la llegada del avión procedente de México"
Luisa:	El avión ya está aquí._____.
Camarera:	Sí , ahora mismo.
Luisa:	_____
Camarera:	Son nueve euros con veinte céntimos.
Juan y Luisa:	Gracias. Adiós.

B Now read the dialogue and complete the conversation, choosing the correct phrases from the box:

> ¿Cuánto es? Para mí, calamares
> La cuenta por favor   ¿Qué tienen?
> Yo, una Coca-Cola

C 🗣 Listen to the recording again and check your answers. Read the transcript, if necessary.

D Now role-play the dialogue with two other people in your group. Here is a menu you can use.

Cafetería Buen Viaje

Bebidas calientes (*Hot beverages*)
café con leche (*white coffee*)
café solo (*black espresso*)
cortado (*espresso coffee with a bit of milk*)
chocolate (*hot chocolate*)

Bebidas frías (*cold drinks*)
agua mineral sin gas (*still mineral water*)
agua mineral con gas (*fizzy mineral water*)
zumo de naranja natural (*natural orange juice*)
limonada (*lemonade*)
té con hielo (*iced tea*)
Coca-Cola
vino tinto / blanco (*red / white wine*)
cerveza (*beer*)
caña (*draught beer*)

Tapas
ensaladilla (*potato salad*)
calamares (*squid*)
tortilla de patatas (*Spanish omelette*)
aceitunas (*olives*)
jamón serrano (*cured ham*)
queso (*cheese*)
patatas fritas (*crisps*)

Role-play 3 Concertando una cita

A Before listening to the first recording, study the information below.

To arrange to meet *Note idiomatic use of* quedar *to suggest an informal social arrangement*	• ¿Quedar + *time* + para + *activity?* • ¿Qué tal si + *activity* + *time?* • ¿Y si + *activity?*	¿Quedamos esta noche para tomar unas copas? *(What about going out for a drink tonight?)* ¿Qué tal si nos vemos mañana? ¿Y si nos vemos por la tarde?
To suggest doing something together	• ¿Ir + *activity?*	¿Vamos al cine?
Arranging when and where to meet	• ¿Cómo + quedar? Quedar . . . • ¿Cuándo + verse? Verse . . . • ¿Dónde + quedar? En . . .	¿Cómo quedamos? Quedamos el jueves a las siete en mi casa. ¿Cuándo nos vemos? Nos vemos mañana a las cinco de la tarde. ¿Dónde quedamos? En el café Derby.
To make an excuse	• Lo siento pero no puedo + *excuse* • Lo siento pero no puedo, es que + *excuse*	Lo siento pero no puedo, tengo otra cita Lo siento pero no puedo, es que tengo que ir a casa de mis padres.
To express agreement		Vale/Muy bien/De acuerdo

To say you agree

B 🎧 Dialogue 1. First listen to the telephone conversation between Luis and his friend Sofía and complete the information.

Actividad propuesta	Hora	Lugar

C 🎧 Dialogue 2. Now listen to the conversation between Lola and Juan Carlos and say if the following statements are *verdadero* (true) or *falso* (false):

	V	F
1 Juan Carlos queda con Lola por la noche.	☐	☐
2 Lola dice que no puede porque tiene otra cita.	☐	☐
3 Juan Carlos le propone a Lola ir al cine al día siguiente.	☐	☐
4 Lola acepta la invitación.	☐	☐
5 Juan Carlos y Lola quedan en verse la semana siguiente.	☐	☐

D Now work with your partner and, using the information from A, arrange to meet him/her.

Role-play 4   Comprando un billete de autobús/de avión

A 🌐 Read the information, then listen to the dialogue and choose which of the phrases you think you hear.

1 Luisa pregunta qué autobuses hay para Madrid
  a por la mañana
  b por la tarde
	2 El horario de autobuses por la tarde es
	  a uno a las 14h y otro a las 22h
	  b uno a las 14.30 y otro a las 21h

3 Por la mañana hay autobuses
  a a las 8.30 y 11:40
  b a las 8:30 y 11:30
	4 Luisa compra un billete para el autobús que sale
	  a a las 11:30
	  b a las 14h

5 Luisa compra un billete
  a de ida y vuelta **b** de ida
	6 El billete cuesta
	  a 20 euros **b** 21 euros

7 Luisa prefiere
  a ventanilla **b** pasillo
	8 Luisa paga
	  a con tarjeta **b** en metálico

B Now role-play with your partner the following situation:

Estudiante A: Estás en Madrid. Hoy es lunes 4 de agosto. El martes próximo tienes que ir a Barcelona y llegar allí antes de las cuatro de la tarde. Vas a una oficina de IBERIA a comprar un billete, de ida y vuelta en clase turista, en un asiento al lado de la ventanilla. No quieres viajar muy temprano. Vas a pagar con tarjeta.

AVIÓN Nº	SALIDA	LLEGADA
740	6:00	6:50
742	8:00	9:50
743	11:30	12:20
745	14:00	15:50
746	16:00	16:50

Estudiante B: Trabajas en IBERIA. Consulta el horario y atiende a tu compañero/a.

Asking for information
- Quería saber qué autobuses/trenes/aviones hay | para Madrid | por la mañana
- ¿A qué hora salen los autobuses/aviones | para Granada | por la tarde?
- Hay uno que sale a las ... y llega a las ... Hay otro a las ... que llega a las ...
- ¿Me podría dar un horario de trenes/autobuses   para Madrid?
- Sí, ¡cómo no! / Por supuesto.

Buying a ticket:
- Quería | comprar | un billete a Madrid | en el autobús | de las diez treinta | para el lunes
-        | reservar | un billete | en el tren | de las quince horas | para el martes
-        | | | en el avión | de las veintidós | para el día 23
- ¿Cuánto es / cuesta?

Describing the ticket
- de ida/de ida y vuelta ... de primera clase/de segunda clase/de turista ... en ventanilla/en pasillo

Paying
- ¿Cómo va a pagar? ¿En metálico? ¿Con tarjeta?
- **En la estación de autobuses/trenes:** andén número ...
- **En el aeropuerto:** puerta número ...

Role-play 5   En el hotel

<u>A</u> Read the vocabulary box below and work out the meaning of the expressions listed:

> Una habitación individual
> Una habitación doble
> De dos camas
> De matrimonio
>
> Para una persona
> Para dos personas
> Para un matrimonio y un niño / dos niños
>
> Con ducha y baño
> Con ducha
> Con cuarto de baño / sin cuarto de baño
>
> Para una / dos / tres noches
>
> Con desayuno
> Con desayuno y cena = media pensión
> Con desayuno, comida y cena = pensión completa
>
> Las llaves
> El ascensor

<u>B</u> 🔘 Listen to the dialogue and complete it.

Recepcionista: *Buenas tardes.*
Cliente: *Buenas tardes.*
Recepcionista: *¿Qué quería?*
Cliente: *Una habitación _____ por favor.*

Recepcionista: *Sí. ¿De dos camas o de matrimonio?*
Cliente: *De _____*
Recepcionista: *¿Para cuántas noches?*
Cliente: *Para __ noches.*
Recepcionista: *¿Con baño y ducha?*
Cliente: *Sí, por favor.*
Recepcionista: *¿Con _____ o media pensión?*
Cliente: *Con _____.*
Recepcionista: *Muy bien. El desayuno es de _____ de la mañana.*
¿Podría dejarme su carnet de identidad?
Cliente: *Aquí tiene.*
Recepcionista: *Firme aquí, por favor. Aquí tiene la llave. Su habitación es la número _____, en el _____ piso. El ascensor está _____.*
Cliente: *Muchas gracias.*

<u>C</u> Practise with your partner. Role-play the following situations.

1 You would like a single room for one night, with shower, with breakfast.
2 You would like a double room with 2 beds and an extra bed for your child for a week, with bathroom and shower, half-board.
3 You would like 2 rooms, one double room with one bed and a single room, for two nights, the double room with shower and bath and the single room only with shower. Full board.

Role-play 6 En el médico

A With the help of your tutor, work out the meaning of the following expressions:

Síntomas
- No encontrarse bien / encontrarse mal: No me siento bien / me siento mal
- Tener dolor de + *part of the body*: Tengo dolor de cabeza, de garganta, de estómago . .

Note: *me / te / le . . . doler* + **definite article** + **part of the body**
To say 'My back hurts' you can use the verb *doler* (radical changing *o>ue*). The verb is used in the third person, in a similar way to *gustar*:
Me *duele* **la** *espalda.* (literally, to me it hurts the back.).
¿Te *duele* **la** *cabeza?* (Do you have a headache?)
Le *duelen* **los** *pies.* (His/her feet are hurting.)

- Doler + *part of the body*: Me duele la espalda / el pie / el tobillo / el estómago . . .
- Tener fiebre / tos: tengo fiebre / tengo 38 grados de temperatura / tengo mucha tos
- Sentirse mareado(a) / cansado(a): Me siento mareado(a) / Me siento (muy)cansado(a)
- Toser; Vomitar

Enfermedades y problemas
Tener + *symptoms*
catarro;
una infección de garganta / de orina
una indigestión
una insolación
una inflamación en la rodilla / en el pie
Tener el brazo / la muñeca / la pierna /
  el tobillo / el pie roto(a)

Remedios
- Tomar aspirinas / paracetamol / antibióticos / jarabe para la tos
- Ponerse una crema antiinflamatoria
- Quedarse en la cama x días
- Descansar
- Beber agua / no beber alcohol
- Comer poco / no comer grasas
- Hacerse un análisis de sangre / de orina / una radiografía

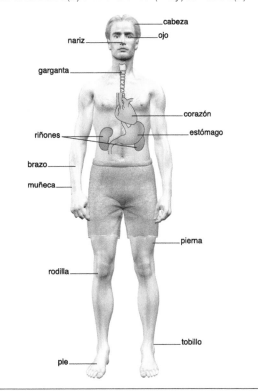

cabeza
ojo
nariz
garganta
corazón
estómago
riñones
brazo
muñeca
pierna
rodilla
tobillo
pie

B Now listen to the conversation between a doctor and his patient to find out:

a the patient's symptoms
b the doctor's diagnosis
c the doctor's advice

C Taking the transcript of this dialogue as a model, work with a partner and role-play a similar situation. Take turns.

Role-play 7   En la farmacia

A Before listening to the recording, read the list of items that appear in the box and classifiy them depending on whether they belong to a first aid kit (B, botiquín) or a toiletries kit (N, neceser).

B Listen to the dialogue between the pharmacist and the customer and tick the items that the *cliente* buys.

C Now, with a partner, role-play a dialogue similar to the one you have just heard. Take turns. Use the role-play you have just heard as a model.

Botiquín: First-Aid Kit

a agua oxigenada: *hydrogen peroxide*

b algo contra la picadura de mosquitos: *something for mosquito bites*

c algo para limpiar las lentillas: *something to clean contact lenses*

d algo para la mala digestión: *something to aid digestion*

e unos antibióticos: *antibiotics*

f una caja de aspirinas: *a box of aspirins*

g una caja de tiritas: *a box of plasters*

h un cepillo de dientes: *a toothbrush*

i crema de afeitar: *shaving cream*

j una crema desinfectante: *antiseptic cream*

k esparadrapo: *sticking plaster*

l unas gotas para los ojos: *eye drops*

m un jarabe para la tos: *cough mixture*

n pasta de dientes: *toothpaste*

o una crema bronceadora: *suntan cream*

p una venda: *bandage*

Role-play 8　En la tienda de ropa

A *¿De qué color es la falda?* Ask your partner what colour the various clothes items in the pictures are. Take turns to answer.

B Now take it in turns to describe what people in your group are wearing.

C Before listening to the role-play, familiarise yourself with the following expressions:

> ¿qué talla?　*what size?* (*for clothes*)
> pequeña / mediana / grande　(*small / medium / large*)
> la 38 / la 42 / la 44 . . .
> ¿qué número?　*what size?*　(*for shoes*)
> el 37 / 38 / 39 . . .
> ¿puedo probarme . . . ?　(*can I try on . . . ?*)
> el probador　(*changing room*)
> quedar bien / mal / pequeño(a) / grande / estrecho(a)　(*to fit well / not to fit (properly) / to be too small / too big / too tight*)
> la camisa me queda bien　(*the shirt fits well*)
> ¿qué precio tiene? / ¿cuánto cuesta? (*what's the price? / how much is it?*)
> caro / barato　(*expensive / cheap*)

D 🕴 Begoña and her friend Olga are looking at clothes in a boutique, *una tienda de ropa*. Listen to the dialogue and complete the information.

	Begoña	**Olga**
Prenda		
Color		
Talla		
Precio		
Compra		
No compra		

E Work with a partner and go shopping for clothes. Take turns. Use the role-play you have just heard as a model.

Role-play 9   En la gasolinera

A Before listening to the dialogue, familiarise
yourself with the following expressions
and vocabulary which you will hear in the
recording:

gasolina *(petrol)*   llenar *(to fill up)*
super *(four star)*   mirar / comprobar *(to take a look at / check)*
normal *(two star)*   la presión de las ruedas *(the tyre pressures)*
sin plomo *(unleaded)*   el nivel de aceite *(oil level)*
gasóleo *(diesel)*   el parabrisas *(windscreen)*

To ask for something
¿(Por favor), podría + *verb* + *noun*? ¿Podría comprobar el nivel de aceite?

To offer a service ¿Le *(indirect object pronoun)* + *verb* + *noun*? ¿Le limpio el parabrisas?

B 🗣 Now listen to the dialogue and tick
the expressions that you hear.

María quiere	El empleado se ofrece a
gasolina sin plomo	mirar el nivel de aceite
gasóleo	comprobar la presión de las ruedas
super	limpiar el parabrisas

María quiere
20 litros
10 litros
lleno

María paga
con dinero
con tarjeta de crédito

C 🗣 Listen to the recording again and
then role-play it with a partner. Use some
of the expressions in the box above.

Role-play 10   Comprando comida

A Before listening to the dialogue, familiarise yourself with the ways to express quantities.

Quantity + *de* + name of product

un cuarto de kilo de . . .	*(a quarter kilo of . . .)*
medio kilo de . . .	*(half a kilo of . . .)*
un kilo de . . .	*(a kilo of . . .)*
cien / doscientos . . . gramos de . . .	*(100 / 200 grams of . . .)*
un cuarto de litro de . . .	*(a quarter litre of . . .)*
medio litro de . . .	*(half a litre of . . .)*
un litro de . . .	*(a litre of . . .)*
una botella de un litro de . . .	*(a litre bottle of . . .)*
un paquete de . . .	*(a packet of . . .)*
una caja de	*(a box of . . .)*
media docena de . . .	*(half a dozen . . .)*
una docena de . . .	*(a dozen . . .)*

■ *¿Qué deseaba?*

B Here is a list of food products. Look up any you don't know in a dictionary. Then, using some of the quantity expressions above, choose one item from each category and say how much you would like to buy.

■ *¿Quería un kilo de manzanas*

verduras y legumbres	fruta	carne	pescado
cebollas	fresas	carne de cerdo	bacalao
coliflores	mango	carne de cordero	bonito
espinacas	melón	ternera / vaca	merluza
lechugas	manzanas	pollo	sardinas
lentejas	naranjas		merluza
patatas / papas	papaya	**embutidos**	trucha
tomates	peras	chorizo	
zanahorias	piña	jamón	**bebidas**
ajos	plátano	queso	agua mineral
		salchichón	leche
			vino

otros

aceite de oliva	café	huevos	sal	aceitunas / olivas	galletas	pan
de girasol	chocolate	mantequilla	vinagre	azúcar	harina	pasta

C In Spain and Hispano-America, there are of course supermarkets (*supermercados*), where you can buy almost everything, but you can also buy your food in traditional markets or in specialised food shops. Here are the names of some of these shops:

carnicería   charcutería   frutería
panadería   pescadería   verdulería

Now say where you would go to buy the following food.

manzanas	pan	merluza	zanahorias	pollo
salchichón	papayas			

D 🔊 Listen to the dialogue and complete:

Dependienta:	Buenos días, ¿qué deseaba?
Cliente:	Quería una _____, por favor.
Dependienta:	¿De litro?
Cliente:	No, _____.
Dependienta:	¿Algo más?
Cliente:	Sí. _____ de chorizo, doscientos de _____ y una _____.
Dependienta:	Aquí tiene. ¿_____?
Cliente:	No, nada más. ¿Cuánto es?
Dependienta:	Son _____.

E Tonight you and your friend are preparing dinner for a friend. Decide what you are going to cook, make a list of the things you need to buy and then go shopping. Don't forget to think about the quantities you need to buy.

Role-play 11   En el restaurante

A Before listening to the dialogue read the menu and find out the meaning of the dishes you don't know. Ask people in your group. If necessary, use a dictionary.

La carta / El menú

Primer plato
Sopa de ajo
Espárragos con mayonesa
Ensalada
Calamares
Paella

Segundo plato
Carne asada
Pollo al ajillo
Chuletas de cordero
Merluza a la romana
Parrillada de mariscos

Postre
Fruta del tiempo
Fresas con nata
Helados variados
Flan de la casa
Tarta de queso de la casa
Quesos

Pan
Bebidas: agua – cerveza – vino
Café

B Listen to the dialogue and complete the information:

	Elena	**Laura**	**Ignacio**
Bebida			
Primer plato			
Segundo plato			
Postre			

C Answer the questions below:

1 Does the waiter when addressing the customers use *tú* or *usted*?

2 What does the waiter say when asking:
 a if they want something to drink,
 b what they're going to have for dinner and
 c if everything is all right?

D Now in a group of four, practise what you have just learnt. Take it in turns to be the waiter.

281

Role-play 12   En la Oficina de Correos

A Match the phrases or words on the left with their equivalent on the right.

1 echar una carta	**a**	the parcel
2 enviar / mandar	**b**	the stamp
3 certificado/a	**c**	the postcard
4 por correo normal	**d**	to post a letter
5 contra reembolso	**e**	registered
6 el sello	**f**	to send
7 el formulario	**g**	the addressee
8 el remitente	**h**	normal post
9 el destinatario	**i**	the form
10 el paquete	**j**	cash on delivery
11 la tarjeta postal	**k**	the sender

B 🎧 Listen to the dialogue and complete the table with the details of items to be posted:

	destino	correo normal	certificada y urgente	¿cuánto es todo?
cartas				
paquete				

C Now role-play with your partner the following situation at a post office. Use some of the expressions shown below in your conversation:

> Estás en España, quieres comprar sellos para mandar dos tarjetas postales, una a Santigo de Compostela y otra a Estados Unidos y una carta a Escocia. Además, tienes que mandar un paquete certificado y urgente a Valencia (España).

> *You're in Spain and want to buy stamps to send one postcard to Santiago de Compostela and one to the USA, as well as a letter to Scotland. Additionally, you need to send a registered urgent parcel to Valencia.*

Role-play 13   En la Oficina de Turismo

A 🎧 Listen to the dialogue and tick the phrase you hear.

1 Offering help

a ¿En qué puedo ayudarle?

b ¿En qué le puedo ayudar?

c ¿Puedo ayudarle?

2 Referring to the price range, location of a hotel and type of room

a Uno barato, en el centro, sin cuarto de baño en la habitación

b Uno no muy caro, en el centro y con cuarto de baño en la habitación

c Uno de lujo, en el centro y con cuarto de baño en la habitación

3 Referring to the specific price of a room in a hotel

a El precio de la habitación es de 80 euros por noche

b La habitación cuesta 80 euros por noche

c El precio de la habitación es de 85 euros por noche

4 Referring to the distance

a Está a quinientos metros andando de aquí

b Está a cinco minutos a pie de aquí

c Está a unos minutos en coche

5 Saying the breakfast is not included in the price

a No, el desayuno es aparte

b No, el desayuno no está incluido

c No, es aparte

6 Asking for information

a ¿Tiene un mapa de la ciudad?

b ¿Tiene unos folletos con información sobre la ciudad?

c ¿Tienes un mapa de la ciudad?

B In the dialogue *tres estrellas* ('three stars') is mentioned when referring to the category of the hotel. Are you familiar with this classification? If not, ask other people in your group or your tutor to explain how the classification system works.

C Work in groups of three and go to an *Oficina de Turismo*. Ask them

a to book two single bedrooms with shower in a hotel for you

b and to give you information about the town or city you are visiting.

Use the transcript as reference but adapt it to your needs.

Role-play 14 En el garaje

A Before listening to the dialogue, familiarise yourself with the new vocabulary shown in the drawings and read the following words and expressions.

> arrancar (un coche) *(to start a car)*
> estar estropeado/a *(to be damaged / have something wrong with it)*
> estar gastado/a *(to be worn [out])*
> la grúa *(breakdown truck)*
> las pastillas del freno *(brake pads)*
> perder aceite *(to lose oil)*
> tener un pinchazo *(to have a puncture)*
> tener una avería *(to break down)*

B First read the list of problems with Carlota's car. Then listen to the dialogue between Carlota and the mechanic and then identify what Carlota says and what the mechanic answers. Write C for Carlota and M for mechanic.

1 El carburador está muy sucio.
2 El coche está estropeado.
3 El faro derecho no funciona.
4 El faro izquierdo no funciona.
5 Hace un ruido muy raro al arrancar.
6 El motor no está muy bien.
7 Las pastillas del freno están muy gastadas, necesita unas nuevas.
8 Pierde aceite.
9 Las ruedas delanteras están muy viejas.

C 🔊 Listen to the dialogue again and answer the following questions.
1 How long does it take the mechanic to find out what is wrong with Carlota's car?
2 How much is it going to cost to repair Carlota's car?
3 When will the car be ready?

D Work with your partner and role-play a similar situation. Use the transcript as a model if necessary.

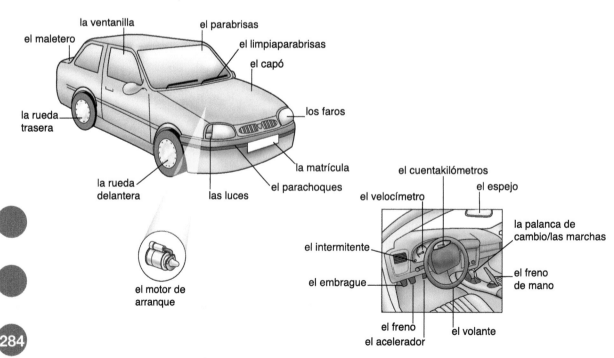

- la ventanilla
- el maletero
- el parabrisas
- el limpiaparabrisas
- el capó
- la rueda trasera
- los faros
- la rueda delantera
- las luces
- la matrícula
- el parachoques
- el motor de arranque
- el cuentakilómetros
- el espejo
- el velocímetro
- la palanca de cambio/las marchas
- el intermitente
- el embrague
- el freno de mano
- el freno
- el acelerador
- el volante

Role-play 15   El pronóstico del tiempo

A Work with your partner and describe today's weather where you live in Spanish.

B Work with your partner and describe what yesterday's weather was like where you live.

C  Listen to the weather forecast for Spain and complete the table.

El tiempo en España			
	En el norte	**En el centro**	**En el resto de la península**
Miércoles:			
Jueves:			

D In a group of four people write down the weather forecast for next weekend and present it as if you were making a TV weather forecast. Don't forget to illustrate your words with a map of the area.

Key to the: 'In class or at home' activities

Unidad 1

A Hola, ¿Cómo te llamas?

A te llamas; me llamo; mi nombre; son mis apellidos.

B **a** me llamo; **b** se llama; **c** Se llama; **d** te llamas; **e** Se llama;

C **a** ¡Hola! Buenas noches; **b** ¡Hola! Buenos días; **c** ¿Cómo se llama? **d** ¿Cómo te llamas? **e** ¿Cómo se llama? **f** Adiós; **g** Hasta luego;

E **a** ¿Cómo se llama? **b** ¿Cómo te llamas? **c** ¿Se llama (usted) Rosalía? **d** ¿Se llama (ella) Dolores?

G **a** ¡Ho-la! Me lla-mo Jo-sé Rei-no-so Ca-o; **b** Bue-nos dí-as ¿Có-mo se lla-ma?; **c** Cas-ta-ño Ca-bre-ra son mis a-pe-lli-dos

B Mucho gusto

A **a** (¡Hola!) Buenos días. ¿Cómo está (usted)? **b** Mira, Sofía, éste es José. **c** El gusto es mío. **d** Encantada. **e** ¿Cómo se escribe su segundo apellido? **f** Mire, señor Márquez, éste es el doctor Fuentes Ramos.

B Miguel: ¿cómo estás?; ésta es la Sra Ventura: El gusto es mío / Encantada

C **1** Hola, **buenos** días. **2** Buenos días. ¿**Cómo** está? **3** Muy **bien**, gracias. ¿Y **usted**? **4** Bien, gracias. Mire, señor García, éste es el doctor Sánchez. **5** Encantado. **6** **Mucho** gusto.

D **1** ¿Cómo te llamas? / ¿Cómo se llama? **2** ¿Cómo se escribe tu / su primer apellido? **3** ¿Cómo se escribe tu / su nombre? **4** ¿Cómo está? **5** ¿Cómo estás?

E Sr, Sra, Srta, Dr, Dra.

C ¿De dónde eres y dónde vives?

1 Yo soy de España. Soy español.
2 Tú eres de los Estados Unidos. Eres estadounidense.
3 Usted es de Rusia. Es ruso.
4 Mi amiga es de Argentina. Es argentina.

B **1** ¿Cómo te llamas? / ¿Cómo se llama?
2 ¿De dónde eres? / ¿De dónde es?
3 ¿Dónde vives? / ¿Dónde vive?
4 ¿Dónde viven Jorge y María?
5 ¿De dónde eres? / ¿De dónde es?

C **1** **trabajar**: trabajo, trabajas, trabaja, trabajamos, trabajáis, trabajan.
comer: como, comes, come, comemos,coméis, comen.
recibir: recibo, recibes, recibe, recibimos, recibís, reciben.
2 **estar**: estoy, estás, está, estamos, estáis, están.
ser: soy, eres, es, somos, sois, son.

D ¿Qué idiomas hablas?

A **estudiar**: estudio, estudias, estudia, estudiamos, estudiáis, estudian.
leer: leo, lees, lee, leemos, leéis, leen.
abrir: abro, abres, abre, abrimos, abrís, abren.

B **a** son **b** son **c** sois **d** es **e** somos **f** soy

C **1** alemán **2** danés **3** finlandés **4** holandés **5** húngaro **6** islandés **7** ruso **8** sueco **9** turco **10** árabe

D **a** cero **b** seis **c** trece **d** veintiuno **e** treinta y siete **f** cuarenta **g** cincuenta y cinco **h** sesenta y cuatro **i** setenta **j** ochenta y ocho **k** noventa **l** noventa y nueve

E **1** Soy, trabajo, vivo, Hablo **2** eres, vives, hablas **3** se llama, vive, vive, trabaja, Habla **4** somos, vivimos, estudiamos, Hablamos **5** estáis, habláis, Estudiáis, aprendéis **6** son, viven, trabajan, estudian, aprenden

Unidad 2

A La familia

A **2** Rafael es el hermano de Rosario y Jorge.
3 Dolores es la suegra de David. **4** Laura es la nieta de Dolores. **5** Luisa es la nuera de Pedro y Dolores. **6** Iván es el primo de Laura y Victoria. **7** Carlota es la hermana de Iván y Marina. **8** Rosario es la cuñada de Luisa. **9** Pedro y Dolores son los padres de Rafael. **10** Iván es el nieto de Pedro y Dolores.

B Pedro; Dolores; Dos; Casada; David; Dos; Casado; Tres; Soltero

El padre de Rosario se llama Pedro y su madre se llama Dolores. Tiene dos hermanos, Jorge y Rafael. Rosario está casada con David. Tiene dos hijos: Laura y Victoria. Su hermano Jorge está casado y tiene tres hijos, dos hijas, Carlota y Marina y un hijo, Iván. Su hermano Rafael está soltero / no está casado y no tiene hijos.

C **1** está / tiene; **2** son; **3** estás; **4** está / tiene (usted); **5** vivimos / vive; **6** es

B ¡Cumpleaños feliz!

A se(p)tiembre, abril, junio, noviembre

B **1** tiene; **2** Qué / es; **3** Es el; **4** Cuándo es; **5** tienes; **6** somos / Tenemos; **7** tienen / cinco hijas; **8** está / vive; **9** hablan

C **1** hermanos; **2** primos; **3** la tía; **4** la sobrina; **5** el primo; **6** la cuñada; **7** el marido; **8** el tío

D **Se** llama Miriam y viv**e** en Lima. **Su** madre es peruana y **su** padre es colombiano. **Tiene** dos hermanos y una hermana. **Su** hermano mayor está soltero y **sus** otros hermanos están casados. **Ella** no est**á** casada, pero **tiene** un hijo. **Su** hijo se llama Francisco. **Sus** hermanos casados tienen dos hijos cada uno. **Su** hermana tiene un niño y una niña y **su** hermano tiene dos niños. El hijo de **su** hermana tiene cinco años como **su** hijo. **Sus** hermanos viven en los Estados Unidos y **sus** padres en España.

C ¿Cómo es?

A **1** ¿Cómo eres (tú) / es (usted)?
2 ¿Cómo tiene(s) el pelo?
3 ¿De qué color tiene(s) los ojos?
4 ¿Es / eres atractiva?
5 ¿Lleva(s) gafas?

This is the description of a woman.

B **a** fe**o**; **b** mal**a**; **c** baj**o** / fuert**e**; **d** viej**o**; **e** grand**es** / bonit**os**

C Mi vecino es un hombre bajo y guapo. Tiene los ojos grandes y el pelo liso. Su nariz es pequeña y proporcionada. Es bastante simpático y alegre.

D **1** El tío de mi padre es mayor.
2 Mi amigo es agradable.
3 El profesor alemán es serio.
4 Nuestro primo tiene los ojos grandes y negros.
5 El niño es trabajador.

E **1**d; **2**e; **3**f; **4**h; **5**b; **6**a; **7**c; **8**g

F **1** Él es un hombre inteligente.
2 Nosotros somos gente bastante organizada.
3 Nuestras hijas tienen los ojos oscuros.
4 Su vecino es bastante antipático.
5 Soy bastante alto.
6 Ella es una mujer muy organizada.
7 Mi hermana es un poco tímida.
8 Mi mejor amigo/a es muy simpático/a.

G **1** es / está; **2** estamos; **3** es / está; **4** estoy / son; **5** están; **6** son / están; **7** eres / estoy

H **Ser:** yo soy; tú eres; usted, él / ella es; nosotros(as) somos; vosotros(as) sois; ustedes, ellos(as) son.

Tener: yo tengo; tú tienes; usted, él / ella tiene; nosotros(as) tenemos; vosotros(as) tenéis; ustedes, ellos(as) tienen.

Llevar: yo llevo; tú llevas; usted, él / ella lleva; nosotros(as) llevamos; vosotros(as) lleváis; ustedes, ellos(as) llevan.

D ¿A qué te dedicas?

A **1** La / trabajador**a**
2 un / monóton**o**
3 La / impacient**e**
4 Los / simpátic**os**
5 una buen**a** / organizad**a**
6 El / peligros**o**
7 un / disciplinad**o**
8 La / interesant**e**

B **1** profesor; **2** estudiantes; **3** traductor; **4** camarera; **5** informático; **6** mecánicos

C **1** falso – cuarenta y ocho
2 falso – cuarenta y seis
3 verdadero
4 verdadero
5 falso – no tiene trabajo / está en paro
6 verdadero
7 verdadero
8 falso – es un chico (yo soy el mediano)

arreglar	trabajar	tener
arreglo	trabajo	tengo
arreglas	trabajas	tienes
arregla	trabaja	tiene
arreglamos	trabajamos	tenemos
arregláis	trabajáis	tenéis
arreglan	trabajan	tienen

Unidad 3

A Cosas de ciudad

A

Tú	Usted
1	¿Cómo se llama?
2 ¿ A qué te dedicas?	....
3	¿Dónde vive usted?
4 ¿ Cuál es tu dirección?	....
5	¿Tiene (usted) móvil?
6	Perdone, ¿hay un banco por aquí?
7 Oye, por favor, ¿dónde está la catedral?	....
8	¿Adónde va (usted)?

B **1** ¿Adónde **vas**? **Voy al** mercado **a** comprar vegetales.
2 ¿Adónde **van** Leticia y Laura? **Van al** restaurante **a** comer.
3 ¿Adónde **vais** vosotros? **Vamos a la** estación **de** tren **a** tomar **el** tren.
4 ¿Adónde **va** José? **va a la** Oficina de Correos **a** enviar **una** carta.

C NOMBRE: Sofía
APELLIDOS: Pérez Domingo
PROFESIÓN: abogada
DIRECCIÓN: Pl. Delicias 16
CIUDAD: Madrid
CÓDIGO POSTAL: 45078
TELÉFONO: 91 319 32 65 90
FAX: 91 320 32 78 00
CORREO ELECTRÓNICO: Sofi3@entel.com

D *Telephone number:* noventa y uno, trescientos diecinueve, treinta y dos, sesenta y cinco, noventa.

Fax number: noventa y uno, trescientos veinte, treinta y dos, setenta y ocho, cero cero

1
Perdona ¿dónde está la calle Fuegos?
La primera calle a la izquierda.

2
Perdone, ¿hay un teatro por aquí?
Sí, la segunda calle a la derecha.

3
Oye por favor, el bar Luna está por aquí ¿verdad?
Sí, sigue todo recto, la segunda calle, a la izquierda.

B Mi casa

A **a** tercer; **b** segunda; **c** quinto; **d** primer; **e** primeros; **f** décima; **g** octavo; **h** sexta

B un / pequeñ**os** / un / grand**e** / una / bonit**a**. La / cuadrad**a** / una / una / grand**e** / una / una

C **a** amarillos; **b** verde; **c** blanca; **d** azul; **e** grises; **f** naranja; **g** negro; **h** roja

D **a** detrás de; **b** delante de; **c** enfrente de; **d** encima de; **e** debajo de; **f** al lado de; **g** dentro de

E **1** ningún; **2** ninguna; **3** una / ninguna; **4** ningún; **5** una / una; **6** uno

F **1** cuántas; **2** cuántos; **3** cuántos; **4** cuántas; **5** cuántos

C La ciudad y el pueblo

A **1** El autobús es menos cómodo que el metro. Es más incómodo.
2 El coche es menos caro que el taxi. Es más barato.
3 La ciudad es menos limpia que el pueblo. Es más sucia.
4 Ir a pie es menos cansado que ir en bicicleta. Es más relajante.

B **1** pref**iero** / barat**a**; **2** pref**erís** / al; **3** pref**ieren** / tiene; **4** hay; **5** pref**ieres**; **6** Pref**iero** / porque

C **1** mejor; **2** mayor; **3** peor; **4** mejor; **5** menor

D **a** Cien españoles.
b Novecientas setenta y ocho personas.
c Cuatrocientos treinta y dos euros.
d Doscientas noventa y nueve alumnas.
e Novecientos veintisiete programas.
f Quinientas cinco lenguas.
g Setecientos sesenta.
h Trescientos diez médicos.
i Ciento cuarenta y un jardineros.
j Ochocientas quince arquitectas.

D **En la ciudad**

A 1b; 2d; 3c; 4a

B **1** ¿Cuál? Lugo (es la más pequeña)
2 ¿Cuál? Barcelona
3 ¿Qué? Barcelona y Cádiz
4 ¿Qué? Sevilla, Cádiz y Murcia

C es / española. Está / la costa / más / moderna / dinámica / variada / importantes / Está a.

D **1** muy fácil / facilísimo
2 muy contaminada / contaminadísima
3 muy feo / feísimo
4 muy aburrido / aburridísimo
5 muy rico / riquísimo
6 muy grande / grandísima
7 muy simpático / simpatiquísimo

Unidad 4

A **¿Qué hora es?**

A **1** ¿Qué hora **es**? **Es la una y media.**
2 Luisa, ¿**tienes** hora? Sí, **son las diez y veinte.**
3 Por favor, señor, ¿tiene (usted) **hora?** Sí, **son las siete menos cuarto**.
4 Señora por favor **tiene (usted)** hora? No, **lo siento**.

B **a** Son las seis y diez de la tarde.
b Es mediodía. / Son las doce del mediodía.
c Es la una y cuarto de la mañana / madrugada.
d Son las once menos veinte de la noche.

e Es la una menos cinco de la tarde / del mediodía.
f Son las ocho y media de la mañana.
g Son las ocho menos veinticinco de la tarde.
h Es la una de la tarde / del mediodía.
i Son las cinco y veinte de la mañana / madrugada.
j Son las cinco menos cuarto de la tarde.

C **a** Juan se viste rápidamente.
b ¿Cuánto cuestan los libros?
c Nos divertimos mucho aquí.
d Mis padres se despiertan muy tempano.
e (Yo) siempre me acuesto tarde los sábados por la noche.
f ¿Entendéis (vosotros) español?
g ¿Quiere (usted) comer?
h Los niños juegan bien al fútbol.
i ¿Ustedes siempre se acuestan temprano los fines de semana?
j Tu hijo mide 2m.

D **a** lunes; **b** jueves; **c** sábado; **d** martes; **e** viernes; **f** domingo; **g** miércoles

E **1** correctamente; **2** perfectamente; **3** maravillosamente; **4** elegantemente; **5** silenciosamente

F se despiertan; van; van; se quedan; ven; duermen; sus amigos van; se acuestan

G

	despertarse	ducharse	vestirse	acostarse
me	despierto	ducho	visto	acuesto
te	despiertas	duchas	vistes	acuestas
se	despierta	ducha	viste	acuesta
nos	despertamos	duchamos	vestimos	acostamos
os	despertáis	ducháis	vestís	acostáis
se	despiertan	duchan	visten	acuestan

H

regular verbs			irregular verbs		
-ar	**-er**	**-ir**	**-ar**	**-er**	**-ir**
desayuno	como	escribo	cuento	entiendo	voy
estudias	bebes	vives	estás	eres	pides
habla	aprende	sube	cierra	tiene	prefiere
nos levantamos	comemos	describimos	estamos	volvemos	corregimos
completáis	corréis	recibís	cerráis	sois	seguís
cocinan	deben	reparten	piensan	quieren	van

B Los horarios

B **1** Desayunan entre las siete y media y ocho y media de la mañana.

2 Comen entre las dos y tres de la tarde.

3 Cenan entre las nueve y diez y media de la noche.

C **1** Mike come menos que Pablo. Pablo come más que Mike.

2 Mi hermano cena tanto como yo. Yo ceno tanto como mi hermano.

3 Teresa se viste más rápidamente / menos despacio que Jacinto. Jacinto se viste menos rápidamente / más despacio que Teresa.

4 Mi abuela merienda menos que mi abuelo. Mi abuelo merienda más que mi abuela.

5 Elena trabaja más horas al día que Carmen. Carmen trabaja menos horas al día que Elena.

6 El banco abre más tarde que el supermercado. El supermercado abre más temprano / menos tarde que el banco.

D **1** A las dieciséis (horas).

2 A las catorce (horas) treinta (minutos).

3 A las seis (horas) cuarenta y cinco (minutos)

4 A las dieciocho (horas).

C La rutina diaria

A **1** Mi hermano y yo siempre desayunamos a las once y diez de la mañana.
¿A qué hora desayunáis (tu hermano y tú)?

2 Francisco normalmente termina las clases a las siete de la tarde.
¿A qué hora termina (Francisco las clases)?

3 Mi familia come a menudo a las dos y cuarto de la tarde.
¿A qué hora come tu familia?

4 Julio y José casi siempre van al bar a las diez menos cuarto de la noche.
¿A qué hora van (Julio y José) al bar?

5 El abuelo a veces cena muy tarde; cena a las doce menos cuarto de la noche.
¿A qué hora cena el abuelo?

6 Las clases empiezan demasiado temprano, empiezan a las ocho de la mañana.
¿A qué hora empiezan las clases?

B **1** se levanta; **2** se ha levantado; **3** desayuna **4** ha desayunado; **5** vuelve; **6** ha tenido; **7** termina; **8** va; **9** ha trabajado; **10** ha ido

C

	-ar	-er	-ir
he	desayunado	comido	vivido
has	estudiado	bebido	escrito
ha	trabajado	aprendido	salido
hemos	estado	visto	ido
habéis	hecho	tenido	dicho
han	se han acostado	sido	abierto

D Tareas domésticas

A **1** conducen; **2** traducimos; **3** conozco; **4** doy; **5** veis; **6** hacen; **7** digo; **8** vienes; **9** tenemos; **10** sé

B **2** La profesora está enseñando matemáticas.

3 Los estudiantes están haciendo un examen.

4 Nosotros estamos limpiando la casa.

5 Vosotros estáis haciendo la cena.

6 La secretaria está hablando por teléfono.

7 La ingeniera está diseñando un puente.

8 Los mecánicos están arreglando los coches.

C **1** llega / se ha levantado / ha llegado

2 he estado / estoy

3 cocina / ha cocinado

4 ha devuelto / he sacado

5 ha ido / tiene

6 estudian / han podido / han tenido, tienen

7 traduzco / he tenido

8 limpiamos / hemos descansado

D **a** Son las ocho de la mañana.

b Son las siete y cuarto de la tarde.

c Son las cinco y media de la madrugada / mañana.

d Son las doce menos veinticinco de la noche.

e Son las seis y diez de la tarde.

E **1** ¿Qué haces? ¿Qué estás haciendo?; Estoy leyendo

2 estoy vistiéndome / me estoy vistiendo

3 está jugando

4 está hablando

5 está descansando

F **1** Hoy hemos comido a las dos y cuarto.

2 Este año Marta ha escrito una novela.

3 Este mes vosotras habéis tenido exámenes.

4 Esta mañana usted ha llegado tarde.

5 Esta tarde ellos han visto el partido de fútbol.

6 Últimamente he estado muy estresado.

7 Este curso tú has estudiado mucho.

8 Recientemente nosotros hemos resuelto muchos problemas.

Unidad 5

A Objetos

A **1** ésa / aquélla; **2** ésa; **3** este; **4** aquél;
5 aquél

B **1** para; **2** para; **3** por; **4** para; **5** para;

B Terminar o no terminar

A **1**a; **2**none; **3**a; **4**a; **5**a; **6**a; **7**none;
8a

B **1** *Lo* mandamos mañana.
2 *Me* recibe por la tarde.
3 *La* he acabado por la mañana.
4 *Lo* tenéis el lunes.
5 *Ellos lo* llevan al aeropuerto.
6 Usted *los* ha entendido.
7 *Lo* queremos alquilar. / Queremos
alquilar*lo*.
8 *La* está haciendo. / Está haciéndo*la*.
9 *Los* tenemos que devolver hoy / Tenemos
que devolver*los* hoy.
10 *Te* veo a las diez.
11 *Las* estamos escuchando. / Estamos
escuchándo*las*.
12 *Lo* están viendo. / Están viéndo*lo*.

C **1** Este pastel *lo* como yo.
2 Nosotros llamamos a Pedro.
3 La clase *la* da la profesora de biología.
4 A los compañeros *los* informáis vosotros.

D **1** No, todavía no / aún no la he cortado.
2 Sí, las hemos empezado esta semana.
3 No, todavía no / aún no la han terminado.
4 Sí, lo he leído al llegar.
5 Sí, la han visto esta mañana.

E **1** ¿Tienes hambre? ¿Por qué no haces un
bocadillo?
Lo acabo de hacer. / Acabo de hacerlo.
2 ¿Tenéis sed? ¿Por qué no compráis una
botella de agua?
La acabamos de comprar. / Acabamos de
comprarla.
3 ¿Tiene (usted) sueño? ¿Por qué no duerme
una siesta?
La acabo de dormir. / Acabo de dormirla.
4 ¿Tienen (ustedes) prisa? ¿Por qué no
terminan la reunión?
La acabamos de terminar. / Acabamos de
terminarla.
5 ¿Tienes calor? ¿Por qué no enciendes el
aire acondicionado?
Lo acabo de encender. / Acabo de
encenderlo.

F **1** conozco / la conozco
2 saben / lo sabemos hablar / sabemos
hablarlo
3 sé / sabemos

C Permisos y préstamos

A **1**f; **2**g; **3**h; **4**e; **5**d; **6**a; **7**b; **8**c

B **1** pon / poned; **2** cuelga / colgad; **3** ordena /
ordenad; **4** haz / haced; **5** pasa / pasad;
6 limpia / limpiad; **7** compra / comprad; **8**
friega / fregad

1 pon**la** poned**la**; **2** cu**é**lga**la** / colgad**la**;
3 ord**é**na**la** / ordenad**la**; **4** haz**la** / haced**la**;
5 p**á**sa**lo** / pasad**lo**; **6** l**í**mpia**lo** / limpiad**lo**;
7 c**ó**mpra**lo** / compradlo; **8** fri**é**ga**los** /
fregad**los**

C **1** **Te** doy dinero.
2 **Les** envías el paquete.
3 No **le** prestamos la casa.
4 ¿**Le** habéis mandado el recibo?
5 ¿**Les** han entregado las notas?
6 Regála**melo** un piso.
7 Leéd**selas** las noticias.
8 Juan **se lo** compra un helado.

1 **Te lo** doy.
2 **Se lo** envías.
3 No **se la** prestamos.
4 ¿**Se lo** habéis mandado?
5 ¿**Se las** han entregado?
6 Regálamelo.
7 leédselas
8 Juan se lo compra

D Los ordenadores

A **1** La casa **que te he dejado** es de mi padre
2 La mujer **que ha entrado** es la directora
de la empresa.
3 Una vídeo-cámara es una máquina **que
sirve para reproducir imágenes y
sonido.**
4 Ese señor **que tiene bigote** es el profesor
de matemáticas de mi hijo.
5 El libro **que tenéis en casa** es de mi tío.
6 El coche **que ha comprado** Pedro es
muy lento.
7 El avión **en que he viajado** hoy por poco
tiene un accidente.
8 La litografía **que ves,** ¿es de Dalí?

B Mi tío Julián **que vive en México** es el
hermano menor de mi madre. Es un hombre
alegre **que siempre está de buen humor**. La
ciudad **en que vive** es una ciudad grande **que
está a unos trescientos kilómetros de la**

capital. Él está casado pero no tiene hijos. Es dueño de un hotel **que está construido cerca de una playa fantástica**. Viene a España una vez cada dos años. Cuando está en España viaja mucho.

C **a** configuración, **b** documentos, **c** disquete, **d** disco duro; **e** ayuda; **f** teclado; **g** cerrar sesión; **h** microprocesador; **i** monitor; **j** ratón; **k** impresora; **l** programas; **m** ejecutar; **n** buscar **o** Cerrar sesión

Unidad 6

A El tiempo libre

A **1** Los domingos nunca dormimos / no dormimos nunca hasta las once de la mañana.
2 Hacemos deporte a menudo. / A menudo hacemos deporte.
3 Siempre salimos con nuestros amigos / Salimos siempre con nuestros amigos.
4 Casi nunca vamos de compras. / No vamos de compras casi nunca.
5 Vemos la televisión casi siempre. / Casi siempre vemos la televisión.
6 Los fines de semana vamos de excursión de vez en cuando. / Los fines de semana de vez en cuando vamos de excursión.
7 Vamos de copas muchas veces.
8 Vamos de compras pocas veces.
9 No navegamos por Internet nunca. / Nunca navegamos por Internet.
10 Casi siempre leemos.
Note: there are other possible answers.

B **1**e; **2**c; **3**f; **4**b; **5**a; **6**d
Note: there are other possible answers.

C **1** ¿Qué va a hacer este domingo?
2 ¿Qué piensan hacer la semana que viene?
3 ¿Qué van a hacer el lunes que viene?
4 ¿Adónde van mañana por la noche?
5 ¿Qué va a hacer el mes próximo?
6 ¿Adónde van en enero?

B El tiempo y el clima

A **1** La primavera . . . el 20 de junio
2 El verano . . . el 20 de se(p)tiembre
3 El otoño . . . el 20 de diciembre
4 El invierno . . . el 20 de marzo

B El tiempo está nublado.
El tiempo está nuboso.
El tiempo está soleado.
El tiempo está ventoso.
El tiempo está caluroso.
El tiempo está frío.

El tiempo está bueno.
El tiempo está malo.

C **a** Hoy hace frío, hace cinco grados centígrados. Tengo frio.
b Hoy hace mucho calor, hace veintiocho grados centígrados. Tengo calor.
c Hoy hace muchísimo frío, hace menos diez grados centígrados. Tengo mucho / muchísimo frío.
d Hoy hace bastante calor, hace veinticuatro grados centígrados. Estoy bien.
e Hoy hace muchísimo frío, hace menos diecisiete grados centígrados. Tengo mucho / muchísimo frío.

D **a** En Barcelona hace sol / buen tiempo. El tiempo está soleado / bueno.
b En Cáceres hay niebla. El tiempo está nublado.
c En Madrid nieva / está nevando. El tiempo está malo.
d En Salamanca llueve. El tiempo está lluvioso.
e En Sevilla hay nubes. El tiempo está nuboso / cubierto.
f En Valencia hay viento. El tiempo está ventoso.

C Gustos

A **1** me gustan . . . me gustan; **2** te gusta . . . me gusta; **3** le interesan; **4** nos interesa . . . le interesa; **5** os gusta; **6** nos gusta; **7** me interesan; **8** les interesan; **9** nos gusta; **10** les gusta; **11** le gusta; **12** le interesa

B . . . me gusta . . . me gustan . . . le gusta . . . prefiere . . . me gusta . . . me gustan . . . le gusta . . . le parece . . . me gusta . . . me parece . . . gusta . . . prefiere . . . me gusta . . . prefiere

C **1** A mí sí.; **2** Sí, ¿y a ti? A mí no; **3** Sí, ¿y a ti? A mí también; **4** No, ¿y a ti? A mí sí; **5** No, ¿y a ti? A mí sí.

D De viaje

A A la señora Mascato le gusta viajar mucho y viaja a menudo. Le gusta viajar con sus amigos. Siempre que puede, viaja en avión. Viaja porque le interesan otras culturas. Le gusta ir a países exóticos. Le encanta visitar ciudades. La verdad es que prefiere las ciudades al campo. Siempre se aloja en hoteles y nunca ha viajado en viajes organizados. Su estación preferida para viajar es el otoño porque hay menos gente.

B **1** ¿Has / Ha viajado (usted) alguna vez por Argentina?
2 ¿Habéis / Han ido (ustedes) alguna vez en globo?
3 Paco y María, ¿han estado en Costa Rica?
4 ¿Has viajado / Ha viajado (usted) alguna vez en avión?
5 ¿Habéis / Han visitado (ustedes) alguna vez el Museo Picasso de Barcelona?
6 Los señores Baltar, ¿han ido alguna vez a España?

C **1** A mí me gusta el sol. Me gustaría ir a la playa.
2 A mi hija le gusta salir de noche. Le gustaría ir a un lugar turístico.
3 A mi hijo le gusta la aventura. Le gustaría ir a un país exótico.
4 A mis padres les gusta la tranquilidad. Les gustaría ir a un hotel de lujo.
5 A mis mejores amigos les gusta la montaña. Les gustaría visitar los Pirineos en España.

Unidad 7

🅰 ¿Qué hiciste?

A **1** vivieron; **2** cerraron / cerró; **3** llegó / llegué; **4** ganó; **5** jugaron; **6** entendiste; **7** llegasteis; **8** compramos; **9** se vistió; **10** realicé

B **1** Cerré las puertas. Las cerré.
2 Visitamos a Pedro. Lo visitamos.
3 Comprendimos la lección. La comprendimos.
4 Pablo y Margarita pintaron el piso. Lo pintaron.
5 Buscasteis a vuestras amigas. Las buscasteis.
6 Los estudiantes ganaron el partido. Lo ganaron.
7 Eliminasteis los insectos. Los eliminasteis.
8 Saludaron a su profesora. La saludaron.
9 Usted firmó el acuerdo. Usted lo firmó.
10 Comprasteis la casa. La comprasteis.

C **1** Les entregué los deberes. Se los entregué.
2 Le explicaron el asunto. Se lo explicaron.
3 Le regalamos un vestido. Se lo regalamos.
4 Me mandaron un paquete. Me lo mandaron.
5 Les escribí una carta. Se la escribí.
6 El jefe os pagó la cena. El jefe os la pagó.
7 Te prestaron dinero. Te lo prestaron.
8 Usted nos compró lotería. Usted nos la compró.
9 Mike les enseñó inglés. Mike se lo enseñó.
10 Os arreglé el coche. Os lo arreglé.

D **1** ¿Con quién trabajasteis ayer / ¿Con gente de qué nacionalidad trabajasteis ayer?
2 ¿A qué hora llegó el tren?
3 ¿Con quién saliste el lunes pasado?
4 ¿Cuándo compraste el coche?
5 ¿Dónde aterrizó el avión?
6 ¿Cuántos vestidos de verano comprasteis?
7 ¿Cuántos pisos vendieron la semana pasada?
8 ¿Qué sofá escogiste?
9 ¿Cuál escogiste?
10 ¿Qué repasaste ayer?

🅱 ¿Qué tal las vacaciones?

A **1** ¿Adónde fuiste de vacaciones el año pasado?
2 ¿Con quién fuiste?
3 ¿En qué mes fuisteis? / ¿Cuándo fuisteis?
4 ¿Cuánto tiempo estuvisteis?
5 ¿Dónde os alojasteis?
6 ¿Cómo viajasteis / fuisteis?
7 ¿Qué hicisteis?
8 ¿Cómo lo pasasteis?
9 ¿Qué tiempo hizo?

B **1** vinieron; **2** estuvieron; **3** viajamos; **4** llevé; **5** visitamos; **6** tuvimos; **7** fue; **8** hizo; **9** llovió; **10** salimos; **11** pudieron; **12** se fueron; **13** fueron; **14** hicieron; **15** anduvieron; **16** pasaron

C **1** Se la explicamos.
2 Se lo compré.
3 No te lo di.
4 Los profesores se lo comunicaron.
5 Os la enviaron por correo.
6 Sus tíos se lo prometieron.
7 Se lo comí.
8 Tuvimos que pagarla. / La tuvimos que pagar.
9 ¿Te lo mandé?
10 Fuisteis a dárselos. / Se los fuisteis a dar.

D **1** recibimos; **2** hemos estado; **3** fui; **4** ha hecho / hicimos; **5** han hecho / hicieron

E **1** había llegado; **2** había terminado; **3** se había ocultado; **4** había tenido; **5** había visto

🅲 La vida de uno

A Goya **nació** en Fuendetodos, España, en **mil setecientos cuarenta y ocho**. **A los veintidós** años se fue a Roma donde pintó algunas obras. Al cabo de un año, en mil setecientos setenta y uno, regresó a Zaragoza. Durante diecinueve años, entre mil setecientos setenta y tres y mil setecientos noventa y dos trabajó en la Fábrica de Tapices donde pintó sus obras más alegres.

Ese mismo año sufrió una crisis profunda. En ese momento se quedó sordo. De mil setecientos noventa y dos a mil ochocientos ocho pintó retratos de aristócratas en los que representó aspectos negativos de los personajes. En mil ochocientos ocho Napoleón invadió la Península. Entre mil ochocientos ocho y mil ochocientos catorce tuvo lugar la Guerra de la Independencia. En esa época Goya pintó *Los fusilamientos de la Moncloa*. En mil ochocientos catorce, Napoleón perdió la guerra y se restituyó la monarquía absoluta. Entre mil ochocientos ocho y mil ochocientos veinte Goya pintó sus *pinturas negras*, obras llenas de horror y brutalidad. Desde mil ochocientos veinte hasta mil ochocientos veintiocho, Goya vivió en Francia donde murió.

Note: other variations are possible.

B **1** Nació en el siglo dieciocho.
   2 Se quedó sordo a los cuarenta y cuatro años.
   3 Napoleón invadió España a principios del siglo diecinueve.
   4 La Guerra de Independencia duró seis años.
   5 Vivió en Francia de 1820 a 1828.

D alcanza . . . empieza . . . alcanzan . . . supera . . . es . . . conquistan

   1 En el siglo cinco.
   2 En el siglo dieciséis.

D Recuerdos del pasado

A **1**h; **2**e; **3**f; **4**g; **5**b; **6**c; **7**d; **8**a

B **1** comíamos
   2 estaba viendo / llamó / me levanté / abrí / había
   3 paseaba / oyó
   4 iba / pudo / se puso
   5 hizo / llovía / decidí / vi / preparaba / terminé
   6 trabajaba / tuvo
   7 volvía
   8 esperábamos / compramos
   9 fuisteis
   10 era / estaba

C nació / se marchó / estaba combatiendo / abandonó / se puso / empezó / descubrió / formó / abandonó / empezó / llevó / era / decía / pensaba / murió

Unidad 8

A ¡Baila conmigo!

A **1** Sí, consúltalo / No, no lo consultes
   2 Sí, tómala / No, no la tomes
   3 Sí, abridlos / No. no los abráis
   4 Sí, tíralos / No, no los tires
   5 Sí, compradla / No, no la compréis

B **1**
Música y baile

nouns	verbs	Perfil de una población
el tango	bailar	blancos
la música	enlazarse	negros
las habaneras		españoles
las polkas		italianos
las mazurcas		alemanes
el vals		húngaros
el candome		eslavos
la danza		árabes
la percusión		judíos
la melodía		
el violín		
la flauta		
la guitarra		
el instrumento		
el bandoneón		
el acordeón		
el ritmo		

C **2 a** v; **b** f bailaba el candombe; **c** v; **d** v; **e** f nadie tenía dinero; **f** f se hablaban lenguas diferentes; **g** v; **h** v; **i** v; **j** f era un baile socialmente poco aceptado

B ¡Siga por ahí!

A Mira, por favor, ¿sabes dónde está el ayuntamiento?
Sí, toma la primera calle a la izquierda, síguela hasta el final y allí está.

Mire, por favor ,¿sabe si hay una tienda de música por aquí?
Uhmm . . Ah sí, siga todo recto hasta el final y después tome la calle de la derecha.

B
tú	usted
1 súbelo / no lo subas	súbalo / no lo suba
2 bájalas / no las bajes	bájelas / no las baje
3 elígeselo / no se lo elijas	elíjaselo / no se lo elija
4 pídeselo / no se lo pidas	pídaselo / no se lo pida
5 averígualo / no lo averigües	averígüelo / no lo averigüe
6 traelos / no los traigas	tráigalos / no los traiga
7 dáselo / no se lo des	déselo / no se lo dé
8 cómprasela / no se la compres	cómpresela / no se la cómpre
9 devuélvesela / no se la devuelvas	devuélvasela / no se la devuelva
10 levántate / no te levantes	levántese / no se levante

vosotros	ustedes
1 subidlo / no lo subáis	súbanlo / no lo suban
2 bajadlas / no las bajéis	bájenlas / no las bajen
3 elegídselo / no se lo elijáis	elíjanselo / no se lo elijan

4 pedídselo / no se lo pidáis — pídanselo / no se lo pidan

5 averiguadlo / no lo averigüéis — averígüenlo / no lo averigüen

6 traedlos / no los traigáis — tráiganlos / no los traigan

7 dádselo / no se lo deis — dénselo / no se lo den

8 comprádsela / no se la compréis — cómprensela / no se la compren

9 devolvédsela / no se la devolváis — devuélvansela / no se la devuelvan

10 levantaos / no os levantéis — levántense / no se levanten

C 1 d, 2 c, 3 e, 4 a, 5 b

D **1** ¡Qué salada! ¡Qué paella tan salada! ¡Qué paella!
 2 ¡Qué malo! ¡Qué café tan malo! ¡Qué café!
 3 ¡Qué interesante! ¡Qué libro tan interesante! ¡Qué libro!
 4 ¡Qué horrible! ¡Qué película tan horrible! ¡Qué película!

E **1** ¡Me encanta / gusta muchísimo la ópera!
 2 ¡Odio / Detesto / Me espanta la cerveza!
 3 ¡Me encantan / gustan muchísimo las películas románticas!
 4 ¡Odio / Detesto / Me espantan las hamburguesas!
 5 ¡Qué pescado tan malo / horrible!
 6 ¡Qué malo!

¿Qué pasará?

A **1** Este año no creo que vaya de vacaciones a México.
 2 Pedro y yo, no pensamos que el jefe nos suba el sueldo.
 3 Los expertos no creen que el problema de la escasez del agua tenga solución.
 4 Nuestro abogado no piensa que mañana firmemos los papeles.
 5 No pienso dejar de trabajar dentro de dos años.
 6 No creéis que los ordenadores dominen nuestra vida, ¿verdad?
 7 No creo que en este siglo vaya a haber muchos terremotos.
 8 Mi hermano pequeño no piensa ser médico.

B ... empezará su ... Va ... va ... sabe ... su ... espera ... Se imagina ... hará ... A ella le gustaría ... viajará ... irá ... supone ... se casará ... tendrá ... le preocupa ... sabe ... acabará ... sabe ... vivirá ... espera

C **1** No sé cuándo terminaré mis estudios, pero espero encontrar un buen trabajo y ganar dinero.
 2 No sé si me casaré, pero me gustaría conocer a un hombre interesante.
 3 No sé dónde compraré una casa en el futuro, pero espero comprarla en una ciudad grande.
 4 No sé cómo haré el experimento, pero espero que salga bien.

¡Espero que tengas mucho éxito!

A **1** vayas; **2** pidieron; **3** salir; **4** terminen; **5** sepa; **6** viajamos; **7** dimos; **8** hable

B **1** llames / que pueda; **2** hagas / tener; **3** mandemos / que / recibáis; **4** hagáis / que / haya; **5** viajéis / que / sea; **6** os reunáis / hablar; **7** vea / que podamos; **8** llame / que planifiquemos

C **1** tiene; **2** tenga; **3** pueda; **4** vieron; **5** tenga

D **1** Vimos un vídeo que nos gustó mucho.
 2 Este es el gimnasio donde entreno todos los días.
 3 Este es el hotel donde vivimos cinco años.
 4 Ellos vieron el accidente que tuvo lugar en la autopista.
 5 Compraron un coche que era de segunda mano.
 6 Este es el pueblo donde mi familia y yo veraneamos.

E **1** la que; **2** el que; **3** las que ; **4** la que; **5** los que

F **1** ¿Tú qué comerías? / comería
 2 ¿De qué le hablaría usted? / usted, le hablaría
 3 ¿Qué llevarías? / llevaría
 4 Tú, en mi lugar, ¿Qué harías? / tu lugar, buscaría

Glossary of grammatical terms

Adjective   Adjectives are words that describe nouns. When we say *Pablo es alto y María es baja* the words *alto* and *baja* are telling us what Federico and María are like; they give us more information about them.

Adverb   Adverbs modify verbs, adjectives or other adverbs by saying how, when, where, how much or how often something is done or happens. Words like *bien* (well), *mañana* (tomorrow), *aquí* (here), *bastante* (enough), *sencillamente* (simply) are adverbs.

Article   Articles are words that indicate if a noun is specific or non-specific. The **definite article** 'the' has four forms in Spanish: *el, la, los, las*, e.g. *el profesor de español* (the Spanish teacher). The **indefinite article** 'a/an, some' also has four forms: *un, una, unos, unas*, e.g. *un profesor de español* (a Spanish teacher).

Conjunction   Conjunctions are words which link two other words, phrases or clauses: *El perro y el gato* 'the dog and the cat'; *Estoy cansada pero lo haré* (I am tired but I will do it); *No salgo porque tengo que trabajar* (I am not going out because I have to work).

Demonstrative   Demonstratives are words that indicate the relative proximity of people, animals or things to the speaker, either in space or in time. They can be **adjectives**: *este coche* (this car) or **pronouns**: *éste* (this one)).

Direct object   A noun or a pronoun that is on the direct receiving end of the action. In the sentence *tengo las tijeras aquí* (I have the scissors here), *tijeras* is the direct object.

Finite verb   A verb whose form changes according to the person, number, tense and mood, as distinct from being an infinitive, present participle or past participle.

Gender   A grammatical term that classifies a word either as masculine or feminine. All Spanish nouns (not only those which refer to people or animals) are either masculine or feminine: *casa* (house) is feminine; *árbol* (tree) is masculine.

Indirect object   A noun or a pronoun that benefits or loses as the result of an action. In the sentence *El profesor entrega los ejercicios a los estudiantes* (the teacher hands the exercises to the students), *a los estudiantes* is the indirect object.

Infinitive   The infinitive is the form of the verb given as the main entry in Spanish dictionaries. It is invariable. Spanish verbs are divided into three categories depending on the endings of their infinitive form, -ar, -er, or -ir: *hablar* (to speak), *comer* (to eat), *vivir* (to live).

Interrogative   A word used to express a question. Interrogative words can be **adjectives**: *¿Qué libro lees?* (What book are you reading?), **pronouns**: *¿Qué lees?* (What are you reading?) or **adverbs**: *¿Cuánto quiere?* (How much/many do you want?)

Mood   A grammatical term used to define the speaker's attitude towards the verbal action. There are three moods, each with their own set of **tenses**: the **Indicative** mood denotes something factual or real: *Vivo en España* (I live in Spain); the **Subjunctive** mood denotes something subjective, unreal or hypothetical: *Quiero que vengas* (I want you to come); and the

Imperative mood is used for commands and instructions: *Ven* (Come).

Noun   Nouns are words for people, animals, things and even ideas, feelings or emotions: *hombre* (man), *gato* (cat), *mesa* (table), *democracia* (democracy), *miedo* (fear).

Number   A grammatical category which indicates whether something is singular or plural: *esta mujer es inteligente* (this woman is intelligent); *estas mujeres son inteligentes* (these women are intelligent).

Object pronoun   A pronoun that replace the direct object and the indirect **object**. There are direct object pronouns (*me, te, lo, la ...* me, you, him, her, it) and **indirect** object pronouns (*me, te, le ...* to/for me, you, him, her, it).

Past participle   A past participle is a non-personal form of the verb: *trabajado* (worked), *comido* (eaten), *dormido* (slept). When used with the verb *haber*, it forms compound tenses, such as the perfect tense: *hoy he trabajado en casa* (today I have worked at home). It can also be used as adjective: *la ventana está abierta* (the window is open).

Possessive   Possessives are words that indicate possession or ownership. They can be **adjectives**: *mi hermano* (my brother) or **pronouns**: *las bicicletas son nuestras* (the bicycles are ours).

Preposition   Prepositions are words that link two other words or groups of words in order to indicate a relationship of time, space, possession, etc: *Llegamos por la tarde* 'We arrive in the afternoon'; *El libro está en la mesa* 'the book is on the table'

Present participle   The present participle is the form of the verb that is used to say what is happening at the moment. It is invariable. In English verbs ending in -ing are present participles and in Spanish -ando or -iendo: *en este momento estoy trabajando* (at this moment I am working).

Pronoun   A word that replaces or refers to a noun: *ella* (she), *éste* (this one), *¿Quién?* (Who?) etc.

Reflexive verb   Verbs such as *me despierto* (I wake up), *te levantas* (you get up), that can express actions done by the subject for or to himself/herself, are said to be reflexive. These verbs are always accompanied by a reflexive pronoun *me, te, se, nos, os, se* (myself, yourself, himself, etc.). Reflexive verbs are an extremely large category in Spanish.

Subject   A word or group of words that perform an action or exist in a state: *Marta y Lola compraron un piso* (Marta and Lola bought a flat); *el coche es viejo* (the car is old).

Subject pronoun   A pronoun representing the person or thing that performs an action or exists in an state: *Ellas compraron un piso* (they bought a flat), *él es viejo* (he is old).

Subjunctive   See **Mood**.

Tense   The form of the verb that indicates the time of the action: past, present or future.

Verb   A verb is a word that indicates an action or an state: *Juan estudia inglés* (Juan studies English), *Emilia es joven* (Emilia is young).